Anti-Semitism in Times of Crisis

Anti-Semitism in Times of Crisis

Edited by Sander L. Gilman
and Steven T. Katz

NEW YORK UNIVERSITY PRESS
New York and London

Library of Congress Cataloging-in-Publication Data
Anti-semitism in times of crisis / edited by Sander L. Gilman and
    Steven T. Katz.
        p.   cm.
    Includes bibliographical references and index.
    ISBN 0-8147-3044-2 (cloth)
    1. Antisemitism—History.   2. Christianity and antisemitism.
    3. Antisemitism in literature.   4. Holocaust, Jewish (1939–1945)—
Influence.   I. Gilman, Sander L.   II. Katz, Steven T., 1944–   .
    DS145.A644   1991
305.892'4—dc20   91-6745
                                                               CIP

New York University Press books are printed on acid-free paper,
and their binding materials are chosen for strength and durability.

Contents

Preface

This volume grew out of a conference held at Cornell University in 1986 under the auspices of the Program in Jewish Studies and the Western Societies Program. The conference was directed by Sander L. Gilman and Steven T. Katz. It brought together scholars from throughout the world to discuss the meaning and nature of anti-Semitism.

One of the topics which was hotly debated (and remains controversial) is the very term *anti-Semitism*. Its use in the conference and its appearance in the title of this volume should be clarified. The term *anti-Semitism* is used because it evokes a specific stage in the history of Western Jew-hatred. Coined by Wilhelm Marr as part of the scientific discourse of race in the nineteenth century, the term *anti-Semitism* arose from half of the dichotomy of "Aryan" and "Semite" which haunted the pseudoscience of ethnology during this period and beyond. Maurice Olender illustrates this extraordinarily well in his *Les Langues du paradis: aryens et semites—un couple providentiel* (Paris: Gallimard, 1989). It is a socially constructed category which was used in Europe specifically to categorize the difference between "Semites" and Others. It has no validity except as a marker of the discourse of Jewish difference. We have selected this term as a blanket label for all stages of Jew-hatred as a means of emphasizing the inherent consistency of Western attitudes toward the Jews. We do not intend it to present a valid category of racial identity. That Jews exist and self-label themselves as Semites is without a doubt the case. The use of the term *anti-Semite* makes no reference to this act of self-labeling. Its use does not imply any transcendent value to this dichotomy, nor does it imply or deny the real existence of such groupings.

Ithaca, New York

Introduction

Sander L. Gilman and Steven T. Katz

This collection of essays on anti-Semitism in times of crisis mirrors the history of the reception of the Jews in exile from the early Christian Church through our contemporary age. It is the image of the Jew which stands at the center of the book; not his/her reality. It is thus, for the most part, a book about Western (in its broadest sense) self-definition, an identity reflected in the structure of the Western fantasy about Europe's ultimate other, the Jew. An extension of this fantasy is to be seen in the chapters discussing the anti-Semitism of the Arabic Middle East, which, as Bernard Lewis has so convincingly shown, has incorporated Western attitudes toward the Jews. It is also to be seen in the chapters on two Eastern European examples of the "Jewish Problem" (that phrase coined by those who saw the Jews as a problem needing resolution), where the question of a pan-European image of the Jews is addressed. For Tsarist Russia, with its image of the Jew shaped by Orthodoxy, and Fascist Latvia, with its image of the Jew shaped by a frontier Lutheranism, are both "European," if the root of the European model of anti-Semitism is sought within the continuity of Christianity's image of the Jew.

But it is not merely that the Jew is the obvious Other for the European, whether the citizen of the Roman Empire or of the Federal Republic of Germany. The special role of the Jew within the mental world of the West as well as that world colonized by the European, is an artifact of the Europeanization of Christianity and the eventual secularization of Christian

1

models of the Jew. Thus the view that "racial" or "scientific" anti-Semitism of the late nineteenth century formed a radical break with the "medieval" religious tradition of Jew-hating because of its self-confessed atheism is rooted in a simple misunderstanding of the nature of the secularization of religious models within the biological sciences of the nineteenth century.[1] The basic model of the Jew found within "religious" contexts is merely secularized in the course of the eighteenth and nineteenth centuries. The blindness and intractability of the Jew in accepting Christianity become the psychological limitations of the Jew which preclude him/her from ever becoming a truly "cultured" member of Western society; the perversity of the Jew's nature in betraying Christ over and over again (throughout history) becomes the biologically determined quality of the Jew which leads to the Jew's heartless role in the rise of capitalism (or communism—take your pick); the Jew's destructive role in literally destroying the life of Christians, whether through the ritual use of Christian blood or the mass poisoning of wells which led to the Black Death, becomes the Jew's biological role as the transmitter of diseases such as syphilis (and, according to at least one commentator in Chicago in 1988, AIDS[2]). The role of the Jew as the essential Other in the Christian West (including Europe's westernmost intellectual provinces, such as the United States) must be raised in any discussion concerning the history of anti-Semitism.

Or, again, put in a different way, we must ask whether anti-Semitism is an unchanging, constant, manifestation of Western religious (and, therefore, political) institutions or whether it only appears sporadically in widely different locations and in variant forms? The examination of this question of the continuity or discontinuity of Jew-hatred, of its fluctuating yet strangely consistent form, provides the bases for a fundamental reevaluation of the history of anti-Semitism in the West. And it is not only in the context of political history that this reevaluation must take place. For cultural and literary history have long been seen as an arena in which the manifestations of anti-Semitism are played out, often in ways that predate their appearance within greater social reality. The text quite often serves as the arena for testing the limits of toleration. Within the present collection a number of essays have addressed this fascinating question—how the nature of the representation of the Jew reflects and shapes (or is reflected and shaped by) the political reality of the Jew within the society of the Diaspora.

This debate has recently resurfaced in a new guise. In the Federal Republic of Germany during the 1950s and 1960s, there had been a traditional, liberal approach (e.g. Ralf Dahrendorf) which tended to see the path of German history as having taken a special turn which led to the exploitation of anti-Semitism as a political platform and, eventually, if not inexorably, to the Holocaust. The literary image of the Holocaust at this time (Andersch, Grass) was of a world of destruction in which the German served as the agent of destruction, destroying not only (not even primarily) Jews but other "good" Germans. Such a view stressed the continuity of German images of the Jew from the early Middle Ages and stressed the inherent function of anti-Semitism in shaping the self-definition of the German.

Following the showing of the American TV show "Holocaust" in 1976, a shift in the perception of the past began to be noticeable. Beginning in the 1970s a number of conservative historians (the best-known among them being the Bonn historian Michael Stürmer) saw a need to reevaluate the past in order to form a new German identity, one free, or at least no longer centrally bound, to the image of a unique German past which focused on the Holocaust and the tradition of German anti-Semitism. Some of these historians, notably Ernst Nolte, have gone so far as to see the Holocaust as being merely a German version of other models of dealing with groups labeled as "dangerous" within recent history (specifically the Soviet treatment of the large landholders during the 1920s).[3] In other words, such scholars would represent the place of Nazi anti-Semitism in German history as inherently discontinuous with the German past. The literary image of the Holocaust becomes tied to a "new" reality, the reality of the present. Thus a spate of autobiographies by the *children* of Nazi figures (such as Arnolt Bronnen) begin to appear. These reflect their trauma as the survivors of this world. The fictional (and filmic) world begins to use the Holocaust as metaphor, a pattern well known from American (Styron) and Australian (White) letters, but rarely found within West German letters until the 1970s. The best example of this is the 1987 novel *Die Taube* by Patrick Süßkind. For Süßkind's novel is about the *condition humaine*, not about Jews in camps or the origin of fascism.

The very history of anti-Semitism becomes part of the shaping of a new identity for the West Germans. And, following the collapse of the Berlin Wall on November 9, 1990, for the Germans in the German Democratic Republic, as can be seen in the final chapter of this volume. To undertake such a reevaluation of history, it is clearly important for them to reread the Western history of attitudes toward the Jews. For any pattern of continuity of anti-Semitism inherent in Western culture would destroy their demand for German anti-Semitism to be seen as unique. It is such a rereading which places the emphasis on the discontinuity of the image of the Jews and makes this just as important as the call for continuity in Western (or at least German) history in the 1960s. This is, of course, lost on many of the participants who simply see their position as "right" and the other position as "wrong."

In this debate, the "Historikerdebatte" in West Germany during the past few years, the question which dominates is not solely whether there is a "special" place for the history of anti-Semitism within the German tradition, or whether the Holocaust was patterned on other events of the twentieth century and had specifically little to do with the history of Western anti-Semitism. What has become central is whether or not the Jew, so long the marker of what the German was not, any longer plays any role in contemporary German thought. It is clear from the attempt of contemporary neo-conservative historians that the role of the Jew has shifted. It is now the burden of this past, a past in which the Jew was the central definition of difference, which the German wishes to shed.

How does the history of anti-Semitism function in a world devoid of Jews, or at least, a world in which the Jew is no longer visible? And how does the now invisible Jew respond? There has been a shift from the earlier model in which Jews internalized the extraordinary visibility given them within the culture of the Diaspora. The process of internalization is now linked to the marginal invisibility of the Jews. Thus many of the essays in this volume chart the Jewish response to the image of the Jew—whether in *Haskalah* Berlin, nineteenth-century Vienna, or contemporary Germany.

While evident parallels can be made to other categories of difference in the West such as antiblack racism, anti-Semitism does provide a self-contained problem which in turn reflects certain basic structures inherent in all manifestations of demonization. Thus anti-Semitism is both paradigmatic, following the embedded attitude of Christians toward the Jews within all communities in the West (and by extension, the Middle East), and representative, since its deep structure is universal. The rhetoric through which such attitudes have been described by historians in modern times has varied from "medieval anti-Judaism" to "scientific (or racial) anti-Semitism." The question which must be asked is whether these are separate manifestations of the same underlying problem? Whether it is the unique role of the Jew as the Other against which, from the history of the early Church to the present, the Christian defines him/herself negatively or whether or not, according to modern social historians, the radical difference of time and locus makes the incidental selection of the Jew the only connecting link? The history of the development of anti-Semitism (to use only one of the labels as a *pars par toto* for all of the manifestations, regardless of their interrelationship) is one with the concept itself and is part of the submerged narrative of this book. What will be illustrated by the wide range of essays collected in this volume is that in the case of the supposed difference between "anti-Judaism" and "anti-Semitism" in the history of the treatment of Jews in Europe, we are dealing with shifts in the articulation of perception, not in the basic perception itself.

Is a negative attitude toward the Jews one which surfaces only sporadically, even though continually present within the culture because of basic structural features of Christianity, and then only in times of crisis? What is it about such times which spontaneously seem to result in the use of the Jews as the essential Other through which to define the integrity of the self? Are there times which, almost of a mechanical necessity, are predisposed, preprogrammed to unloose the evil genie of anti-Semitism, or is it rather, that whenever there is a need for a "true" devil, a "real, palpable enemy," that the search always culminates in discovering the Jews as a natural reflex of the Western mind-set concerning difference? Throughout this volume the specific studies reflect the problem of dealing with the "meaning" of anti-Semitism in the Diaspora.

Each of the chapters serves as a case study for the appearance and structure of anti-Semitism in very different times and places. All of them reflect the complexity of examining anti-Semitism within the historical, cultural, or national contexts. All seek to uncover the root question: Why the Jews? Which is, of course, the real "Jewish Question."

Nicholas de Lange, in his important discussion of "The Origins of Anti-Semitism," begins by making it clear that the notion of anti-Semitism, especially racial anti-Semitism, did not exist in the ancient, or even medieval period. Turning to the classical era he makes two important points. The first is that anti-Jewish prejudice in the classical era is "in very short supply." And secondly, that there are "severe" problems connected with the correct interpretation of the material that does exist. These difficulties recognized, what does the evidence reveal? De Lange makes it clear that the evidence does not support the well-known, widely disseminated theory of "eternal anti-Semitism," i.e., that such Judeophobia existed universally in the Hellenistic and Roman world. Anti-Jewish sentiments did exist, it would appear from the fourth century B.C.E., and were accentuated from the second century B.C.E., on, but the evidence from this epoch suggests that anti-Judaism was neither universal nor virulent, certainly not when compared to the ferocity of anti-Jewish sentiments within Christianity. It was the coming of Christianity, as James Parkes and most recently Rosemary Ruether make evident, that transformed anti-Judaism into the extraordinarily complex, historically significant force that it became. And yet, as de Lange wisely points out, this thesis too is not without its difficulties, for anti-Judaism does predate Christianity and, secondly, the evidence, as John Gager has recently argued, is more complex than usually allowed in this reconstruction. Accordingly, while we have preconditions, antecedents, precedents for that later, mature, deadly anti-Semitism of the post-crusader and modern era, we are dealing with material that reflects a far more ambiguous legacy of group hatred than is usually thought. There are a number of elemental issues whose continuity is attested in the later history of anti-Semitism, but great caution, must be employed in evaluating them in their own context, as well as using them in attempting to decipher the roots and causes of later anti-Semitism.

Moshe Lazar's essay on the images of the Jew in medieval art and literature reflects the process of dehumanization which accompanies the creation of the stereotypes of the Jew. In "seeing" the Jew as different, as grotesque, as related to other categories of difference, such as the demonic, Christian Europe during the Middle Ages provided a means of differentiating between the true believer and his/her antithesis. One could literally "see" the difference. There was no confusion possible, for Jews looked different. This fantasy of difference was played out within the social reality of the Middle Ages, with the creation of distinctive clothing required for Jews and, indeed, in the institution of the "ghetto" as a locus that labeled its inhabitants as Jews. If the "Jew's hat" was grotesque, if the "ghetto" stank of garbage and effluvia, that was because the Jews looked and smelled different. Thus the boundary between the self and the Other was drawn. The Jew was made to look different. This problem was one long ascribed to the European Enlightenment—what happens when you can no longer distinguish between yourself and that individual who represents the definition of what you are not. In the High Middle Ages the Jews came to be integrated in many ways into European society. Thus the language of the Jews in the Holy Roman Empire of the German Nation came to be the Middle High German dialects of the Rhine Valley. At this time the Jew dressed, sounded, and looked like—everyone else. Thus the need to draw lines, to demonize the Jew, both within the visual representation of the Jew and through the abstract signs associated with the Jew (the Jew's hat, the Jew's star). From this grew the idea of the "ghetto," a locus for the Jew. And in that "ghetto" the language which made the Jew indistinguishable from his Christian neighbor was isolated and became—Yiddish, the language which came to mark the inherent, degenerate difference of the Jew within the German-speaking world.

Jeremy Cohen's essay makes a fundamental contribution to an understanding of the anti-Judaism of Martin Luther. Concentrating upon three elements in Luther's anti-Jewish arsenal, (1) the contrast between old and new covenants central to Luther's theology, (2) his disapproval of the study of Hebrew and Judaica by Christians, and (3) his personal dislike for Jews and Judaism, Cohen makes evident that Luther was not an innovator in any of these polemical areas. He repeated the classical arguments of the *Adversus Judaeos* tradition but was in large measure derivative in his attack. Whatever the historical novelty of the post-Reformation context, Luther's anti-Jewish concerns, arguments, and visceral antipathies were deeply conservative and represent a recycling of inherited themes. But beyond this conclusion, the value of Cohen's essay lies in his rich description and articulate deconstruction of these central Christian motifs which throw light on the entire medieval Jewish-Christian encounter.

R. Po-chia Hsia's brilliant essay, "Jews as Magicians in Reformation Germany," constitutes a major contribution to our understanding of the role of the Jew, and of anti-Semitism, in the Reformation era. Hsia argues that between 1450 and 1550 "the medieval ambivalence concerning Jews as magicians eventually gave rise to a new view of German Jews which dissolved the medieval foundations of pogroms but established simultaneously the basis of modern anti-Semitism." The basis of this radical trasmutation lies in the changed status of the Jew as magician. In the late medieval era this role was especially connected with the Blood-libel myth wherein Jews repeated their role in the Crucifixion, and Christians in exposing this malevolence protected and cleansed their social order. And Luther, too, was prone to repeat these views, another instance of Jeremy Cohen's contention regarding Luther's theological and sociopolitical conservatism vis-à-vis the Jews. Yet, at the same time, the Reformation undertook, represented, a fundamental effort to demagicize the Jew, or at least to control his magical power. This it did in three ways: (1) through its own appropriation of the magical knowledge of the Jews, especially through the study of Hebrew; (2) through a study of Jewish rites; and (3) by creating ghettos in which to confine, and

hence control, Jewish magic; or by expelling Jews altogether. Hsia illuminat-
ingly reviews each of these three aspects of the Reformation demagicization
of the Jew and Judaism. Through a wealth of historical detail he defends this
reading of the Reformation attitude toward Jews and demonstrates that
ultimately Reformation theology, with its own demagicizing of the mass and
its new "rationalistic" theological emphasis, undermined the medieval mind-
set which was essential to the particular association of Jews and magic and
which, in turn, was integral to late modern anti-Semitism.

Pinchas Hacohen Peli considers the Jewish response to anti-Semitism as
seen in rabbinic *midrash*. He recognizes that midrashic hermeneutics operates
by creating a complementary "reality" to that of the brute empirical and in
this "other reality" more satisfying "answers," replies, defenses, and national
hopes can be found. In such a second dimension, which for the sages was a
more authentic dimension revealing as it did God's ultimate teleological and
providential order, the problem of anti-Semitism appears very different from
when it is perceived as a simple, contingent, historical fact. Indeed, from
the midrashic perspective, anti-Semitism reflects fundamental ontological
givens which are neither easy to comprehend nor to overturn. Seen thus,
Judeophobia is the legacy of the archetypal conflict of Jacob and Esau, a
conflict that transcends socioeconomic or political causations. All later
historic manifestations of anti-Judaism are, from this interpretive angle,
reincarnations of this original fratricidal collision. This "metaphysical" enmity does, of course, have social, juridical, economic, political, and theological implications, but none of these is its cause, and hence no simple
tinkering with these concrete forms of life can obviate the "disease." Only
the messianic future can provide, can ensure, the necessary corrective. This
eschatological hope provides the basis for Jewish survival in the present
persecutory interim.

It is within the writings of the first generation of acculturated German
Jews that the complexity of the internalization of the Western idea of the
Jew for Jews themselves can truly be judged. Liliane Weissberg's subtle
reading of Rahel Varnhagen's letters, in the light of Hannah Arendt's
assumption of a radical line between the early religious image of the Jew and
that of racial anti-Semitism of the nineteenth-century, illustrates both the
argument of discontinuity as well as the internalization of the image of the
Jew. The creation of the persona of the woman as emancipated Jew with all
of the ambiguities of both roles at the turn of the nineteenth century
illustrates that Jews, once they understood themselves to be (or were prom-

ised that they would be) part of the body politic, shared the very same set of assumptions concerning the nature and meaning of "Jewishness" that dominated the culture into which they sought admission. Rahel Varnhagen is an especially important "object" for such a study, as she inspired Hannah Arendt's first independent book. Her biography of Rahel has formed the basis for much of the discussion of the self-image of the Jewish woman in Western culture. Liliane Weissberg's reinterpretation of this seminal figure for twentieth-century discussions of Jewish identity better helps place her in the context of her own time.

The models which structured the nineteenth-century German image of the Jew were often taken (and as often again applied) to other arenas of thought. Walter Sokel's study of the image of the Jew within the "dualistic" paradigms of nineteenth-century German thought shows how the philosophical implications of antithesis form the locus where the Jew is represented. Beginning with the figure of the robber, Franz Moor in Friedrich Schiller's *The Robbers*, Sokel illustrates the power of the categories of difference. Once this is established, the role of the category of the Jew, understood as an ontological category, can be placed within the worldview of nineteenth-century literature. His central example is the widely read novel *The Hunger Pastor* (1864) by Wilhelm Raabe, about the clash of civilizations, in which the Jew is the antithesis of all morality. The movement from this dichotomy to Friedrich Nietzsche's antithetical view of the Jews as part of his radical critique of Western culture is, however, not as great as it seems. For Nietzsche glorifies precisely what Raabe condemns. Here, too, the models of "philo-Semitism" which haunt the Western image of the Jews can also be placed within the generalized models of understanding the Jew as the critical measure of the Western world.

With Walter Sokel's chapter the structure of the German (or what would in 1871 become the German) perception of the Jew is circumscribed. With Ruth Kluger's essay on the internalization of the idea of anti-Semitism with the work of Austrian Jews of the nineteenth and twentieth centuries, there is a further examination of how Jews within the world of the Diaspora dealt with their "literary" image of the Jews. The Austrian situation was in many ways quite different from the German, even though the illusion was that a shared language implied a shared culture. The growth of Prussian hegemony and the gradual dissipation of Austro-Hungarian power (within the "royal and imperial" monarchy as well as without) meant that Austrian Jews found themselves in a world which they and those about them felt was in decay.

And the difference between the implications of "political" anti-Semitism for the Germans (who saw this as part of the initial political process of the new state) and the Austrians (who saw this as part of the petty nationalisms inherent in the Empire itself) was important for the Jews in each realm. But Jews in both Germany and Austria accepted the basic premise of their own difference. Whether this was in the form of self-abnegation (such as in the work of Otto Weininger) or self-glorification (as in the dramas and political writings of Theodor Herzl), the Jews always assume that there is a "Jewish Problem." Only through the purgation of the Holocaust does at least one Jewish writer, Ilsa Aichinger, come to see the "Jewish Problem" not as the outsiderdom of the Jew but as the role of the Jew in Austrian life. It is thus an "Austrian" rather than a "Jewish Problem."

Leonard Dinnerstein's study, "Anti-Semitism in Crisis Times in the United States: The 1920s and 1930s," helps us understand both the continuity and uniqueness of anti-Semitism in the United States. While the Depression, anti-Semitic agitation, and World War II all helped to heighten anti-Semitism in the United States in this period, a proper decoding of the sentiment in this context must also consider the more general intolerance of American society in this period, the xenophobia, bigotry, and fear directed at many groups other than Jews, as well as the simple human jealousy at the already upwardly mobile successes of the Jewish community. This fear mixed with jealousy produced the social exclusion manifest in many social clubs and organizations, as well as in the quotas that began to exist in education, housing, employment, and the professions. Spurred on by hate-filled publications such as Henry Ford's *Dearborn Independent*, these sentiments spread throughout the American body politic. But the events of the 1920s were, as Dinnerstein describes them, "only a warm up for the next decade when an 'ominous' new wave of anti-Semitism occurred." In the 1930s anti-Semitic pressure increased dramatically, calling for the exclusion of the Jew from all the main organs of American social, political, and economic life. Like the Russian Slavophiles, American anti-Semites emphasized Jewish "foreignness" and disloyalty, supporting their arguments with the new racial and anticommunist rhetoric as well. And like European anti-Semites, American Judeophobes blamed all the ills of modern American life on "the Jews," especially on Roosevelt's liberal policies which were sitgmatized by their enemies as the "Jew Deal." Yet Roosevelt did not back away from his appointment of Jewish advisors and officials, and the campaign against American Jewry failed to institutionalize anti-Semitism in America as it was legitimated and institutionalized in Europe.

The nature and development of racial anti-Semitism in the Weimar Republic is the subject of Steven Katz's essay. He indicates how the German loss of World War I and the consequent instability of the Weimar Republic led to a radicalization of German political and ideological life. The historical context of the lost war fostered conditions in which the expression of extreme racial anti-Semitic notions found an hospitable reception in at least certain considerable segments of the German body politic. Katz considers four major and recurrent themes of the Weimar years: (1) the German military defeat in World War I; (2) the indignity of the Versailles Treaty; (3) the image of the Jew as revolutionary; and (4) the caricature of the Jew as supranationalist capitalist. He shows how each issue was manipulated by anti-Semitic ideologies, and how all were "explained" not by any rational appeal to economic or sociopolitical factors, but rather by recourse to the pseudoscientific, yet immensely powerful and persuasive concept of race, i.e., racial anti-Semitism. All the ills of German (and more broadly European) society were not the consequence of political errors or economic miscalculations but the consequence of an international, metapolitical conspiracy predicated upon racial imperatives. The merit of Katz's chapter lies in its detailed exploration and decipherment of this rancid, but immensely consequential, ideology that, with the rise of Hitler, finally succeeded in reversing the whole trend of modern Jewish history since the Enlightenment.

In the United States there has been a tradition of seeing literary anti-Semitism as a fringe manifestation of nineteenth-century xenophobic "know-nothingism." The post-Holocaust world of American culture dominated, as it seems, by Jews in every medium, would have to be free of such images. In reality, "Jews" no more dominate the contemporary American culture industry than they did the culture industry of the Weimar Republic, and within this industry, as Guy Stern shows so very well, there is a broad and constant critical portrayal of the Jew as the antithesis of all American values. Stern's subtle discussion of the range of the image of the Jew points toward the stereotypical function of these images as images of the outsider group. Thus the figure of Jack Benny in (the then) LeRoi Jones's play *Jello*, not merely represents white society exploiting the black, but the essential "Jew" as the force behind American racism. Stern's analysis of the role that such images play in post-World-War-II American culture illustrates the extraordinary continuity of the negative image of the Jew which is present within the entire history of the Diaspora.

In a courageous and revealing chapter Andrew Ezergailis explores the role of Latvian anti-Semitism and its contribution to the destruction of Latvian Jewry during the Holocaust. That Latvians were involved in the three Einsatzgruppen actions that took 90,000 Jewish lives in Latvia is certain. The question that this essay probes is why? Ezergailis explores the two main explanations offered to account for this phenomenon, that of anti-Semitism per se, and that of Latvian revenge for Jewish "crimes" against Latvians during the Soviet occupation of Latvia in 1940–41, and he finds both wanting as fully sufficient explanations of the deadly actions that transpired. His close analysis of the historical record indicates the limited applicability of these widely held contentions. In their place he offers his own novel reconstruction of events that accounts for the behavior of the Latvians by recourse to a more pluroform structural explanation that emphasizes the political and social chaos that existed in Latvia just before and during the Nazi invasion. As a consequence of the indigenous Latvian dictatorship of Ulmanis and its overthrow by the Soviets in 1940, and then the subsequent invasion of the Nazis in June 1941, Latvia was in a state of disarray. In this situation five things happened. Some Latvians saw the Nazis as liberators and joined them in their anti-Semitic barbarities. Secondly, the Latvian pro-Nazi leadership was able to attract a variegated group of teenagers, gymnasium students, university students, soldiers, and policemen, plus others, who were looking for "useful" employment quite incidental of any special feelings about or against Jews per se. Thirdly, there was a significant group of individuals who joined in these murderous activities because of their anti-Bolshevik sentiments which linked Jews with Soviet domination. Fourthly, the Latvian killing squads attracted certain unsavory psychological types who found comradeship and other forms of psychological support and fulfillment in these murderous circles. As Ezergailis notes: "the membership of the Arājs Kommando perhaps represented a cross-section of Latvian society, a strong component of it consisted of soliders, athletes, fraternity brothers/students, men of homophilic associations." Fifthly, there was simple avarice, the desire to steal the property of the Jewish population. In sum, Latvian behavior was caused by more than simple prejudice, and it therefore forces us to reconsider the entire question of how and why events like the Shoah are not only possible but become realities.

If the American situation after 1945 would have led one to have imagined a shift in the image of the Jew, how much more so would the situation in Germany (both West and East) have presumed an alteration in the image of the Jew. Showing the powerful continuity of the image of the Jew's language and discourse in the most important post-World-War-II writer in German, Günter Grass, Sander L. Gilman illustrates how such images are internalized and restructured by two "Jewish" writers in contemporary letters, Jurek Becker and Edgar Hilsenrath. These authors had to deal with their own labeling as "Jews" through their treatment in the concentration camps under the Nazis, as well as the complex image of the Jew which they found within postwar culture in both the German Democratic Republic (Becker) and the Federal Republic of Germany (Hilsenrath). What this chapter illustrates is that the power of the continuity of images shapes the response of those labeled as Jews, and that this response can often be a creative answer to the problem of the ambiguities of an inherently anti-Semitic culture. Nowhere is the problem of the representation of the Jew more complex than in the German-speaking world after the Holocaust. Here the world of the murders collides with the victims—not the dead, not the more easily categorized victims of the past, but the living, breathing, functioning Jew. The difficulties which Jews, specifically Jewish writers, have in such a context cannot be underestimated.

The European model of the Jew permeates the image of the Jew in the Middle East, as Bernard Lewis indicates, replacing a model which had dominated Islam from the time of the Prophet. The power of this Western model is tied to the role which colonialism played in the Middle East through the nineteenth and twentieth centuries. Its parallel can be found within the image of the Jew in present-day Japanese culture which is an artifact of the Christianization of Japan beginning with the Dutch and continuing with various and sundry groups after the opening of Japan in the mid-nineteenth century. It is important to recognize that the acceptance of this image for the present-day image of the Jew, whether Israeli or European, has had *real political* consequences. The roots of this can be traced to the beginning of the twentieth century. But the importance of Islamic fundamentalism in shaping the received "Western" image of the Jew for its own political ends cannot be underestimated. For the "devil" now has a specific locus, the state of Israel, and the Jew is no longer to be tolerated within the Islamic state. The Jew has become the enemy, and the face of the enemy is that of the Western Jew seen through the nightmare fantasy of the anti-Semite. As throughout European history, the image of the Jew provides a matrix for political action against Jews. It is not merely that the image of the Jew is a negative one, it provides the rationale for destructive acts against those labeled as "Jews."

Nowhere is this fact better illustrated than in David Menashri's chapter on the Jews of contemporary Iran before the death of Khomeini. A "Westernized" society (with all of the negative, Western images of Jewish difference) which collapsed into religious fundamentalism, Iranian society today reflects all of the ambiguities of a society under stress. The role of the Jew is one of the images of "evil," cursed by God, which defines the mental boundaries of the Islamic Republic. The Jews, as they had in the Middle Ages, form the definition of the Other, in a model of difference shaped as much by Western images of the Jew as by the more traditional Islamic ones. But the image of the Jew is not merely a "religious" image, for the Jew also serves within the representation of the power struggle within the Middle East as the image of the political enemy. Given the complex relationship of Islam with Judaism; of the former British colonies, such as Iran and Palestine, with European images of the "Oriental"; and of newly fundamentalist Islamic states with the state of Israel, it is no wonder that the image of the Jew within contemporary Iran is as complex as it is.

The final chapter by Sander L. Gilman, written before German unification in October 1990, raises the question of the Jewish response to the spectre of German reunification. As radical as the collapse of the regime of the Shah, the political changes in Central Europe begun during 1989 have evoked the history of anti-Semitism and the Shoah. It is in the fetishization of the Jew within the discourse of the reemerging Central European nation-states and the understandable Jewish response that the most recent chapter in the history of "Anti-Semitism in Times of Crisis" can be seen.

Throughout this volume, the individual case studies serve as a series of exempla in the ongoing history of anti-Semitism in the West as well as the measure of the Jewish response. The periods examined are all periods of "stress," of disequilibrium, where the function of categories of difference seems a necessity in preserving the boundaries of the world in which there is a sense of imminent dissolution. The source of such fears must be located somewhere. In the West, the traditional locus of these fears has been the Jews. For the tradition of Christianity, as embodied in the central text, the New Testament, is one which labels the Jew (at least in the later Gospels) as the antithesis of the healthy, sound, perfect world of the Christian communion. The Jews are the "natural" locus for the origin of all senses of dissolution. Even in those Western situations where a "philo-Semitic" image of the Jews seems to dominate (as in the fundamentalism of American evangelical Protestantism or of Cromwell's Puritans) the covert image of the Jew is that shaped by the New Testament. Christianity carries the virus of anti-Semitism, not necessarily in its institutions, which can and often are beneficient toward the Jews (because of the function which the Jews and their conversion are thought to play in bringing about the second coming of Christ), but in its central text. And it is this text which forms the basis for the antithetical image of the Jew which dominated the Western discourse about the Jew.

The stereotype of the Jew is rooted in the earliest history of the rise of Christianity (or rather in the historical record of the separation of the early Church from Judaism) and is mirrored in a static manner in a series of texts —the Gospels, or as the early Christians referred to them "The New Testament"—which were generated dynamically over time.[4] As early as Eusebius and Athanasius (in the fourth century C.E.) these texts come together to be the central canon of Christianity while the so-called "pseudo-Gospels" (such as the gospel of Nicodemus) are removed. In the Gospels, Christians are given a static representation of the Jew and a direct message about the inherent difference of the Jew. It is the Jew who is the marker of difference. It is in the continuity of the Gospels at the center of Christianity—not in the theology or indeed in the practice of the Church—that the negative representation of the Jew is preserved. And it is to this central stereotype that Western (that is, Christian or secularized) society turns when it needs to provide itself with a vocabulary of difference for the Jew.

This can be understood by examining/comparing four analogous passages in/of the Gospels. Focusing on the presentation, we see that in the first set of passages Jesus Christ speaks in Aramaic. Let us turn to the Gospels in their canonical order and read one passage, the last words of Christ in all of them. Matthew, the first gospeler, represents a Christ whose last words are as follows: "And about the ninth hour Jesus cried with a loud voice, saying, 'Eli, Eli, Lama Sabachthani?' that is to say, My God, My God, why hast thou forsaken me?" (27: 46). In Mark we find Christ: "at the ninth hour . . . [crying] with a loud voice, saying 'Eloi, Eloi, Lama Sabachthani? which is, being interpreted, My God, My God, why hast thou forsaken me?" (15: 34). The significance of this lies in the presentation of Christ as speaking the same language of the Jews: his words need to be translated into Greek, Latin, or English for the reader to understand. The reader is thus made aware of the foreignness of Christ's language—he speaks the language of difference; he is a Jew who is identified by his very language and discourse. Placed in the mouth of Christ, the language of the Jews is the magical language of a positive difference.

But in the second set of passages, Christ speaks directly to the reader. If we take the parallel passage from Luke we can trace the same course with very different results. Christ is taken to Calvary and there he is crucified. "And when Jesus had cried with a loud voice, he said, Father, into thy hands I commend my spirit: and having said thus, he gave up the ghost" (23: 46). In John, the last of the Gospels which related the life of Christ, he is taken to Golgotha and there "he said, It is finished: and he bowed his head, and gave up the ghost" (19: 30). In Luke and John there is no need for translation or interpretation. The language of this passage is completely transparent to the reader. The reader of the passage understands that Christ speaks the same language as the reader. This "lucanization," according to Morton Scott Enslin, "reflects a marked sameness of tone, their smoothness and freedom from the little idiosyncrasies which stamp the man himself."[5] More so, the later Gospels provide a verbal sign of difference between the image of the Jews and that of the early Christians represented in the text— Jews who were at the time becoming Christians in a world in which the valorized language was Greek. Thus the existence of a "hidden" language which would mark Christ as a "real" Jew, i.e., as a non-Greek-speaking Jew, and therefore of lower status, was impossible.

This movement in the Gospels from the image of Christ as a talking Jew to that of the Christian, whose discourse is separate and distinct from that of the Jew becomes clearest in the writings which codified the views of the early Church. In Acts, Peter's first speech to his fellow Jews in Jerusalem is recounted in a manner that differentiates between Greek, the language of his readers (now feeling themselves to be "Christians"), and the representation of the Jews' discourse. He writes, for example, "And it was known unto all the dwellers at Jerusalem; insomuch as that field is called in their proper tongue, Aceldama, that is to say, The field of blood" (1: 19). But the utterances of Jesus in Acts never need this type of translation. His language is consistently accessible.

A similar movement of the text is to be found in the recounting of the defense of the first Christian martyr, Stephen. The movement away from the "hidden" language of the Jews reveals itself to be more than a rejection of the language of the Jews. It is also an appropriation of the discourse of the

Jews which Stephen reveals to the reader as having been misused by the Jews themselves. By stripping away the polluting nature of the "hidden" language of the Jews Stephen reveals to the reader that the very discourse of the Jews was never really their own.

Stephen, a Greek-speaking Jew, had begun successfully to evangelize among the Jews. He was prosecuted by Jewish priests who brought false witnesses to accuse him of blasphemy. His defense is quite extraordinary. He begins by recounting to his Jewish accusers a synoptic history of the Jews as represented in the Torah from the appearance of God to Abraham though the building of the Temple to—the coming, death, and resurrection of Christ:

Ye stiffnecked and uncircumsized in heart and ears, ye do always resist the Holy Ghost: as your fathers did, so do ye. Which of the prophets have not your fathers persecuted? and they have slain them which showed before of the coming of the Just One; of whom ye have been now the betrayers and murderers. . . . But he, being full of the Holy Ghost, looked up steadfastly into heaven, and saw the glory of God, and Jesus standing on the right hand of God . . . (Acts 7: 51–55)

The entire story of the Jews is reduced to a preamble to the coming of Christ. The sense of continuity between the "real" Jews of the past and the "new" Jews (read: Christians) of the early Church, between the "true" Jewish experience actually written "on the heart" and not merely inscribed on the skin, becomes his defense. The act of circumcision, which had become the sign of the special relationship between the (male) Jew and God becomes a false sign, a sign written on the body of the hypocrisy of the hidden language of the Jew. The continuity between the Torah and the Gospels, the Christian demand that the Jews of the Torah prefigure (and thus are replaced by) the Christian experience removes the discourse of the Jews about their own history from their own control. As St. Augustine stated in his manual for new converts to Christianity: "the New Testament is concealed in the Old; the Old Testament is revealed in the New."[6] The Torah suddenly becomes the Old Testament. The "hidden" language of the Jews disappears from the tradition of the early Church even though it is preserved in what now comes to be called the "New" Testament as a sign of the difference of Christ's nature from that of the Jews. The successful separation of the "Church" from the "Synagogue," is indicated in the latest of the Gospels, Revelations, as well as in the Pauline epistles, where the separation between the divine discourse of the Church and the corrupt discourse of the Jews is absolute.

The rhetoric of European anti-Semitism can be found within the continuity of Christianity's image of the Jew. It is Christianity which provides all of the vocabularies of difference in Western Europe and North America, whether it is in the most overt "religious" language or in the secularized language of modern science. For it is not merely that the Jew is the obvious Other for the European, whether the citizen of the Roman Empire or of the Federal Republic of Germany. Anti-Semitism is central to Western culture as the rhetoric of European culture is Christianized, even in its most secular form. This made the negative image of difference of the Jew found in the Gospel into the central referent for all definitions of difference in the West.

In this present volume the interaction between overt and covert representations of the Jew as the Other and the internalization of such images with the self-representation of a number of Western Jews has also been documented. This is an important moment. For it is impossible to break out of this devil's circle of argument—the negative image of the Jew which dominates the Western representation of the Jew finds resonance among those Jews who accept the central value system of the West. In accepting this system—and the inherent negative self-image of the Jew embedded in it— they prove the validity of the charges of difference lodged against the Jew. Thus anti-Semitism may be quite able to exist virtually without Jews immediately present within a society in stress (as in the present-day German Democratic Republic), but when Jews are present they cannot stand apart from this corrosive image of the Jew. Thus to understand Jewish identity in the Diaspora one must also understand the creation, generation, and perpetuation of the negative images of the Jew, those images forged in times of crisis.

Notes

1. See Sander L. Gilman, *Difference and Pathology: Stereotypes of Sexuality, Race, and Madness* (Ithaca, N.Y.: Cornell University Press, 1985), pp. 191–216.
2. Ann Marie Lipinski and Dean Baquet, "Sawyer Aide's Ethnic Slurs Stir Uproar," *Chicago Tribune* (1 May 1988), p. 1; Anthony Lewis, "A Dangerous Poison," *New York Times* (31 July 1988), p. E25; and Cheyrl Deval, "Sawyer Won't Fire Aide over Ethnic Slurs," *Chicago Tribune* (5 May 1988), p. 1.
3. See Roderick Stackelberg, "1986 vs. 1968: The Turn to the Right in German Historiography," *Radical History Review* 40 (1988): 1–13.

4. See Rosemary Reuther, *Faith and Fratricide: The Theological Roots of Anti-Semitism* (New York: Seabury Press, 1974).
5. Morton Scott Enslin, *Christian Beginnings* (New York: Harper Bros., 1938), p. 421.
6. St. Augustine, *The First Catechetical Instruction*, trans. Joseph P. Christopher (Westminister, Md.: Newman Bookshop, 1946), p. 45.

[1]

The Origins of Anti-Semitism: Ancient Evidence and Modern Interpretations

Nicholas de Lange

"I'll tell you what I'm going to do," said Solomon. "I'm going to go and explain everything to Mister Hitler properly, and when he realizes how our poor brothers over there are suffering he'll weep his heart out. There, that's my plan."

"Gentlemen, let us form a Committee Against Anti-Semitism," proposed Mangeclous.

His proposal was accepted, but the discussions turned out to be difficult because the first task was to define the terms. Was there such a thing as a Jewish people? And what was a committee? And how should one interpret the term "anti-Semitism"? Michael stated calmly that the next man to talk politics would feel the sharp end of his jacknife in his belly.

"Let's talk about love instead," he suggested.

—Albert Cohen, *Mangeclous*

It is by now a truism that the subject of anti-Semitism is a controversial one, and part of the problem does indeed reside in the interpretation of the term *anti-Semitism.* * On the technical level, of course, there is not much to argue about. Anti-Semitism is the name of a political movement, founded on group prejudice and a pseudo-scientific theory of race, which belongs to the history of Europe in the period, roughly speaking, between the Franco-Prussian War and the Second World War. The name anti-Semitism was chosen and used by the participants in this movement, and it is itself anti-

21

Semitic, in that it assumes the existence of a Semitic (i.e., Jewish) race. No doubt anti-Semitism has its precursors, and no doubt it has left a residual legacy to our own time, but it was only in the period in question that the movement had an openly organized political structure of any consequence, and that the label was borne with self-confidence and pride. In our day the term *anti-Semitism* (rather like the term *fascist*) has become, on most lips, a term of abuse, except in the context of political and historical investigation. And it is at this point that the trouble begins. Who decides what constitutes anti-Semitism? The term can be found nowadays applied to almost any manifestation of anti-Jewish sentiment or action, ranging from personal prejudice to state policies. This confusion of terminology serves almost any interest rather than that of the pursuit of historical objectivity. It leads to a blunting of arguments, a blurring of valid and important distinctions. If it is not already too late, I should like to put in a plea for this objectionable term to be reserved and restricted to its proper use.

In this study I shall be concerned with one particular aspect of the prehistory of anti-Semitism, namely the claim that the origins of anti-Semitism, or at least of certain distinctive elements of anti-Semitism, are to be found in the ancient world. This quest for the remote origins of anti-Semitism is not the same thing as the assertion that anti-Semitism itself existed in the ancient world, and it is important not to confuse the two. Whether from carelessness or from perversity, it has become not uncommon now to speak of "ancient anti-Semitism." But this is to beg the crucial question: is there such a thing as anti-Semitism in antiquity, or indeed at any time before the modern age?

Anti-Semitism, in the strict sense of the term, cannot be detached from the racial theories which exercised such an important influence on the ethos of Western politics and thought from the middle of the nineteenth century to the middle of the twentieth. The term itself is a reminder of the work on the classification of languages to which those theories tended to appeal for scientific support: because Hebrew (a language closely identified with the Jews although not their spoken language at the time) is a Semitic language, it was argued that the Jews were an alien race in predominantly Aryan Europe. Alien—and inferior, since the Aryan race was superior to all the others. The argument from the scientific classification of languages in physical anthropology, may seem with hindsight to have been logically defective, but in its day it was remarkably influential. And it was something genuinely new in the history of European ideas. It is true that Christian theologians had been preaching for centuries that every Jew was born with a stain of inherited guilt for the crucifixion of the Christian saviour, and the late medieval church in Spain had even employed a system of certificates of "purity of blood," certifying the holder free from Jewish ancestry and giving him access to various positions of authority not open to descendants of Jews, but by and large the church had never held to a theory of racial determinism, but had considered all men, whatever their origin, to be essentially equal and equally capable of being "saved." The fact that racialism, in the modern sense, did not exist in the ancient world,[1] should make one chary of speaking of "ancient anti-Semitism": at the very least, this cannot be anti-Semitism as we know it.

However there are other elements bound up in anti-Semitism, apart from straight racialism. In practical terms, the singling out of the Jews as an alien race in nineteenth-century Europe resulted not just from a theory about languages (the Jews in nineteenth-century Europe overwhelmingly spoke Aryan languages: the only noteworthy exception were those Hungarian Jews who spoke Magyar, which was the language of their Christian fellow countrymen). The Jews were generally despised, resented, ridiculed and feared, and without this deeply entrenched preexistent prejudice it is highly doubtful that anti-Semitism would ever have existed, or at least taken hold in the way that it did. If racism is characteristic of late nineteenth-century Europe, anti-Jewish prejudice had been characteristic of Europe for a long time before. We can study the various forms and degrees of this prejudice well back into the Middle Ages, at different levels of society and in different places, through literature, art and history. We can study, for example, the language of anti-Jewish rhetoric and invective, by which the people were schooled to hate and fear the Jews; we can read the reasoned arguments which attempt to put a rational mask on the irrational prejudice. We can read in texts and see in paintings and statues how the Jews demonified, made into incarnations or partners of the devil. We can read in the chronicles how mob violence was turned against the Jews, as at the time of the First Crusade and often later; how the Jews were liable to become the scapegoat in times of crisis, as at the time of the Black Death. We can see how the Jews were segregated from Christians, deprived of access to the culture and occupations of the majority, forbidden to intermarry with Christians, compelled to live apart and wear distinctive clothes. All these long-established factors, promoted and fomented by the Christian church, contributed to the shameless emergence of anti-Semitism as a secular political philosophy. The question then presents itself *when* and *why* the Jews were singled out to be treated in this way: is anti-Jewish prejudice linked to particular factors in medieval European society or religion, can it be traced back to the early church, or to pre-Christian times? What are the origins of the attitudes that led to anti-Semitism?

The academic study of ancient attitudes to the Jews began only in the past hundred years or so, either as part and parcel of modern anti-Semitism or as a reaction to it. In this time various different views and explanations have been advanced, of which the main trends will be examined in what follows. Despite almost a century of research, however, there is no real consensus, and it is worth asking ourselves why. Part of the answer lies no doubt in the controversial nature of the subject and in the prejudices of the investigators, and also in the difficulty of defining terms. But another serious problem lies in the nature of the ancient evidence. In the first place, the evidence is in very short supply. Most non-Jewish writers (and such evidence as there is comes almost exclusively from written sources) have little or nothing to say, for good or ill, about the Jews, at least before the second or third century C.E. Jewish sources are more forthcoming, and sometimes they preserve valuable extracts from lost works of non-Jewish authors, but they frequently fall under suspicion of casting a somewhat oblique light on the facts, and in general we have to reckon with a severe problem of interpretation: we often have difficulty in assessing the context, the audience addressed and the tone of voice, as it were, of a text.

There are various compendious collections of texts, which are intended to facilitate the study of the subject. In practice, they have not always had the desired effect. In the first place, they tend to present only one part of the evidence—there is no collection that brings together the pagan, the Christian and the Jewish sources. Secondly, they tend by their nature to highlight conflict, controversy and disparagement: and even if explicitly favourable comments are included, we are not given the crucial evidence of silence. Thirdly, we lack the commentary which would make clear the historical or literary context which is normally essential for an understanding of such fragments. It is presumably the uncritical use of such compendia that gives rise to sweeping statements like, "a survey of the comments about Jews in the Hellenistic Roman literature shows that they were almost universally disliked, or at least viewed with an amused contempt."[2] That such attitudes existed in antiquity is beyond question; that they were almost universal can

only be asserted by generalizing boldly from part of the evidence and ignoring
the rest. What needs to be discovered is who held such attitudes, and why,
and what effect they had.

Of the large-scale theories concerning anti-Jewish sentiment in antiquity,
the most sweeping is the "eternal anti-Semitism" theory. According to this
view, anti-Semitism has no beginning: it is as old as time, or at least "as old
as Judaism," as the nineteenth-century French Jewish scholar Théodore
Reinach put it.[3] This theory was highly influential from the late nineteenth
century until after World War II, and is expounded in detail by any number
of authors of the period, many—though by no means all—of them apologists for anti-Semitism. The weakness of the "eternal anti-Semitism" theory
is that it is a theological, an ideological construct. That was also its strength
——if it held its ground for so long (say from the 1880s to the 1950s) it was
because it corresponded to an image which is in the foreground of the Jewish
and Christian theology of election: the image of the Suffering Servant, the
faithful, persecuted people of God, surrounded by enemies and repeatedly
sacrificed on the altar of the pagan rejection of the One God.

However, this theological program which makes the Jewish people into
the eternal victim could not stand up to serious historical examination.
Widely accepted in its day, it was very quickly and easily demolished in the
1950s by historians such as Jules Isaac[4] and Léon Poliakov.[5] For the fact is
that hatred and persecution of Jews are neither eternal nor ubiquitous. For
Poliakov, the fact of the matter is so obvious that he contents himself with
pointing out that the persecution of Jews is virtually limited to the world of
Christianity (and Islam—subject of a subsequent volume in his *History of
Antisemitism*), and he dismisses pre-Christian anti-Semitism in ten short
pages, before turning to the theme announced in his title: anti-Semitism
"from Christ to the Court Jews."

Even in the heyday of anti-Semitism, however, more critical minds
accepted that it had not always existed, although they insisted that it had
very old roots, and sought for its beginnings in the ancient world. According
to the great Roman historian Theodor Mommsen, for example, "hatred of
Jews is as old as the Diaspora."[6] This is also the view of the doyen of early
students of anti-Semitism, Bernard-Lazare: "There is no real anti-Semitism
until the Jews, abandoning their homeland, settled in foreign lands and
came into contact with native or long-established peoples, whose customs,
race and religion were opposed to their own."[7] Bernard-Lazare dated this

phase of Jewish history to the fourth century B.C.E., to the time of Alexander the Great, although he admits that the story of the Diaspora could be traced back earlier, to the Babylonian Exile.

Some scholars have seen the first concrete event in the history (or rather prehistory) of anti-Semitism as the destruction of a Jewish temple in Elephantine in Upper Egypt in the summer of 410 B.C.E., which is documented in Aramaic papyri. Egypt was under Persian rule at the time. Taking advantage of the absence of the Persian satrap, Arshama, some Egyptians sacked the temple and raided the homes of the Jews. Why did they do it? We do not know, and this ignorance poses a problem for any investigation. However, it is interesting that a good deal of the early evidence for anti-Judaism comes from Egypt, the possible reasons for which will be discussed in this chapter.

For many other modern investigators, the beginnings are in the second–first century B.C.E. For Jules Isaac, the "decisive event"[8] is the Jewish resistance to Hellenism at the time of the Hasmonean revolt, giving rise to a self-confident Judaism which clashed with Hellenism in the Greek cities of the East. It is only in the last century B.C.E., however, that Greek, or Greco-Egyptian, anti-Judaism appears as a reaction to the success of Jewish propaganda about the primacy of Jewish ideology. From Alexandria and the other large Greek cities it spread to Rome and to the whole Roman Empire. However, it must be added that for Isaac this early "pagan anti-Semitism," is very weak and pale compared to the slightly later "Christian anti-Semitism."

The thesis that the real roots of anti-Semitism are to be sought in the early Christian church was pioneered before the war by the English Christian James Parkes. In the face of the rise of Hitlerism, Parkes was asked by the International Student Service to investigate the history of anti-Semitism. In the preface to his seminal book, *The Conflict of the Church and the Synagogue,* dated May 1934, he explains

as the collection of material progressed, I became more and more convinced that it was in the conflict of the Church with the Synagogue that the real roots of the problem lay.

At the time this was a revolutionary thesis. Now it has become almost banal, thanks to the work of such scholars as Marcel Simon, whose *Verus Israël* was first published in 1948, and Jules Isaac, whose *Genèse de l'antisémitisme* appeared in 1956.

The "Christian anti-Semitism" theory asserts (broadly speaking) that the roots of modern anti-Semitism can be traced to the anti-Jewish teaching which was deliberately and consciously elaborated in the early church over a number of generations, as a central and essential part of the Christian message. It is not denied that some hostility to Jews existed in the world into which Christianity was born, but it was very limited, and above all it was never developed into an official teaching as it was in the church. Why did the early church choose to build hatred of Jews into its platform? There are various explanations, centering for the most part in the rivalry between Christianity and Judaism in the early Christian decades, the Jewish rejection of Jesus and his message, and the needs of Christian missionary propaganda, which had to undermine the attraction of Judaism while laying claim to the Jewish scriptures.

The "Christian anti-Semitism" thesis has received its strongest statement in Rosemary Ruether's influential book *Faith and Fratricide*, published in 1974. Ruether traces what she calls the "anti-Judaic myth" right back to the foundation documents of Christianity, the New Testament writings, and she insists repeatedly that this anti-Judaism is "neither a superficial nor a secondary element in Christian thought" (p. 226), but "an intrinsic need of Christian self-affirmation" (p. 181). Her major aim is to examine what can be done today to remedy the "teaching of contempt"; in this context she goes so far as to write: "Possibly anti-Judaism is too deeply embedded in the foundations of Christianity to be rooted out entirely without destroying the whole structure" (p. 228).

The "Christian anti-Semitism" theory has a number of strong points in its favour. In the first place it is susceptible of serious historical investigation. In fact it is very well documented, and from "official" Christian sources. Although there are still many question marks—as there always are in ancient history—we can trace the development of what Isaac called the "teaching of contempt" in some detail, from the earliest Christian documents of the apostolic age, through the apologists of the second–third centuries, to the great Christian authors of the classical period of ancient Christian theology in the fourth and fifth centuries; we can also trace the practical consequences of this teaching in the Roman laws, and in the riots and massacres of Jews, the forcible baptisms, and so forth. This is precisely what Christian historians such as James Parkes and Marcel Simon did in their classic works.

A second strength of the "Christian anti-Semitism" theory is that it shifts the responsibility from the victims to the aggressors. It is true that much of the ancient literature on the Jews, whether written by pagan or by Christian authors, is devoted to explaining why the Jews have incurred the justifiable anger or hatred of ordinary peace-loving, law-abiding people (and in the case of Christian authors why they have earned the wrath of God himself). But no critical historian would consider taking such arguments at their face value, and in fact they are likely to tell us more about their authors than their victims. So long as it was maintained that anti-Semitism was as old as Judaism, it was easy enough to argue that the blame must lie with the Jews themselves. Once it was accepted that hostility against Judaism began at a particular time, which more or less coincided with the rise of Christianity, it became necessary to explain why it began when it did, and what it was about early Christianity that favored the development of such hostility.

The "Christian anti-Semitism" thesis is open to two major challenges. One is that it does not do justice to the full evidence for non-Christian anti-Judaism. The second is that it does not do justice to the evidence from the early church.

The first objection — that it does not do justice to non-Christian anti-Judaism — is set out in most detail by J. N. Sevenster, in his book *The Roots of Pagan Anti-Semitism in the Ancient World* (1975). Sevenster takes issue with Jules Isaac for belittling pagan anti-Semitism. "Such anti-Semitic pronouncements as are found in the diverse ancient writers may not be treated as insignificant trivialities. . . . Sometimes Isaac gives the impression of representing that ancient pagan anti-Semitism as unimportant as possible, so that he can let the blame for the later anti-Semitism fall with full force on the Christian Church" (p. 6f.). Sevenster claims to find ample evidence for ancient pagan anti-Semitism. This is not quite a return to the "eternal anti-Semitism" thesis—Sevenster is careful to concede that, so far as "anti-Semitism indeed" is concerned, it is not attested before the second century B.C.E. (p. 181), although he believes that "anti-Semitism in word" can be traced back to the previous century. But it does mark a return to the argument that the Jews themselves are responsible for anti-Semitism:

The most fundamental reason for pagan anti-Semitism almost always proves to lie in the strangeness of the Jews midst ancient society. . . . The Jews were never quite like the others; they were always inclined to isolate themselves; they had no part in the morals and customs of the people about them.

This argument is put even more strongly by E. M. Smallwood, whose book *The Jews under Roman Rule* appeared in 1976, the year after Sevenster's:

One of the most striking characteristics of the Jew has always been his ability to preserve his national identity even after generations of residence among gentiles and to resist assimilation except in superficial matters of language-assimilation or everyday contacts. . . . Their refusal to compromise one jot or tittle of their religion either by abandoning or modifying their own practices or by making courteous concessions to paganism turned them into closely-knit, exclusive groups. Their exclusiveness bred the unpopularity out of which anti-Semitism was born. (P. 123)

This new argument is in essence a revival of the theories of an earlier age. Leaving aside the mildly offensive language in which it is couched, and the questions which should be raised by any theory of aggression which attributes the responsibility for it to the victims rather than the aggressors, it is worth observing that it turns completely on its head that part of the "Christian anti-Semitism" thesis that sees the isolation of the Jewish communities as the consequence of a Christian policy of segregation. Which view is more correct? The pagan polemic certainly accuses the Jews of *amixia*, of not mixing with outsiders, but, as I have already remarked, it is rash to take the language of group prejudice at its face value. On closer examination it would seem that many of the problems of the Jews in the Greek cities arose precisely from their desire to be more assimilated: this is notoriously the case at Alexandria, the one city which is relatively well documented, and it is interesting that the recently published corpus of Jewish inscriptions from Cyrene, where terrible fighting was to break out between Jews and gentiles in 116 c.e., shows that of 170 youths listed as ephebes in the army records, about forty are Jews.[9] And, despite the often-quoted occasions of conflict, there is abundant evidence (mainly archaeological) of Jews in the Greek cities living in close and apparently harmonious contact with their non-Jewish neighbors.

But to refute an *explanation* of pagan anti-Judaism is not to dispose of the phenomenon itself. It is true that hatred of Jews was not a Christian invention. There were people in Egypt at the beginning of the 1st century b.c.e., according to a private letter on papyrus, who felt disgusted by Jews,[10] and there is a clear continuity between the specific myths and slanders put about by certain pagan writers and those found in much later works by fathers of the church. On the other hand, the chronological limits of the pagan hostility are very suggestive: most of the evidence comes from the last century b.c.e. and the first century c.e., and what is earlier comes from Egypt, which appears to be a special case. In other words, it is an aspect—and perhaps not a very widespread aspect (especially given the evidence for pagan converts to Judaism at this time) — of the world into which Christianity was born. After the early second century c.e., the pagan anti-Jewish invective seems to die out,[11] and had it not been for its survival in the church it would presumably have disappeared forever, apart from a few stray remarks in Tacitus and some other classical authors, who quote it or are influenced by it.

The second objection to the "Christian anti-Semitism" thesis—that it does not do full justice to the Christian evidence—has been put forward very forcefully in the recent book by John Gager, *The Origins of Anti-Semitism* (1983). While not denying that "the bulk of early Christian literature" deals "harshly with Judaism," Gager insists that "this undoubted fact must be interpreted in light of the strong likelihood that the surviving Christian writings comprise a deliberately selective sample." And, more specifically, "the voice of the Judaizing Christians—those who saw no need to tie their acceptance of Christianity to a repudiation of Judaism—is scarcely heard at all" (p. 7).

From a historical viewpoint, there is a good deal of sense in Gager's argument: there is abundant evidence in the patristic writings of Christians being attracted to Judaism and accepting many of its teachings and practices. What is more, this evidence comes to us in the form of vehement denunciations of such Christians by other Christians—such as Origen in the third century or John Chrysostom in the fourth—who represent the intellectual and institutional elite in the early church. In other words, theirs is the attitude that won the day, and the voice of the other side—the Judaizers— was suppressed. A comprehensive record of relations between Christianity and Judaism in ancient times has to take account of these facts. Unless Christianity is defined as the Christianity which eventually came to be recognized as Orthodox, it is certainly an exaggeration to claim that early Christianity was uniformly hostile to the Jews and Judaism. In fact it is clear that some groups of Christians were strongly attracted to Judaism, without feeling that this in any way detracted from their Christian commitment.

Gager's book is indicative of a new departure in the study of the subject. The thrust of his argument is twofold: not only does the "Christian anti-Semitism" thesis exaggerate and generalize the Christian antagonism to Judaism, but the "pagan anti-Semitism" thesis exaggerates and generalizes pagan antagonism to Judaism. For Gager, each piece of evidence has to be analyzed both within its own immediate context and against the wider backcloth of its times; the negative evidence has to be fairly balanced by consideration of the positive evidence; due attention must be paid to the evidence of silence; and, above all, one must start with an openness to the *multiplicity* of ancient attitudes to Judaism, and not try to force all the evidence into the straightjacket of a single schema. The result is a complete rereading of the ancient evidence which yields a far more complex picture than has hitherto been offered.

Gager's study of the pagan evidence is facilitated, as he willingly acknowledges, by the work of Menahem Stern, the compiler of the latest and most thorough compendium of texts by Greek and Roman authors bearing on the Jews and Judaism.[12] Stern's compendium is well-nigh exhaustive, so far as pagan authors are concerned, and he is careful to distinguish between different types of material and to comment on the background to the various texts. Stern thus prepares the ground for Gager's more wide-ranging study. In a survey of the material down to the end of the first century C.E.,[13] he makes explicit several of the themes that were to be taken up by Gager. Among their more important general observations are the following:

1. Jews are first mentioned explicitly in Greek literature in the late fourth/early third century B.C.E., and at this time the attitude towards them is molded by a respectful and curious interest in Near Eastern civilizations.

2. In Egypt a disparaging version of the Egyptian origin of the Jews was elaborated to counter the account in the biblical book of Exodus. This mythical history was exploited, together with other material, by the Hellenized Egyptians Chaeremon and Apion in Alexandria at the time of the violence between Jews and gentiles which erupted in 38–41 C.E. It also surfaces in some other Greek and Latin authors.

3. Elsewhere in the Greek East there is surprisingly little in the way of references to Jews in the literature, and few of them are unambiguously hostile. Some express admiration.

4. In Rome a distinctly hostile and contemptuous tone can be discerned in certain writers in the period from Nero to Hadrian, including such well-known figures as Seneca, Persius, Martial, Tacitus and Juvenal. (Gager relates this phenomenon directly to the attraction of Judaism among Romans at the time, and to a reaction among conservative Romans to the success of foreign religions.)

This bare sketch does not begin to do justice to this revised and carefully differentiated interpretation of the evidence for the attitudes to Judaism expressed in the pagan literature, and it is not possible for me here to explore the subject more deeply. Suffice it to say that the abandonment of sweeping generalizations and of the search for a unitary phenomenon with a unitary cause yields, to my mind at least, a far more convincing portrayal of the situation than earlier interpretations. It is a pity that neither Stern nor Gager brings in the evidence of the Jewish literature, which is surely an important part of the picture. Neither of them, for example, mentions the book of Esther, which contains a text which, of all those commonly quoted, comes closest to encapsulating what we normally think of as anti-Semitism, namely the words of Haman to the king at Esther 3:18:

there is a certain people scattered and dispersed among the many peoples in all the provinces of your kingdom, who keep themselves apart; their laws are different from those of every other people and they do not keep your Majesty's laws; it does not benefit your Majesty to tolerate them; if it please your Majesty, let an order be made in writing for them to be exterminated.

However fictional the events narrated in the book of Esther, these words testify at least to a fear of extermination on the part of some Jews, possibly at the time of Antiochus Epiphanes, although this is by no means certain. Such a fear must surely have had some basis in reality, and the reason given —the "otherness" of the Jews—is specific enough to be highly suggestive. We know of no actual attempt to exterminate the Jews in antiquity, but is it perhaps a hint of what some gentiles were saying? Texts like this—and there are others, including the rabbinic texts attributing to the emperor Hadrian the aim of stamping out the teaching and practice of Judaism—should be taken seriously, not as evidence of actual events, but as testifying to certain attitudes on the part of some Jews, certain impressions of what might conceivably happen.

Gager's work, as it applies both to the pagan and to the Christian evidence, marks an important step forward;[14] its main merit is to divert attention away from large-scale interpretations of the evidence towards specific treatment of particular authors and episodes. Nevertheless, it is only a beginning, and the need remains for a good deal of further study of the very complex questions involved. In offering a few tentative conclusions, I wish to do no more than indicate some of the general considerations that might be investigated further.

1. Taking the evidence as a whole, it would seem that the period to which we need to look for the origins of widespread anti-Jewish prejudice is the millennium from the third century B.C.E. to the seventh century C.E.

This period begins with a predominantly favorable attitude to the Jews among those Greek writers who mention them and ends with attempts at forcible baptism and the implementation of a policy of subjugation and isolation, however inconsistently applied. We should not think in terms of a single continuous process: the details are actually very complex. Each stage needs to be considered in its own context, but a certain continuity can nevertheless be discerned. And we must allow for the fragmentary nature of the surviving evidence. To give one example, the Greek translation of the Torah, which played such an important part in the religious life and thought of Jews and Christians, and which must have been familiar to a large public of interested pagans, has left hardly a trace in the writings of pagan intellectuals on which so many arguments have been constructed. If we did not have the surviving Jewish and Christian literature, we would have only the foggiest idea of the contents of the sacred scriptures on which the Jewish and Christian religions were based. Accidental discoveries made in modern times, such as the manuscripts from the Judaean Desert, the Nag Hammadi gnostic manuscripts, or the papyrus fragments of the "Acts of the Alexandrian Martyrs," have enabled us to hear voices which were silenced for centuries, and by the same token have made us only too painfully aware of how many pieces of the jigsaw puzzle we are still missing.

2. Even if the concept of race in the modern sense did not exist in antiquity, peoples in the ancient world tended to have a strong sentiment of national pride extending to a feeling that outsiders were, at least culturally and perhaps even inherently, inferior. This observation can be applied, in various ways, to Greeks, Jews and Romans, and much of the evidence for so-called "anti-Semitism" in antiquity needs to be understood against this background. Remarks by Greeks about Jews need to be compared to remarks by Greeks about other "barbarians," or remarks by Jews about Greeks. The comparison would reveal the existence of quasi-racial prejudice, but not necessarily prejudice of which Jews were the particular victims.

3. The Jews were an important presence in the ancient world. Precise statistics are beyond our grasp, but it can be deduced that the Jews were more numerous, particularly in the eastern Mediterranean region, than in any country today outside Israel; in the main cities, where they were mainly concentrated, they must have constituted a very visible and significant element of the population, and they generally enjoyed some degree of internal self-government. Many aspects of relations between Jews and gentiles fall under the heading of straightforward political life. Naturally there

were conflicts, but such conflicts do not necessarily result from (although they may of course engender) prejudice and hatred.

4. The Jewish religion, as religions go, was well thought of, by and large, in antiquity. It won widespread respect, and many adherents. This continued to be so even after several centuries of Christian propaganda and persecution, and in the Middle Ages there are examples of people risking their lives to become Jews. This needs to be borne in mind, not only as an antidote to the notion that the Jews were universally despised and detested, but also as a possible explanation for some of the antagonism to Judaism, among people striving to preserve their own traditional religious structures or to propagate a rival religion.

5. Prejudices can be infectious. They are transmitted from one generation to the next, and from one country to another. (An outstanding example of anti-Jewish prejudice maintained in the absence of Jews is *The Merchant of Venice,* written three hundred years after the Jews were banished from England.) In Hellenistic Egypt there was a story that the Jews were descended from some lepers who were driven out of Egypt many centuries before (a story which may well have been invented to counter the Jewish version of the Exodus from Egypt, with its evident anti-Egyptian bias). This story seems to surface first in the writings of the Egyptian priest Manetho in the third century B.C.E., although it may be even older.[15] It reappears subsequently in a whole succession of Greek and Latin writers in different parts of the world, coupled to various other disreputable stories about the Jews, some but not all of them of probable Egyptian origin. How exactly were these myths transmitted? Were they propagated deliberately and with hostile intent, or did they disseminate more innocently (though no less harmfully)? And if they appear in the writings of an author who is otherwise neutral or even favorably disposed towards the Jews,[16] do they necessarily betoken anti-Jewish prejudice? There is need for a great deal of more and careful research on the problems of continuity and transmission.

6. There is also need for more research on Christian attitudes to Judaism, particularly against the background of internal tensions within Christianity, of the continuing presence and activity of Jews, and of the relationship between church and state. Some Christian texts which seem to be diatribes against Judaism are really directed against Christians: this is not to belittle the anti-Jewish animus which is a strong feature of much Christian writing, but it suggests that care is needed in the reading of texts. Again, it is important to examine how far Christian authorities, in acting or preaching

against the Jews, were responding to real dangers emanating from Jews, or perhaps taking sides in conflicts or power struggles in which the Jews were not directly implicated.[17] Moreover, any judgment on the Christian treatment of Jews should also take account of the treatment of other religions, and indeed of dissident movements within Christianity. Against this background, the treatment of the Jews can actually seem astonishingly humane and generous.

7. Finally, although this may appear too neatly schematic, it is possible, surveying the period as a whole, to discern a certain progression—not so much in general prejudice and antagonism towards the Jews and Judaism, which is too nebulous a concept to be pinned down, but in the emergence of specific elements of later anti-Semitism of the type I mentioned at the outset:

1. The treatment of the Jews as a scapegoat, an innocent victim in a larger crisis: this may be the explanation of the attack at Elephantine in 410 B.C.E. and again in Alexandria under Caligula in 38 C.E.—at least if we accept the interpretation that the native population was striking vicariously against an imperial power which was too dangerous to provoke directly. (It is possible, however, that, in either case, the Jews were not chosen at random, but that there were other factors that made for conflict.)

2. The erection of an anti-Jewish ideology, including rationalized justifications for hatred and also a demonification of the Jews: this can be traced in Christian writers of the second–fourth centuries.

3. When does it become part of the public policy of the state, as opposed to being limited to individuals or particular interest groups? The answer must be in the fourth century, when the offensive language of the theologians enters Roman legislation, and the previously privileged and protected status of Judaism in Roman law begins to be replaced by adverse discrimination. This is also the time when church synods begin to legislate to restrict relations between Christians and Jews.

4. Unprovoked violence against Jews: this first breaks out in the early fifth century, presumably as a result of hatred stirred up by the preachers.

5. Extermination of the Jews or Judaism: there was no attempt to exterminate the Jews (the book of Esther notwithstanding), but there was a series of edicts decreeing forcible baptism, in the Byzantine Empire,

in Merovingian Gaul and in Visigothic Spain, in the late sixth and early seventh centuries. These have been interpreted as part of an attempt to weld the populations of the empire into a single, homogeneous whole,[18] rather than as a theologically founded attack on the Jews as such. Nevertheless, it represents a dangerous precedent, and a further step down the road to destruction.

Notes

* I have revised the text of my paper in the light of comments made during the discussion and the subsequent proceedings of the conference on "Anti-Semitism in Times of Crisis," held at Cornell University, April 10, 1986. I should like to record my thanks to the organizers of the conference for their kindness in inviting me to take part, and for giving me this opportunity to reconsider a subject which has been preoccupying me, in various ways, for the past twenty years.

1. See A. N. Sherwin-White, *Racial Prejudice in Imperial Rome* (Cambridge, 1967), and the discussion in J. N. Sevenster (English translation by Mrs. de Bruin), *The Roots of Pagan Anti-Semitism in the Ancient World* (*Novum Testamentum*, Suppl. 41, Leiden, 1975), pp. 36ff.

2. This quotation, from J. L. Daniel in *Journal of Biblical Literature* 98 (1979), p. 46, is given merely as an example; others could be quoted, e.g., E. M. Smallwood, *The Jews under Roman Rule* (Leiden, 1976), p. 123: "The Jew was a figure of amusement, contempt or hatred to the gentiles among whom he lived."

3. *Grande Encyclopédie*, art. "Juif."

4. Jules Isaac, *Genèse de l'antisémitisme: essai historique* (Paris, 1956). Cf. his later work, *L'enseignement du mépris: vérité historique et mythes théologiques* (Paris, 1962), English translation by Helen Weaver, *The Teaching of Contempt: Christian Roots of Anti-Semitism* (New York, 1964).

5. Léon Poliakov, *Histoire de l'antisémitisme, tome I: Du Christ aux Juifs de cour* (Paris, 1955), English translation by Richard Howard, *The History of Anti-Semitism, Vol. 1: From Roman Times to the Court Jews* (New York, 1965; London, 1974).

6. Theodor Mommsen, *Römische Geschichte* (Berlin, 1894), 5th edn, vol. 5, p. 519. For a collection of such views, see F. de Fontette, *Histoire de l'antisémitisme* (Paris, 1982), p. 9; Isaac, *Genèse* (supra, n. 4), pp. 29–31.

7. Bernard-Lazare, *L'antisémitisme, son histoire et ses causes* (Paris, 1894), 1969 edn, pp. 21–22, English translation, *Antisemitism, Its History and Its Causes* (London, 1967), p. 19. On Bernard-Lazare, see Nelly Wilson, *Bernard-Lazare: Antisemitism and the Problem of Jewish Identity in Late Nineteenth-Century France* (Cambridge, 1978), especially chapter 5, "Antisemitism, Its History and Causes" (pp. 90–109).

8. Isaac, *Genèse* (see n. 4), p. 127. Cf. Joseph Mélèze-Modrzejewski, "Sur l'antisémitisme païen," in M. Olender (ed.), *Le racisme: mythes et sciences* (Brussels, 1981), p. 427: "la convergence des facteurs . . . désignent le milieu du IIe siècle av. n.è. comme l'époque où aurait pris corps l'antisémitisme."

9. Gert G. Lüderitz, *Corpus jüdischer Zeugnisse aus der Cyrenaica* (Wiesbaden, 1983).

10. V. A. Tcherikover and A. Fuks (eds.), *Corpus Papyrorum Judaicarum*, vol. 1 (Cambridge, Mass., 1957), p. 141. Cf. R. Rémondon, "Les antisémites de Memphis," *Chronique d'Egypte* 35 (1960), pp. 244–61, and the remarks of Mélèze-Modrzejewski, op. cit. (n. 8), p. 416.

11. See D. Rokeah, *Jews, Christians and Pagans in Conflict* (Jerusalem/Leiden, 1982), esp. pp. 58, 210.

12. M. Stern, *Greek and Latin Authors on Jews and Judaism*, 3 vols. (Jerusalem, 1974–84).

13. Menahem Stern, "The Jews in Greek and Latin Literature," in S. Safrai and M. Stern (eds.), *The Jewish People in the First Century*, vol. 2 (Assen/Amsterdam, 1976), pp. 1101–59.

14. Together with other recent work, such as R. L. Wilken, *John Chrysostom and the Jews: Rhetoric and Reality in the Late 4th Century* (Berkeley/Los Angeles/London, 1983).

15. Stern, "The Jews" (supra, n. 13), pp. 1111ff.

16. The historian Pompeius Trogus is a case in point: see Stern, ibid., pp. 1146ff.

17. See, for example, Brian Brennan, "The Conversion of the Jews of Clermont in AD 576," *Journal of Theological Studies* NS 36 (1985), pp. 321–27, or Wilken, *John Chrysostom* (supra, n. 14).

18. See Michel Rouche, "Les baptêmes forcés des juifs en Gaule Mérovingienne et dans l'Empire d'Orient," in Valentin Nikiprowetzky (ed.), *De l'antijudaïsme antique à l'antisémitisme contemporain* (Lille, 1979), pp. 105–24.

[2]

The Lamb and the Scapegoat: The Dehumanization of the Jews in Medieval Propaganda Imagery

Moshe Lazar

Si Christianum est odisse Iudeos,
hic abunde christiani sumus omnes.
("If hating Jews makes one a true Christian,
then we all are outstanding Christians.")
—Erasmus

The rise and the growing presence of the Devil, in earlier and later Christian culture, and his powerful role in the shaping of medieval Christian mentality have inscribed deep grooves in the psyche and imagination of the evangelized pagan populations. The physical existence of the Devil and the reality of his actions in daily life, his terrifying presence lurking from behind every thought and event in the world (the *satanos energumenos*), were as much a part of the believer's faith and mind as the divine incarnation of Christ and the Holy Trinity. The conceptualization and the visual articulation of Satan's image in the Gospel and patristic literature were a mirroring process of the parallel development of christological typology. As in the symbolic antinomy of spirit and matter, light and darkness, the Holy Trinity saw the shaping of an antagonistic *Luciferian Trinity* (Devil-Antichrist-Jew), the negative reverse image of the divine power in a world conceived along lines not so far removed from ancient gnostic and dualistic visionary literature.

The growing corpus of christological exegesis was matched step by step with an increasing volume of diabological treatises. The intensified diffusion of Saints' lives and miracle tales documenting the ongoing beneficial intervention of Christ and Mary in this world is shadowed by the same profusion of "documented" stories relating the evil deeds, under disguises both human and animal, of the Devil and his netherworld hosts. While the image of a "lost paradise" was but faintly perceived at a distant horizon in history, the diabolic landscape with its dreadful creatures was always very close, day and night, whether in the desert cave of the hermit or at prayer in the church, haunting every Christian from the cradle to the grave.

In the process of shaping the cathedrals' pictorial programs, theatrical performances as well as popular mass movements, the divine and the diabolic, Christ and Satan were the primordial energizers of the creative imagination of preachers, writers, and artists. Never was there a serious doubt about the real existence of both. The reality of heavenly paradise, in fact, could not match up in inventiveness with the detailed realistic and dramatic presentation of the demonic netherworld. Whereas fiction and utopia were essential to the former, disfigured reality and dystopia provided the framework of the latter. If God was conceived as the creator of the stage and the author of the play, Christ's rewriting of the biblical play—and functioning as both the stage director and central protagonist—offered to Satan, his grotesque antagonist and buffoon, his ape (*simia dei*), an occasion to steal the show and captivate the audiences. And while the demonic jester provided the comic relief needed in a play loaded with typological-didactic lessons, he remained under various disguises—Lucifer, Satan, Antichrist, Jew, Dragon, Dog, Woman—the most feared creature in the daydreams of the monk, the sermons of the preachers, the imagination of the artists, and the anxious psyche of Everyman.

The symbolization process of both good and evil cuts through anthropology, zoology, botany, biology, linguistics, astronomy, and delineates the realms of the divine and the diabolic: the Christian and the Other, the dove and the raven, the lamb and the goat, the lily of the valley and the *auriculae judae* (Judas's ears),[1] the sun and the moon, young and old, etc. Bestiaries, herbaries, lapidaries, nothing is left untouched. Geography, cartography, and historiography are not exempt from similar types of demarcation. Demonic anthropoids of imaginary monstrous races, zoomorphic humanoids, and fantasmagoric sea and land beasts extend the limits of reality in the vast enterprise of teaching the christological interpretation of the universe and mankind. The process of demonization of the material world and human existence, the diabolization of any reality outside Christianity, from the Gospel and Paul to Bosch and Luther, through thousands of verbal and visual representations, both sophisticated and popular, have created over the centuries some of the most memorable landscapes of fear in the mental makeup of Christianized Europe.

In its enterprise of demonizing non-Christian reality, adopting the structure and language of ancient Near Eastern, platonic, and gnostic dualisms (spirit/matter, sons of light/sons of darkness, *agnostos theos/demiurgos*), emerging Christianity engages in a relentless anti-Jewish campaign as part of its differentiation process from ancient Israel and its Torah. In the course of evangelization of the Gentiles, subverting the literal meaning of historical texts and events, translating into a dualistic typological system characters and metaphors related to good and evil, to past and future, to sin and bliss, the various writers of the Gospel and, later, the Church Fathers, organize a body of literature in which "true Israel" (*Versus Israel*, i.e., Christianity) is the realm of the Sons of Light whereas the people of unfulfilled messianism represent the Sons of Darkness. The Church is defined as godly, the Synagogue as satanic. Building on this predicament its theology, its liturgy, its predication, and eventually also a social, political and economic ideology, Christianity writes simultaneously its gospel of love for the Gentiles[2] and a gospel of hatred toward the Jews. With Christianity coming into power in the fourth century, Anti-Judaism becomes more forcefully a doctrinal necessity, a guide for the "teaching of contempt," as Jules Isaac has defined it,[3] articulating a series of myths: the myth of a degenerate Judaism at the time of Jesus; the myth of a Jewish diaspora as God's punishment of the Jews for the crucifixion; the myth of the Jews as Christ's killers; the myth of Israel's rejection by God. Described as descendants of Cain and identified with the Devil, the Jews are given all the possible attributes and qualifications, all the images and symbols that pertain to the prince of the netherworld. The Devil is Jewish and the Jew is the Devil, or his servant, his mediator on earth.[4] Let us briefly examine the enterprise of demonization and dehumanization developed during the first millennium which saw the metamorphosis of the Jews into a nation of the Beast and a congregation of devils and gargoyle-like creatures.

It has frequently been stated, contrary to what J. Parkes had already clearly indicated in his pioneering work *The Conflict of the Church and the Synagogue*,[5] that pagan Anti-Judaism in Hellensitic and Roman times is what essentially became Christian Anti-Judaism or Antisemitism several centuries later. Most of the slanderous anti-Jewish statements by Mnaseas of Patara and Manetho orginate in Alexandria, in the neighborhood of a thriving Hellenized Jewish community, as a sort of reaction against the Exodus saga of the Bible. Some of their writings were preserved by Josephus Flavius in his *Contra Apion*.[6] Among their fabulations: the Jews were all leprous before being enslaved in Egypt; they were expelled from Egypt, not divinely delivered; they adore the golden head of a donkey in the Temple's sanctuary; Moses was an Egyptian priest, and taught the Hebrews to destroy altars of other gods, to show no mercy to others, etc. Some of these stories were repeated by Greek authors. Posidonius tells that Antiochus IV Epiphanes, upon entering the Temple in Jerusalem, found a statue of a bearded man riding a donkey and holding a book; he thought him to be Moses. He then ordered to sacrifice a fat sow on the altar of their God. Apion, adding to the preceding materials, borrows from Posidonius the story that the Jews capture every year a stranger, preferably a Greek, sacrifice him in the Temple, eat his flesh, and swear to remain enemies of the Greek.[7] He also mentions that the Jews are separatists, hate other nations and other gods.

Several Roman writers, in their historical or geographical descriptions, repeat some of these fables. For example, Tacitus: "The Jews reveal a stubborn attachment to one another, an active commiseration, which contrasts with their implacable hatred for the rest of mankind. They sit apart at meals, they sleep apart, and though, as a nation, they are singularly prone to debauchery, they abstain from intercourse with foreign women."[8] Tacitus, though repeating all the fables of his predecessors, does not mention the "ritual murder" episode. On the other hand, contrary to most of his predecessors or contemporaries, he describes many positive qualities of the Jews, among them: they don't kill children; they believe in the immortality of the soul; they are against visual representations of God; and this God is eternal and cannot die. Juvenal expresses contempt for those Romans who convert to Judaism. Celsus, who was opposed to both Jews and Christians, writes: "If the Judeans would stick to observing their laws, nothing could be said against them; we have to confound those who abandon their own law to follow the Judeans."[9] The common denominator of these stories and calumnies is a reaction against the active Jewish proselytism in the Greco-Roman world, and denigration of the monotheistic faith and the Mosaic Law (observance of the Sabbat, circumcision, dietary laws, etc.) of which they knew in fact very little. Nevertheless, "the Hellenistic period is striking not just for the absence of Anti-Semitic actions and the low level of Anti-Semitic beliefs but for the indications of active interest in Jewish history and religion."[10] The Jews in the Roman Empire were granted important civil and religious rights, were active in a variety of trades and professions, and did not suffer from social, racial, or economic discrimination.[11] The major distinction between them and the general population was their attachment to monotheism and observance of the Mosaic Law. "Essentially, Christian anti-Judaism," writes Rosemary Ruether, "grew from a quite separate and distinct motivation, rooted in the interreligious antagonism between Judaism and Christianity over the messiahship of Jesus, whereas the motivations of pagan anti-Judaism were found in their reaction to Jewish anti-paganism."[12] In any case, anti-monotheistic utterances and slanderous fables concerning the Jews remained quite isolated in the works of Greek and Roman historians and writers, and did not develop into an organized doctrine with its propaganda machinery. Except for their religious beliefs and rituals, the Jews were culturally quite well assimilated in the Hellenistic and Roman societies. Anti-Jewish riots, as for example in Alexandria, were localized phenomena and very short-lived.[13]

An abyss separates, both in content and intent, the defamatory rumors of pagan antiquity from the anti-Jewish ideological elaborations at the time of the redaction of the Gospels and their interpretation by the earliest Church Fathers,[14] and this abyss widens considerably when Christianity begets an Empire and political power at the time of Constantine. "We may now put to rest the notion," writes J. Gager, "that Gentile converts to Christianity brought with them, *as Gentiles,* the pervasive anti-Semitism of the Greco-Roman world. Not only was there not such pervasive anti-Semitism, but it is safe to assume that many Gentile converts were drawn from those already attracted in some fashion to Judaism."[15] Another major gulf seems to separate the teachings of Jesus, a Jewish preacher—not yet named Christ, i.e., "annointed," "Messiah"—from the evangelical and christological interpretations of his teachings. Whereas the former was not advocating the abrogation of the Law (Torah) and certainly not the demonization of his fellow brethren, the latter elaborated after his death a different platform which may be summed up as follows: those who refuse Christ as the Messiah don't see that Israel has been rejected by God, that the election has been transferred from the *older* to the *younger* synagogue (now called *ecclesia,* with the same meaning as *synagoga*: assembly, congregation);[16] they are not the true Jews anymore but the killers of Christ and belong to the Devil; if the Jews were really faithful to their election they would renounce their "Jewishness," i.e., their attachment to the Torah. "The Church was at enmity with *this* Judaism, not because it was obsolete, but because it refused to be obsolete and threatened, again and again, to become compellingly relevant in a way that could call into question the very foundations of the Christian claim."[17]

In an interesting essay,[18] D. Hare considers three distinguishable phases in the elaboration of Anti-Judaism, which might, for our purpose here, describe three consecutive sources of anti-Jewish imagery in early Christianity: (a) *Prophetic Anti-Judaism:*[19] namely language borrowed from prophetic wrath in the Old Testament, used to chastise the wicked among the Israelites,—not yet part of christology; (b) *Jewish-Christian Anti-Judaism:* following the Passion of Christ, it adopts the preceding language of prophetic wrath and adds new elements about the apostasy of Israel, its blindness, its deafness, its refusal to recognize the Saviour (in Luke and Acts but not in Mark), and Israel as a whole being guilty of Jesus' death; (c) *Gentilizing Anti-Judaism:* mainly in Matthew; incorporating in its teaching the components of the preceding phases but stressing now God's absolute rejection of Israel; borrowing from the Old Testament expressions and parables relating to separation between husband and wife, i.e., God and Israel, the latter having been replaced by a new spouse, the Church of the Gentiles. Whereas all of Israel are guilty of Christ's death, Pilatus and the Romans are exonerated; and, finally, the Jews bring upon themselves the Christian's blood vengeance forever: *"His blood be on us and on our children!"* (Matthew 27:25). But compared to Paul and John, Hare argues, Matthew's christology is low key, "functional, not ontological."[20]

While these distinctions might be extremely interesting from a theological point of view, and whether Matthew's gospel in his anti-Jewish stance is more functional than ontological, the fact remains that all the phases described by Hare have generated in Christian exegesis a thesaurus of vilifying, demonizing, and dehumanizing expressions concerning the Jews. These expressions, it may be argued, belong more to the domain of rhetoric and allegory,[21] used at a certain time in history and for a specific audience, but we know much better now: they have been understood as addressed to the Jews at any future time and accepted most often in their literal meanings. The Fathers of the Church, from Origen to Saint Augustine, certainly knew how to distinguish between history and allegory, between functional and ontological pronouncements, but what they conveyed through their teachings and to those who preached to the illiterate masses was unmistakably accepted as relating to the Jews living in their midst: "His blood be on us and on our children!"[22]

The demonization process and, ultimately, its dehumanizing result, emerge on the scene within a more clearly structured framework of ideology and propaganda in the writings of Paul and John. "The sad truth of religious history," writes Ruether, "is that one finds that special virulence, which translates itself into diabolizing and damnation, only between groups which pose rival claims to exclusive truth within the same religious symbol system"; and adds: "the basic line of vilification which he [Matthew] represents is common to the entire synoptic tradition and did not originate with him."[23] In his fascinating and controversial book, *The Scapegoat,* René Girard analyzes a wide range of "persecution texts" with inherent or hidden scapegoats (generally defined by him as "victims of a hatred without cause," as Jesus in the Passion story), but fails to perceive the multiple "persecution texts" in Matthew, Acts, Paul, and John, in which both the scapegoat *of* the text and *in* the text—to use Girard's distinctions—are one and the same: the Jews were certainly no less "victims of a hatred without cause" than Jesus, if one considers history rather than myth.[24] A good number of scholars have pointedly noted the shifting from the use of *Hebrews* to *Pharisees* to *Jews* (Fig. 9), particularly in Paul and John, with a strong derogatory and aggressive emphasis on the word Jews.[25] It has also been similarly noted how the guilt of Jesus' death had been transferred from the Roman political authority to Jewish religious authority and to Jews in general. Origen, for example, will present as fact and gospel truth the statement that the Jews "nailed Christ to the cross." In a number of medieval illustrations one finds even a hyperpropagandistic transformation of Pilate himself into a Jew (see Fig. 13). Whereas the role of the Romans is being neatly muted, the conspiratory plot of the Jews is being dramatically highlighted:[26] a collective premeditated murder of the true Messiah by those whose fathers had already been branded as killers of prophets.[27]

Among the variety of negative qualifiers used to transform the Jews from human beings into a mythical and monstrous race the most radical one, without any doubt, originates with John. He seems to be the first one to identify the Jew with the Devil in a statement—not extant in the other Gospels—he attributes to Jesus himself:

"Ye do the deeds of your father." Then said they to him: "We be not born of fornication; we have one father, even God." Jesus said unto them: "If God were your Father, ye would love me; for I proceeded forth and came from God; neither came I of myself, but he sent me. Why do ye not understand my speech? even because ye cannot hear my word. Ye are of *your father the devil,* and the lusts of your father ye will do. He was a murderer from the beginning, and abode not in the truth[. . . .] he is a liar, and the father of it." (8:41–44; emphasis added)

Branded as the son of the Devil, the latter being the most absolute incarnation of Evil and destined to become the most dreaded monstrous creature, the Jew was thus cast in a mythical image from which all the other negative attributes were to be genealogically derived: liar, deceiver, agent of corruption and debauchery, treacherous, poisoner and killer, horned beast, etc. Any new verbal or visual characterization of the Devil in the following centuries is then automatically applied to the Jews.

Following the letter and the spirit of John's demonization of the Jews, the book of Revelation—attributed to John but probably written by a disciple— develops even more the archetypical mythic image of the Jews as a commu- nity of devil worshippers:

I know thy works, and tribulation, and poverty, (. . . but thou art rich) and I know the blasphemy of them which say they are Jews, and are not, but are the *synagogue of Satan;* . . . Behold, I will make them of the *synagogue of Satan,* which say they are Jews, and are not, but do lie. (2:9 and 3:9; emphasis added)

In the apocalyptic landscape of the book of Revelation the Synagogue of the Jews is now transformed into a Synagogue of the Devil, "the dragon, that old serpent, which is the Devil, and Satan." Confronting the mythical slain Lamb ("having seven horns and seven eyes, which are the seven Spirits of God") and those who "have washed their robes and made them white in the blood of the Lamb" are various mythical beasts (denomic locusts, scorpions, a great red dragon "having seven heads and ten horns", the riding satanic Woman ("Babylon the Great, the Mother of Harlots and abominations of the earth") representing Satan and those who worship him, the slayers of the Lamb.

These early texts disseminating concepts and imagery identifying the Jews as satanic creatures are crowned with the elaboration of the supreme mythi- cal and terrorizing figure of Antichrist. The allusions to Antichrist in the Gospels are few and ambiguous. The only mentions of Antichrist (or even *antichrists*) occur in the epistles of John:

Little children, it is the last time: as ye have heard that Antichrist shall come, even now are there many antichrists; whereby we know that it is the last time. They went out from us, but they were not of us[. . . .] Who is a liar but he that denieth that

Jesus is the Christ? He is antichrist, that denieth the Father and the Son. (John 2:18–19, 22)[28]

The legend of Antichrist, originating within the rich corpus of Christian apocalyptic literature,[29] develops typologically an antithetic story to that of Christ. The life of Christ serves as a model for the life of Antichrist. In a treatise on Antichrist, Saint Hippolyte (d. 236) establishes the main framework for all future theologians:

For the deceiver seeks to liken himself in all things to the Son of God. Christ is a lion, so Antichrist is also a lion; Christ is a king, so Antichrist is also a king. . . . The Saviour came into the world in the circumcision, and he will come in the same manner. The Lord sent apostles among all the nations, and he in like manner will send false apostles. . . . The Lord gave a seal to those who believed in Him, and he will give one in like manner. The Saviour appeared in the form of man, and he too will come in the form of a man.[30]

Origen, his contemporary, describes Antichrist as the supreme Imposter, an actor who is able to imitate Christ and almost all of his deeds: "Invenimus omnes virtutes esse Christum, et omnes simulatas virtutes Antichristum." ("We find that all virtues pertain to Christ, and all simulacres of virtues to Antichrist!")[31]

Figuratively represented as the Beast—in the way Christ is as the Lamb—but as Christ appearing incarnated in a human form, Antichrist is given a biblical ancestry and a Jewish identity. (In some medieval illuminations, Antichrist is shown wearing the Jewish badge of infamy.) Born in Babylon (a name associated with sin and the "great whore"), conceived in the womb of a Jewish prostitute by the Devil, Antichrist grows up in Bethsaida and Chorazain (villages cursed by Christ), and is educated by Satan, magicians, and false prophets. A Jew by birth through his mother—a descendant from the tribe of Dan[32]—and recognized as a Jew through circumcision,[33] Antichrist's mission on earth is to undermine the evangelization process, to corrupt and destroy Christianity, and to establish himself as messiah and king. This Jewish Antichrist, as Satan/Beast and as a grotesque *rex judaeorum*, represents thus the third and crucial phase in the diabolization process of the Jews in early Christianity: (1) Devil, father of the Jews; (2) Satan's Synagogue, both as congregation and house of prayers; and (3) Antichrist as Jewish/satanic messiah, still expected by the Jews and, periodically, manifesting himself in the world with the help of the latter (Fig. 27).[34]

The "teaching of contempt" and the dissemination of anti-Jewish pronouncements find their most eloquent expression in patristic literature after

Constantine's conversion. "For Judaism," writes Father Edward Flannery, "the fourth century was a prelude to millennial misfortune. . . . By the end of the fourth century, the Jew's civil status was precarious, and his image had greatly deteriorated. At the close of the previous century, he was no more than a special type of unbeliever; at the end of the fourth, he was a semisatanic figure, cursed by God, and marked off by the state."[35] As we have seen, the Jew had become long before that time more than a "semisatanic figure"—a mirror-image of Satan and Antichrist. Saint Gregory of Nyssa presents the following synthetic portrait of the Jews:

murderers of the Lord, assassins of the prophets, rebels against God, God haters, . . . advocates of the devil, race of vipers, slanderers, calumniators, dark-minded people, leaven of the Pharisees, sanhedrin of demons, sinners, wicked men, stoners, and haters of righteousness.[36]

Saint Jerome, who frequently consulted with rabbis, uses nevertheless similar qualifiers when speaking about the Jews: serpents; in the image of Judas; their praying is as pleasant to God as a donkey's braying. Saint Ephraim likens the synagogue to a prostitute. Saint Augustine calls the Jews descendants of Cain and from the seed of Esau. Socrates, a continuator of Eusebius, is one of the first to spread the *ritual murder* libel, accusing Jews in Imnestar (Syria) of having crucified a Christian boy during the feast of Purim.[37] Sergius the Stylite calls his contemporary Jews "sons of 'the sons of vipers,' " "offspring of iniquity and a fornicating false seed," and "sons of darkness." Pope Gregory the Great presents the Jews as "preachers of Antichrist"; a nation of the Beast; the devil dwells in the heart of the Jews. Agobard proclaims that Jews should be segregated, for they are "Antichrists," "sons of the devil," "Satan's synagogue," the "filth of society," seducers and debauchers of Christian women ("these sons of the devil seduce them, disguising their hate while offering them false caresses").[38]

But no one more than John Chrysostom, in the patristic enterprise of vilification of the Jews and in the entire corpus of *Adversus Judaeos* apologetics,[39] has contributed a greater share to the formation of the anti-Jewish propaganda imagery while at the same time making the Jews as Christ killers and the Jewish dispersion as punishment for deicide a major cornerstone of his theology.[40] In the first of his homilies against the Jews Chrysostom uses in each sequence of his discourse a central anti-Jewish qualifier upon which he dwells at length, garnishing it with typologically arranged quotations from the Scriptures:

the Jews are *dogs, stiff-necked, gluttonous* and drunkards; "*beasts* unfit for work, they are *fit for killing*, . . . *fit for slaughter*" [quotes Luke, 19:27, 'But as for these my enemies, who did not want me to be king over them, bring them here and slay them']. . . .

"These Jews are gathering choruses of effeminates and a great rubbish heap of harlots; they drag into the synagogue the whole theater, actors and all. For *there is no difference between the theater and the synagogue.*" . . .

"Where a harlot has set herself up, that place is a brothel. But *the synagogue is not only a brothel and a theater; it is also a den of robbers and a lodging for wild beasts.*" . . .

The "*synagogue is a dwelling of demons*"; God is not worshipped there, for it is a "*place of idolatry.*"

The shrines (i.e., the "ridiculous and disgraceful synagogues") of the Jews are filled with "bugbears and hobgoblins" which frighten the "simpler-minded Christians." . . .

The Jews "live for their bellies," like "*pigs* or *goats.*" . . .

"Inns are not more august than royal palaces. Indeed the *synagogue is less deserving of honor than any inn*. It is not merely a *lodging place for robbers* and *cheats* but also for *demons. This is true not only of the synagogues but also of the souls of the Jews.*" . . .

"Is it not strange that those who worship the Crucified keep common festival with those who crucified him?" ("with those who shouted 'Crucify him, Crucify him' and 'his blood be upon us and upon our children' ")[41] . . . .

Because the Jews fail to "see" the many prefigurations of Christ in the Old Testament, "*we must hate both them and their synagogue.*" . . .

The synagogue, even "if there is no idol there, still demons do inhabit the place." . . .

"*Here the slayers of Christ gather together*, here the cross is driven out;" "does not greater harm come from this place since *the Jews themselves are demons?*" . . .

There is no difference between a pagan temple of Apollo and a synagogue, between pagans and Jews. "But the Jews practice a deceit which is more dangerous. In their synagogue stands an invisible altar of deceit on which *they sacrifice not sheep* and calves *but the souls of men.*" . . .

"*Demons dwell* in the synagogue, not only in the place itself but also *in the souls of the Jews,*" who are "the common disgrace and infection of the whole world," "wild beasts," "brute beasts," thieves, plunderers, "cheating in trade." (Homily I; emphasis added)

All these and more in only one of the many homilies preached by Chrysostom (the "*golden mouthed*") against the Jews. In his sixth sermon, he sums up his definition of the synagogue: "Now you give it a name more worthy than it deserves if you call it a *brothel*, a *stronghold of sin*, a *lodging-place for demons*, a *fortress of the devil*, the destruction of the soul, the precipice and pit of all perdition, or whatever other name you give it." And, finally, in the opening sentences of his seventh homily: "Have you had enough of the fight against the Jews? Or do you wish me to take up the same topic today? . . . The man who does not have enough of loving Christ will never have enough of fighting against those who hate Christ"; "their trumpets [the *shofar* on the Day of Atonement] were a greater outrage than those heard in the theaters; their fasts were more disgraceful than any drunken revel. So, too, the tents [the *sukkah* of the Feast of Tabernacles] which at this moment are pitched among them are no better than the inns where harlots and flute girls ply their trades." Following closely in the footsteps of Paul and John, Chrysostom's dramatic and violent anti-Jewish propaganda will find, centuries later, its equivalent in another "golden-mouthed" preacher, Martin Luther.[42]

Marked with the sign of Cain or the seal of Antichrist on his forehead— later to be made visible and explicit through the yellow badge of infamy on his garment[43]—branded as Christ killer and possessed by the devil, hated by God and his preachers, the mythical Jew of Christian theology became superimposed on the real Jew living in the shadow of the church. The lines of demarcation between reality and myth concerning the Jews and the synagogue were further blurred by translating the metaphors of hatred and contempt, elaborated in patristic literature, into codified systems of social vilification and juridical ghettoization of people who had been stripped of their human features.[44]

When we arrive at the end of the first millennium, the diabolization and dehumanization process of the Jews has run its full course and reached a major phase in its verbal representation of the Synagogue as the house of devils and vipers, the Jews as Christ killers and a nation of the Beast. In the ensuing centuries, building on a millennium of demonization and vilification, medieval Christianity disseminates the grotesque and dehumanized image of its mythical Jews through a masterful use of its mass media: sermons, plays, and visual arts. A *canned* image of the Jew and Judaism had been created and adopted as an integral part of the "literature of the illiterate."[45] The simply articulated and canned stereotypes were now going to translate theological anti-Jewish doctrine into mass consumers' imagery which would easily be conjured up in times of crisis, in periods of social, political, and economical unrest. The final canned product of the mythical Jew was now marketable, under a concise dehumanizing label, throughout the Christianized world. Slight changes in style, technique, or iconography are of no consequence to its effectiveness and popularity, much in the same way, if we may borrow a contemporary marketing device, as Coca-Cola—the *classic and new formula.*[46]

If the fourth century witnesses a major development from evangelical to patristic anti-Jewish propaganda, and from archetypical diabolic metaphors to an organized theological system of vilification with its own enriched dehumanizing lexicon, the eleventh century shows their integration into the daily life and mentalities of Christianized Europe, their increased dissemination through the popularizing mass media (sermons, theatre, visual arts), and their efficacity in a mythical-demagogic manipulation of human illusions and fears. The importance of the millennium phenomenon, and the related First Crusade for understanding this transformation of anti-Jewish propaganda can hardly be overstated. The historical period surrounding the millennium offers a prototypical case of a society in spiritual, social, political, and economic crisis, deeply steeped in utopic and dystopic exaltation, inspired and manipulated by zealous and political leaders who know the art of exploiting the people's fear of the Devil and Antichrist, and know how to conjure up the earthly double of the latter: the mythical and demonized Jew in their midst. "The coming of Antichrist," writes Norman Cohn,

was even more tensely awaited. . . . People were always on the watch for the "signs" which, according to the prophetic tradition, were to herald and accompany the final "time of troubles"; and since the "signs" included bad rulers, civil discord, war, drought, famine, plague, comets, sudden deaths of prominent persons and an increase in general sinfulness, there was never any difficulty about finding them. . . .[47]

In the eyes of the crusading *pauper* the smiting of the Moslems and the Jews was to be the first act in that final battle which . . . was to culminate in the smiting of the Prince of Evil himself. Above these desperate hordes, as they moved about their work of massacre, there loomed the figure of Antichrist. . . . It is the will of God— Urban is made to announce at Clermont—that through the labours of the crusaders Christianity shall flourish again at Jerusalem in these last times, so that when Antichrist begins his reign there—as he shortly must—he will find enough Christians to fight. . . .[48]

But if the Saracen (and his successor the Turk) long retained in the popular imagination a certain demonic quality, the Jew was an even more terrifying figure. Jews and Saracens were generally regarded as closely akin, if not identical; but since the Jews lived scattered through Christian Europe, they came to occupy by far the larger part in popular demonology. Moreover, they occupied it for much longer with consequences which have extended down the generations and which include the massacre of millions of European Jews in mid-twentieth century. . . .[49]

It was believed that in preparation for the final struggle Jews held secret, grotesque tournaments at which, as soldiers of Antichrist, they *practiced stabbing.* Even the ten lost tribes of Israel, whom Commodianus had seen as the future army of Christ, became identified with those hosts of Antichrist, the peoples of Gog and Magog— peoples whom the *Pseudo-Methodius* described as *living off human flesh, corpses, babes ripped from their mothers' wombs, and also off scorpions, serpents* and all the most disgusting reptiles.[50] (Emphasis added)

It is against this background that one has to analyze the variety of themes, genres, techniques, styles, and expressions relating to the proliferation of anti-Jewish imagery during the second millennium. The following subjects, of which only some brief examples will be given here,[51] represent the most important lines of anti-Jewish propaganda on stage, in art, and in real life.

1. The dramatization and visualization of christological typology and diabological typology as they were elaborated in patristic literature. The opposites right and left, high and low, young and old, straight and crooked lines, sublime and grotesque expressions, balanced and violent gestures, symbols of light and darkness, portraits and caricatures are used to characterize the forces of good on the one hand, and the agents of evil (Lucifer, Antichrist, Pharaoh, Herod, Nero, Jews) on the other. (Fig. 14, 16). Medieval drama and art are didactically, rather than esthetically, oriented and structured, and the dualistic typological system determines their thematic choices as well as their formal solutions.[52] The devils and the Jews (Cain, Judas, Herod, medieval Jews) play the roles of the hideous villains and antagonists both for a didactic purpose and for comic relief.[53]

2. The confrontations between *Ecclesia* and *Synagoga*, or a Christian and a Jew, in plays and in art. These are inspired by a long tradition of the literary-theological genre of the polemic dialogue between the old/veiled and the new/unveiled Testaments, and in particular by the most popular pseudo-Augustinian *De Altercatione Ecclesiae et Synagogae* which became the model for the medieval *Ordo Prophetarum* type of plays or scenes.[54] By setting up against each other two opposing factions, one of which served as foil to amuse the audience through grotesque gesticulations, asinine stubbornness, comic jargon, and ultimate crushing defeat, the disputation was used as shattering, irrefutable proof of the Christian truth. In the twelfth-century *Jeu d'Adam*, for example, during the procession of the prophets, the disputation begins with the arrival of Isaiah, who announces that "A virgin shall come forth from the race of Jesse." The Prophets of Israel, with the christianized interpretation of their prophecies and metaphors, are mobilized against the historical Jews of later centuries in dramatized evangelization scenes as well as in pictorial and sculptural representations. The comic intention becomes immediately apparent in the words and gestures of the Jew, as revealed in the following interchange:

JEW: Now answer me, sir Isaiah:
Is this fable or prophecy?
What is this you have said?
Did you invent it? *Where is it written?* [55]
You were sleeping, you dreamed it!
Is this the truth or is it a jest?
ISAIAH: This is no fable, but complete truth.
JEW: Now *make us see it!*
ISAIAH: What I have said is prophecy.
JEW: *In what book is it written?*
ISAIAH: In the book of life. I didn't dream it.
I saw it!
JEW: How did you do it?
ISAIAH: With the help of God.
JEW: You seem to be an old fool,
Your mind is quite disturbed!
You're old and narrow-minded . . .
Now, look at this hand of mine?
See if I am sick or healthy!
ISAIAH: You have the felon's disease,
From which you will never be cured!
JEW: Am I really sick then?
ISAIAH: Yes, sick with error! (*Jeu d'Adam,* ll. 883–903; emphasis added)

The terror of being struck down by an incurable disease leads the Jew to accept conversion—the miraculous cure which metamorphoses wolves into sheep, demonized Jews into baptized human creatures—the conventional wishful-thinking finale in almost all of the Judeo-Christian encounters in medieval drama.

In another play, *The Presentation at the Temple,* described by an eyewitness at its theatrical performance,[56] the confrontation between Ecclesia and Synagoga represented the didactic and grotesque highlight of the show. The contrast in their costumes, symbolic emblems, style of speech, and general demeanor was meant to evoke admiration of the former and contempt for the latter.

Ecclesia is dressed completely in gold, in the clothes of a deacon, her beautiful hair flowing down her shoulders; on her head she wears a crown of gold with lilies and precious stones; and on her breast a kind of chalice which shall signify the New Testament; and in her left hand she will carry a cross the size of her body, and the cross will be of pure gold. . . . In her right hand she will carry a kind of round fruit completely golden, signifying the universal dominance of the Church.

Synagoga, on the other hand, is dressed in an *old tunic reaching her ankles . . .* and with a *black, torn cloak.* Her head covered in the fashion of an *old woman,* with a veil of obscure color, and *over her eyes and face she shall wear a black veil. . . .* In the left hand, she will carry a certain standard which will appear as a broken black spear. *. . .* And in the right hand she will carry *two stone tablets pointing toward the ground,* on which there will be inscribed letters in Hebrew script, which will signify the Law of Moses and the *Old* Testament. (See Figs. 9, 10, 11, 12)

Finally, when Ecclesia is received with rejoicing, Synagoga is ridiculed and brutally thrust off the stage by the archangels Gabriel and Raphael, her fall provoking waves of laughter and verbal abuse in the audience. Throwing away the tablets of the Law, Synagoga, in tears, escapes from the church. Instruments of music are played out loud to calm the excited public ("tantum quod populus quietetur a risu propter Synagogam expulsam"). In addition to the grotesque appearance of Synagoga or the Jews, in even a stronger contrast with the saintly and soft-spoken Ecclesia, these caricatural characters are made to mouth a stream of insulting invectives, curses, Hebrew nonsense words[57] and obscenities[58] which, while provoking laughter in the crowd, also helped arouse its hatred toward the Jews living amidst them. Special measures had often to be taken to protect the Jewish quarters during performances of Passion and Mystery plays. In various places, Jews had to participate in the production costs of these performances and to be present at the show to see their disgraceful status reflected and explained on the stage.

In the Benediktbeuern *Ludus de Nativitate*[59] we find the arbitrator of the disputation, Saint Augustine, with the prophets on his right, Archisynagogus and the Jews on his left (always on the *sinister* side). Archisynagogus and the Jews, as well as the Hebrew prophets, are not presented as the contemporaries of Jesus but as the contemporaries of the medieval spectators, caricatural representatives of the Jews in general. (See Figs. 1–7)

Let Archisynagogus with his Jews, having heard the prophecies, make an excessive clamor; and, pushing forward his associate, *agitating his head and his entire body and stamping the ground with his foot, and imitating with his sceptre the manners of a Jew in every way,* let him say indignantly . . . with immoderate and violent laughter [follows a lengthy sarcastic speech concerning the Immaculate conception in the style of]:

"Who would predict that a camel / could be born from a cow? / Whenever a virgin will conceive / the river Xanthus will flow backwards, / the wolf will flee from the lamb, / the plain will become hilly." . . .

Archisynagogus will bawl and shout, agitating his body and head, and deride the prophecies [but in the end, he and his Jews will see the truth and convert]. (Emphasis added)

The Jews (including Cain, Herod, the Pharisees, the crucifiers) are represented in similar ways as Synagoga and Archisynagogus in most of the medieval plays: gesticulating, shouting, ranting, and raving like mad dogs, cursing and blaspheming the holy beliefs and rituals of the Church, resembling the medieval stage devils in every aspect. The Jews *"out-Herod Herod"* in their frenzied and demonic acting on the stage.[60]

The most frequent expressions associated with the Jews, in the Latin and vernacular plays, relentlessly repeat and act out the traditional qualifiers of their nature on the stage: gesticulate, jump, dispute, spit, make noise, laugh, conjure up the devil, rage, curse, act as madmen, hate Christ and Mary, mock, deceive, steal holy host and stab them, torture and crucify holy icons, blind, deaf, felony, perfidy, gluttony, hypocrisy, savage, hard necked, treacherous, sinister, mad dogs, wolves, false dogs, scorpions,[61] pig [or Jewish sow, *Judensau*][62] [see Figs, 23, 28, 29, 31], demons, etc.

One cannot overstate the theatrical effect on the audiences achieved through the combination of grotesque costumes, gestures, and language in the presentation of the Jews on stage. In thousands of illuminations, paintings, stained-glass windows, sculptures, ivory carvings, and engravings, in every possible style, technique, and format, originating from all over medieval Europe, the confrontation between Ecclesia and Synagoga is a visual counterpart to what we find in drama. Invariably Ecclesia on the right hand of the cross, a beautiful crowned Queen, holding the scepter of domination and often collecting Christ's blood in a chalice, paradise and the sun in her corner; on the left hand of the cross, Synagoga, in the guise of a disgraced Queen, an old and bent over woman, her eyes veiled, blindfolded, or covered by a devil's hand (Fig. 8), her crown or tables of the Law escaping from her grip, her broken scepter—rather resembling a lance—threatens Christ's body or pierces the Holy Lamb (Figs. 12, 18), hell and the moon in her corner. In other works, Synagoga will be shown mounted on a ridiculous and stubborn ass (Fig. 11), riding a donkey or a pig while seated backwards on the animal (Figs. 27, 29, 30), having a goat [i.e., the devil] on her shoulder, holding a goat's head in one hand, nursing a goat or holding it in her lap (Figs. 10, 11), an arrow being shot in her eye by a devil, sometimes a purse in her hand as symbol of usury, etc.[63] Ridiculing the old Synagoga, surrounding her with negative symbols and showing her defeat convey the theological message in a simplified interpretation; but when she is shown

with a devil-goat the images of Satan's Synagogue and the Mother of Antichrist are unequivocally conjured up in the mind of the faithful who
visualize the preacher's sermons. This is even more dramatically so when
synagogue is represented as piercing the Holy Lamb or holding a chalice (an
oil lamp?) upside down—demonstrating the ongoing crucifixion by the Jews
(Fig. 17), Here, as in the plays, Synagogue, in the confrontation scene, is
literally represented as a congregation of Jews, dressed in their medieval
garments, inflicting upon the cross or Christ's body identical tortures.

3. The growing number of narrative poems, plays, or scenes dealing with
Antichrist and his Jews. This trend follows Adso's very popular *Libellus de
Antichristo*, written during the effervescence of the Millennium syndrome.
The latter inspired such plays as the *Ludus de Antechristo* (c. 1150), *Jour du
Jugement* (early fourteenth century), and *Mystère de l'Antéchrist et du Jugement
de Dieu* (sixteenth century), as well as narrative poems such as *Le Tournoie-
ment Antecrist*, etc. The artistic treatment of the Antichrist legend and the
Apocalypse is a major contributor to the shaping of the medieval landscape
of fear.[64] The Jewish Antichrist, wearing the badge of infamy, and even
some of the demonic locusts with "Jewish" round cap hats, are a constant
reminder of the diabolic conspiracy aiming to destroy the Christian world.

4. The typological use of the bestiaries: the contemporary Hebrews of
Jesus, brothers in the same monotheistic faith, became in the writing of his
history identified with the treacherous Judas, labeled as Pharisees and, in the
process, losing even his name, to be simply called Jews. As traitors and
murderers, as money-changers and thieves, the Jews still retained some
semblance of human physionomy. Being repeatedly called carnal, lecherous,
avaricious, malicious, blind, deaf, rich, idle, filthy, idolatrous, demonic,
etc., the Jew still remained a human being, albeit a descendant from the
seed of Cain. But once identified with the Devil, the Jews not only enter the
imaginary domain of the mythical monstrous races but become mythical
beings themselves. The mythicization and diabolization of the Jews led
consequently to their dehumanization. They become now *serpents, vipers,
aspics, basiliscs, goats, pigs, ravens, vultures, bats, scorpions, dogs, cormorants,
hyenas, jackals, vermine,* to name only a few among the most frequent
zoological qualifiers, to which are added mytho-zoological ones according to
the talent and fertile imagination of individual theologians and artists. From
a lexicological perspective the technique consists, in a first phase, to borrow
from the Old Testament all the poetic metaphors and images used by the
Prophets in the expression of their wrath, selecting those that bear negative

connotations and applying them to the Jews in general. In the next phase, with the symbolic demonization of the animal kingdom and the formation of a mythical zoology, the range of lexical dehumanization is further extended. Among the numerous mytho-zoological beasts, the *manticore* of the bestiaries is described as a "beast born in the Indies. It has a threefold row of teeth meeting alternately, the face of a man, with gleaming blood-red eyes, a lion's body, a tail like the sting of a scorpion, and a shrill voice which is so sibilant that it resembles the botes of flutes. It hankers after human flesh most ravenously."[65] In some illustrations the manticore wears the *pileum cornutum* (horned hat) of the Jew (see Fig. 25).[66]

Whereas the christological imagery, *dove, lamb, eagle, lion, pelican, unicorn,* and its positive application to the good Christians, retains its metaphoric character, the diabological one is interpreted literally. The former humanizes the animal world and domesticates it into a familiar one; the latter animalizes the Jews, dehumanizes them, and metamorphoses them into dreadful and nightmarish creatures (Fig. 26).

5. The Jews in miracle stories, miracle plays, narrative poems, and the visual arts are presented (a) as mediators between a Christian and Satan or (b) as thieves, liars, and cheaters. The works in the second group, generally, not only have the Jew caught but show him repenting and converting to Christianity. Contrary to those in the first group they represent a minor genre, whereas the former constitute a successful and long-lasting tradition. The most popular and central to this tradition is the legend of Theophilus, the unhappy and despairing cleric who sold his soul to the Devil—a Jewish magician acting as mediator between them—but who later repented and gained salvation through the intercession of Notre Dame. The story first appears in a sixth-century Greek narrative by Eutychianus, but was reworked by Paul the Deacon of Naples in the ninth century; it is his Latin version which became the source of numerous adaptations in poetic narratives and drama,[67] chiefly among them *Lapsus et Conversio Theophili Vicedomni* by Hroswitha of Gandersheim, *Comment Theophilus vint à pénitence* by Gautier de Coincy, *Miracle de Théophile* by Rutebeuf, an anonymous *Miracolo di Teofilo* in Italian, a Galician-Portuguese version in the *Cantigas de Santa Maria* by Alfonso X the Wise, and three anonymous plays in Middle Low German. The development of the Jew's role in these eight versions, from an anonymous *nefandus Hebreus* to a Jewish magician and later to a group of Jews, as well as the relationship between the Jew and the Devil need to be carefully analyzed. The illustrations of the Theophilus legend in manuscripts, stained-glass windows, and the sculptural programs of cathedrals

have been preserved in great numbers and show their relationship to the poetic and dramatic narrative over several centuries (see Fig. 15).

6. The Jews and the desecration of holy icons (Christ, Mary, Saints): This trend appears most often in the framework of the miracle-tale genre (including in some instances the punishment of the Jewish culprit, and generally his conversion), and includes stealing, torturing, stabbing or burning holy icons, or for this purpose making waxen images. It seems to have been extremely popular among the masses, given the enormous quantity of texts and artistic representations which have been preserved.

7. The Jews and the desecration/stabbing of the Holy Host, in general also within the structure of the miracle tale: A Jew, or several Jews, participate in the stabbing (Fig. 19). This group of works, both in drama and art, achieves a deeper emotional impact on the masses with its high degree of violent anti-Jewish propaganda, almost equal to that of the ritual murder libel. Among the most virulent dramatizations are *Le Jeu et Mystère de la Saincte Hostie par Personages* in France and the *Play of the Sacrament* in England.

8. The Jews and the ritual murder libel: This was represented through four major topical groups:

A. Jew accused of killing a Christian child;
B. Jew accused of killing his own son after he becomes a Christian (through baptism or his partaking in the eucharist);
C. A congregation of Jews involved in killing one or several Christian children;
D. A Jewess entraps a Christian boy and kills him.

Group A is represented by the chronicle relating the William of Norwich blood libel (1144) and the numerous literary-artistic versions it has inspired (Fig. 22).

Group B is mainly derived from a story elaborated in the works of Gregory of Tours and Evagrius Scholasticus: a Jewish boy follows his friend to church, partakes in the communion, thus becoming a Christian, and upon his return is thrown by his father into a furnace; the boy is saved by the Virgin, the father is punished and the mother converts (Fig. 20), or both and an entire congregation convert. Some forty different versions of the story have been preserved in a great number of copies, representing a wide variety of languages (Greek, Latin, Old French, German, Spanish, Arabic, Ethiopian).

Group C (a variation of Group A) includes major historical blood libel incidents, followed by tragic results, which have inspired during centuries hundreds of illustrations: the Simon of Trent legend (Figs. 23, 24, 29, 31) —the most disseminated one, and the Santo Niño de la Guardia libel fabricated by the Spanish Inquisition, among many others. The diffusion of these illustrated horror stories all over the world (Fig. 21), from the Middle Ages to the twentieth century, creates a propitious and fertile soil which sprouts in turn new historical calamities for Jews targeted as scapegoats. The horror produced by the Simon of Trent illustrations is paralleled in drama by a most violent anti-Jewish play, *Das Endinger Judenspiel.*

Finally, Group D includes the Hugh of Lincoln legend (or *The Jew's Daughter*), disseminated through a host of English and Scottish ballads, Chaucer's *The Prioress's Tale,* and multiple versions in France, Spain, etc.

9. The "pound of flesh" story. From the Italian narratives and the French *Marchand Chrétien de Constantinople et Usurier Juif* to Shakespeare's *Merchant of Venice,* we witness essentially another type of variation on the Jew as killer of Christian children, this time in Christ-like protagonists.

The works in categories 6 to 9 represent fundamentally a series of creative variations on one central theme: the reenactment by the Jews of the crucifixion of Christ. The Jews *literally* torture Christ, spill his blood, and kill him in the body of the Christian child, do so *symbolically* in stabbing the Host or spilling the chalice of wine, or by asking for a "pound of flesh," and historically by refusing to convert. These works provide the most important ingredients in the anti-Jewish propaganda imagery: Jews as Christ killers, agents of Satan and Antichrist, old and degenerate blood suckers, dehumanized man-eaters—mythical creatures, between Frankenstein and Dracula, growing like the phantasmagoric manticore in the fearful minds of the untutored masses. For three centuries in England, the Jew survived in a Jewless land as a powerful mythical monster, useful in a time of crisis and change to project local and national frustrations and guilt feelings on him rather than on the Christians themselves. Who was in Marlowe's and Shakespeare's time the real merchant of London, the real money-lender? Needless to say, he was not in the synagogue. With Shakespeare's *Merchant of Venice* we are back again in the genre and framework of the medieval miracle play structure: Antonio as Christ, Shylock as Antichrist, and Portia as Virgin Mary. Shylock, combining in his character and dramatic role the composite image of the cormorant and the manticore, the bloodsucking usurer and the devil, powerfully fashioned by Shakespeare's theatrical talent, brings with him into the modern world a revigorated image of the mythical Jew, fathering a rich lineage of monstrous Jews from Fagin to Jud Süss.

1 Prophet Joel. St. Urbain church, ca. 1270.

2 Jacob. Bourges Cathedral; 13th c.

3 Drawing of Prophet.
Victoria and Albert Museum; 13th c.

114

5 Dispute between Christians and Jews. Engraving, 16th c.

4 English Jew. Victoria and Albert Museum; 1275.

6 Jews bringing Jesus before Caiphas. London, British Museum; ca. 1280.

7 Jesus and three Pharisees. Paris, B.N., Ms.Fr.403; 13th c.

8 Matfre Ermengaud, *Breviari d'Amor*. Escorial, 14th c.

9 Moralized Bible,
14th c. Ecclesia,
God the Father, bearded
Jew as Synagoga, and Devil.

10 Ecclesia and Synagoga.
Verdun, Municipal
Library, Ms.119; 12th c.

11 Crucifixion, *Hortus Deliciarum*, 12th c.

12 Ecclesia and Synagoga.
Montpellier, Ms. 399.

13 Pilate as Jew. Amiens, 13th c.

14 Nero, Devil and Jew persecute
martyr. Poitiers, 12th c.

15 Legend of Theophilus. Paris, Notre Dame, 13th c.

16 Jew and Devil crushed by Saints. Paris, Notre Dame.

18 Synagoga pierces Holy Lamb. Ivory cross, England, ca. 1180.

17 Synagoga spilling wine (blood) from chalice. Sens, ca. 1520.

19 Stabbing of the Holy Host. Sternberg, 1492.

20 Jew throws his son in a furnace. Book of Hours, England, 14th c.

21 Ritual murder. Poland, 16th c.

22 William of Norwich. *The Nuremberg Chronicle,* 15th c.

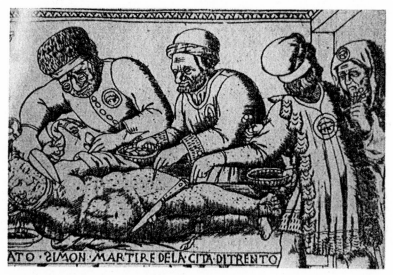

23 Simon of Trent. Pigs on the Jews' badges.
Engraving, Florence(?), 15th c.

24 Simon of Trent. *The Nuremberg Chronicle*, 15th c.

25 Manticore with Jewish head. *Royal Bestiary*; London, British Museum.

26 A member of the monstrous races.
The Nuremberg Chronicle, 15th c.

27 *The Future Messiah of the Jews.* Broadsheet. Woodcut, Germany 1563.

28 Big Jewish sow (Judensau). Germany, 15th c.

29 Jew riding backwards on sow.
Glass painting, 17th c.

30 Jew Riding backwards on monstrous
beast. Aershot, Notre Dame, 15th c.

31 Jews riding goat, Jewish sow,
Jewish devil, and martyrdom
of Simon of Trent; 17th C.

32 Grotesque Jewish devils.
Title page of satiric
broadsheet, Germany, 1571.

Notes

1. Also called "Jews' Ears"; *auricularia sambucina;* see Fr. *oreille de Judas;* It. *orecchio di Giudá;* Ger. *Judasohr, Judasöhrlein;* Sw. *Judasöra;* Pol. *Judaszowe ucho.* For these and many more examples, see Wayland D. Hand, "Dictionary of Words and Idioms Associated with Judas Iscarioth," *University of California Publications in Modern Philology,* 24 (1942), 229–356; s.v. Judas-Ear.
2. Paul: "I am the apostle of the Gentiles" (Romans 11:13); "the Jews, Who both killed the Lord Jesus, and their own prophets, and have persecuted us; and they please not God, and are contrary to all men; Forbidding us to speak to the Gentiles that they might be saved" (1 Thessalonians 2:14–16). Whether Paul's preachings were addressed to Jews refusing the Gospel and opposing its dissemination, or to the pagan community, has no particular relevance to the fact that he contributed in a major way to the vilification process of the Jews and Judaism as was also the case with John Chrysostom centuries later.
3. See Jules Isaac, *Genèse de l'antisémitisme* (Paris: Calman-Levy, 1956).
4. Joshua Trachtenberg's book, *The Devil and the Jews: The Medieval Conception of the Jew and Its Relation to Modern Antisemitism* (New Haven: Yale University Press, 1943), represents an important pioneering work on the demonization of the Jews, but some of its basic tenets are in need of being newly elaborated; in particular, his thesis that anti-heretic propaganda was a sort of matrix for anti-Jewish accusations after Jews were identified with infidels and heretics in the wake of the First Crusade. See also Leon N. McCrillis, *The Demonization of Minority Groups in Christian Society during the Central Middle Ages* (Ph.D. diss., University of California, Riverside, 1974); Eric M. Zafran, *The Iconography of Antisemitism: A Study of the Representation of the Jews in the Visual Arts of Europe 1400–1600* (Ph.D. diss., New York University, 1973).
5. James Parkes, *The Conflict of the Church and the Synagogue. A Study in the Origins of Antisemitism* (London: Soncino Press, 1934; repr. New York: Atheneum, 1969). See Preface (1934): "Much more evidence could be produced to support the thesis that the hostility of the Roman world to the Jew offers no explanation of the creation and survival of antisemitism. . . . I became more and more convinced that it was in the conflict of the Church with the Synagogue that the real roots of the problem lay." See also C. H. Moehlman, *The Christian-Jewish Tragedy: A Study in Religious Prejudice* (New York: Colgate-Rochester Divinity School, 1933). The thesis of pagan anti-Judaism as the source of Christian antisemitism was strongly rejected by J. Isaac *(Genèse de l'antisémitisme),* and later by Gavin Langmuir, "Anti-Judaism as the Necessary Preparation for Anti-Semitism," *Viator,* 2 (1971), 383–89; Rosemary R. Ruether, *Faith and Fratricide* (New York: Seabury Press, 1974); John J. Gager, *The Origins of Anti-Semitism: Attitudes toward Judaism in Pagan and Christian Antiquity* (New York and Oxford: Oxford University Press, 1983); but is maintained generally, for a variety of reasons, by Marcel Simon, *Verus Israël. Etude sur les relations entre Chrétiens et*

Juifs dans l'empire romain (Paris: E. de Boccard, [1948] 1964); F. Lovsky, *Antisémitisme et mystère d'Israël* (Paris: Seuil, 1955); N. Sevenster, *The Roots of Pagan Anti-Semitism in the Ancient World* (Leiden: Brill, 1975).

6. Josephus, *Complete Works*, trans. William Whiston (Edinburgh: W. P. Nimmo, 1867; repr. (Grand Rapids, Mich.: Kregel Publications [1960], 1981), pp. 607–36.

7. *Contra Apion*, vol. 2, pp. 13, 137.

8. Tacitus, quoted in Theodore Reinach, *Texes d'auteurs Grecs et Romains relatifs au Judaïsme* (Paris, 1895; repr. Hildesheim: Georg Olms Verlag, 1963), pp. 306–8.

9. Celsus, in Origen's *Contra Celsus*, quoted in T. Reinach, p. 168.

10. J. Gager, p. 43; see also p. 57: "it is a serious mistake to infer from these texts that their individual authors or Roman literary circles in general harboured strong negative feelings about Judaism."

11. See the most solid contribution to the history of the Jews in the Roman Empire by J. Juster, *Les Juifs dans l'empire romain* (Paris: P. Geuthner, 1914), 2 vols; also H. J. Leon, *The Jews of Ancient Rome* (Philadelphia: Jewish Publication Society, 1970); E. M. Smallwood, *The Jews under Roman Rule: From Pompey to Diocletian* (Leiden: Brill, 1976).

12. R. Ruether, p. 30.

13. See James S. Seaver, *The Persecution of the Jews in the Roman Empire* (Lawrence, Kans.: University of Kansas Press, 1952.)

14. See beside the studies of R. Ruether and J. Gager, Paul Démann, "Israël et l'unité de l'Eglise," *Cahiers Sioniens*, 7,1 (March 1953), 1–24; Karl Thieme, *Biblische Religion Heute* (Heidelberg: L. Schneider, 1960); Edward H. Flannery, *The Anguish of the Jews* (New York: Macmillan, 1964), pp. 60–61: Gregory Baum, *Is the New Testament Anti-Semitic?* (New York: Paulist Press, 1965), a completely revised version of his earlier *The Jews and the Gospel* (New York: Newman Press, 1961), p. 6: "what Paul and the entire Christian tradition taught is unmistakably negative." See also P. Richardson, *Israel in the Apocalyptic Church* (Cambridge: Cambridge University Press, 1969); A. T. Davies, ed., *Antisemitism and the Foundations of Christianity: Twelve Christian Theologians Explore the Development and Dynamics of Antisemitism Within the Christian Tradition* (New York: Paulist Press, 1979), p. xiv, after quoting J. Isaac ("Christianity, in its essence, excludes antisemitism") states:

    In the larger sense, of course, all Christians would have to accept this proposition, or else cast off their faith as hopelessly derelict and irreformable. But if the essence of Christianity is defined strictly in terms of the *classical* christological formulations of the Church about Jesus, or later orthodox interpretations of what these classical statements were intended to mean, it is not impossible that 'essential' Christian beliefs contain an antisemitic principle that has warped the Christian mind on the subject of Jews since early times.

15. J. Gager, p. 112; see also his statement (p. 114): "once again the tone and substance of Christian pronouncements against Judaism must be seen as shaped by Christianity's relative social and religious inferiority vis-à-vis Judaism within pagan society and culture."

16. See Paul's interpretation of Genesis 15:23: "And the first-born [not the *older*] will serve the younger."
17. R. Ruether, p. 63. See also J. Isaac, pp. 161–62, on the myth of a degenerate Judaism at the time of Jesus.
18. D. R. A. Hare, "The Rejection of the Jews in the Synoptic Gospels and Acts," in *Antisemitism.*, ed. A. T. Davies, pp. 27–47. See also P. Richardson, pp. 188–94.
19. J. Gager, who accepts Hare's main outline, would prefer to use here, quite understandably so, the expression "intra-Jewish polemic."
20. Hare follows here the views of R. H. Fuller, *The Foundations of New Testament Christology* (New York: Scribner and Sons, 1965), pp. 247–49.
21. It has also been frequently argued apologetically that John's use of *sons of light* and *sons of darkness* was not meant to symbolize Christians and Jews respectively but represented only a sort of "demythologized allegory." See Ruether, p. 116, and her strong rejection of this view: "Unfortunately, for almost all of Christian history, this antithesis has not been read in this demythologized way, but literally. This is because John himself, as well as the other New Testament writers, did not demythologize this antithesis. On the contrary, they mythologized it. . . . John gives the ultimate theological form to that diabolizing of 'the Jews' which is the root of anti-Semitism in the Christian tradition." See also J. T. Townsend, "The Gospel of John and the Jews: The Story of a Religious Divorce," in *Antisemitism*, ed. A. T. Davies, pp. 72–97. In the apocryphal Acts of John we read: "the Jews received their law from the lawless serpent" (quoted by R. Wilde, *The Treatment of the Jews*, p. 220).
22. Due to the limitations of this study, a detailed presentation of the anti-Jewish language not only in the Synoptic Gospels but particularly in Paul, John, and the writings of the Church Fathers, will be given in my book, *Satan's Synagogue* (in progress).
23. R. Ruether, pp. 30 and 75.
24. R. Girard, *Le bouc émissaire* (Paris: Grasset et Fasquelle, 1982; trans. Yvonne Freccero, *The Scapegoat* (Baltimore: The Johns Hopkins University Press, 1986), p. 118. See also a more specific study, and from a different perspective, by Hyam Maccoby, *The Sacred Executioner. Human Sacrifice and the Legacy of Guilt* (London: Thames and Hudson, 1982), chapters 1, 8–12.
25. On the semantic and functional relationship between Judea, Judas, and Jews, see L. Poliakov, *The History of Anti-Semitism* (London: Elek Books, 1965), p. 24: "the fact that the name of the apostle to betray his Lord appears to be derived philologically from Judea, the fatherland of the Jews, might of course be merely a coincidence. But the coincidence is too remarkable not to suggest a deliberate desire to symbolize the opprobrium henceforth heaped upon the chosen people." The word Jews, rather than Pharisees or Hebrews, appears more than forty times in Paul and some seventy times in John.
26. See H. Maccoby, *The Sacred Executioner*, p. 137: "[Paul] imitates the pro-Roman, anti-Jewish version of the Crucifixion, in a form even more extreme

than that found in the Gospels"; see also his monographic study, *The Mythmaker: Paul and the Invention of Christianity* (New York: Harper and Row, 1986).

27. See P. Winter, *On the Trial of Jesus* (Berlin: W. de Gruyter, 1961); H. Cohen, *The Trial of Jesus* (New York: Harper and Row, 1971); R. Ruether, pp. 88ff. On the role of Paul, see H. Maccoby, *The Mythmaker*; H. J. Schoeps, *Paul: The Theology of the Apostle in the Light of the Jewish Religious History* (Philadelphia: Fortress Press, 1961); R. Ruether, pp. 95–111; P. Richardson, ch. 5; G. F. Moore, *Judaism in the First Centuries of the Christian Era: The Age of the Tannaim*, 3 vols., Cambridge, Mass.: Harvard University Press, 1927), vol. 3, pp. 151ff; [reprt. New York: Schocken, 1971].

28. See also 1 John 4:3, and 2 John 7.

29. On the various sources of themes and motifs in the Antichrist story, and its dissemination during centuries in theology, literature, drama, and art, see below, note 64.

30. *Ante-Nicene Fathers*, ed. A. Roberts and J. Donaldson (New York: Scribner Sons, 1903), vol. 5, p. 206.

31. See L. U. Lucken, *Antichrist and the Prophets of Antichrist in the Chester Cycle* (Washington, D.C.: Catholic University Press, 1940), p. 17: "It was, accordingly, easy for the medieval mind to conceive him as the 'simia Christi,' just as his master, Satan, was the 'simia Dei.' " On this question, see H. W. Janson, *Apes and Ape-Lore in the Middle Ages and the Renaissance* (London: the Warburg Institute, University of London, 1952), in particular ch. 1.

32. For the typological connexion Antichrist-serpent-Dan, see Genesis 49:17: "Dan shall be a serpent by the way, an adder in the path, that biteth the horse heels, so that his rider shall fall backward."

33. In the late medieval *Passion Play of Luzern*, Antichrist's father is characteristically named Abraham.

34. See the following entry in a fifteenth-century personal chronicle, *Journal d'un bourgeois de Paris à la fin de la guerre de Cent Ans*, ed. Jean Thiellay (Paris: Union Générale d'Editions, 1963, p. 107): In April 1429 brother Richard, a Cordelier, came to announce to the Parisians that "he had recently returned from Syria and Palestine, and that in Jerusalem he had been told by many Jews about the birth of their Messiah who would give them back the Promised Land; they were hastily heading in groups toward Babylon, and this Messiah is according to the Holy Scriptures Antichrist who was to be born in Babylon." Our translation.

35. E. H. Flannery, p. 45. See D. P. Efroyimson, "The Patristic Connection," in *Antisemitism*, ed. A. T. Davies, pp. 98–117; R. Wilde, *The Treatment of the Jews in the Greek Christian Writers of the First Three Centuries* (Washington: Catholic University of America Press, 1949).

36. *Homilies on the Resurrection*, 5 (Migne, *PG*, 46:685).

37. See J. Isaac, p. 185; M. Simon, p. 160; Cecil Roth, "The Feast of Purim and the Origins of the Blood Accusation," *Speculum*, 8 (1933), 520–26.

38. See J. Isaac, pp. 277ff.

39. On the *Adversus Judaeos* tradition, see M. Simon, pp. 165–213; R. L. Wilken, *Judaism and the Early Christian Mind* (New Haven: Yale University Press, 1971);

R. Ruether, pp. 124–81; J. Gager, chs. 8–10; B. Blumenkranz, *Les Auteurs chrétiens latins du moyen âge sur les juifs et le judaïsme* (Paris-La Haye: Mouton, 1963); A. B. Hulen, "The 'Dialogues with the Jews' as Sources for the Early Jewish Argument against Christianity," *Journal of Biblical Literature*, 51 (1932), pp. 55ff; D. Judant, *Judaïsme et Christianisme. Dossier pastristique* (Paris: Editions du Cèdre, 1969); A. Lukyn Williams, *Adversus Judaeos. A Bird's-Eye View of Christian 'Apologiae' until the Renaissance* (London: Cambridge University Press, 1935). It is interesting to note here that while James Parkes was engaged in his research to unmask the various disguises of Antisemitism, Lukyn Williams was teaching the *adversus Judaeos tradition* to "a class of young men preparing for Christian work among the Jews!"

40. We are quoting from *Saint John Chrysostom. Discourses against Judaizing Christians*, trans. by Paul W. Harkins (Washington: Catholic University of America Press, 1975). The use of "against judaizing Christians" rather than the traditional "against the Jews" is intended by Harkins, as by some other religious scholars, to apologize for Chrysostom and mitigate the circumstances of his virulent attacks; but see J. Gager, p. 119: "But if loyal Christians are the audience of the sermon, the Judaizers are the targets of his wrath and the Jews its victims." A close analysis of his homilies shows clearly that, while speaking *about* judaizing Christians, Chrysostom lashes out *against* Judaism and Jews.

41. P. Harkins, p. 18, n. 63: "Chrysostom obviously holds the position, which was common for centuries, that all Jews are responsible for Christ's passion and death."

42. See Heiko. A. Oberman, *The Roots of Anti-Semitism in the Age of Renaissance and Reformation* (Philadelphia: Fortress Press, 1984); Johannes Brosseder, *Luthers Stellung zu den Juden im Spiegel seiner Interpreten* (Munich: Max Hueber Verlag, 1972).

43. See Ulysse Robert, *"Les signes d'infamie au moyen-âge,"* *Mémoires de la Société des Antiquaires de France*, 49 (1888), 60–125 [reprt. as book, Paris 1891]. Guido Kisch, "The Yellow Badge in History," *Historia Judaica*, 4 (1942), 95–144; Ruth Mellinkoff, *The Mark of Cain* (Berkeley: University of California Press, 1981); and "The Round-Topped Tablets of the Law: Sacred Symbol and Emblem of Evil," *Journal of Jewish Art*, 1 (1974).

44. See J. Parkes, *The Jew in the Medieval Community* (London: Soncino Press, 1938); Y. Baer, *A History of the Jews in Christian Spain* (Philadelphia: Jewish Publication Society, 1966), 2 vols; Guido Kisch, *The Jews in Medieval Germany. A Study of their Legal and Social Status* (Chicago: University of Chicago Press, 1949; repr. New York: Ktav Publishing House, 1970); A. Scharf, *Byzantine Jewry from Justinian to the Fourth Crusade* (London: Routledge and Kegan Paul, 1971); J. R. Marcus, *The Jew in the Medieval World* (New York: Atheneum, 1972); S. Grayzel, *The Church and the Jews in the XIIIth Century*, rev. ed. (1933; repr. New York: Hermon Press, 1966); Clyde Pharr, *The Theodosian Code and Novels and the Sirmondian Constitution* (Princeton: Princeton University Press, 1952); S. Katz, *The Jews in the Visigothic and Frankish Kingdoms of Spain and Gaul* (Cambridge, Mass.: Harvard University Press, 1937); S. L. Greenslade, *Church*

and State from Constantine to Theodosius (London: SCM, 1954); B. Blumenkranz, *Juifs et Chrétiens dans le monde occidental* (Paris-La Haye: Mouton, 1960); and a good overview in R. Ruether, pp. 183–225.

45. The visual arts, and certainly also the theatre, were an effective instrument of the Church in teaching the typological interpretation of the Scriptures to the illiterate masses. See Walafrid Strabo's statement "pictura est quaedam littera-tura illiterato," followed by Pope Gregory the Great: "Paintings are placed in the churches to enable the illiterate to read on the walls what they cannot read in the books"; quoted by L. Réau, *L'Art du moyen âge* (Paris: 1935, p. 2). Sergius the Stylite, defending the use of images in the church against accusations of idolatry, argued: "And we depict in the church for the teaching and admonition of men every narrative which the scripture regarded worthy of being a reminder, that whatever the scripture relates for the hearing of the ear, the eye might see in the form of a picture" (*The Disputation of Sergius the Stylite against a Jew*, ed. A. P. Hayman [Louvain: Universities of Louvain and Washington, 1973], vol. 2, p. 60). See also Robert Grigg, "Constantine the Great and the Cult without Images," *Viator*, 8 (1977), 1–32.

46. This would also be our basic response to those historians who oppose the theory of a continuity of Antisemitism from its Christian beginnings to our time. In spite of the differences between the traditional articulations of antisemitic pro-paganda and modern ones which include racial overtones, the commonality of ideas and imagery as well as their dehumanizing purpose and effect are a clear testimony of continuity rather than of rupture.

47. Norman Cohn, *The Pursuit of the Millennium: Revolutionary Millenarians and Mystical Anarchists of the Middle Ages* (1957; rev. expanded ed., New York: Oxford University Press, 1970), p. 35.

48. N. Cohn, p. 75.

49. N. Cohn, p. 76.

50. N. Cohn, pp. 78–79.

51. All texts and topics (among many others) alluded to in the next pages of this study are dealt with in great detail in my forthcoming book, *Satan's Synagogue*.

52. See M. Lazar, "Enseignement et Spectacle: la *disputatio* religieuse dans le drame médiéval," *Scripta Hierosolymitana*, 19 (1967), 126–51; "Satan and Notre Dame: Characters in a Popular Scenario," *A Medieval French Miscellany*, ed. N. Lacy (Lawrence: University of Kansas, 1972), pp. 1–14; "The Saint and the Devil: Christological and Diabological Typology in Fifteenth Century Provençal Drama," in *Essays in Early French Literature Presented to Barbara M. Craig*, ed. Norris J. Lacy and Jerry C. Nash (York, S.C.: French Literature Publications Co., 1982), pp. 81–92; *Lo Jutgamen General: Drame provençal du XVe siècle* (Paris: Klinck-sieck, 1970); W. E. Meyers, *A Figure Given: Typology in the Wakefield Plays* (Pittsburgh: Duquesne University Press, 1969), ch. 3.

53. See David Bevington, *Medieval Drama* (Boston: Houghton Mifflin, 1975), pp. 274, 322; T. McAlindon, "Comedy and Terror in Middle English Literature: The Diabolical Game," *Modern Language Review*, 60 (1965), 325–332; M. Lazar, "Les Diables: Serviteurs et bouffons," *Tréteaux*, 1 (1978), 51–69.

54. See B. Blumenkranz, *Die Judenpredigt Augustins* (Basel, 1946); *Altercatio Aecclesie contra Synagogam* (Strasbourg, 1954); *Le Juif médiéval au miroir de l'art chrétien* (Paris: Etudes Augustiniennes, 1966); Wolfgang Seiferth, *Synagogue and Church in the Middle Ages: Two Symbols in Art and Literature* (New York: F. Ungar, 1970); H. Walter, *Das Streitgedicht in der lateinischen Literatur des Mittelalters* (Munich, 1920); H. Pflaum (Peri), "Der allegorische Streit zwischen Synagoge und Kirche in der europäischen Dichtung des Mittelalters," *Archivum Romanicum*, 18 (1934), 243–340; M. Sepet, *Les prophètes du Christ* (Paris, 1878); K. Young, "Ordo Prophetarum," *Transactions of the Wisconsin Academy of Sciences, Arts and letters*, 22 (1922), 1–82; M. J. Rudwin, *Die Prophetenspruche und-zitate im religiosen Drama des Mittelalters* (Leipzig, 1913).

55. These questions are put in the mouth of the Jew (here and elsewhere), or indicated in art by the Jew pointing his index to a scroll or book, to signify that the Jews understand only the letter, not the spirit of the Scriptures, i.e., the allegorical-typological meaning of the texts. Hand movements and index finger pointing to a scroll are generally signifying discussion and dispute (see Figs. 1, 4, 5, 6, 7).

56. Philippe de Mézières (1327–1405); see Karl Young, *The Drama of the Medieval Church* (Oxford: Clarendon, 1933), vol. 2, pp. 227–42.

57. See Moïse Schwab, "Le Credo traduit en hébreu et transcrit en caractères latins," *Revue des Etudes Juives*, 45 (1902), 206–8; "Mots hébreux dans les mystères du moyen âge," *REJ*, 46 (1903), 148–151.

58. See D. Bevington, p. 274: "the perpetrators of evil are generally noisy, brash, and obscenely humorous, whereas the defenders of virtue are serene and idealized."

59. D. Bevington, pp. 180ff.

60. See Richard B. Donovan, *The Liturgical Drama in Medieval Spain* (Toronto: Pontifical Institute of Medieval Studies, 1958), p. 95:

   The expression [out-Herod Herod] has generally been considered Shakespeare's own. That it was current already around the year 1200, however, is shown by its appearance in the Vich *consueta* written about that time. The Catalan scribe lists as one of his reasons for not reciting the *Invitatorium* on the Feast of the Epiphany: *Ne Herodidemus Herodes!*. . . Shakespeare in medieval Latin! Here the phrase has the connotation of "seen to outdo Herod in hypocrisy and deceit," but it may well be an indication that as early as 1200 Herod the actor had given special vogue to the expression by his antics and extravagance.

61. See Marcel Bulard, *Le Scorpion, symbole du peuple juif dans l'art religieux des XIVe, XVe, XVIe siècles* (Paris, 1935).

62. See Isaiah Shachar, *The Judensau. A Medieval Anti-Jewish Motif and its History* (London: The Warburg Institute, University of London, 1974).

63. For examples illustrating several of these symbolic and emblematic representations, see W. Seiferth, *Synagogue and Church*, Figs. 18, 20, 22, 28, 30, 42, 59, 60, and 65; B. Blumenkranz, *Le Juif médiéval*, Figs, 55, 57, 68, 70, 78, 119, 121; H. Pflaum [Peri], "Der allegorische Streit," all the reproductions; M. Lazar, "Enseignement et spectacle," Pls. IX, X.

64. See Wilhelm Bousset, *The Antichrist Legend*, trans. A. H. Keane (London:

Hutchinson, 1896); Emile Roy, *Le Jour du Jugement. Mystère français sur le Grand Schisme* (Paris: Emile Bouillon, 1902); Lucken, *Antichrist and the Prophets of Antichrist*; Hans Preuss, *Die Vorstellungen vom Antichrist im späteren Mittelalter, bei Luther und in der Konfessionellen Polemik* (Leipzig: J. C. Heinrichs, 1906); Horst P. Rauh, *Das Bild des Antichrist im Mittelalter: von Tyconius zum deutschen Symbolismus* (Beiträge zur Geschichte der Philosophie und Theologie des Mittelalters, n. s. 9, Münster: Aschendorff, 1973); Jessie Poesch, *Antichrist Imagery in Anglo-French Apocalypse Manuscripts* (Ph.D. diss., University of Pennsylvania, 1966); Richard K. Emmerson, *Antichrist in the Middle Ages: A Study of Medieval Apocalypticism, Art and Literature* (Seattle: University of Washington Press, 1981).

65. See *The Bestiary. A Book of Beasts [Latin Bestiary]*, trans. and ed. T. H. White (New York: Putnam's Sons, 1954), p. 51. "The name [manticora] is derived from an old Persian word meaning 'man-eater,' and some have suggested that the Manticore is simply a man-eating tiger. . . . Another suggestion is man, tiger, i.e., an uncanny creature like the Werewolf. . . . Mermaids, mermecoleons, manticoras, mantiserras and half a dozen others have at one time or another been scrambled together by interpreters like Isidore of Seville, not in pursuit of natural history, but in that of language, or even in that of morals" (p. 2, n. 1).

66. Reproduced in Anne Clark, *Beasts and Bawdy* (New York: Taplinger 1975), Fig. 6, from *The Royal Bestiary* (British Library). Both Clark and White (who illustrates his text with a drawing of the manticore wearing the Jewish hat) fail to notice its identification as a demonized "Jewish" beast.

67. See M. Lazar, "Theophilus: Servant of Two Masters. The Pre-Faustian Theme of Despair and Revolt," *Modern Language Notes*, 87 (1972), 31–50.

[3]

Traditional Prejudice and Religious Reform: The Theological and Historical Foundations of Luther's Anti-Judaism

Jeremy Cohen

The early sixteenth century marked a critical period of transition for European Jews and Christians alike.* In the wake of a flurry of expulsions from England, France, Spain, Portugal, Southern Italy, and much of Germany, Jewish life in Western Europe came to a virtual standstill. By mid-century, Jews could reside only in portions of Germany, in the papal states, and in the Northern Italian cities, areas where most Jewish communities encountered increasingly harsh forms of discrimination. In Eastern Europe, however, Ashkenazic Jewry had discovered refuge and opportunity; several generations of unprecedented material prosperity and intense cultural creativity now awaited the Jews of Poland and Lithuania, prior to the Chmielnitzski massacres and the socioreligious decay which would ensue in their aftermath.

While Jews still struggled to cope with the alienation and political subjugation that life in the Diaspora had entailed for over a thousand years, for the Christian society of Western Europe the Middle Ages had ended. The mold of the mystical body of Christ, conformity to whose design the Roman Church repeatedly demanded of all components of European Christendom, had suffered a series of permanent dismemberments. The Scholastic synthesis succumbed before the critique of the nominalists and the vitality of Renaissance humanism. Catholic discipline could not restrain the free spirit of

81

popular heresy which threatened the very credibility and survival of holy mother Church. The throne of St. Peter had fallen prey to schism, opportunism, and abuse. The conciliar movement which attempted to mend these wounds awakened new debate over the propriety of monarchic rule in the community of God's faithful. National states and independent principalities now replaced the feudal organization of medieval polities. Concisely put, the foundations of medieval civilization were giving way to those of modernity.

Much of the distinctive spirit of the sixteenth century is exemplified in the career, the writings, and the personality of Martin Luther. One might gain valuable insight into the man and his age by considering how the prime mover of the Protestant Reformation confronted the quintessentially medieval problem of the European Jew. Despite the flurry of academic and ecumenical conferences which recently commemorated the passage of five centuries since Luther's birth, scholarly debate over Luther's pronouncements concerning the Jews continues. Such discussion has typically focused on the virulent anti-Jewish polemic of Luther's later years, still endeavoring to gauge the relative degrees of continuity and change marked by this polemic in Luther's own life and thought.[1] Yet many participants in this discussion have failed to evaluate Luther's overall contribution to the history and development of Christian anti-Judaism. Did the transitional nature of the early sixteenth century move its most influential spokesman to formulate a new Christian program for dealing with the European Jewish minority? Or did the traditional nature of the Jewish problem co-opt Luther into responding traditionally, with an answer conceived by his patristic and medieval predecessors?

As a preliminary step in response to these questions, I propose in this essay to reorient the chronological framework of the discussion, and to consider the depth and complexity of the interactions between postbiblical Judaism and classical Christianity underlying Luther's anti-Jewish ideology. Specifically, I shall depart from three characteristics of Luther's teaching and explore their antecedents in the ancient and medieval history of the Church: (1) the contrast between old and new covenants so fundamental to Luther's theology, (2) his misgivings concerning the propriety of Judaic study among Christian scholars, and (3) the revulsion with which he reacted to contemporary Jews and Judaism. This chapter will not duplicate the extensive scholarly analysis that these components of Luther's anti-Judaism have already undergone. In studying his forerunners, however, it may advance the proposition that Luther contributed little, if anything, new to the Jewish-Christian controversy.

Law, Gospel, and *Adversus Judaeos*

What good does it do them to know and to possess God's commandment? Let them boast that this makes them God's own special, dear angels, in comparison with whom other angels are nothing! How much better off they would be if they did not have God's commandment or if they were ignorant of it. For if they did not have it, they would not be condemned. The very reason for their condemnation is that they possess his commandment and yet do not keep it, but violate it constantly.[2]

Beneath much of Luther's thought lies a sharp, uncompromising dichotomy between Law and Gospel, in all of their respective ramifications. Yet such a chasm between Synagogue and Church derives from the earliest days of the latter's history, when the original disciples of Jesus, in the wake of the crucifixion, asserted their Christianity in terms of a negative of Judaism. If the abstract principles of apostolic theology *need* not have entailed anti-Jewish hostility, the belief of Jesus' disciples that their master had initiated the realization of Jewish messianic expectations, coupled with the increasingly staunch opposition of first-century Jewry to the new Christian sect, dictated otherwise: The early Church came to view itself as the living embodiment of God's covenant with Israel; admission to the newly inaugurated kingdom of heaven demanded the affirmation of Nazarene Christology; ·the disbelieving Jews, whose leaders should have accepted Jesus but instead attempted to expel his followers from their community, became the enemies of Christ *par excellence*. Hence the ambivalence toward the Synagogue at the heart of the Christian worldview, which resulted in the ideology of *Adversus Judaeos*. The Church expressed its identity as the medium of the divine plan for the salvation of mankind, in the language of Jewish Scripture and Jewish history. The Jew was valued insofar as he preserved these, but his persistent claim to represent God's chosen people undermined the legitimacy of the *Ecclesia*. For Christian doctrine to be validated, Judaism had to be proven wrong and inferior; its survival had to be rationalized and, when it eventually became possible, carefully regulated.

Various stages of the widening rift between the early Church and the Synagogue illustrate how this ambivalent outlook took shape. The followers of Jesus whose faith withstood the trauma of the crucifixion explained the death of their savior with an appeal to Hebrew Scripture, at the same time as their growing isolation in Roman Judea gave rise to the theologically grounded motif of the Jew as Christ-killer. For all of his startling successes in opening the doors of the Church to the Gentiles, itself an expression of the "cognitive dissonance" which social scientists deem a characteristic result of "the crisis of non-fulfillment" in a messianic movement, the apostle Paul never did enunciate an entirely clear-cut, consistent approach to the Jews. "God has no favorites," Paul proclaimed to his Roman correspondents (Romans 2:11); "the true Jew is not he who is such in externals, neither is the true circumcision the external mark in the flesh. . . . We are discharged from the law, to serve God in a new way, the way of the spirit, in contrast to the old way, the way of a written code" (2:28, 7:6). Nevertheless, Paul still acknowledged the precedence of Jew over Greek, the holiness and utility of the Torah, and the continuing significant role of the Jews in biblical *Heilsgeschichte*. The eleventh chapter of his epistle, which not long ago prefaced an issue of *The Lutheran World* (October 1963) calling for renewed Jewish-Christian dialogue, looks forward to the salvation of all of the Jews, asserts the irrevocability of God's gracious gifts to them, and posits the temporary nature of their disobedience (vv. 25–31). Paul perpetuates the ambiguity in primitive Christian attitudes toward the Jews, laying the groundwork for the doctrine that they must be preserved in order to be completed, and thus to realize God's plan for the salvation of all mankind. Following the Romans' destruction of Jerusalem and the Temple in 70 C.E., the anti-Nazarene policies of the rabbis of Yavneh strove to exclude Jewish Christians from the synagogues, solidifying and formalizing the gap between the two religious communities. The first and fourth Gospels testify well to this hostility. Yet even as Matthew casts the Jews as collectively guilty of deicide in perpetuity, and as his Jesus' parting words instruct the apostles "to make all nations my disciples"—not merely "the lost sheep of the house of Israel" as before—his Jesus clearly marks the climax of a Jewish scheme of salvific history; the evangelist unhesitatingly compels his scriptural evidence to validate his contentions in Judaic terms. Even as John the evangelist perceives the antagonism between Synagogue and Church as beyond the point of reconciliation, likening them to the cosmic foes of darkness and light, biblical imagery pervades his Gospel, as do the cosmological and mystical ideas of Greek-speaking Jews. As wide as the rupture between parent and child religions grew, the ambivalence of the latter toward the former remained unmitigated. Paradoxically, it was the overwhelmingly

Gentile church of the second century that first appropriated for itself, to the exclusion of the Jews, the title of the true Israel, though it too justified this appellation with an allegorical brand of exegesis borrowed from Philo Judaeus.[3]

The Church of the patristic age readily absorbed the ambivalent *Adversus Judaeos* tendencies of its apostolic predecessor, and it incorporated them into the worldview which was to dominate the Western mind for the next millennium and beyond. As the fathers of the Church struggled to promote, define, and systematize the tenets of their theology, defending the *Ecclesia* against its various enemies, anti-Jewish polemic continued to constitute an important means for asserting Christian beliefs. It is no accident or coincidence that most of the important Church fathers of the period—Justin Martyr, Tertullian, Cyprian, Origen, John Chrysostom, Ambrose of Milan, Augustine of Hippo, Gregory the Great, Isidore of Seville, and others—all polemicized strenuously against the Jews throughout their writings, many in sermons, treatises, and dialogues composed specifically for that purpose. *Adversus Judaeos* became a literary genre unto itself in the propagation of Christian theology. It usually comprised "a stereotyped enumeration of proofs taken from the Bible for the truth of Christianity, and the detection of prophecies and prefigurations that were enriched from the present status of the Jews in 'servitude' and dispersion."[4] Patristic authors used the anti-Jewish treatise methodically to review and expound upon Hebrew Scripture, demonstrating how Jesus and the Church had fulfilled its manifold prophecies, if they would only be interpreted allegorically or spiritually, not historically or carnally. The evil of the Jews' rejection of Jesus was frequently set against the background of a national history of moral and spiritual villainy. Some found biblical evidence for the election of the Gentiles prior to the Passion, apportioning everything positive and pleasant in Scripture to the true Israel of the spirit, but reserving the condemnatory and the wrathful for the Jews of the flesh. The nature of Judaism was exemplified in Cain (the despised fratricide), Hagar (the abandoned spouse), Esau (the son dispossessed of his birthright), Simeon and Levi (the murderers among Jacob's children), the bitter waters of Marah, the veil which covered Moses' face, the adulteress of Hosea's prophecies, and the like. The respective rituals of Synagogue and Church were similarly characterized so as to buttress the categorical distinction between the two institutions. As such, the utility of *Adversus Judaeos* literature depended little on its ability to convert the Jews. God would provide for them in due course; in the interim, they extended the scripture basis for enhancing the faith of Christians. Augustine explained in his own sermon against the Jews, "When these scriptural works are quoted to the Jews, they scorn the Gospel and the Apostle; they do not listen to what we say because they do not understand what they read." Yet the Christian duty to argue against them remained. "Testimonies are to be selected from sacred Scripture, which has great authority among the Jews, and if they do not want to be cured by means of this advantage offered them, they can at least be convicted by its evident truth."[5] John Chrysostom employed his anti-Jewish polemic, likewise based primarily on a reading of the Hebrew Bible, to try and prevent all contact and conversation between Christian and Jew.

Where Christ-killers gather, the cross is ridiculed, God blasphemed, the father unacknowledged, the son insulted, the grace of the Spirit rejected. . . . If the Jewish rites are holy and venerable, our way of life must be false. But if our way is true, as indeed it is, theirs is fraudulent. I am not speaking of the Scriptures. Far from it! For they lead one to Christ. I am speaking of their present impiety and madness.[6]

In a word, Christianity and Judaism were mutually exclusive. The dramatic opposition between them was essential to the integrity of the Church, and the *Adversus Judaeos* polemic, regardless of its effect on contemporary Jewry, served to enhance that integrity.

That the Church fathers employed anti-Jewish polemic above all to assert the truth of Christianity to a Christian audience points to another significant aspect of patristic anti-Judaism. The virulence of pronouncements against the Jews notwithstanding, the primarily theological-pedagogic—as opposed to conversionist—motives of the polemics resulted in their characterization of the Jew as the stereotypical representation of the Old Testament, and not in accordance with historical reality. Judaism embodied the decadent, obsolete covenant of the letter, the law, and the flesh—all that Christianity had supplanted and replaced. No matter that the patristic era also witnessed the crystallization of classical rabbinic Judaism and the compilation of the Talmud, processes of intensive cultural vitality and creativity that enabled Judaism to survive the destruction of the Temple and the loss of a national center in Palestine. For the Church fathers, as Augustine proclaimed, the Jews "have remained stationary in useless antiquity."[7] Christian theology insisted that they did. The ambivalence, whereby the Church needed Judaism in order to divest it through polemic of its biblical covenant and election, to cite one historian's apt metaphor, "had built a [characterological] prison for the Jewish people."[8]

Beginning in the fourth century, in the wake of its successful bid for the allegiance of the emperor of Rome, the Church endeavored to translate its *Adversos Judaeos* ideology into a policy that would shape Jewish history. While political rulers, both before and after the fall of the Western Empire, frequently treated the Jews in ways other—usually more favorable—than that advocated by the clergy, prelates and theologians worked to institutionalize the ambivalence of which we have spoken. The mixed blessing of alliance with the state induced the Church to define its attitudes toward Jews in very pragmatic terms, in line with the perfect Christian order it hoped to introduce into Western society and civilization. On the one hand, the Jews might live in peace and practice their religion. "Slay them not," Augustine instructed his congregants, alluding to Psalm 59:12.[9] "For if they had been annihilated as they deserved," Cassiodorus commented on the same verse, "the hope for their conversion would have perished completely. Thus the Jews have been scattered [the verse continues: "scatter them by thy might and bring them to ruin"] whether to be induced to desire conversion, or (as some profess) that in struggling against heretics the Church might have testimony furnished by its enemies from the Old Testament."[10] God had ordained the survival of the Jews, as living relics of the Old Testament, to validate the claims of the Church. "They were dispersed," quipped Augustine, "and thus by the evidence of their own Scriptures they bear witness for us that we have not fabricated the prophecies about Christ."[11] On the other hand, the Jews' fulfillment of this role depended in large measure on their enforced inferiority and subservience to Christians; how otherwise could their existence testify to the rectitude of faith in Christ? Theologians and Church councils alike continually inveighed against excessive fraternization between Christians and Jews, strove to restrict Jews from owning Christian slaves or otherwise wielding authority over Christians, and clamored against any opportunity granted the Jew to enhance the stature of his religion. Under the threat of excommunication, Bishop Ambrose of Milan accordingly forbade Emperor Theodosius the Great of Rome from forcing Christians who had destroyed a synagogue to make restitution to the Jewish community.

The Study of Judaica and Anti-Jewish Polemic

Shall a place be provided out of the spoils of the Church for the disbelief of the Jews, and shall this patrimony, given to Christians by the favor of Christ, be transferred to the treasuries of unbelievers? . . . Will you grant the Jews this triumph over God's Church? this trophy over Christ's people? these joys, O Emperor, to unbelievers? this festival to the synagogue? this grief to the Church?[12]

In *The Last Words of David*, Luther lauds the great fourteenth-century Christian exegete, Nicholas of Lyra—"by far the most faithful and pure interpreter, and far before all the ancient and modern Hebraists"—for his defense of Christianity against Jewish criticism. Yet "how frigid, how futile is that same man," he asks, when he relies on rabbinic exegesis in explaining the meaning of Scripture? "For a superstitious regard to the letters and the text that are received by the Jews . . . soon bring on a darkness; and at length, the true sense and understanding of the scriptures concerning Christ are lost, and judaizing imaginations creep upon us unawares when they ought not."

Luther lived in an age of noteworthy Christian Hebraic scholarship, which early Protestantism undoubtedly helped to promote. If his comments on Nicholas of Lyra exemplify his emphatic demarcation between Law and Gospel, they also reveal regret concerning the Christian valuation of Judaic texts, the "Judaizing" tendency of certain sixteenth-century reformers which contributed so heavily to the acrimony of Luther's anti-Jewish polemic. This concern of Luther, the interconnection of exegetical method in the academy with the essential demands of *Adversus Judaeos* ideology, likewise antedates him.[13] For while the reliance of Christian theology on the doctrines of the Old Testament was always self-evident, the patristic and medieval Church could never forget that the text and literal observance of these biblical teachings continued to reside within a community of infidels.

As patristic and early medieval theologians explained what they claimed to be the true, spiritual sense of Scripture, they simply assumed that contemporary Judaism embodied the obsolete and no longer edifying, literal sense. And if the ideological importance of the biblical Jew blinded churchmen to the *realia* of Jewish history, so too did the Augustinian notion that all theological truth could be derived entirely from the text of the Bible—when properly interpreted—militate against the maturation of biblical exegesis as a sound academic discipline. When the Bible had to meet all of the theologian's needs, those needs *a priori* colored one's appreciation of the scriptural text. According to Augustine, the perfection and goal ("plenitudo et finis") of the Bible and biblical study were the love of God. Such a consideration not only relegated non-canonical texts to a markedly inferior status, but it also determined the appropriateness of literal or figurative exegesis for any specific passage of Scripture. Simply put, "whatever in the word of God cannot be related in its literal sense to moral virtue or doctrinal truth, you may recognize as figurative." As a result, Heiko Oberman has correctly observed, "there is no objective standard by which to separate the literal sense—or the clear places in Scripture—from the allegorical sense—or the obscure places. This difference is not contained in the text . . . but largely dependent on the relation of the reader to God."[14] No wonder that the historical sense of the Old Testament was usually neglected during the early Middle Ages, or that churchmen generally failed to procure the tools that would promote it: familiarity with the Jewish traditions that embodied it, and knowledge of Hebrew. Instead, owing to their preoccupation with the contrast between *Ecclesia* and *Synagoga*, Christian theologians continually identified the latter with all that the covenant of grace had superseded. The interests of pedant or antiquarian aside, how could the literal sense of Scripture enhance one's appreciation of the kerygma of Christ? If many publicly advocated the study of Hebrew for the sake of understanding the Bible, few bothered to act upon their own advice.[15] A figurative reading of the Bible, hand in hand with a blindness to postbiblical developments in Judaism, perpetuated *Adversus Judaeos* polemic as a means of teaching Christianity to a Christian, not a Jewish, audience. As late as the eleventh century, Peter Damian, cardinal, papal legate, and an avid exponent of ecclesiastical reform, authored two anti-Jewish treatises which merely rehashed the usual scriptural testimonies and their established patristic interpretations. Of note is the juxtaposition of Damian's confidence that his biblical citations will triumph—in actual face-to-face debate—over "every insanity of Jewish depravity," and his remark that disputing with contemporary Jews need not rank high among the priorities of the Church.[16]

The cultural awakening or "renaissance" of the twelfth century, and particularly the shift of the focus of medieval scholarship from monastery to urban school, heralded a new critical spirit in the medieval mentality.[17] A rebellion against patristic methodology, the insistence upon a more scientific explication of texts, the demand that religious ideas bespeak the *realia* of history—all these contributed to renewed interest in and greater influence of the Old Testament in twelfth-century Christendom. Numerous scholars have demonstrated the resurgence of literalist exegesis of the Old Testament, the widening tendency to view the observance of Mosaic law as meritorious and justificatory in its own time, and the greater use of the Old Testament to explain and authenticate contemporary Christian institutions and practices. Concern for the *hebraica veritas* now enjoyed considerable prominence in Christian Old Testament commentary, and exegetes began to involve themselves in the study of the Hebrew language, either with the help of converted Jews or with that of medieval rabbis themselves. Yet Christian commentators sought far more than linguistic instruction from the Jews. For who could better understand the original meaning and significance of the covenant of Moses than those who continued to observe and promulgate its literal teachings? Beryl Smalley has put it well: "When the medieval scholar talked to a Rabbi he felt that he was telephoning to the Old Testament." [18] Literally minded commentators borrowed extensively from rabbinic scholars and from rabbinic literature, with the paradoxical result that in the realm of Christian exegesis evidence gleaned from contemporary Jewish tradition frequently was deemed authoritative *prima facie!* The forthrightness and ease with which Hugh of St. Victor, his student Andrew, Peter Comestor, and Stephen Harding (to list only a few) justified their instruction from rabbis, juxtaposed rabbinic traditions and traditional Christian exegesis, and even preferred the former over the latter has been much discussed in recent scholarship, but it still cannot fail to astound the student of Christian-Jewish relations.

One would expect that the perception of the medieval Jew as spokesman for the Old Testament would have reinforced the anti-Jewish polemical tendency of the earlier period, grounded as it was in the premises that the biblical character of Judaism had not changed since antiquity, and that the Jews served to convey the meaning of the Old Testament to the Christians who tolerated them. Most of the extant Christian polemics from the twelfth century do validate this assumption. Peter of Blois, for instance, whom R. W. Southern views as exemplifying the distinctive "humanism" of the period, began his own treatise *Against the Perfidy of the Jews,* "Even today the Jews are to be allowed to live, because they are our enslaved book-bearers [*capsarii*], as they carry around the prophets and the law of Moses for the assertion of our faith. Not only in their books but also in their faces do we read of the passion of Christ." [19]

Yet such an outlook—that is, renewed interest in Hebrew and rabbinic exegesis, coupled with the retained conviction that Judaism was essentially biblical—evoked serious questions among various churchmen of the twelfth century. For a Christian valuation of the *hebraica veritas* and its literal meaning, which cast a presumption of authenticity upon Jewish interpretation of the Old Testament, appeared to undermine the basic contrast between carnal Judaism and spiritual Christianity at the core of the patristic *Adversus Judaeos* tradition. The opposition between letter and spirit had always rested at the foundation of Christianity's claims to validity, and it had facilitated the stationary, antique conception of Judaism which prompted seeking Jewish help on the literal sense in the first place. As twelfth-century Christian exegesis proceeded to attribute relevance and importance to the Jewish understanding of the letter, it unintentionally threatened to subvert the very set of theological assumptions which had spawned it! Alongside the new literalism of twelfth-century Christian exegesis, reliance on rabbinic interpretations in explaining the Old Testament could prove equally problematic. In seeking instruction from a contemporary rabbi, the churchman inadvertently accorded respect to postbiblical, talmudic Judaism as the bearer of the literal understanding of the Hebrew Bible. Yet the rabbinic tradition also demonstrated that Judaism had *not* remained "stationary in useless antiquity" ever since the day of the crucifixion, as Augustine had presumed; this assumption, now questionable, had provided primary theological justification for tolerating Europe's growing Jewish community, as well as for the Church's claim to have inherited God's biblical covenant from a stagnant, moribund Judaism. The enthusiasm with which some prominent Christian exegetes now sought rabbinic instruction awakened doubts among others.

The mystical exegete and theologian Richard of St. Victor composed an entire treatise to condemn the preference of the literalists, dubbed "our [Christian] Judaizers," for Judaic over ecclesiastical instruction; they interpreted the Old Testament independently of the Gospel, enhancing the stature of Judaism at Christianity's expense.[20] In their decretist commentaries, Rufinus, Huguccio, and other noted canonists impugned the reliability of contemporary Jewish books, including the Masoretic Text of the Bible, owing to deliberate rabbinic corruption and distortion.[21] And some scholars, like the English Herbert of Bosham and Abbot Peter the Venerable of Cluny, proceeded to suggest tentatively that medieval Jews had forsaken their biblical heritage. Peter in particular is noted for his indictment of the Talmud as "diabolical" and expressive of doctrine inherently "blasphemous, sacrilegious, ridiculous, and false"; commitment to the Talmud revealed the "bovine intellect" of medieval Jews, whose persistent refusal to accept Christianity ostensibly relegated them to a subhuman status. Yet even for Herbert and Peter, the patristic conception of the Jews and of Judaism as quintessentially biblical ultimately prevailed. According to Peter, talmudic doctrine antedated Jesus and exemplified the Judaism which Christianity came to replace; he thus could identify talmudic homilies with "the endless fables, and the traditions utterly foreign to the law of God, of which the Lord said to the Pharisees in the Gospel (Matthew 15:7), " 'You must have abandoned the precepts of God for the sake of your own traditions.' " Most importantly, talmudic error derived directly from the mentality which insisted on inter-preting sacred text only literally, admitting "neither metaphor, nor allegory, nor any of the customary modes of figurative speech, through which all these things may rightfully be interpreted as applying to God." As a result, Euro-pean Jews still played their instructive part in the divine economy of salva-tion. "There is fulfilled in you, O wretched people, what your apostle by birth, ours in terms of doctrine, said of such things: 'The time will come when they will not stand wholesome teaching, but follow their own fancy and gather a crowd of teachers to tickle their ears. They will stop their ears to the truth and turn to mythology' " (2 Timothy 4:3–4).[22]

Only in the thirteenth century did Christian scholars display a responsive-ness to the inconsistencies which underlay the twelfth century's valuation of rabbinic instruction in biblical exegesis, growing sensitive to the interplay of their use of Jewish tradition with the logical demands of their *Adversus Judaeos* polemic. Freed from enslavement to the field of theology, thirteenth-century biblical commentary formalized the distinction between literal and spiritual sense, placing greater emphasis still on the former. Recognition of the value of the *hebraica veritas* therefore became more widespread, and the number of Christians adept in Hebrew increased markedly. The new Aristo-telian rationalism also infused vitality into the endeavor to understand Old Testament teaching as purposeful in its own original context. At the same time, however, the thirteenth century saw a new polemical rejection of the contemporary Jew as no longer valuable in facilitating the encounter be-tween Latin Christendom and the Old Testament. The thirteenth-century Church—perhaps as an indirect result of its promotion of Hebraic scholar-ship—gained considerable familiarity with the Talmud and Midrash; and it now could perceive the historical evolution which separated antique biblical Judaism from the religion of medieval Jewry. Some deemed the European Jewish community unfit for toleration on theoretical grounds, given its abandonment of the stagnant, Old Testament way of life on the basis of which Augustine had justified its preservation. No longer was Judaism a mere foil that facilitated the Christological assertions of the polemicist. Anti-Jewish polemic assumed a much more direct and aggressive character;

it aimed to undermine the presence and security of the Jew in a properly ordered Christian society.[23]

In a variety of contexts, Christian theologians now sought to liberate the edifying instruction inherent in Judaic sources from the inauthentic, contemporary Jew. Thirteenth-century scholastics approached the *ideas* of Moses Maimonides—especially those asserting the right, rational purpose of Mosaic law in its original, historical setting—as expressive of classical Judaism in its most rational, coherent formulation, as an exemplary blend of Aristotelian science and biblical faith.[24] Nevertheless, this positive estimation of some of his opinions did not prevent the Inquisition from burning Rabbi Moses' works, or Thomas Aquinas from reproaching him for abandoning the literal meaning of Scripture, or Giles of Rome from condemning him for forsaking the rational truth of biblical revelation.[25] Throughout his postils, Nicholas of Lyra drew extensively on the glosses of Rashi (Solomon ben Isaac of Troyes, 1040–1105) and on other rabbinic works, but he maintained that rabbinic Judaism and its contemporary spokesmen had deviated deliberately from Old Testament religion and were essentially heretical as a result; one could no longer casually presume Jewish exegesis to be authoritative.[26] Most illustrative of the new tendency was the condemnation of the Talmud by the thirteenth-century Church. At the same time as the decrees of Popes Gregory IX and Innocent IV consigning the Talmud to the flames stimulated clerical interest and scholarship in rabbinics, they disavowed the rationale for the positive side of the old *Adversus Judaeos* ambivalence: the premise that the Jew had, in fact, remained stationary in useless antiquity. In the words of the chancellor of the University of Paris, appointed in 1247 to head a papal commission to pass judgment on the Talmud, "these books turn the Jews not only from an understanding of the spirit, but even of the letter."[27] When the burgeoning of Christian Hebraic scholarship, which invariably enhanced respect for the traditions of rabbinic exegesis, fueled his anti-Jewish polemic, Luther followed well-established precedents of the later Middle Ages.

The Legacy of Mendicant Anti-Judaism

I shall give you my sincere advice . . . to set fire to their synagogues or schools . . . , that their houses also be razed and destroyed . . .—instead they might be lodged under a roof or in a barn . . .—that all their prayer books and Talmudic writings, in

which such idolatry, lies, cursing, and blasphemy are taught, be taken from them
. . . , that their rabbis be forbidden to teach henceforth on a pain of loss of life and
limb . . . , that safe-conduct on the highways be abolished completely for the Jews
. . . , that usury be prohibited to them, and that all cash and treasure of silver and
gold be taken from them. . . . But if we are afraid that they might harm us . . . ,
then eject them forever from the country.[28]

Luther's polemics cannot fail to convey their author's abhorrence for the
Jews of sixteenth-century Europe, an emotional response to their presence
which transcended and preceded any considerations of abstract doctrine or
theology. Simply put, the Jews did not belong in Luther's Christian world.
This attitude too originated in late medieval Christendom, deriving from
the generally increasing intensity and friction in Jewish-Christian relations
during the twelfth, thirteenth, and fourteenth centuries.

The Crusades, which broadened the social, economic, and cultural fron-
tiers of Europe in multifarious ways, also highlighted the problematic status
of the Jewish community, owing to the massacres of Ashkenazic Jews that
accompanied the crusading movements of 1096, 1146, and 1190. Holy wars
brought sizeable Jewish settlements in Palestine, Sicily, and Spain into the
orbit of the Roman Church for the first time; and the focus of Jewish
socioeconomic and religious creativity gradually shifted away from the world
of Islam to a Christian, European environment. Simultaneously, the growth
of Western cities, commerce, and industry, linked to the emergence of a
Christian middle class and a European economy oriented more and more to
money than to land, stimulated increased hostility toward the Jewish merchant, whose investment capital continued to be deemed an invaluable asset
by kings and princes. And the medieval Church was itself experiencing the
zenith in its development and rise to power, calling for a vast program of
socioreligious reform to insure the adherence of all components of Western
Christendom to the ideals and behavioral patterns of the exemplary *societas
christiana*. The synthesizing spirit of the age, evident in theology and eccle-
siology alike, sought an absolute harmony between theory and practice, the
conformity of social structures and individual lifestyles with the logic and
principles of sacred doctrine.

Most active in the implementation of this ecclesiastical policy were the
Dominicans and Franciscans, the two mendicant orders licensed by the
papacy early in the thirteenth century, whose friars quickly came to dominate the theological faculties of important universities, the inquisitorial
prosecution of heretics, conversionist missions to the infidels, the propaga-

tion of spirituality among the laity, and the interaction between the Church and the Jew. Inasmuch as their role in Christendom bridged theoretical academic scholarship and militant pastoral activism, both as individuals and certainly as orders, not illogically did they enunciate and disseminate the new ideas which upset the precarious balance of the patristic *Adversus Judaeos* tradition. It was the Dominicans and Franciscans who spearheaded the attack upon the Talmud, espousing the view of postbiblical Judaism as a heretical deviation from the biblical faith, supposed fidelity to which had entitled the Jews to survive in a properly ordered Christian society. The Jew was no longer cast as blindly allegiant to the letter of Mosaic law, but as a deliberate unbeliever, whose first-century Jewish ancestors had actually recognized Jesus as their savior, perhaps even as the son of God (according to Thomas Aquinas and Nicholas of Lyra), and had killed him spitefully nonetheless. In the wake of this conscious betrayal of the divine covenant, the rabbis could no longer maintain the Mosaic religion with honest intentions. Either they had to accept Christianity, or they had to fabricate a qualitatively new religious system, entirely beyond the purview of biblical salvation history. Concerned above all with their own power and stature, motivated not by ignorance but by envy, depravity, and guile, the rabbis chose the second alternative, willfully allying themselves with the devil, supplanting the Bible with their Talmud. Such a schema of Jewish history found expression in numerous contexts, ranging from the theological and exegetical works of mendicant professors at the University of Paris, to the polemical arguments of the Spanish Dominican school of Raymond de Peñaforte, to the popular sermons of the German Franciscan Berthold von Regensburg and the Italian Dominican Giordaro da Rivalto.

The friars' attack upon rabbinic literature persisted throughout the late medieval period. Following the initial condemnations of the late 1230s and 1240s, many anti-talmudic treatises appeared reviewing the accusations against the Talmud and often including lists of offensive quotations. By the middle of the fourteenth century, at least ten additional popes and kings had ordered the Talmud confiscated, and then either censored or burned at the hands of the mendicants. The Inquisition subsequently burned the Talmud in Bourges, Toulouse, Paris, Pamiers, and again in sixteenth-century Rome—on one occasion (1310, in Toulouse) even after the Jews had been banished from the community several years previously.

The indictment of postbiblical Jewish literature provided the logic for a new, aggressive brand of anti-Jewish polemic aimed directly at European

Jewry and intent upon its downfall; it too was undertaken by the friars from the thirteenth century onward. Dominican and Franciscan preachers regularly compelled Jewish scholars to dispute with them publicly, often securing royal sanction to invade Sabbath synagogue services for that purpose—a privilege typically exercised at the head of an angry Christian mob. Although the jurisdiction of the Inquisition over the Jews was technically limited, its agents exploited and contrived all possible excuses for harassing them, a practice which boded ill for a number of Jewish communities. In the early 1290s, the Dominican inquisitor Bartolomeo de Aquila received royal permission virtually to obliterate the Jewish communities of Southern Italy, on the grounds that their members had aided the relapse of several Christian proselytes to their former Jewish observances; by 1300, the Neapolitan area was practically *Judenrein*. The thirteenth century witnessed the first officially sponsored ecclesiastical attempt to convert the Jews en masse. Mendicant missionaries trained themselves in Hebrew and rabbinics, so as to communicate with the Jews effectively on their terms. Schools were established expressly for this purpose. (Among their first graduates was Raymond Martini, professor of Hebrew at the Dominican *studium* in Barcelona, whose mammoth polemical *Pugio fidei* helped to mold the arguments of Nicholas of Lyra and Paul of Burgos, who in turn figured so prominently in Luther's writings.) Did not conversion to Christianity offer the best means for purging Europe of its Jewish presence? For such indeed was the friars' ultimate goal. The Franciscan tertiary Raymond Lull, missionary *par excellence* of the period, accordingly entreated the papacy, "if they [i.e., the Jews] do not convert, let them be ejected from Christendom."[29]

With clerical help, the new perception of contemporary Judaism soon gained a strong foothold among the Christian laity, who now beheld in the Jew not an authentic proponent of Old Testament religion, but the embodiment of all that was unnatural, satanic, and inimical to the welfare of Christendom. The Jews were now deemed the logical compatriots of Christian heretics, who likewise detracted from the ideal organismically conceived unity appropriate to Christian society. The charge of ritual murder, the blood libel, as well as the accusations that Jews desecrated the host and poisoned wells, first appeared in medieval Europe only in the twelfth and thirteenth centuries. The Jew was conceived as possessing grotesque physical characteristics, from a pointed nose to a distinctive and foul odor. By the fourteenth century, the iconographic contrast between *Synagoga* and *Ecclesia*, directly expressive of the old patristic ambivalence toward the Jews, had lost its popularity in Christian art. Artists now focused upon the blasphemy and treachery of the European Jew, represented the Jewish—and even Roman—enemies of Jesus in late medieval Jewish garb, and graphically portrayed the affinity between the devil and the Jews. The pathetic, but dignified, female personification of the Synagogue, which had captivated the attention of churchgoers for most of the Middle Ages, slowly gave way to wretched motifs like the *Judensau*, which depicted contemporary Jews sucking at the teats or basking in the dung of a female swine and to which Luther himself appealed in his *Vom Schem Hamphoras und vom Geschlecht Christi*.[30] To be sure, the new image of the Jews so opposed to that of the Church fathers never went unchallenged in Christendom; popes and kings at times resisted it, and perhaps even Luther himself may have had his doubts. By the sixteenth century, however, the friars and their legacy had certainly made their mark. Most European kingdoms had expelled their Jews; and had Augustinian anti-Judaism remained in vogue, the expulsions could not have proceeded so smoothly, free of ecclesiastical opposition and interference. The idea of a Europe *Judenrein* began to take its place in the mentality of Western Christendom.

In his important monograph on *The Roots of Anti-Semitism in the Age of Renaissance and Reformation*, Heiko Oberman insightfully describes the setting for Luther's encounter with the Jews:

In the sixteenth century, the Jewish question in the empire was as virulent and pressing as ever, even after the great wave of the earlier expulsions had ebbed away. It is true that violent measures such as mass expulsions or forced conversions occurred for the most part before the turn of the century. But humanism and Reformation carried on the struggle against the Jews with their own weapons. These movements could not realize their hopes for a reconstruction of church and society without first settling their spiritual score with the Jews and with Judaism. The intensification and deepening of the ideological conflict was in fact a characteristic feature of the incipient new era. Both humanism and Reformation, soon completely allied in several ways, together diagnosed the affliction of the age as symptomatic of its deepest disorders: reform demanded the absolute renunciation of a "Judaism" that had infiltrated into all aspects of life—the church and the monastery, the schools and the universities, the imperial free city and the episcopal see.[31]

As the present study itself suggests, the seriousness and urgency of the perceived Jewish problem in Western Europe had loomed to unprecedented heights by the end of the Middle Ages. One cannot but concur with Professor Oberman that early modern anti-Judaism was in many ways a new creature, deserving of evaluation within the elaborate matrix of social, political, and economic transformations which characterized its age. Nevertheless, we must humbly take issue with Oberman's subsequent conclusion, that vis-à-vis "the preliminary question, to what degree Luther's [anti-Jewish] perceptions are a reflex of the continuity of the age . . . , there are no problems and have been none for some time." [32] If Luther's attack upon the Jews derived from a new, peculiar meeting of unique individual and critical circumstances, then the weapons of his polemical arsenal, the ideas of his anti-Judaism, were distinctively anachronistic. Luther's preoccupying concern with Judaism and its role in the divine economy of salvation, his attitude toward the *Biblia hebraica* and rabbinic literature, his impassioned appeals for dealing with the Jews of his day, and his sensitivity to "Judaizing," the alleged encroachment of Judaism upon contemporary Christian society—all these had ample precedent in the patristic and medieval Church. However great Luther's role in embedding anti-Judaism in the foundations of modern Western civilization, and however much his ideas responded directly to the crisis of age, the ideas of his polemic—like their target— remained traditional and conservative indeed.

Notes

*   I am deeply grateful to Professors Mark Lee Raphael of the Ohio State University and Paul Minus of the Methodist Theological School in Ohio, who read an earlier version of this chapter, for their helpful criticisms and comments.
1. Recent works on the subject include Mark U. Edwards, Jr., *Luther's Last Battles: Politics and Polemics, 1531–46* (Ithaca, 1983), ch. 6; Heiko A. Oberman, *The Roots of Anti-Semitism in the Age of Renaissance and Reformation*, trans. James I. Porter (Philadelphia, 1984), throughout; and Heinz Kremers, ed., *Die Juden und Martin Luther—Martin Luther und die Juden: Geschichte, Wirkungsgeschichte, Herausforderung* (Neukirchen, 1985). Johannes Brosseder, in his *Luthers Stellung zu den Juden im Spiegel seiner Interpreten*, Münchener Universitäts-Schriften, Katholisch-theologische Fakultät, Beiträge zur Ökumenischen Theologie 8 (Munich, 1972), carries the story forward into the subsequent history of anti-Semitism, but he does not measure Luther's ideas against those of his medieval predecessors. As recently as the December 1976 meeting of the American Historical Association, Oberman and James Kittelson debated their markedly conflicting assessments of Luther's later works concerning the Jews. See Kittelson's *Luther the Reformer: The Story of the Man and His Career* (Minneapolis, 1986), pp. 273–75; and the detailed critique by Kittelson's doctoral student Ken Schurb, "Luther,

the Jews, and Apocalyptic: An Evaluation of Heiko Oberman's Position," forthcoming in the *Concordia Journal*.

2. Martin Luther, *On the Jews and Their Lives*, trans. Martin H. Bertram, in *Luther's Works*, ed. Jaroslav Pelikan and Helmut T. Lehmann, 47 vols. (Philadelphia, 1971), 47:168.

3. Among many others, see Rosemary Ruether, *Faith and Fratricide: The Theological Roots of Anti-Semitism* (New York, 1974), pp. 64–116; John Gager, *Kingdom and Community: The Social World of Early Christianity* (Englewood Cliffs, 1975), and *The Origins of Anti-Semitism: Attitudes Toward Judaism in Pagan and Christian Antiquity* (New York, 1985); Paul Richardson, *Israel in the Apostolic Church* (Cambridge, 1969); and C. F. D. Moule, *The Birth of the New Testament*, 3rd ed. (San Francisco, 1982). For more specific, technical treatments of some of the particular issues over which I have hurriedly glossed, see E. P. Saunders, *Paul and Palestinian Judaism* (Philadelphia, 1977); W. D. Davies, "Paul and the People of Israel," *New Testament Studies* 24 (1977), 4–39, and *The Setting of the Sermon on the Mount* (Cambridge, 1966); Lloyd Gaston, *No Stone on Another: Studies in the Significance of the Fall of Jerusalem in the Synoptic Gospels*, Supplements to *Novum Testamentum* 23 (Leiden, 1970); and J. Louis Martin, *History and Theology in the Fourth Gospel*, 2nd ed. (Nashville, 1979). On cognitive dissonance in particular, see Leon Festinger et al., *When Prophecy Fails: A Social and Psychological Study of a Modern Group that Predicted the Destruction of the World* (New York, 1956), esp. ch. 1, and Gager, *Kingdom*, pp. 37ff.

4. Amos Funkenstein, "Basic Types of Christian Anti-Jewish Polemics in the Later Middle Ages," *Viator* 2 (1971), 374. The history and substance of patristic polemic against the Jews have been discussed most instructively by A. Lykyn Williams, *Adversus Judaeos: A Bird's-Eye View of Christian Apologiae until the Renaissance* (Cambridge, 1935); Marcel Simon, *Versus Israel: A Study of the Relations between Christians and Jews in the Roman Empire (135–425)*, trans. H. McKeating (New York, 1986), esp. pt. 2; Bernhard Blumenkranz, *Die Judenpredigt Augustins: Ein Beitrag zur Geschichte der jüdisch-christlichen Beziehungen in den ersten Jahrhunderten* (1946; repr., Paris, 1973), and *Les auteurs chrétiens latins du Moyen Age sur les Juifs et le Judaïsme* (Paris, 1963); and Heinz Schreckenberg, *Die christlichens Adversus-Judaeos-Texte und ihr literarisches und historisches Umfeld (1.–11. Jh.)*, Europäische Hochschulschriften 23, no. 172 (Frankfurt, 1982).

5. Augustine, *In Answer to the Jews* 1.2, in *Treatises on Marriage and Other Subjects*, ed. Roy J. Deferrari, The Fathers of the Church: A New Translation 27 (New York, 1955), p. 392.

6. John Chrysostom, Homily 1 *Against the Jews*, trans. in Wayne A. Meeks and Robert L. Wilken, *Jews and Christians in Antioch in the First Four Centuries of the Common Era*, Society for Biblical Literature sources for Biblical Study 13 (Missoula, 1978), p. 97.

7. Augustine, loc. cit. 6.8, p. 400.

8. Beryl Smalley, *The Study of the Bible in the Middle Ages*, 2nd ed. (1952; repr., Notre Dame, 1964), p. 26.

9. Augustine, loc. cit., 7.9, p. 403.

10. Cassiodorus, *Expositio* in Psalmum 58.12, CCSL 97:525–26; cf. Rufinus, *In Psalmos Commentarius* 58.12, PL 21:880.

11. Augustine, *Concerning the City of God against the Pagans* 18.46, ed. David Knowles, trans. Henry Bettenson (Harmondsworth, 1972), pp. 827–28.

12. Bishop Ambrose of Milan, *Letter* 40.10, 20, trans. Mary Melchior Beyenka, The Fathers of the Church: A New Translation 26 (New York, 1954), pp. 10–11, 14.

13. *The Last Words of David*, in *Select Works of Martin Luther*, trans. Henry Cole, 12 vols. (London, 1824), 2:183–84. On sixteenth-century Christian Hebraic scholarship in general and Luther's approach to such study in particular, see the recent analysis of Jerome Friedman, *The Most Ancient Testimony: Sixteenth-Century Christian Hebraica in the Age of Renaissance Nostalgia* (Athens, Ohio, 1983). This section of my essay summarizes arguments of a more detailed study, "Scholarship and Intolerance in the Medieval Academy: The Study and Evaluation of Judaism in European Christendom," *American Historical Review* 91 (1986), 592–613. For other considerations of the trends in question, see above all the works of Beryl Smalley, especially *The Study of the Bible* and essays collected in *Studies in Medieval Thought and Learning from Abelard to Wyclif* (London, 1981), Henri de Lubac, *Exégèse médiévale; Les quatre sens de l'écriture*, 2 pts. in 4 vols., vol. 1 "Théologie," pp. 41–42, 59 (Paris, 1959–64); Herman Hailperin, *Rashi and the Christian Scholars* (Pittsburgh, 1963); Aryeh Grabois, "The Hebraica Veritas and Jewish-Christian Intellectual Relations in the Twelfth Century," *Speculum* 50 (1975), 613–34; Amos Funkenstein, "Changes in the Patterns of Christian Anti-Jewish Polemic in the Twelfth Century [Hebrew]," *Zion*, n.s. 33 (1968), 125–44; and C. Merchavya, *The Church versus Talmudic and Midrashic Literature, 500–1248* [Hebrew] (Jerusalem, 1970).

14. Augustine, *De doctrina christiana* 1.84–85, 2.99ff., 3.33–34, CSEL 80:30, 63–73, 88, Heiko Oberman, *Forerunners of the Reformation: The Shape of Late Medieval Thought* (New York, 1966), pp. 283–84.

15. On the Christian knowledge of Hebrew, see also Berthold Altaner, "Zur Kenntnis des Hebräischen im Mittelalter," *Biblische Zeitschrift* 21, *Hebraischkenntnisse des früheren Mittelalters*, Biblioteca degli studi medievali 4 (Spoleto, 1973).

16. Peter Damian, *Antilogus contra Judaeos* and a companion *Dialogus inter Judaeum requirentem, et Christianum e contrario respondentem*, PL 145:41–68. On both *opuscula*, see David Berger, "St. Peter Damian: His Attitude toward the Jews and the Old Testament," *Yavneh Review* 4 (1965), 80–112; and Blumenkranz, *Les auteurs*, pp. 265–71.

17. In addition to the works cited above in n. 12, see also M.-D. Chenu, *La théologie au douzième siècle*, Etudes de philosophie médiévale 45 (Paris, 1957); R. W. Southern, *Medieval Humanism and Other Studies* (Oxford, 1970); and G. R. Evans, *Old Arts and New Theology: The Beginnings of Theology as an Academic Discipline* (Oxford, 1980).

18. Beryl Smalley, *Hebrew Scholarship among Christians in XIIIth Century England as Illustrated by Some Hebrew-Latin Psalters*, Lectiones in Veteri Testamento et in rebus judaicis 6 (London, 1939), p. 1.

19. Peter of Blois, *Contra perfidiam Judaeorum*, PL 207:825
20. Richard of St. Victor, *De Emmanuele*, PL 196:601–66.
21. See Gratian, *Decretum*, D. 9, c. 6: "Libris veterum ebrea volumina, novis greca auctoritatem impendunt"; and Rufinus, *Summa decretorum*, ed. Heinrich Singer (Paderborn, 1902), p. 23. See also the comments of Johannes Faventinus, *Summa Decreti* (Vat Reg. lat. MS 1061, fol. 53ra), Huguccio, *Summa Decreti* (Admont Stiftsbibliothek Ms 7, fol. 11v), the *Glossa palatina* (Vat Reg. lat. MS 977, fol. 3vb) and the *Glossa ordinaria* of Joannes Teutonicus, ad loc. I am grateful to Mr. Steven Horwitz of the Institute of Medieval Canon Law at the University of California, Berkeley, for supplying me with photoprints of the relevant portions of the mss. cited.
22. Beryl Smalley, "A Commentary on the *Hebraica* by Herbert of Bosham," *Recherches de théologie ancienne et médiévale* 18 (1951), 29–65; Raphael Loewe, "Herbert of Bosham's Commentary on Jerome's Hebrew Psalter," *Biblica* 34 (1953), 44–77, 159–92, 275–98; Peter the Venerable, *Tractatus adversus Judaeorum inveteram duritiem*, PL 189:507–650, esp. 539, 622–23, 627, 648–49. Peter's understanding of Matthew 15:7 is echoed in Ludolf of Saxony, *Vita Jesu Christi* 1.88, 4 vols. (Paris, 1878), 2:314–17.
23. In addition to the works cited above in n. 12, see my studies of *The Friars and the Jews: The Evolution of Medieval Anti-Judaism* (Ithaca, 1982), and "The Jews as the Killers of Christ in the Latin Tradition, from Augustine to the Friars," *Traditio* 39 (1983), 1ff. Specifically with regard to the Christian knowledge of Hebrew texts, see Smalley, *Study*, ch. 6; Samuel Abraham Hirsch, *Early English Hebraists: Roger Bacon and His Predecessors* (London, 1905); and Altaner, "Zur Kenntnis."
24. Beryl Smalley, "William of Auvergne, John of LaRochelle and St. Thomas of Aquinas on the Old Law," in *St. Thomas Aquinas, 1274–1974*, 2 vols. (Toronto, 1974), 1:10–71; Jacob Guttmann, "Der Einfluss der maimonidischen Philosophie auf dds christliche Abendland," in *Moses ben Maimon: Sein Leben, seine Werke und sein Einfluss*, ed. W. Bacher et al., 2 vols. (1908; repr., Hildesheim, 1971), 1:135–230; and Wolfgang Kluxen, "Maimonides im lateinischen Abendland als Beispiel einer christlich-jüdischen Begegnung," in *Judentum im Mittelalter: Beiträge zum christlich-jüdischen Gespräch*, ed. Paul Wilpert, Miscellanea mediaevalie 4 (Berlin, 1966), pp. 146–66.
25. On the inquisitorial burning of Maimonides' works, see Cohen, *The Friars*, pp. 52–60; for Aquinas's rebuke of Maimonides, *In Sententiarum* 48.2.3, and 6, and Hans Liebeschütz, "Eine Polemik des Thomas von Aquino gegen Maimonides," *Monatsschrift für die Geschichte und Wissenschaft des Judentums* 80 (1936), 93–96; and Giles of Rome, *Errors of the Philosophers* 12.1–11, ed. Josef Koch, trans. John O. Riedl (Milwaukee, 1944), pp. 58–67.
26. See Nicholas's two anti-Jewish treatises published in *Biblia sacra cum glossis etc.*, 6 vols. (Venice, 1588), 6:275E–285D, and Cohen, *The Friars*, pp. 174–95.
27. Solomon Grayzel, ed., *The Church and the Jews in the XIIth Century*, rev. ed. (New York, 1966), pp. 278–79n.
28. Luther, *On the Jews and Their Lies*, pp. 268–72.

29. Raymond Lull, *"Le Liber de acquisitione Terrae Sanctae"* 2.3, ed. Ephrem Longpré, *Criterion* 3 (1927), 274. See also Cohen, *The Friars*, throughout, and "The Jews as the Killers of Christ," 1ff.

30. See Raoul Manselli, "La polémique contre les Juifs dans la polémique antihérétique," in *Juifs et Judaïsme de Languedoc, xiiie siècle–début xive siècle*, Chaiers de Fanjeaux 12 (Toulouse, 1977), pp. 251–67; Cohen, *The Friars*, pp. 231ff.; Joshua Trachtenberg, *The Devil and the Jews* (New Haven, 1943); Wolfgang S. Seiferth, *Synagogue and Church in the Middle Ages: Two Symbols in Art and Literature,* trans. Lee Chadeayne and Paul Gottwald (New York, 1970); Bernhard Blumenkranz, *Le Juif médiéval au miroir de l'art chrétien* (Paris, 1966); and Isaiah Shachar, *The Judensau: A Medieval Motif and Its History* (London, 1974). For Luther's allusion to the Judensau, see *Vom Schem Hamphoras* in *D. Martin Luthers Werke: Kritische Gesamtausgabe,* 58 vols. (Weimar, 1920), 53:600.

31. Heiko Oberman, *The Roots of Antisemitism in the Age of Renaissance and Reformation* (Philadelphia: Fortress Press, 1984), p. 36.

32. Oberman, *The Roots of Antisemitism,* p. 37.

[4]

Responses to Anti-Semitism in Midrashic Literature

Pinchas Hacohen Peli

Midrash represents a huge corpus of postbiblical literary creativity by the rabbis of the land of Israel. Midrashic literature spans many generations, yet it is held together by the oneness of Scripture to which rabbinic minds always returned, seeking old answers to new questions arising out of constantly changing times and situations.

Midrashic literature, in its numerous extant collections,[1] reflects the multifaceted events which took place from the late fourth century c.e. to the first half of the seventh century c.e., i.e., from the coming of Hellenism to Israel to the rise of Islam, a period of over one thousand years. In this millennium, we witness a great variety of anti-Semitic forms and attitudes.

A close study of the Midrashic texts proves the veracity of the statement, quoted in the name of the contemporary historian Salo Baron, that "there is nothing new in modern Anti-Semitism." Every kind of argument and counterargument for and against the Jews has already been expressed before and history does in this respect repeat itself over and over again.

The vast Midrashic literature indeed presents us with a rich quarry of historical information[2] on this subject and its various modes, from antiquity down to medieval times. However, our purpose here is not to dig up historical evidence of Anti-Semitism in the rabbinic sources, but to try to deduce from the Midrashic material available to us what the Jewish self-understanding of the anti-Semitic phenomenon was and how Jews "responded" to it. It should be understood that we are not dealing here with "disputation" material used at public debates between Jews and their opponents, although this too can be found in the Midrash.[3] Rather, our interest lies in the literary evidence of the Jewish confrontation with Anti-Semitism produced primarily for "inner consumption."

In order to understand the nature and scope of our undertaking, a word must be added on the ways in which the Midrashic texts came into being. While most of them were attributed to well-known rabbis of their generation, they were not in the strict sense of the term, solely the creation of these rabbis. The Midrash emerged first as an ongoing oral tradition in which at least three "partners" shared: the scriptural text, the rabbinic authorities of this later period and their audience.[4] The interaction of these three elements is represented, had its source, in the weekly reading of the biblical "portion of the week." This was the text on which, according to a very ancient custom,[5] the preacher would expound. Each and every Sabbath (either Friday night or Sabbath afternoon) the rabbi of the congregation would preach and conduct a dialogue in front of a full house audience, including both men and women.

The congregation that would flock to the sermon came with the expectation of being taught Torah as well as of being informed regarding worldly affairs, of being entertained, and of being provided with the courage to go on living another week under the unbearably hard circumstances in which Jews frequently found themselves.

The subject of the weekly sermon was never remote nor far-fetched. Judging by the kind of audience they had and gauging their expectations, the rabbis would address themselves to the actual problems the week had left on the minds and hearts of the people. Using their ingenuity to link what they said with the weekly reading of the Torah (the five books of Moses divided in a fifty-four annual cycle, or in a triennial cycle of 154 "portions," one "portion" for each Sabbath),[6] they helped the people draw instruction and guidance and derive encouragement and inspiration to sustain them for the week ahead. The Midrash appears to have served as a powerful weekly flight into "another reality," a different cosmos in which not even the sky was the limit for its imaginative fancies. Its only parameters were those of the Bible, which was the sole concrete element of this Midrashic-Aggadic cosmos beyond which nothing else mattered.

Some of those homilies originally delivered in hundreds of synagogues in Judea and Galilee over the centuries were eventually committed to writing to make up the body of Midrashic literature, also known as Aggada (lit.

"tale," or "lore" in contrast to Halachah representing "the law" and the legal literature).

The enchanted world of Aggada transcends time and space. It is composed, according to Isaac Heinemann's fundamental understanding of the subject[7] of "creative historiography" and "creative philology" in which "organic thinking" deliberately disregards gaps of time and space. History is not viewed as a lineal listing of chronological "facts," nor are words monolithic in their meaning. Both historiography and philology can be stretched as far as the creative imagination can take them. In the eyes of the Midrash it is not at all surprising for Abraham to strike up a conversation with Queen Esther, since they both inhabit the biblical universe, just as Moses could carry on a dialogue with King David—and we can listen in.

In this classical Midrashic ambiance[8] how did Jews react to Anti-Semitism in its manifold expressions? How did they deal first in their encounter with heathen peoples and later with their Christian or Islamic neighbors and rulers, who believed the "mother" religion must die or be put to death now that the "daughter" religions are here? The question we pose is not what they said or how they acted towards their assailants, but rather how did they explain this negative phenomenon to themselves? Did they accept, wholly or partially, the wild accusations so often leveled against them or did they reject them out of hand? Did they bemoan their bitter fate or did they learn to accept it as one does vis-à-vis any unexpected, unexplained, natural disaster?

A close examination of the Midrashic material suggests that none of these reactions, which manifest themselves in response to Anti-Semitism in modernity, mark the tone of the classic rabbinic response. The attitude of the rabbis in the Midrash, undoubtedly shared by the people who listened to them over the generations, represents an altogether different posture in facing up to the Anti-Semitism manifested in their days.

I

The rabbinic posture is manifested in the typical Midrashic way in which they applied biblical precedents, arising from that "other" literary Aggadic "reality," to the issues at hand. In the particular manner of their response to Anti-Semitism, however, we find a rare example of a specific typology which runs through the entire literature, covering, as it were, the full range of the varying eventful historical changes. History continued to turn pages, but the typology remained, fixed and unchanged, as though awaiting its full resolution some time in the future.

The story of Anti-Semitism in its variegated manifestations is typified according to the Midrash by the animosity originating in the relationship between Jacob and Esau. The struggle between the two brothers is not seen by the rabbis as a totally irrational phenomenon, neither are its causes "explainable" as racial, economic, or xenophobic. On the contrary, Jacob and Esau issue from the same mother and father, they are brothers, they are equals, but the animosity between them is inevitable.

The famous second-century sage R. Simeon bar Yochai states: "Halacha be'yadua sh-esaw soneh l'yaakov" (*Sifrei, Behaalotcha,* 9), namely, "it is a well known (legal) rule that Esau hates Jacob." This formulation is puzzling. Many have asked, what does Halachah mean in this statement about an historical phenomenon? What kind of legal decision did R. Simeon wish to postulate here? It seems to us that what R. Simeon bar Yochai was trying to establish was the fact that the animosity between Esau and Jacob is axiomatic, and although often irrational, it could not be changed, having the same fixity as any established Halacha!

The struggle between Jacob and Esau is prenatal and is recorded as originating during the pregnancy of Rebekah: "The children struggled in her womb, and she said: 'If so, why do I exist?' " (Gen. 25:22).

What these words mean precisely is difficult to say,[9] for the Hebrew original is itself not wholly clear. But that the mother-to-be was thoroughly distraught and that there was anxiety due to imminent trouble cannot be doubted, for ". . . she went to inquire of the Lord." And the answer she receives to her inquiry informs her that the offspring she is carrying are not just two innocent babes, but that: "Two nations are in your womb, Two peoples apart still in your body; One shall be mightier than the other, And the older shall serve the younger" (Gen. 25:23).

The notion of viewing the two infants in Rebekah's womb as a metaphor for two peoples in competitive rivalry is biblical and is supported by the stories that follow (the sale of the birthright; the blessings of Isaac), which also underscore the differences in personality type between the two brothers, culminating with the phrase "And Esau hated Jacob . . ." (Gen. 27:41). It is evident again when, years later, the brothers get together: "And Esau ran to meet him, and fell on his neck, and kissed him and they wept . . ." (33:4). This is followed by a seemingly "happy ending" where the two brothers, now well established heads of large families of their own, agree to go their separate ways: "So Esau returned that day to his way unto Seir. . . . And Jacob journeyed to Succoth, and built him a house, and made booths for his cattle" (33:16–17).

While the biblical story ends here in a relatively idyllic mood, this is not true of the rabbinic commentary on this material. In the Midrash the story of the relationship between Jacob and Esau, from this point on, is spun out in an ongoing drama which takes us up to the present and even into the remote eschatological future. Only then will Jacob's promise to follow Esau to Seir (35:15) be fulfilled, but on wholly different terms, in the ominous words of the prophet Obadiah (2:21): "And liberators shall march up on Mount Zion to judge Mount Esau." What transpires between these two poles in history, between the birth of the two children and the eventual triumph of Jacob over his brother Esau, is taken by the rabbis as a typological representation of the confrontation between Jews and Gentiles down through the ages.[10]

Everything that happens in this conflicted realm is reflected in the Midrashic portrayal of these two main archetypes: Jacob and Esau. Both are of the same race and the same breed, children of the same mother and father and yet representing contrasting worlds.[11] Their juxtaposition is not a one-time affair or an antiquated myth; it is enacted and re-enacted anew every day. Any attempt at an understanding of what one may call by extension Anti-Semitism must take into account the primal Jacob-Esau encounter. What transpires at any later time as a result of Jew-hatred must be evaluated and understood in the light of the alternative "other reality" formulated by the Midrash.

II

In reading the events as the Midrash does, the fact stands out that Esau is the progenitor of Edom, or is Edom himself.[12] Does scripture not explicitly declare "Esau is Edom" (Gen. 36:8–9)? Moreover, Esau is also the direct grandfather of the biblical Amalek (ibid. 36:12). The future bloody encounters with these two representative descendants of Esau are clearly marked on the historical record which serves as the backdrop for the conflict as it is drawn in Midrashic literature. Edom, the false neighbor-brother who pretended to represent brotherly love excelled in "violence against your brother Jacob . . . and stood aloof while strangers carried off his wealth" (Obadiah 1:10–12), becomes identified with Rome and subsequently with Christianity. The outer historical trappings change, but Esau-Edom remains the same. Esau in his extreme form of Amalek also keeps reappearing in brutal confrontation with Israel. At the supreme moment of the Exodus, Amalek is there (for no obvious reason) to block Israel's way (Exodus 17:8–16). Again, the mastermind behind the diabolic plan to exterminate the entire Jewish people a thousand years later in the lands of Ahasuerus is a descendant of Esau-Amalek, none other than Haman, the Agagite.[13]

The fates of the two—Esau-Edom-Amalek and Jacob-Israel—are forever intertwined. Anti-Semitism in all its various garbs is only one of the expressions of the bond between them. It does not warrant a cause and effect explanation. It is unavoidably, irrevocably, just there. It begins with the very birth of Jacob-Israel and it is marked by the struggle between Jacob and the mysterious "man" who comes to attack him in the darkness of the night, identified by the rabbis (Gen. Rabba 75:3) as "the angel of Esau." Jacob emerges from this struggle limping, but also with a new name YISRAEL, "He who wrestled with God and with man and overcame . . ." (Gen. 32:28). This wrestling and destined overcoming of Jacob-Israel will remain from now on one of his distinguishing marks.

The struggle takes place in history, but its "real" arena is that of the "other reality" created by Midrash. Historical stages come and go in the one temporal reality, but the scene is dominated by the Jacob and Esau of the "other." Both worlds, the mundane and the Aggadic, are not completely detached from each other, nor does the Midrashic reality represent a full escape from the actual world. On the contrary, the two fortify each other. The Midrashic reality provides the proper perspective from whence to view the scene and acquire that insightful self-understanding of the phenomenon in its totality. Its implications, very often, even bear practical results.

Let us now turn to a sample selection of some Midrashic text from Genesis Rabba.[14] They deal with the biblical figures of Jacob and Esau of yore, but actually represent, beneath the surface, an attempt at understanding the phenomenon of Anti-Semitism in the generation of the rabbis to whom the tests are attributed, some time between the second and fourth centuries of the common era. Those years saw many remarkable changes, among them the turning of pagan Rome to Christianity, yet there was hardly any change in the essence of the relationship between Jew and Gentile as it goes back to the Jacob-Esau typology.

The text (Genesis Rabba 63:3) starts with the beginning of the story:[15]

AND THE CHILDREN STRUGGLED TOGETHER (WAYYITHROZAZU) WITHIN HER (Gen. 22:22). Rav Yohanan and Resh Lakish discussed this. Rav Yohanan said: Each ran to slay the other. Resh Lakish said: Each annulled (*mattir*) the laws (*ziwuyaw*) of the other. Rav Brechiah observed in Rav Levi's name: Do not think that only after issuing into the light of the world was he [Esau] antagonistic to him, but even while still in his mother's womb his fist was stretched out against him . . .

What we are presented with here is not an innocent picture of three sages (who were among the great minds of their generation) sitting around chatting and musing over just another verse of Torah. In actuality, what we have are three different views of the "reasons" for Anti-Semitism, couched in the typology of Jacob and Esau. How is this animosity, they ask, to be explained? Rav Yohanan: "Each ran to slay the other" (*wayyithrozazu* is derived from *raz*, to run, and *razaz*, to crush, slay). It is part of human nature to clear the ground of competition, even at the price of murder and so Jacob and Esau were out to kill each other as part of a fight for "space" and *Lebensraum*. Resh Lakish has a complementary opinion. There is more than a struggle for space involved here. The two infants represent a clash of cultures, two conflicting worldviews. They annual each other's taboos. According to Resh Lakish, coexistence between two cultures or two *Weltanschauungen* is an impossible undertaking. The third rabbi, Rav Brechiah seems to reject both of the above "explanations" of Anti-Semitism and states that there is no rational explanation at all. It is something inherent in the very nature of the two brothers, even before they appeared in this world.

There is yet a fourth, anonymous, view in the Midrash, immediately following the above text:

They sought to run within her [deriving *wayyithrozazu* from *ruz*, to run]. When she passed near a synagogue or houses of learning, Jacob struggled to come out. . . . While when she passed idolatrous temples, Esau eagerly struggled to come out . . .

This last explanation sees the conflict as a religious struggle. While it is possible, perhaps, to arrive at some kind of cultural pluralism, religion demands exclusivity. Mother Rebekah was terrified: how could one person identify simultaneously with both pagan temples and with the synagogue? She was somewhat comforted only when told that there were two children within her womb, although she also realized that the two would not be able to live in peace with each other.

What all Midrashic views have in common is that they do not deal with Anti-Semitism as with a completely one-sided deplorable act committed by

Gentiles who are out to attack or to kill Israel. Rather, they treat Judeophobia as an inevitable reality that Jews have to learn to live with without giving up in despair on the one hand, or trying in vain to "correct" its causes on the other. Part of the method of learning to live with the conflict is not to passively accept things, but to try and give as good as one gets. If this cannot be done by exerting real power, of which Jews were long deprived, there are other levels of consciousness and expression on which to respond.

The Midrashic texts that follow probe further into the essence of the Jacob-Esau confrontation as it emerges within its historical context.

TWO NATIONS ARE IN THY WOMB: There are two proud nations in thy womb, each taking pride in his world, and each in his kingdom. There are two rulers of nations in thy womb: Hadrian of the Gentiles and Solomon of Israel. Another interpretation: Two peoples hated by the nations are in thy womb: All heathens hate Esau (nations feared and hated Rome, the conqueror of the world) and all heathen hate Israel . . .

This anonymous rabbi transfers the weight of the confrontation from the cultural and religious to the political, and asserts that there are two superpowers in the world. In many ways they are a match for each other, but only one can rule at any given time.

Caeserea (representing Edom-Rome) and Jerusalem — if one says to you that both are destroyed, do not believe him; if he says that both are flourishing, do not believe him: if he says Caeserea is waste and Jerusalem is flourishing, or that Jerusalem is waste and Caeserea is flourishing, you may believe him. I shall be filled, she is laid waste (Ezekiel 26:2), if this one is filled that one is laid waste, and if that one is filled, this one is laid waste . . . (B. Talmud, Megillah 6a)

This view puts Israel on the same level as imperial Rome, two equal rivals rather than an imperium vis-à-vis an insignificant fringe state. Hadrian and Solomon, although centuries apart, stand together as two examples of great sovereigns.[16] Even in being objects of hatred, the Jews are no exception. Rome too is hated.

This motif is further developed in the Midrashim that follow. Till now, one of them says (63:7), the world was a faceless conglomerate of many small nation-states; with the emergence of Esau and Jacob, "two peoples shall be separated from thy womb." From now on, the world is divided between two kinds of people: Romans and Jews. Rav Brechiah derives from this prooftext something else: "This ["from thy womb"] shows that [Jacob] was born circumcised," in other words, Jacob had no choice in the matter; he is irrevocably tied to the Jewish fate and to Jewish destiny.

The Midrash is not unaware of the vicious attacks against Jews and Judaism which proliferated on the other side, but tries in its own way to fight back. The counterattack was never as venomous as the attacks directed at them from both pagans and Church Fathers, yet in the face of the uncontrolled attacks on Jacob-Israel the sages created their own image of Esau as they saw him now in the form of the Roman Empire or the Christian Church.[17] Here is one example of many taken from our Midrash Genesis Rabba 63:12:

> Rav Phineas said in Rav Levi's name: You find that Abraham lived a hundred and seventy-five years. Isaac one hundred and eighty. . . . God withheld these five years from Abraham's life because Esau violated a betrothed maiden and committed murder. . . . Rav Berachiah and Rav Zakkai the elder said: He also committed theft. . . . Said the Holy-One-blessed-be-He: I made a promise to Abraham, assuring him: thou shalt go to thy fathers in peace, is this a good old age when he sees his grandson practicing idolatry, immorality and murder! Better that he quit this world in peace!

What a subtle (and very "Jewish"!) way—by the grandfather embarrassed by the acts of the grandson—of responding to vicious attacks by pointing to the corruption in the Roman Empire or the hypocrisy in the Church. Often in this vein of rebuttal, they resorted to the sophisticated sword of irony. Consider, for example, the following Midrashic exegesis:

> HE CALLED ESAU HIS ELDER (GREATER) SON (27:1). Rav Leazar ben Rav Simon said: This may be compared to a country that was levying a bodyguard for the king. Now a certain woman there had a son, a dwarf, whom she used to call "Tallswift." Said she: "My son is tall and swift; why then do you not appoint him?" "If in your eyes he is tall and swift," they retorted, "in ours he is but a dwarf. . . . In like manner, his [Esau's] father called him great. . . . His mother called him great: And Rebekah took the choicest garments of Esau her great son (27:15). Said the Holy One, blessed be He, to them: "If in your eyes he is great, in Mine he is small" as it says, behold I make thee small among the nations (Obadiah 1:2). (Genesis Rabba 45:11)

The fact that you are great in the eyes of your mother who sees you as "tall and swift" does not make you such in actuality, especially in the Midrashic "other reality," which is the one that really counts.

The Midrash also casts doubts on what look like generous overtures from Esau's side. Thus the verse describing the reconciliation between Esau and Jacob which reads: "And Esau ran to meet him, and fell on his neck, and kissed him, and they wept" (Gen. 33:4), is traditionally written in the Torah with dots over it. Why so? Because, say some of the sages, the word *wayyishakehu* (and he kissed him) could also be used phonetically as "and he bit him." And the Midrash continues: "A miracle happened and Jacob's neck turned into marble so that the bite could not hurt him. Thus, 'and they wept,' Jacob over the pain in his frozen neck; Esau over his teeth trying to bite into the marble." Such musings, of course, offered only partial comfort, but what was of great importance in such verbal maneuvers was the teaching and the hope it inspired that some day in the future, a future that may not be so far off, things will be altered.

This hope pervaded Jewish life. The Midrash tells us:

AND AFTER THAT CAME FORTH HIS BROTHER (25:25). A Roman prefect asked a member of the family of Salu: 'Who will enjoy power after us?' [In reply] he brought a blank piece of paper, took a quill and wrote upon it, AND AFTER THAT CAME FORTH HIS BROTHER, AND HIS HAND HAD HOLD ON [ESAU'S] HEEL. Upon this the comment was made: See how ancient words become new in the mouth of a sage! Moreover, it teaches how much suffering was endured by the righteous man. (Genesis Rabba 63:12)

In this last instance, the answer to "the question" is not offered by a rabbi but by a layman, a member of the family of Salu. What he did not dare say in an open debate he wrote down on a slip of paper, hinting, alluding, where the future lies.

It was this kind of Midrashic "response," proud, controlled, self-assured, that kept generations of Jews ever looking to inquire "how ancient words become new." While realizing "how much suffering was endured by the righteous," Judaism and the Jewish people never disintegrated under the indescribable pressures of irrational animosity.

Notes

1. For a listing of available Midrashic collections, see *Midrash and Literature*, edited by Geoffrey H. Hartman and Sanford Budick (New Haven: Yale University Press, 1986).
2. On the historical aspects of Misrash, see the bibliographical references in C. G. Montefiore and H. Loewe, *A Rabbinic Anthology* (New York: Schocken Books, 1974). An example of its actual application can be found in Gedaliah Alon, *The Jews in their Land in the Talmudic Age*, translated and edited by Gershon Levi (Jerusalem: Magnes Press, 1980).
3. Regarding the nature of the extensive literature known as *adversus Judaeos*

(against the Jews), see the Introduction and Bibliography in *Disputation and Dialogue*, edited by E. E. Talmage (New York: Ktav Publishing House, 1975).

4. J. L. Zunz and C. Albeck, *Haderashot be-yisrael ve-hishtalshelutan hahistorit* (Jerusalem: Mosad Bialik, 1947) [in Hebrew].

5. The weekly reading of the Torah is traditionally accredited to Moses himself. See Maimonides, *Mishne Torah*, Laws of Prayer, ch. 12, 1. See also *Encyclopedia Judaica*, "Torah, Reading of", vol. 15 (Jerusalem: Encyclopedia Judaica, 1973), pp. 1246–55.

6. Jacob Mann, *The Bible as Read and Preached in the Old Synagogue* (New York, 1940), idem and I. Sonne, *The Bible as Read and Preached in the Old Synagogue*, 2nd edition (New York, 1966).

7. Isaac Heinemann, *Darkei ha-Aaggada* (Jerusalem: Magnes Press, 1974) [in Hebrew].

8. On the Midrash as a distinct literary genre, see James L. Kugel, "Two Introductions to Midrash," in Hartman-Budick (note 1 above); Addison G. Wright, *The Literary Genre Midrash (Pauline Fathers and Brothers* (Staten Island, N.Y.; Alba House, 1967); Jose Faur, *Golden Doves with Silver Dots* (Bloomington: Indiana University Press, 1986); and the important contributions of Susan Handelman, in particular: "Everything Is in It: Rabbinic Interpretation and Modern Literary Theory," in *Judaism* 35 (Fall 1986), pp. 429–40.

9. Nahum M. Sarna, *Understanding Genesis* (New York: McGraw-Hill, 1986).

10. The fact that such a typology is used only rarely, as Jewish Bible interpretation shuns moving away from the plain meaning of the text, is pointed out by André and René Rinah Neher in their *Histoire biblique du peuple d'Israël* (Heb. trans.) vol. 1 (Yerushalayim-R. Mass, 1985–1986), p. 55.

11. There are many rabbinic attempts to define the two contradictory worldviews representing Esau and Jacob. Some find it in Esau's preference for this world, while Jacob prefers the world to come. Others find the difference, in the words of Isaac (Genesis 22:22), "The voice is the voice of Jacob, but the hands those of Esau." Jacob's strength is in the vocal practice of prayer and learning, while Esau's lies in the skill of his hands. See B. *Talmud Gittin 57b*, where the two can use each other's "specialization."

12. On Esau as the father of Edom who is but a prototype of Rome and also identified with Amalek, see Solomon Schechter, *Some Aspects of Rabbinic Theology* (New York: Schocken Books, 1961), pp. 99ff. For a more detailed comparison, see p. 108. H. Loewe (in the *Anthology*, note 2 above) suggests another reason why Esau came to be regarded as the prototype of the wickedness of Rome, i.e., because Herod was an Idumean, hence Herod-Edom-Esau. An extensive collection of Midrashic material connecting Edom to Rome and the Church is in Michael Guttmann, *Clavis Talmudis*, "Maphteach ha-Talmud," vol. 1 (Budapest: Waitzen, 1901), pp. 498–504.

13. This is a typical example of "creative philology" and "creative historiography," connecting the campaign against Amalek conducted by King Saul who spares the life of Agag the king of Amalek against the wishes of the Prophet Samuel

(1 Samuel 15:32) and Haman "the Agagite" (Esther 3:1) his representative descendant who falls into the hands of Mordechai, the son of . . . Kish (ibid., 2:5), Kish being also the name of the father of Saul (1 Samuel 9:1) which, in a way, completes the full cycle of events.

14. There is, of course, much more Midrashic material on the subject. Our selection is but a sampling from two chapters of Genesis Rabbah. Even in this sample there is another, very interesting cluster of Midrashim dealing with the confrontation of Esau and Jacob (chapters 75–78), but we shall not deal with it here.

15. We follow in our quotes (with minor changes) the edition of *Midrash Rabbah*, translated into English, with notes, glossary and indices, under the editorship of H. Freedman and Maurice Simon (London: Soncino Press, 1983).

16. "Two peoples," *shnei goyim* (Genesis 25:23) was also read by the rabbis as *shnei gaiim*, two proud ones, and was applied not only to the great kings of both Rome and Israel, but also to great and proud sages like Antoninus and Rabbi Judah the Prince *(B. Talmud, Berachot 57b; B. Talmud, Avoda Zarah 11a)*.

17. Verbal attacks against Judaism and Jews both among pagans and Christians were most vituperous, filled with hatred and mendacity. See Victor Tcherikover, *Hellenistic Civilization and the Jews* (Philadelphia: Jewish Publication Society, 1979), pt. 2, ch. 4; and James Parkes, *The Conflict of the Church and the Synagogue* (New York: Meridian Books, 1961). Compare also E. E. Urbach, *Hazal, Emunot V'deot* (Jerusalem: Magnes Press, 1969), p. 486 [in Hebrew].

[5]

Jews as Magicians in Reformation Germany

R. Po-chia Hsia

As Marcel Mauss points out, the continuity between religion and magic is predicated upon a structural similarity between the two systems.[1] Both have to do preeminently with power, the act of creating, be it the creation of the universe out of nothing, or gold out of base metals. Both specify techniques of power, in rites, incantations, prayers, in systems of symbolic representations to implore, coerce, and encapsulate divine forces for the benefit of the community of believers.[2] The three essential elements of magic (and by implication religion) are the practitioner, rites, and a system of representations. Hence we find a mirror image, albeit somewhat distorted, between religion and magic: one has its priest, the other its magician; both have rites of sacrifice, formulae of prayers and incantations, rituals incomprehensible to the larger community of laymen; and both rely on linguistic and nonlinguistic representations of supernatural forces. But a mirror image also implies otherness. The structural similarities between religion and magic cannot obscure the functional differences between the two institutions. Religion is public. It functions as a social institution whereby the central act of sacrifice bears witness not only to the coercive moral obligations entertained by the community of believers but also to the expectations of divine beneficence and goodwill in exchange for the collective act of propitiation. Magic is secret. As an institution it is without distinctive compartments or boundaries, a confusing mass of rites and representations, not codified, except by philosophers who study it, and practiced in occult for the benefit or to the detriment of select individuals or groups within society.[3]

In medieval Europe, religion and magic functioned as two autonomous systems with porous and ill-defined boundaries between them. Belief in magical forces underpinned popular faith in the efficacy of Christian sacraments; the latter were, in turn, applied by the laity and by the parish clergy, together with a vast ecclesiastical paraphernalia of objects and rites, for the alleviation of daily life. All that matters was that things should work. Thus necromancy, geomancy, amulets, talismans, spells, incantations, fortune-telling, herbal medicine, holy water, relics of saints, prayers, and sacraments formed the cultural universe of peasants, priests, townsfolk, princes, and kings.

The magical reputation of Jews was already firmly established before the Christianization of the Roman Empire. But in medieval Christianity Jewish magic came to be seen as essentially demonic. In its fight to establish orthodoxy and control, the medieval church gradually eroded away any conceptual distinctions between heretics, magicians, and Jews, lumping all under the realm of darkness, attacking all as the enemy of true religion.[4] Charges of enchantment sparked mob violence against Jews in England in 1189, and accusations of ritual murder, whereby the blood of Christian boys was purportedly used by Jews for magical rites, led to the 1235 pogrom in central Germany.[5] In late fifteenth-century Germany, on the eve of the Reformation, there was in existence an extensive folklore concerning Jews as magicians: they were reputed to be highly skilled diviners, fortune-tellers, physicians, and medicine men, but also evildoers, murderers of Christian children, torturers of the host, and, in the not too distant historical memory of Christendom, poisoners of wells and instigators of the Black Death.

The remarkable development in the century between 1450 and 1550 was that the medieval ambivalence concerning Jews as magicians eventually gave rise to a new view of German Jews which dissolved the medieval foundations of pogroms but established simultaneously the basis of modern antisemitism. We need to understand the intensity of ritual murder and host desecration accusations in the Reformation century by taking seriously the literal and symbolic meanings they had for contemporaries, instead of dismissing them out of hand as products of a bigoted age. In the remainder of this essay I propose to examine the significance of this crisis of antisemitism and document the changes within German society which eventually accounted for the disappearance of ritual murder trials and the subsequent articulation of a new antisemitism. In a supposed ritual murder, one or several Jews were accused of kidnapping and murdering Christian children, almost always boys, in order to seek revenge on Christians, but more especially to use their blood for magical purposes, in the preparation of poison, for circumcision, for Passover service, for the ritual purification of rabbis, and for stopping menstrual and other kinds of bleeding.[6]

We can clearly distinguish a structure of the blood libel by analyzing it as a discourse, in which various social voices made use of the ensemble of religious, political, and magical vocabulary to contest and define the nature of social reality, and we can begin to understand the multiplicity of meanings the language of accusation had for the participants involved. The three levels of this structure include an initial process of rumor or gossip, when a Christian heard about the need of blood on the part of the Jews and made an attempt to sell it to them, or when a corpse of a child was discovered, or actually when the murder has just been committed. This initial process can be described as the appropriation of an immemorial myth—one transmitted by folk songs and tales, by pictorial depiction, pilgrimages, and shrines— namely, that Jews had murdered Christian children in the past, and that blood played a central role in Jewish magic; it activated oral legends about Jews and applied it toward the explanation or resolution of an immediate problem in daily life. The dialogue was between an impersonal discourse— articulated in part by historical facts, transmitted by the various media of popular culture, sanctioned in part by ecclesiastical authorities, authenti- cized by chronicles—and a particular actor, be it a peasant, a nobleman, a journeyman, or a city council.

The second level of a ritual murder discourse moved from accusation to interrogation. Here, the murmurs and whispers of village gossip became submerged in the official voice of the judicial apparatus and the protestations of the suspects. The discourse was between officers of the law in the Holy Roman Empire, who drew both from the discourse of legends about Jews and from local customs and the written laws of the Empire, and the Jews, who were interrogated under judicial torture to confess to the crimes. The inter- locution was an uneven one, as the magistrates called in witnesses, weighed the evidence, and applied torture, while the Jews tried steadfastly to main- tain their innocence. At this stage, the discourse became a political one as well: friends and relatives of the suspects appealed to imperial authorities; city councils exchanged queries and warnings about other possible ritual murders; and there was often a contestation of judicial competence, because many of the Jews were under imperial jurisdiction. If the evidence proved inconclusive, or when the real causes of the murders came to light, the Jews were set free. But too often, the Jews were forced to admit their "guilt" under judicial torture, thus retroactively confirming the initial rumor of ritual murder.

The third and final level was the sentencing and public execution of the Jews. Banished were the discordant voices of unequal contestation in the process of interrogation: the "crime" has been confessed; the voice of the evildoers muted; replacing the voice of angry accusation, stern interrogation, and tormented protestations was the voice of unison. Now, the discourse resounded in the voice of a vindicated and triumphant Christian community. The public execution itself served as a dramatic representation of the "evil" of Jews and the triumph of Christianity: folk songs and tales were composed; eyewitness accounts were written down and sold in cheap fly-sheets and pamphlets; entries were recorded in chronicles; and in the case of the 1470 Endingen trial, a morality play was composed to commemorate the Christian triumph over Jews. [7]

These alleged "ritual murders" shared certain characteristics: the victims were usually pre-pubescent boys; their corpses showed signs of torture, sometimes prick marks, dismemberment, or wounds similar to the crucifixion; the ritualistic shedding of blood supposedly played a central role in the murder.

The structure of ritual murder discourse resembles a pyramid in that a broad base of popular legends and folktales provided the universal grammar for the articulation of more specific forms of antisemitic language. I have chosen to call this "popular culture" without restricting the currency of these ideas to only the lower social groups. The fact that these beliefs functioned as myths implied that they constituted the common cultural universe for society. Out of this common expectation about Jews as magicians and their need for Christian blood arose incidents in which Jews came under suspicion. Once they were denounced to the authorities, the realm of popular discourse and magical beliefs interacted with the realm of legal discourse and politics. Depending on the judicial outcome and the political pressure surrounding a trial, the case would either be resolved at this level or transformed into an execution. The process from accusation, interrogation, to execution would be like the ascension of a pyramid; out of the many potential cases only a few actually resulted in executions.

There were two crucial components underlying the structure of ritual murder discourse: the role of magic in popular religion, and the tensions between a learned religion and traditions of folk beliefs in Christian society. As Mauss suggests, a magician is not really a free agent; he is forced to play out a role assigned to him by tradition or defined by the needs of his clients. In Reformation Germany, the needs of the common folk created the roles which were then enforced on reluctant Jewish "actors": they were to play the part of magicians, be it as fortune-tellers, finders of lost objects, makers of amulets, or, in these alleged crimes, as ritualistic murderers. If we understand one of the central functions of magic as the fulfillment of the gap between wish and reality, then the magical role forced upon Jews in ritual murders can be understood as the need by pre-Reformation German society to create an immediate salvific presence. It provided a discursive outlet for the unspeakable crimes committed against children, be it infanticide, or child murders, perhaps sexual in origins, or resulting from the domestic violence of late medieval society. It disguised the real event by creating an alternative explanative model of a dialectical opposition between the two binary opposites of Jew/magician/murderer and Christian/believer/victim, between black, demonic magic and life-giving, godly religion. At a deeper level, it produced a powerful experience of sacrifice which was so central to the self-expression of late medieval piety, in a century of the imitation of Christ and the many moving and gruesome depictions of the crucifixion. In a ritual murder discourse two sacrifices were involved: by torturing and murdering a Christian boy, the Jews were reenacting the crucifixion, giving it a salvific immediacy and power which the mass could not rival; by exposing the "crimes" of the Jews and avenging the "murder," sacrificing the evildoers to an offended deity, the triumph of Christianity was celebrated and the crucifixion of Jesus avenged and vindicated. A ritual murder was an imitation of Christ par excellence; both the *Judenspiel* of Endingen, which commemorated the 1462 "murder," and the *Passionspiel* of Freiburg, performed on Corpus Christi Day, drew from a common structure of ideas and events, represented by a similar dramatic conception, and reflected the obsession with sacrifice.

The explicit connections between the crucifixion and ritual murder accusations were also manifest in the writings of the learned theologian Johann Eck, Luther's chief opponent during the early Reformation years. In the wake of the 1529 Pösing ritual murder trial, the reformer in Nuremberg, Andreas Osiander, composed a spirited defense of the Jews, denying the reality of ritual murders.[8] In 1540, when another ritual murder charge was raised against the Jews in Sappenfeld, Eck wrote *Refutation of a Jewish Booklet* in which he explains that Jews needed Christian blood in order to wash away their own blood stains which God had inflicted on them because they had crucified Christ.[9] He concludes that "it is no wonder that the Jews now buy the blood of innocent children, just as their fathers had bought the innocent blood of Jesus Christ from Judas with thirty pennies."[10] In a tone charged with emotions, Eck relates his own personal experience: in 1504, when he went as a young student from Cologne to the University of Freiburg, he witnessed a ritual murder case. A father in the village of Waldkirch near Freiburg sold his son to two Jews because they wanted some blood; he didn't know they were going to kill him. The two Jews were arrested and brought to trial in Freiburg. Eck describes how the small corpse was bled white and pale; that he saw and touched the wounds of the boy with his own hands.[11] The child could have become a saint just as Simon of Trent had been blessed, and his corpse would have been a relic bestowing salvific merit on those who behold and touch, if not for the fact that the Jews refused to confess under repeated torture and, after repeated orders from Emperor Maximilian, had to be let go.[12]

Christian blood could wash away the stains of blood on the Jews, so Eck argued. Eck's ideas reflected the fundamentally magical mental structure of an educated doctor of theology and university professor in early sixteenth century Germany. It was sympathetic magic at work: opposites attract one another, and a sympathetic substance forces the other out; thus Jews needed Christian blood to cleanse their own blood stains from Christ.[13] The potency of blood in a ritual murder discourse derived from the fact that it was spilled from a sacrificial victim. Sacrifice, death, and magic formed a continuum in this mental world. Magic is power. And one could find a host of legends in Germanic folklore concerning the power of blood: it heals diseases, stops bleeding, and spellbinds reluctant lovers.[14] Violent death creates magical power, and in the late sixteenth century the Rhinish physician Johann Weyer recorded many examples of folk beliefs in infanticide and witchcraft which were similar to ritual murder legends.[15]

A sacrifice, performed in a magical or religious rite, is essentially a coercive act: either the victim is an unwilling one, or the deity is forced into manifesting his divine power in exchange for the sacrificial gift.[16] Through the double sacrifice in a ritual murder discourse, a Christian community cleansed itself of a polluting element, namely the magicians, Jewish murderers, and coerced God to manifest his divine power in response. The idea of religious contamination was reflected in the symbols and metaphors of folk literature of the time. The identification of feces with demonic pollution is well known in Luther's writings; his scatology, in fact, reflected the symbolic structures of popular culture. In the popular folk tales of the peasant rogue Till Eulenspiegel, the crafty peasant tricked some Frankfurt Jews into buying his own feces as medicine (story 35); Thomas Murner, Luther's Franciscan foe, lampooned the reformer with literary and pictorial feces;[17] in the poem *Of Jewish Honor*, published anonymously in 1571, the poet chanted that Jews should not be tolerated because their very presence polluted the purity of Christian communities.[18] And what was purer in a community than its children? The alleged child murders by Jews were particularly horrendous to late medieval Germans because of the identification of their ideal family life with the image of a holy kinship *(die heilige Sippe)*, with Joseph, Mary, and the baby Jesus.[19]

As I have argued earlier, a sacrifice is essentially an exchange; and in response to this ritual murder discourse, God was supposed to manifest his salvific grace. Reports of miracles all followed upon the convictions and executions of Jews in these trials. In the 1540 Sappenfeld case, the sacrificial and miraculous nature of the death showed itself in a subsequent folk song. It narrates how the Jews tortured the boy for three days, piercing his ears, castrating him, cutting off his fingers and toes, stabbing him all over, and cutting three crosses on his body. More revealing was the subsequent event after the execution of the Jews. The corpse of the infant boy was put on display and five weeks later it bled, showing God's mercy, so says the song.[20] As we shall see later, the bleeding eucharist was the central element in a purported host desecration and one of the most powerful salvific images of pre-Reformation piety. The complete confusion of images between Christ and the child, the eucharist and the corpse created an immediate salvific presence "showing God's mercy" to the authorities and peasants of Sappenfeld. It was nothing less than an eucharistic sacrifice, a social mass, enacted in a discourse, with a language partially drawn from the liturgy of the ecclesiastical hierarchy and partially from the vocabulary of popular magical beliefs, with a set of interlocutors encompassing the Christian community and the "other," resulting in the reaffirmation of the unity and boundary of the collectivity and the reassurance of God's grace, similar to the social function of the mass. Miracles, apparitions, healings, the erection of shrines, the beginning of pilgrimage were all signs of the divine response to this double sacrifice. The benefit to the community was more than spiritual;

pilgrimage brought a temporary prosperity to the locality. Seen from one perspective of the evangelical movement, folk superstitions and greed went hand in hand. Osiander accused greedy monks and priests of fabricating the myth of blood ritual murders. In investigating these charges, a magistrate must ask himself, Osiander cautioned, "whether the priests or monks were not themselves eager to obtain the appearance of greater sanctity, more miracles, and to establish new pilgrimages, or whether they were much inclined to exterminate the Jews."[21]

A variant of ritual murder discourse was the accusation of host desecration, in which Jews allegedly stole or bought stolen consecrated host in order to torture Christ. Similar to the ritual murder discourse, a host desecration discourse manifests a parallel narrative structure: a wicked priest or Christian sells consecrated host to the wicked Jews, usually at Passover, whereby the Jews applied all kinds of torture with knives and fire, but eventually someone discovers the bleeding host which cannot be destroyed, thus uncovering the "crimes" of the Jews; at last, a miracle, a moment and a locus for salvation, was created by the establishment of chapels, shrines, and pilgrimages. Woodcuts, pamphlets, and folk songs, commemorate the triumph of sacrifice over magic. Aside from the celebrated 1337 case in Teckendorf, Bavaria,[22] the other incidents occurred within the forty years before the Reformation: Passau (1477), Sternbach in Mecklenburg (1492), Brandenburg (1510), and Halle in Saxony (1514).[23] Again, like the ritual murder discourse, there is no evidence that host desecration legends had any grounding in reality.

Both forms of discourse narrate the role of Jews as evil magicians, but the translation of legend into trial and execution depended upon the cooperation of the elite. In other words, popular belief in magic alone cannot explain the intensification of magical discourse from legend to interrogation; moreover, many ordinary Christians went to Jews for fortune-telling and medicine. Obviously, magic and Jewish magicians played an ambiguous role for Christians; they could heal as well as kill. It was really the confluence of a particular event and the participation of the elite in a mental universe of magic which precipitated the escalation of the levels of discourse. The crucial element leading to a trial and persecution was the displacement of a legal discourse by a magical discourse: all these cases were heard by secular authorities, few with training in civil and canon law. Paradoxically, for the magistrates and clerks, the crucial question was not one of the unconscious subtext of magic, but the language of common law, which functioned to articulate and mask a myth, and read more like a liturgical, dramatic text than a legal document. The 1470 Endingen trial record was copied down in the Freiburger Kopialbuch, a compilation and a copy book of the texts of all the privileges accorded to the city. When the Freiburg city fathers were confronted with a purported ritual murder case in 1504, they could rely not only on living memory of the Endinger trial but also on the actual, authentic judicial proceedings thirty-four years back. Likewise, in 1504, the magistrates in Mulhouse in Alsace wrote to the city fathers in Freiburg asking for detailed information on the current trial for their own judicial reference because their own Jews also came under the suspicion of ritual murder.[24]

There are three important conclusions we can draw from an analysis of these ritual murder and host desecration discourses. First, they represented attempts to fabricate and sustain a myth: that Jews were black magicians and Christians their innocent victims, and that God would ultimately vindicate their sacrifice and expose these "crimes." The function of the myth in fact masked the real motives behind some of the accusations, be it a personal grievance by a Christian debtor against a Jewish moneylender, or a general hatred of Jews, or a need to explain a gruesome murder, or a desire by the local clergy and authorities to create a moment of sanctity and fame. Crucial was not the real events or nonevents behind the discourse but the representations. Secondly, for Christians, these discourses represented triumphs and vindications in the battle against false religion. Suspicions arose always around Easter, when the conjunction of Passover and the commemoration of the passion of Christ created powerful emotions. The accusations demonstrated to the Christians that the crucifixion was not only a historical, unrepeatable event, but a recurring tragedy or "crime," perpetrated even by the Jews of the Holy Roman Empire. Its recurrence was thus both a source of passion and sorrow as well as comfort, because of the ritualistic, hence repeatable and reliable, nature of the sacrifice. For German society on the eve of the Reformation, these discourses meant nothing less than the triumph of true religion over false magic. Lastly, looking at ritual murder and host desecration discourses from our perspective, they were indeed magical representations, but the magic was performed by Christians, not by the accused Jews. A double sacrifice, a twofold rite, transformed reluctant Jews into magicians, and then destroyed their malevolent "magic" by a powerful ritual of Christian sacrifice and exorcism, in which, quite literally, the communities were cleansed of magical pollution and became, so to speak, "Judenfrei."

But the fabrication of myth and battle against Jewish magic were not confined to late medieval Christianity alone; these efforts continued through
the first decades of the Reformation in Germany, under a different ecclesiastical leadership and a new system of theology and rites, using new strategies
to disenchant the Christian community of magical possession.

No one embodied the ambivalence toward magic more vividly than
Luther himself; he both believed in it and condemned it. From the Wittenberg professor's table talks there emerges a picture of the reformer which
rounds out the image of the passionate theologian and writer of vehement
antisemitic tracts. Especially toward his latter years, Luther was preoccupied
with the malevolent forces of magic, particularly that of the Jews. In *Vom
Schem Hamphoras* (1543), a work which attacks the cabala as mere superstition and magic, Luther exclaims that "a Jew fabricates as much idolatry and
magic as the hair on nine cows, that is, countless and infinite."[25] He had
believed for some time that Jews were poisoners, influenced most probably
by legends of well poisonings by Jews prior to the Black Death.[26] For Luther,
the "Jewish danger" was the product of a mind which placed true, evangelical Christianity on one side, and all opponents of the Reform, real or
imaginary, on the other. Thus he attacks Jews, papists, and Turks in one
breath in *Von den Juden und ihren Lügen* (1543);[27] they were all idolators,
blind believers in the false religion of the flesh and of the law, whereas the
evangelicals trusted in the vital religion of the spirit. The binary opposition
between old and new law, flesh and spirit, superstition (*Aberglaube*) and faith
(*Glaube*), magic and religion resulted in a renewed and stricter attempt to
define the boundaries of the sacral community. Jews were assigned a prominent role as the quintessential *other* in Luther's social and psychological
drama of salvation.

The need to delineate a new community of evangelical Christians was
particularly acute in the early Reformation years because opponents of the
reform accused the movement as instigated by the Jews. When Osiander
ventured to publish an anonymous tract defending Jews against the charge of
ritual murder, Eck, knowing the true identity of the author, calls him the
"evangelical scoundrel" (*evangelischer Lumpen*) who dared to defend the
"bloodthirsty Jews."[28] The Lutherans, Eck curses on, were all evil monks
who had stirred up the Peasants War and were now defending the archene-
mies of Christendom.[29] Host desecrations by Jews were no different from the
Lutheran desecration of the eucharistic sacrament.[30] Eck concludes his long-

winded vituperation by accusing Osiander of slander against the whole of
Christianity, because by denying the truth of ritual murders, the evangelical
reformer was in essence accusing Christians of murder, magic, and lies.[31]
Some of the evangelicals were actually attacked by their enemies as Jewish
converts: Osiander's friend, Johann Böschenstein, was accused by a cleric of
being a Jewish convert and his father of being a learned rabbi, only because
he preached against icons and statutes; he felt compelled to compose a tract
in defense of his pristine Christian honor.[32] In turn, the evangelicals would
label their more radical competitors, including the Anabaptists of Münster,
as Judaizers, who had deviated from the true path of reform by their excessive
fundamentalist zeal.[33]

If we remember that Mauss characterizes a magical system as consisting of
three elements—a system of representation, rites, and practitioners—we
can better understand the strategies employed by the Reformation to disenchant Christianity of magical possession by the Jews. The first method of
disenchantment was the dissection and appropriation of the magical system
of representation, namely, the Christian appropriation of Hebrew.[34] Another approach was the study or exposition of the rites of Judaism. Finally,
the practitioners of magic, the Jews themselves, were rendered harmless by
confinement in ghettos or by expulsions.

A magical language consists of signs and symbols accessible only to a
small circle of practitioners and hence is a closely guarded secret. Its very
power lies not in the meaning of the text but in the coercive force of the
incantations and magical formulae. The immense popularity of the writings
of Cornelius Agrippa, replete with angelic names and formulae of incantations in Hebrew, both inside and outside Germany, testified to the fascina-
tion with magic; possession of a magical language fired the hopes of those
who would gain wealth, recover health, know fortune, crush enemies, in-
duce love, or simply share the secrets of the universe.[35] Moreover, magic
enabled one to cheat even the crafty Jews, as the legend of Faust offered an
example of the black magician cutting off his own leg as collateral to a
Jewish usurer and winning back more than his share of wealth in the end.[36]
While a handful of Christian scholars avidly learned Hebrew in order to read
cabalistic books and to gain access into the mystical, magical world of
ultimate knowledge of the divine, the common people did not hesitate to
procure amulets and talismans inscribed with Hebrew letters.[37] When a
visitation of the Saxon parishes turned up amulets, Luther bitterly denounced the village pastors, still clinging to their old ways and beliefs, and

in whose possession were found magical books with spells, charms, prayers, and names of angels and demons written in Hebrew.[38]

For Luther, the attack on Catholic superstitions paralleled the campaign to unmask Jewish magic as mere superstitions: in his expansive moments at table, Luther exclaimed that Jews were already superstitious in classical antiquity, as Cicero had noted, "and that we can see in all of Germany their vestiges";[39] or that "Jews and priests are scoundrels. . . . In sum, Jews are a most haughty people and most devoted to superstitious glosses."[40] To unmask, to expose, one has to know the language of one's opponents. While a defender of the old faith like Eck attacked the Lutherans for insisting the study of Hebrew was essential for recovering the true Christian faith,[41] for the Wittenberger and many evangelical clerics, knowledge of the Old Testament in its original represented a rescue of the true Christian heritage from rabbinic glossators and Jewish captivity. It was the only way to break the spell of a magical language, and through its appropriation, evangelical Christianity would triumph over Jews and Catholics. Thus when three rabbis came to Luther in 1540 to understand what seemed to them to be the philosemitic attempt to study Hebrew, they found out just the opposite. Samaria the rabbi told Luther that: "we rejoice because you christians are studying our language and reading our books such as Genesis and others; we hope that you will all become Jews." To this the reformer shouted: "Never! We hope that you will become Christians."[42]

Once a magical language is dissected and studied, it loses its force of enchantment. Furthermore, the knowledge of Hebrew made possible a better understanding of Jewish liturgy and helped to dispel the mystery surrounding Passover service, which had sustained many ritual murder and host desecration suspicions. The writings of Johannes Pfefferkorn provide a most instructive example. In spite of the fervor of this one convert who wanted to burn all Jewish prayer books, force Jews to baptize and do hard labor, he also showed an urgency and a sincere desire for his former coreligionists to convert. He composed two tracts to explain to Christians the observance of the Sabbath and the Passover: *A Booklet on Jewish Confession* (1508) and *Explication on How Jews Observe Passover* (1509).[43] While one of the aims of these tracts was to expose Jewish superstitions and "blasphemies" against Christianity, Pfefferkorn was careful to show that they were not magical rites in which Jews slaughter Christian children. In an earlier work exhorting the Jews to convert, Pfefferkorn refutes the legend believed by "the vulgar

Christians" that Jews needed Christian blood; if one by chance came across Jews who murder Christian children, it was out of hatred and not magical necessity.[44] It was only later, when the Jews rejected Pfefferkorn and when Reuchlin openly derided him as merely another "Jewish convert," that Pfefferkorn's attitude hardened. But even then, in his many vituperative tracts against Jews and Reuchlin, he only mentions ritual murder and host desecrations twice, and both times in a guarded tone of received knowledge from the collective wisdom of the Christian church.[45]

Whereas Pfefferkorn merely described the celebration of Sabbath and Passover, another convert, Anton Margaritha, the son of the chief rabbi in Regensburg, baptized in 1521, translated the entirety of the prayer book used by the Jewish communities in early sixteenth-century Germany.[46] For the first time, Christians could read in German the liturgy and prayers of Jews which contain no traces of magical incantations.[47] Nonetheless, Margaritha admits that Jews had murderers, adulterers, and other criminals as well, the greatest crime among them being hatred and cursing among themselves and betraying one another to the Christian authorities.[48] The only place where magic is mentioned is when Margaritha laments the cabala and the magic of the Jews, superstitions which did not help them for "there is no people who gets run over, robbed, and killed more often on the open roads than Jews."[49] *Der gantz Jüdisch Glaub* exerted a profound influence on the evaluation of Jews by the new Lutheran church: Luther read it, praised it, and was confirmed in his belief that both Jews and Catholics were superstitious and believed in good works;[50] after the first Augsburg edition of 1530, it was reprinted once in 1531 in Augsburg, at least three times in Frankfurt (1544, 1561, 1689), and in 1731 in Leipzig; it provided the standard text for introducing Lutheran pastors to the customs and ceremonies of the Jews.[51] The exposition of Jewish rites aimed at knowledge over an alien religion; it resulted in the mastery and ridicule of what was once an unknown magical system. Magic was now transformed into superstition.

The final attack on Jewish magic concentrated on suppressing the practitioners. From the 1450s to 1521 town after town in the Holy Roman Empire expelled its Jews; by the mid-sixteenth century, only the two imperial cities of Frankfurt and Worms had any recognizable Jewish communities.[52] Economic and political considerations stood behind many of these expulsions. Usury was the universal charge; and the fact that citizens of imperial cities got entangled in legal disputes with Jews under the protection of princes and lords, who were often hostile to civic freedom, moved the city fathers to

expel Jews. In the fourteen years before the magistrates of Nuremberg expelled the Jewish community in 1498, they registered over 23,000 civil cases
related to Jews; all of them arose from moneylending, and a substantial
portion represented lawsuits between Jewish creditors and Christian debt-
ors.[53] But religious concerns were no less urgent. In Regensburg, the magistrates wanted to expel their Jews in the wake of the 1475 ritual murder
investigation but were thwarted by imperial opposition. A later generation
succeeded in 1519.[54] The continuity between late medieval piety and the
new evangelism was embodied in the Regensburg case by the pivotal role
played by Balthasar Hubmaier in expelling the Jewish community. He studied under Eck at Freiburg and Ingolstadt; and after receiving his doctorate in
canon and civil law, he was called to serve as cathedral preacher in Regensburg. Hubmaier arrived just when the evangelical movement was gathering
momentum, and he excoriated moneylenders and Jews, enjoined his audience to do penance, and called upon the city fathers to purify the Christian
community of "polluting" Jews.[55] On the site of the razed synagogue, the
citizens erected a chapel to honor the Virgin Mary; it prospered as a pilgrimage shrine for Upper Bavaria until the city adopted an evangelical church
ordinance in 1521.[56] Hubmaier himself was to become an Anabaptist and
died in 1528 for his faith in Vienna.

Central to the undermining of the elements of a belief in Jewish magic was
the elevation of true religion, or more precisely evangelical faith, over folk
superstitions and false, magical religion. Keith Thomas has argued for the
rise of religion and the decline of magic in early modern England, and a
similar process can be discerned in sixteenth-century Germany.[57] As an
intellectual revolution as well as a social movement, the Reformation profoundly altered the consciousness of the educated elite. When everyone was
a sinner, when true sainthood was invisible, when the earthly church comprised both the good and the bad, the traditional boundaries between holiness and profanity began slowly to lose the force of their former permanence.
The rapid decline of pilgrimages and the veneration of saints in reformed
areas finally undermined the foundations which gave rise to ritual murder
and host desecration accusations. Similarly, when new doctrines of the
eucharist expounded on the symbolic and commemorative nature of the
sacrament, when Christ's sacrifice was understood to be historic and eternally efficacious, when the mass was attacked as a concoction of monkish

magic, a crucial foundation underlying the discourse of Jewish magic was dissolved.

The gradual change in the mentality of the elite was reflected in the replacement of a magical discourse by a legal discourse in ritual murder charges. After the 1540 Sappenfeld case, suspicions and accusations did not vanish, but a new generation of magistrates, with more training in jurisprudence, handled the matter very differently.[58] In 1563, a leathermaker journeyman in Worms went before the city council and reported that he saw the Jew Abraham carrying a Christian infant under his overcoat into the Jewish quarter.[59] The magistrates held both Abraham and the journeyman. They interrogated Abraham on March 18, failing to get any confession. The matter might have ended there if not for the fact that Abraham's relatives filed a lawsuit in the Reichskammergericht in Speyer, citing violation of imperial injunction against ritual murder trials.[60] Thoroughly entangled in a lawsuit which threatened to bring imperial sanctions against the city, the magistrates dragged their feet and negotiated a face-saving solution, releasing Abraham on bail after more than a year's imprisonment.[61]

The decline of magical discourse was also manifest in the way historical documents were interpreted. Whereas the 1470 Endingen trail record provided historical "proof" of the magical crimes of the Jews when it was entered in the Kopialbuch of Freiburg, serving moreover as a historical reference for the 1504 Freiburg trial, a different approach to historical and legal records can be seen one century later.

On September 9, 1611, the officials of the Cologne archiepiscopal government in Arnsberg wrote to the city council of Frankfurt.[62] In the letter they reported on the arrest of several Jews who were accused of torturing and murdering a child in the town of Brilon. Further charges were brought to their attention that Frankfurt Jews had committed similar crimes. The imprisoned Jews maintained their innocence and begged the Cologne officials to write to Frankfurt so that the city fathers "might open up their old and new protocol and find out for themselves whether such stories had ever been recorded."[63] The Frankfurt magistrates spent a month examining councillor protocols for the last century and a half and replied on October 7. Upon investigation of their own archives, the city fathers found two cases. In 1504, the shoemaker Bryhenn came under suspicion because of the sudden death of his stepson and his own hasty departure from the city. Arrested in nearby Hanau, Bryhenn confessed that he had struck and killed his stepson.

But when the jailors wanted to apply more torture, he confessed further that "he had stabbed him to death with needles," collected the blood, and sold it to the Jew Gumpricht. Although Gumpricht was arrested and interrogated under torture in Frankfurt, he maintained his innocence. When Bryhenn was condemned to death, he retracted his accusation, and Gumpricht was set free without compensation. Another case came up almost a century later. In 1593, Abraham of Dublin came begging from Poland; he received only one and a half talers from the Frankfurt Jews and was openly scorned by them. In anger, he took oxen blood from a butcher and hid it in the synagogue, so that the Frankfurt Jews might come under the suspicion of ritual murder. The magistrates arrested him but eventually set him free.[64] Other than these two incidents, the Frankfurt magistrates reported, they could not find any more evidence in the archive. Regarding the painting on the Brückenturm, one of the watchtowers of the city known for its depiction of ritual murder of Simon of Trent in 1474, the magistrates wrote that it did not depict a murder in Frankfurt but one in far away Trent many years ago, and they refused to have the painting removed. At the further request of the Frankfurt Jews, the magistrates enclosed a copy of the imperial mandate of Rudolf II (1577) confirming the privileges of the Jews and condemning ritual murder charges.[65]

In Worms and Frankfurt, suspicions and accusations escalated into official investigations, but did not become condemnations and executions. In other words, the structure underlying ritual murder and host desecration discourse was undermined. Not only was the magical discourse about Jews repressed by a legal-political discourse, when imperial mandates and magisterial jurisprudence dismissed charges, but the dissolution of the tripartite structure of ritual murder discourse allowed for new and differentiated articulations of the individual components which formerly comprised a magical disource. Thus, the disenchantment of Christianity and the dismissal of Jews as magicians did not have to result in a self-critical, self-conscious confrontation with a dubious past; rather, the single magical myth, fabricated out of diverse events in the century between 1450 and 1550, was transformed into differentiated historical "facts," and further transmitted by theological dissertations, academic studies of Jews, history books, and folktales. Although the evangelical movement attacked superstitions, the unmasking of magic did not lead to self-unmasking; Jews might not have been magical murderers by the end of the sixteenth century, but they were once, as attested to by history, and their "criminal nature" would still manifest itself in greed and deceit, in usury and false religion, if no longer in magic and murder.

Concomitant with the decline of ritual murder condemnations, cases of child murders were beginning to be publicized in Germany. But the suspicion of Jewish magic lingered on, even if ritual murder trials were suppressed. In 1573 when the Jew Leopold of Berlin was broken on the wheel and quartered, he was accused of being a "conjuror of the Devil," having pledged his soul and body to him, and lying with Christian women; he was executed as a murderer, thief, traitor, and magician.[66] In 1591, Johann Georg Godelmann, a doctor of canon and civil law, accused Jews of being a blasphemous and magical people in his learned Latin treatise on how to recognize and punish magicians and witches.[67] Gradually the image of the Jew as murderous magician became the Jew child kidnapper: in early eighteenth-century Frankfurt, when small children were missing, their parents would worry that they had gone into the Jewish ghetto and been killed.[68]

Displaced by a new legal-political discourse, the myth of Jewish magic nevertheless got passed on into the realm of cultural and historical discourse. Myth was no longer a part of a living magical world in which ideas and events flowed in and out of a unified, reality-ordering structure, it became history. The Frankfurt magistrates who replied to the Cologne officials in 1611 that they could find no documentary evidence of ritual murders in Frankfurt were also the ones who refused a petition by the Jewish community to remove the depiction of the ritual murder at Trent on the Brückenturm two years earlier, although the Jews argued passionately how the picture aroused great hatred against them and constantly endangered their lives.[69] To the city fathers perhaps, the ritual murder at Trent was a historical event which was just as real as the innocence of the Frankfurt Jews; both facts were attested to by written discourse, in the one by chronicles and pamphlets, in the other by the archival sources of the city.[70] Songs and folktales commemorating host desecrations and ritual murders often passed into print and were collected and studied by the folklorists of the nineteenth century.[71] The transformation of magic/myth into knowledge/religion eventually laid the foundation for the Enlightenment in Germany, when Christian scholars of Judaism at the end of the seventeenth century such as Johann Christof Wagenseil (1633–1705)[72] and Johann Jacob Schudt (1664–1722)[73] tried to educate at least the learned reader about the falsity of ritual murder charges, although their books are filled otherwise with attacks on usury, false religion, and the character of German Jews.[74] But the power of collective knowledge and the aura of the printed word in preserving and transmitting ritual murder discourse were strong. In the same decades when Wagenseil and Schudt were cautiously offering German society a relatively more accurate picture of Jewish life and history, another *érudit*, Johann Andreas Eisenmenger (1654–1704), professor of Oriental languages at Heidelberg, affirmed their historical veracity. In his massive and pretentious tome, *Judaism Discovered* (1700), he recounted the history of ritual murders from the fifth century onward.[75] In addition to the many history books and theological treatises, Eisenmenger cites as authority the picture in Frankfurt under the Brückenturm which depicted the death of Simon of Trent. After giving contemporary examples of ritual murders in Poland, Eisenmenger concedes that

one does not hear nowadays any more of these gruesome acts in Germany, except that, if I remember correctly, I had read in the newspaper some years ago that in Franconia a murdered child was found and therefore the Jews were held on suspicion. But since one has in the past dealt most stringently with the Jews wherever such things were committed, it is thus beyond doubt that they refrain from such bloodshed out of fear of punishment, although their hatred of Christians is just as great now as it might have been at any time past.[76]

He repeats the catalogue of magical beliefs surrounding blood and speculates that perhaps rabbis used Christian blood in writing down spells on amulets.[77] At the end of this section, Eisenmenger grudgingly concedes that perhaps in the past some instances of injustice were involved but that he himself was inclined to believe in a core element of truth in these charges because so many authorities had written about them and so many examples were cited. He concludes "that the Jews committed child murders mostly during Easter . . . because our savior Christ was crucified at Easter, and they did this to scorn him."[78]

From the perspective of Germans of the late seventeenth century, especially from those of Lutheran faith, it seemed that Christians were finally disenchanted from Jewish magic. Deprived of their magical power, exposed as superstitious, and rendered harmless in ghettos, Jews remained nonetheless an alien, potentially dangerous element in a rejuvenated, but divided, Christian society. The academic study of Judaism and Jewish life in Protestant Germany served only in passing to dispel popular legends; for many, its chief meaning was to document and ridicule Jewish superstitions, and to celebrate the triumph of Christian faith over medieval magic, a victory achieved by the heroic struggles of the Reformation.

Notes

For comments and criticisms on an earlier version of this chapter, I would like to thank Sander Gilman, Barry Strauss, and Ruth Angress. The arguments and historical examples in this chapter are developed in greater length in my forthcoming book, *Murderous Magic: Jews and Ritual Murder Discourse in Reformation Germany*.

1. Marcel Mauss, *A General Theory of Magic*, trans. Robert Brain (London, 1972).
2. Ibid., p. 18–22.
3. Ibid., pp. 10, 23–24, 86ff.
4. See Edward Peters, *The Magician, The Witch and the Law* (Philadelphia, 1978), pp. 12–13, 94 and Joshua Trachtenberg, *The Devil and the Jews* (New Haven, 1943), pt. 2.
5. Joshua Trachtenberg, *Jewish Magic and Superstition. A Study in Folk Religion* (Philadelphia, 1939), pp. 2, 7.
6. See Heinrich Strack, *The Jew and Human Sacrifice*, trans. Henry Blanchamp (New York, 1909), throughout.
7. See Karl von Amira, ed., *Das Endinger Judenspiel* (Halle, 1883).
8. The anonymously published tract was republished by Moritz Stern who correctly identified the author; see *Andreas Osianders Schrift über die Blutbeschuldigung*, ed. Moritz Stern (Kiel, 1893).
9. Johann Eck, *Ains Judenbüchlins Verlegung: darin ain Christ/gantzer Christenhait zu schmach/will es geschehe den Juden unrecht in bezichtigung der Christen kinder mordt* (Ingolstadt: Alexander Weissenhorn, 1541), sig. J⁴ʳ–K¹ʳ. For a brief description of the polemics between Eck and Osiander, see Heinrich Graetz, *Geschichte der Juden von der ältesten Zeiten bis auf die Gegenwart*, vol. 9 (Leipzig, 1891), pp. 309–11.
10. "Nit ist zu verwundern: dz die juden jetzt kaufen das blut der unschuldigen kinder, so ir väter kauft haben das unschuldig blut IHESU Christ vm 30. pfennig von Judas." Ibid., sig. K²ʳ.
11. Ibid., sig. B³ᵛ⁻⁴ᵛ.
12. Stadtarchiv Freiburg A1 XII C, nos. 28 and 29 for the correspondence on the trial; for the confessions of the Jews, see Ratsprotocol 1504 B5 (P) XIIIa, no. 9, fos. 4ᵛ–5ʳ.
13. On sympathetic magic, see Mauss, p. 72.
14. See *Handwörterbuch des Deutschen Aberglaubens*, ed. Hanns Bachtold-Stäubli and E. Hoffmann-Krayer (Berlin/Leipzig, 1927–42), entry "Blut," cc. 1434–1442; and Throndike, *History of Magic*, vol. 5 (pp. 101–2, 462, 602, 639, 660), vol. 6, pp. 240, 243, 292, 484.
15. Johann Weyer, *De praestigiis daemonum. Von Teuffelsgespenst, Zauberern und*

Grifftbereytern Schwarzkünstlern, Hexen und Unholden . . . (Frankfurt: Nicholaus Basseum, 1586), bk. 3, ch. 4, p. 152; for folk recipes using blood to stop bleeding, see p. 311f.

16. Marcel Mauss, *The Gift: Forms and Functions of Exchange in Archaic Societies*, trans. Ian Cunnison (London, 1969).

17. See his "Von den Grossen Lutherischen Narren," in *Thomas Murners Deutsche Schriften*, ed. Paul Merker, vol. 9 (Strasbourg, 1918), p. 267.

18. *Der Iuden Erbarkeit* (n.d., 1571), sig. B^{2v}. In her book, *Purity and Danger: An Analysis of Concepts of Pollution and Taboo* (London, 1966), Mary Douglas argues that the fear of religious pollution is fundamental in delineating religious communities.

19. John Bossy, *Christianity in the West 1400–1700* (Oxford, 1985), pp. 10–11.

20. *Ein hübsch new lied von Zweyen Juden/ vnd einem Kind/ zu Sappenfelt newlich geschehen* [n.p., n.d.] sig. F^{3-3v}.

21. Stern, ed., *Osianders* . . . *über die Blutbeschuldigung*, p. 42: ". . . ob nicht pfaffen/ oder munch da selbst/ den schein grosser heyligkeyt zu erlangen/ grosse wunderwerck/ vnd newe walfarten an zu richten/ begirig/ oder sunst die Juden zu vertilgen seer geneygt weren."

22. The Teckendorf case was publicized with the advent of printing; it was recorded in the Nuremberg chronicle of Hartmann Schedel (1493) and later commemorated in a 1520 pamphlet. The Nuremberg chronicle was first published by Anton Koberg in 1493; I have used the 1497 Schönsberg edition of Augsburg. See Hartmann Schedel, *Liber Chronicarum cum figuris et imaginibus ab initio mundi* . . . (Augsburg: Johann Schönsberg, 1497), fo. 258^v. See also *Von Tegkendorff das geschicht wie die Juden das heilig sacrament haben zugericht werdt is in disem büchlin verston was den schalckhafftigen Juden ist worden zu lon* (Augsburg: S. Otmar, 1520).

23. Eck. *Ains Judenbüchlin Verlegung*, sig. T^2–V^{3v}. On the Passau host desecration case, see *Geschichte der Juden von Passau mit dem Sacrament im Jahr 1477*. There are two editions, one by Kaspar Hochfeder of Nuremberg, the other by Johann Forschauer of Augsburg: see *Einblattdrucke des XV. Jahrhunderts*, ed., *Kommission für den Gesamtkatalog der Wiegendrucke* (Halle, 1914), p. 290. The woodcuts are reproduced in W. M. Schmid, "Zur Geschichte der Juden in Passau," *Zeitschrift für die Geschichte der Juden in Deutschland* 1, no. 2 (1929), p. 129. On Mecklenburg, see the pamphlet, *Ein wunderbarlich geschichte. Wye dye Merckischen Juden das hochwirdig Sacrament gekaufft und zu marten sich verstanden. Anno Domini 1510*, reprinted in Heiko A. Oberman, *Wurzeln des Antisemitismus* (Berlin, 1981), pp. 197–200.

24. Stadtarchiv Freiburg: C1 Judensachen, letter from city council of Mulhouse to city council of Freiburg, dated July 27, 1504.

25. *D. Martin Luthers Werke. Kritische Gesamtausgabe* (Weimar, 1883–), vol. 53, p. 602. Hereafter cited as *WA Br (Briefwechsel)* and *WA Tr (Tischreden)*.

26. *WA Br* 3, p. 821. On legends of well poisonings prior to the Black Death, see for example, Heinrich Schreiber, ed., *Urkundenbuch Freiburg* vol. 1, (Freiburg, 1829), pp. 379–83.

27. WA 53, pp. 542, 544.

28. Eck, Ains Judenbüchlin Verlegung, sig. A^4.

29. Ibid., sig. N^{4v}–O^{1v}.

30. Ibid., sig. V^4.

31. Ibid., sig. Z$^{4–4v}$.

32. See Johann Böschenstain, Ain Diemietige Versprechung/ durch Johann Böschenstain/ geborn von Christenlichen Öltern/ auss der stat Esslingen/ wider etlich die von im sagen/ Er seye von Jüdischem stammen/ und nit von gebornen Christen herkommen zügesant . . . (n.p., n.d.).

33. See Klaus Deppermann, "Judenhass und Judenfreundschaft im frühen Protestantismus," in Die Juden als Minderheit in der Geschichte, ed. Bernd Martin and Ernst Schulin (Munich, 1981), pp. 110–30; here, 120–21.

34. For a succinct introduction to the history of Hebrew learning by Christians in Germany, see Otto Kluge, "Die hebräische Sprachwissenschaft in Deutschland im Zeitalter des Humanismus," Zeitschrift für die Geschichte der Juden in Deutschland 3 (1931), pp. 81–97, 180–93.

35. For the writings of Heinrich Cornelius Agrippa of Nettersheim, see his Magische Werke, 5 volumes in 3 books (Berlin, 1921). See also Charles Nauert, Agrippa and the Crisis of Renaissance Thought (Urbana, 1965).

36. See Historia von D. Johann Fausten dem Weitbeschreyten Zauberer und Schwarzkünstler, ed. Richard Benz (Stuttgart, 1977), pp. 81–83.

37. On Christian Hebraica, see Jerome Friedman, The Most Ancient Testimony. Sixteenth Century Christian-Hebraica in the Age of Renaissance Nostalgia (Athens, Ohio, 1983). For the history and preparation of Hebrew amulets, see T. Schrire, Hebrew Amulets: Their Decipherment and Interpretation (London, 1966), esp. pp. 69–72 on Christian-Hebrew amulets and the use of Hebrew inscriptions by Christians.

38. "Vom Schem Hamphoras," WA 53, p. 614.

39. WA Tr 4, 3990.

40. WA Tr 4, 4019.

41. Eck, Ains Judenbüchlin Verlegung, sig. P^{4v}–Q^{2v}.

42. WA Tr #4, 5026: "Nos laetamur, quod vos christiani discitis nostram linguam et legitis nostros libros ut Genesis et reliquos; spes est futuros vos omnes Iudaeos. Nihil est! Nos speramus vos futuros christianos."

43. Eyn buchlijn der iudenbeicht (Cologne: Johann von Landen, 1508); a Latin and a Low German edition were also published by Landen in 1508: Libellus de Judaica confessione sive sabbato afflictionis and Eyn boichelgyn der ioeden bicht. The tract on Passover is Explicatio quomodo ceci illi iudei suum pascha servent: et maxime quo ritu paschalem eam cenam manducent (Cologne: Heinrich von Nussia, 1509).

44. Johannes Pfefferkorn, Speculum adhortationis iudaice ad Christum (Speyer: C. Hist, 1507); reprinted by M. von Werden of Cologne in 1508. See sig. D^{1}–^{1v}.

45. See his Handt Spiegel wider und gegen die Jüden (Mainz: J. Schoeffer, 1511), sig. A^4 and Streydt Puechlyn. Vor dy warheit vnd eyner warhafftiger historie Joannis Pfefferkorn Vechtende wider den falschen Broder Doctor Joannis Reuchlyn und syne jungern Obscurorum virorum . . . (n.p., 1516), sig. C$^{2v–3}$.

46. See Anthonius Margaritha, *Der gantz Jüdisch Glaub mit sampt eyner grundtlichtenn und warhasstigen anzeygunge, aller satzungen, Ceremonien, gebetten, heymliche und offentliche gebreuch, deren sich die Juden halten, durch das gantz Jar . . .* (Augsburg: Heinrich Steiner, 1531). For Margaritha himself, see Josef Mieses, *Die älteste gedruckte deutsche Übersetzung des jüdischen Gebetbuchs aus dem Jahre 1530 und ihr Autor Antonius Margaritha* (Vienna, 1916); for the conflict between Margaritha and the Jewish communities, see Selma Stern-Taeubler, *Josel of Rosheim, Commander of Jewry in the Holy Roman Empire,* trans. Gertrude Hirschler (Philadelphia, 1965).

47. See Margaritha, *Der gantz Jüdisch Glaub,* sig. D²ff. for translation and commentary of the Passover service.

48. Ibid., sig. L²ᵛ⁻³.

49. Ibid., sig. Y⁴ᵛ.

50. *WA Tr* 5, 5504.

51. The 1544 Frankfurt edition was published by C. Egenolff; the 1713 Leipzig edition by Friedrich Lanckischen. The Leipzig edition has a forword by Magister Christian Reineccius, Bachelor of Theology, who writes on the book's important influence on Luther and on subsequent generations of Lutheran theologians. The 1531 Augsburg edition that I used shows three provenances, with the last owner one by a Magister Johann Joachim Prickler bearing the year 1684. This particular work is in Benecke Rare Books Library, Yale University (Mck 50 530mc).

52. The most comprehensive source for the study of the expulsion of Jews, prior to the completion of the *Germania Judaica,* is the multivolume reference work, *Deutsches Städtebuch,* edited by Erich Keyser and later with the collaboration of Heinz Stoob. Articles on individual cities are written by archivists, who provide information of varying reliability on the history of Jews in their home towns. Although there are some omissions, this is on the whole a reliable reference guide; see *Deutsches Städtebuch. Handbuch städtischer Geschichte,* ed. Erich Keyser and Heinz Stoob, 5 vols. in 9 books (Stuttgart, 1939–74). For a purely economic and political interpretation of the motives for expulsion, see Markus J. Wenninger, *Man bedarf keiner Juden mehr. Ursachen und Hintergründe ihrer Vertreibung aus den deutschen Reichsstädten im 15. Jahrhundert* (Cologne, 1981), esp. pp. 54–199.

53. Stadtarchiv Nürnberg, repertorium B14/V no. 2, four volumes of register of the *Schuldverbriefungsbücher* of the city court between 1484 and 1498. These are alphabetically entered according to the legal parties involved, and a brief description of the case is noted as well. For secondary literature on the expulsion of the Nuremberg Jews, see Philip N. Bebb, "Jewish Policy in Sixteenth Century Nürnberg," *Occasional Papers of the American Society of Reformation Research* (1977), pp. 125–36.

54. On the expulsion of the Regensburg Jews, see Raphael Straus, *Die Judengemeinde Regensburg im ausgehenden Mittelalter* (Heidelberg, 1932).

55. See Torsten Bergsten, *Balthasar Hubmaier. Seine Stellung zu Reformation und Täufertum 1521–1528* (Kassel, 1961), pp. 76–86.

56. For a contemporary description of the expulsion of the Jews, the erection of the

Marian chapel, the miraculous cures and the pilgrimage, see *Wie die new Capell zu der schönen Maria in Regenspurg erstlich auff kommen ist . . .* (Nuremberg: H. Höltzel, 1519); for folk songs celebrating the purification and rejuvenation of Regensburg, see *Die Historischen Volkslieder der Deutschen von 13. bis 16. Jahrhundert*, ed. Rochus von Liliencron (Leipzig, 1867), pp. 316–39.

57. Keith Thomas, *Religion and the Decline of Magic* (New York, 1971).

58. On the changing legal status of the Jews and the displacement of theological discourse by the language of Civil (Roman) Law among German jurists of the sixteenth and seventeenth centuries, see Renate Overdick, *Die rechtliche und wirtschaftliche Stellung der Juden in Süddeutschland im 15. und 16. Jahrhundert, dargestellt an den Reichsstädten Konstanz und Esslingen und an der Markgrafschaft Baden* (Constance, 1965); Wilhelm Güde, *Die rechtliche Stellung der Juden in den Schriften deutscher Juristen des 16. und 17. Jahrhunderts* (Sigmaringen, 1981); and Guido Kisch, *Zasius und Reuchlin: eine rechtsgeschichtlich-vergleichende Studie zum Toleranzproblem im 16. Jahrhundert* (Constance, 1961).

59. See Stadtarchiv Worms 2030. For Abraham's interrogation, see fos. 1–22.

60. On the citation by the Reichskammergericht, see StdA Wo 2030, fos. 32–33, Urkunde of March 26; and two copies, fos. 35–37. For the legal brief prepared by Abraham's lawyer in Speyer, see fos. 38–48.

61. On the back of a letter of supplication written by Buttlin, Abraham's wife, dated September 10, 1563, urging the magistrates to quickly settle the affair, the city secretary noted the consensus of the magistrates "to settle the matter as best as possible." StdA Wo 2030, fos. 276–79. For Abraham's sworn bail document, see fos. 359–67.

62. This letter, together with the reply of the city council of Frankfurt, are deposited in StdA Fr Ugb E 47p.

63. StdA Fr Ugb E 47p: "Sie wolten Ihre alte unndt neuwe Prothocolla aufschlagen unndt sich darauss erkundigen lassen, ob solch geschicht sich daselbst jemahls zugetragen."

64. See letter of the city council of Frankfurt to Cologne officials in Arnsberg, StdA Fr Ugb 47p.

65. Another copy of the mandate can be found in StdA Fr Ugb E 46y.

66. See L.T.Z.T. [pseu.] *Warhaftige Geschicht vnd Execution Leupoldt Judens/ welche an ihme seiner wolverdienten grausamen und unmenschlichen thaten halben (so er an dem unschüldigen Christlichen Blut begangen) den 28. Jenners/ 1573 zu Berlyn/ nach innhalt Götliches und Keyserliches Rechten vollnzogen worden ist* (1573), sig. A².

67. Quoted by Throndike, *History of Magic*, vol. 6, pp. 535–37.

68. Johann Jacob Schudt, *Jüdischer Merckwürdigkeiten*, 4 parts (Frankfurt/Leipzig, 1714–17; repr. Berlin, 1922, with continuous pagination), p. 1335: "Und weil dann diese Beschuldigung wider die Juden noch heut zu Tage währet/ dahero auch/ wann sich in dieser Stadt ein Kind verläufft oder verliehrt/ ist der Eltern grösste Sorge/ es möge in die Judengasse gekommen/ und von Juden umgebracht worden seyn." In other places, Schudt, in spite of his general hostility toward Jews, emphatically denied that Jews had killed Christians for blood; see pt. 2, bk. 36, S.4 (p. 1355) and pt. 4, bk. 36, S.4 (p. 2587).

69. StdA Fr Ugb E 46y, letter of petition by the Judischeit to the city council of Frankfurt, dated November 21, 1609. Another letter of petition was written on April 30, 1612, to which the magistrates agreed to cover the picture on the occasion of the gathering of the electors. The picture was not destroyed until the 1760s.

70. For an example of the historical record and illustrative woodcut of the ritual murder at Trent, see Schedel, *Liber Chronicarum*, fos. 254^v (Nürnberg Koberger edition) and fos. 285^v–286^r (Augsburg Schönsberger edition).

71. Folktales about Jews have passed on into the collection by the Grimm brothers; the motives have been classified in the Aarne-Thompson Index of Folktale motives; see Stith Thompson, *The Folktale* (Berkeley, 1977), pp. 488–500: "ritual murder" (V361); "The Wandering Jew" (Q502.1); "Solomon as Master of Magicians" (D1711.1). See also *Handwörterbuch des deutschen Märchens*, ed. Johann Bolte and Lutz Mackensen (Berlin/Leipzig, 1930–36).

72. Born in Nuremberg to a prominent merchant family, Wagenseil studied at the universities of Altdorf and Orléans; he served for some years as *Hofmeister* to various Austrian noblemen before returning as professor of Oriental languages to Altdorf where he taught for thirty-eight years. See *Allgemeine Deutsche Biographie* *(ADB)* 40, pp. 481–83.

73. Born in Frankfurt to a pastor's family, Schudt studied in Frankfurt and Wittenberg. He taught at the gymnasium in Frankfurt, eventually becoming its rector in 1717. See *ADB* 32, pp. 652–63.

74. In his *Benachrichtigungen wegen einiger die Judenschafft angehenden wichtigen Sachen* pt. 1 (Frankfurt, 1705), p. 126ff, Wagenseil writes that "der Denen Juden fälschlich beygemessene Gebrauch der Christen-Bluts. Das ist Unwidersprechliche Widerlegung der entsetzlichen Unwarheit, dass die Juden zu ihrer Bedurfnis Christen-Blut haben müssen, welche so viel tausend dieser unschuldigen Leute um Haab, Leib und Leben gebracht."

75. *Entdecktes Judenthum: oder Gründlicher und Wahrhaffter Bericht, welchergestalt die verstockte Juden die Hochheilige Dreyeinigkeit . . . erschrecklicher Weise lästern und verunehren, die Heil. Mutter Christi verschmähen . . . Dabey noch viele andere, bishero unter den Christen entweder gar nicht, oder nur zum Theil bekantgewesene Dinge und Grosse Irrthüme der Jüdischen Religion und Theologie, wie auch viel lächerliche und kurtzweilige Fabeln und andere ungereimte Sachen an den Tag kommen; Alles aus ihren eigenen . . . Büchern* (Frankfurt, 1700), pp. 220–24.

76. Eisenmenger, *Entdecktes Judenthum*, pp. 224–25: "Mann höret aber jetziger zeit nichts mehr von solchen grausamen thaten in Teutschland/ ausser dem das ich/ wann ich mich recht erinnere/ vor etlichen jahren in der zeitung gelesen hab/ dass in Franckenland ein ermordetes kind seye gefunden worden/ und habe man die Juden desswegen im verdacht gehabt: dann weil mann vor diesem mit den Juden sehr scharff verfahren ist/ allwo solche dinge seind begangen worden/ so ist nicht zu zweiffelen/ sie auss furcht vor der straff/ sich nun solches blutvergiessens enthalten/ wiewohl ihr hass gegen die Christen eben so gross ist/ als er jemahls vor diesem gewesen sein mag."

77. Ibid., p. 225.

78. Ibid., p. 227: "Das aber die Juden den Kinder-mord meisterns auff Ostern begangen haben/ wird ohne zweiffel desswegen geschehen sein/ weil unser Heyland Christus auff Ostern ist/ gecreutziget worden/ zu dessen verachtung sie solches thun."

[6]

Stepping Out: The Writing of Difference in Rahel Varnhagen's Letters

Liliane Weissberg

Nation f. vor Ende des 14. Jh. entlehnt aus lat. *natio(nem)*, das als Ableitung von *natus* "geboren" . . . die blutmässige Einheit des Volkskörpers bezeichnet.
—Kluge, *Etymologisches Wörterbuch*, 1967

natio, s. Nascio, war eine Göttin, so die Gebuhrt eines Menschen dirigiren sollen.
—Herderich, *Gründliches Antiquitätenlexikon*, 1743

I

The term *antisemitism* was coined in the late nineteenth century and designates, as a political term, a negative attitude towards Jews that no longer finds its cause in issues of religion, but instead derives from a concept of human races and the difference of human "natures." Hannah Arendt, in her preface to the first part of *The Origins of Totalitarianism*, entitled "Antisemitism," elucidates this shift:

Antisemitism, a secular nineteenth-century ideology—which in name, though not in argument, was unknown before the 1870's—and religious Jew-hatred, inspired by the mutually hostile antagonism of two conflicting creeds, are obviously not the

140

same; and even the extent to which the former derives its arguments and emotional appeal from the latter is open to question.[1]

Arendt proceeds to go beyond this name, and to describe its unnamed prehistory. For her, the "birth" of antisemitism is set earlier in the century, with a redefinition of Judaism in and with the conception of the nation state.

To provide evidence for her thesis, Arendt traces the interaction of Jews and gentiles at the turn of the nineteenth century. She examines the protective gestures of a Jewish community that tries to prevent a progressive assimilation, as well as the gentile reinterpretation of the alien character of the Jews. While illustrating her thesis, she introduces the heroine of one of her earlier books, Rahel Varnhagen.[2]

Like all true heroines, Rahel rises above her peers, even in this description. According to Arendt, Rahel held the most exciting but also "most representative" of the Berlin salons. She compared well to other hostesses, and other Jewish women frequenting the salons: "Her original, unspoiled, and unconventional intelligence, combined with an absorbing interest in people and a truly passionate nature, made her the most brilliant and the most interesting of these Jewish women"(59). Elsewhere, Arendt poses Rahel in a more problematic setting. In her book on *Rahel Varnhagen: The Life of a Jewish Woman*, as well as in related articles, Arendt elaborates on the distinction between *pariah* and *parvenu*,[3] terms she had coined to describe the social position of Jews in the eighteenth and early nineteenth centuries.

While Jews had only limited legal rights and were suffered within the walls of German cities by letters of protection, Berlin Jews in the late eighteenth century felt a chance to leave their outsider or "pariah" existence, and enter gentile society. Social historians like Reinhard Rührup or Arno Herzig are eager to stress the coming together of Jewish emancipation and the rise of the new bourgeoisie.[4]

Arendt, as well, points to the bourgeois ideals of education (*Bildung*) and financial power that gave Jews the hope that assimilation could be within reach. The possible "entrance" into gentile society was not just a matter of religious conversion; the acceptability of the converted as well as the unconverted Jews was at stake. According to Arendt, acculturation, or the striving for the *Bildung* of the gentile world, proved to be a peculiar one-way street, however. Instead of leading to a Jewish emancipation, Arendt describes this process as a bad theatrical: "No one fares worse from this process than those bold spirits who tried to make of the emancipation of the Jews that which it really should have been—an admission of Jews *as Jews* to the ranks of humanity, rather than a permit to ape the gentiles or an opportunity to play the *parvenu.*"[5]

Arendt's term *parvenu* describes Jews striving for assimilation as individuals who are failing in their task. Their wish to assimilate results in a step that marks a lower, and not a higher civilization; its symbol is not the human being but the imitating ape. The act of "aping" does not lead to any adjustment, but reveals precisely the difference between the copy and the "original" proper behavior and education that assimilation tries to emulate. Neither education nor wealth proves to be a stable, neutral, or undifferentiated term.

In the study of Rahel Varnhagen, Arendt describes her as a pariah who became a parvenu. In *The Origins of Totalitarianism,* however, Rahel's life seems untouched either by her social ambition or by her failure to succeed. Instead, her story offers a glimpse of a utopia that stands out from antisemitism's prehistory:

> The charm of the early Berlin salons was that nothing really mattered but personality and the uniqueness of character, talent, and expression. Such uniqueness, which alone made possible an almost unbounded communication and unrestricted intimacy, could be replaced neither by rank, money, success, nor literary fame. (60)

Arendt indeed seems to echo the words of Rahel, who describes herself as a "unique personality": "I am as unique as the greatest being [*grösste Erscheinung*] on this earth."[6]

After 1806, Arendt admits, the utopia disappears. Again, using Rahel's words, she likens this disappearance to a disaster at sea: the Berlin salon "foundered like a ship containing the highest enjoyment of life"(60). The Prussian defeat in the Napoleonic Wars, the peace treaty of 1807, and the legal affirmation of civic, but not political rights for Jews in 1808 mark the steps that ended this state of "innocence and splendor"(60). The historical events shaped the "accident" that separated Jews again from gentiles, and turned many of the "unique personalities" of Rahel's salon into antisemitic thinkers. But was the ship holding tight at sea before it reached these fateful cliffs?

In my reading of Rahel's letters, I will follow Arendt's thesis of the interrelatedness of the rise of antisemitism and the concept of the nation-state by tracing Rahel's definitions of Judaism and of nation. I will question, however, the exceptional status granted to Rahel in *The Origins of Totalitarianism*, and instead claim a relationship between the concept of the "unique personality," as put forward by Rahel and insisted upon by Arendt, and the concept of nation itself. Arendt, looking for the origins of antisemitism, may too arduously avert her gaze from the Berlin salons. In her sketch of the utopia we may find the searched-for scene of birth.

II

Rahel Levin was born in Berlin in 1771, the daughter of the merchant Levin Markus Cohen and his wife Chaie. Already as a young woman, and shortly after her father's death in 1789, Rahel opened her doors for the first of her famed salons. Jews and aristocrats, actors and diplomats gathered in her parents' house in the Jägerstrasse to engage in conversation, and listen to Rahel's "truths of the attic" which she named after the room in which she lived. In 1813, Rahel left Berlin due to the war. She returned in 1819, and soon thereafter opened the second of her salons. By this time, she had already converted to Protestantism and married Karl August Varnhagen, a historian and Prussian state official on leave, and later the editor of several collections of her letters.

Rahel's literary production is her letters. She wrote thousands of them, messages, descriptions, notes, and commentaries that were to produce an autobiography in the dialogic form. David Veit, a young Jewish contemporary of Rahel's, became one of her closest friends and earliest correspondents. Veit grew up in Breslau and moved to Berlin in 1788. While still in Breslau, he had been tutored by a Christian schoolmaster, and after completing his general education in Berlin, he left the city in 1793 to study medicine, first in Göttingen and then Jena. Clearly, these opportunities for study and travel were not available to every Jew, and were certainly not available to women.[7]

Veit's letters to Rahel often center on the notion of *Bildung* and the need for acculturation. They encourage her in her self-education, and they are filled with descriptions of the world outside the ghetto and the Berlin gates. Rahel in turn, seemingly engaged in an "unbounded communication," reports to him the daily occurrences at home, her impressions and opinions, and the progress of her didactic enterprise. "Unbounded communication," however, has its own limits. Rahel's letters, dealing with her "unique personality," reflect this matter of problematic social "bondage." By singling herself out, moreover, this same "bondage" makes the writing of her epistolary autobiography possible. By doing so, she establishes her life as prominent, and her story as an important one to read.

In one of her letters to David Veit, Rahel writes that she is bound to her home by sickness. An aching foot serves as the excuse for her tardy response to Veit's last letter, and she explains her lack of news by her own forced inactivity. Rahel makes up for this lack of news with a fantasy, however, a fantasy that deals with her "origin" and the story of her own birth:

> I have such fantasy, as if an extraterrestrial [*ausserirdisch Wesen*], while I was forced into this world, had stabbed, right with a dagger, these words into my heart: "yes, have sensations, see the world, as only few can see it, be great and noble, an eternal thinking I cannot take from you as well. One thing, however, was forgotten: be a Jewess!" and now my whole life is a bleeding to death; if I keep still, it can last a while; each movement, made to stop the bleeding, is a new death; and immobility is only possible for me in death itself. [8]

Rahel, shifting the attention from her foot to her heart, seems to describe her Judaism as her fate, a birth defect, an ailment, just like her own physical immobility. Judaism is a fateful blemish.

But the passage itself is difficult to read. Joined to eternal thought, greatness, and nobility, Judaism may be the cause of, or is at least a necessary accompaniment to the extraterrestrial's gifts. The Jewess, like the romantic consumptive, is a being whose affliction confers upon her heightened sensibility. The rhetoric of the passage is at odds with the image, however; Judaism joins the other properties as an afterthought. Eternal thought or increased vision may not necessarily have to lead to sorrow; Rahel's Judaism may indeed be an unrelated attribute, but one that spoils her possible perfection. Not only working against perfection, it may turn a heightened sensibility into a curse, and lead the dagger. On the occasion of her birth, it "was forgotten": Rahel's words bear the full force of ambiguity. Perhaps its cause is an extraterrestrial's absentmindedness; perhaps, however, Judaism is this tricky absence, the forgetting, itself. Blemished, and loosing further hold of her own body's integrity, there seems to be no hope for restoration. Rahel's sickness changes the potential ideal into its counterpart; perfection turns into the model of an in-valid: a person of no value.

The story itself relates a scene of judgment. A sentence, voicing the forgotten, or spoken in forgetfulness, accompanies a dagger, that hits her heart while sparing her head. It enacts a death penalty that turns life into a torture. An angel, not a storm at sea, causes Rahel's shipwreck, marks the turning of a utopia into the living death of Judaism. Instead of external storms, Rahel describes her own tempestuous nature, one that can do nothing else but try to cope with the loss of blood by just remaining still. Fury in stillness: Rahel calls this a furious madness, and one that is her truth. It is a frenzied movement and displacement (*Raserei*) and it can therefore be "translated" and "cross over" (*übersetzt*): it is a step done in immobility (134).

Resting at home, Rahel turns her sickness into the image of her own "misfortune." In the continuation of her narrative, the story of the heart again becomes that of the foot; the wound affects her gait. Judaism can turn into a lame foot, and the lame foot into Judaism. Immobility, and the frenzied movement seem to contradict each other, but are able to meet on a linguistic ground. Lameness designates the immobility, but also, as a metaphor, the movement of translation. Stillness and movement coincide in a rhetorical figure that marks her ailment and defect; a figure that can never produce any perfection (or beautiful language), but which is able to produce her "truth." Her/its individual birth is unthinkable without the general, judgmental sentence.

Rahel's lame foot can tell the truth about her injured heart. Several years later, she describes her truth as that of the paradox, and this in turn is nothing but a dislocation, a sprain. In a letter to Varnhagen, she tells another story of birth:

This week, I have invented what a paradox is. A truth, that has not yet found any room to produce itself [*sich darzustellen*]; that is forcing itself violently into the world, and breaks forth with a sprain [*Verrenkung*]. U n f o r t u n a t e l y, this is how I am! — and herein lies my death. — [9]

The story of birth is one of death; this time, it does not follow a slow bleeding, but lies in the sprain of the injured body itself, in the truth that is born. The term *Darstellung* unites the notion of representation with that of a theatrical production. By claiming this story of paradox's birth as one of the birth of truth, and of her own truth, Rahel herself is able to turn the story into a rhetorical figure of translation, an allegory: "this is how I am." To be able to describe herself, to be able to write about herself, Rahel has to change into her former fantasy's other role, become the "extraterrestrial," the outsider who is able to speak her own sentence. She does not describe what is, or invent what could be, but she invents her truth's existence. This is how a paradox is.

The paradox and Rahel, Judaism and the lame foot can always be metaphors for one another. The rhetorical figure has, with force and by displacement, to move linguistically where the room otherwise would not hold. Only here, in this sprain, can Rahel identify her "truth," putting itself/ herself forth, acting itself/herself out as as dislocation, in a movement necessary for any birth. She is able to find her truth only in the displaced narrative of a "fantasy," a story she quotes from an outsider who is even more alien than herself, the extraterrestrial stranger.

In the fantasy of her birth that she recounted to Veit, the family situation is peculiar. Rahel, while being born, has to borrow the voice of an extraterrestrial, the witness of her birth; it is a neutral witness, granting the properties of a parent, but giving death instead of life. The mother from whose womb Rahel is born is not mentioned, nor does she point to any father. Perhaps Rahel does not need to claim any father, if she is addressing her story to a man, David Veit, the authority of her new education; a man who is not living outside earth, only in far-away Jena. But who can be responsible for her conception and birth?

III

Does Rahel's insistence on the origin of her Judaism in a forgetful sentence hide its accidental link to her biological birth? A mark, a sign, an ailment: neither conversion, nor the signature of the legal pen can change what is neither viewed as a religious question, nor as a matter of gaining civic rights. Judaism, conceived as sentence at birth, becomes an anthropological distinction; an individual human fate and the name of a nation itself. Responding to Veit's description of his new residence, Rahel writes elsewhere: "I c o n- g r a t u l a t e you sincerely on the fact, that there are no Jewish students in Jena. I appreciate, by the way, what you have said about the nation, and one has to leave it nevertheless."[10] How is one supposed to leave this nation into which one is born, however; and how can one ever be able to enter another?

The etymology of "nation" derives from the scene of birth. In the fourteenth century, the term "nation" was used to describe a people born in a fixed geographical realm. When the term came into prominence in the political discourse of the eighteenth century in Germany, this prior use was not forgotten. Herder and Fichte, describing and addressing the "German nation," stressed its meaning independent of any structure of the state; it was used to designate a common biological, geographical, and cultural bond. While the French usage since 1789 referred to it in a contractual sense, and as a historically grown unity, "nation" was used in Germany at this time to establish a past history and common future for a group of principalities that did not form a political unity, or a nation state. Germany could exist as a nation, even if one could not find "Germany" on the political map.

Berlin Jews received their legal rights as Prussian citizens during the period of the French occupation—during the time that ended, according to Arendt, the "innocence" of the salons. To gain civic rights, however, was not sufficient for becoming German. To be German meant to belong to a nation that did not define itself by an act of will alone. Made Prussian by the French, Berlin Jews were also made to doubt their German as well as their Prussian identity. Jews, born as Jews, were defined, and defined themselves, as a nation, too, if only of a less desirable kind. How could one choose one's birth?

One way, perhaps, would be to tell one's story; to stage oneself as an orphan ready for adoption. Perhaps one could grow into one's proper birth. Rahel herself believes in the path of evolution. Not only is birth important, but growth and development as well. Education and *Bildung*, these Enlightenment values, should, after all, have some effect. To her advisor Veit, she explains her model of acculturalization. Only individuality seems to ease the burden; the Jews, taken one by one, suffer fewer risks, be they the risks of the strange place or those of a hostile encounter with the other nation. Veit's situation in Jena seems to her explicable:

In Berlin, one can come to terms with the Jews [*Judenheit*] with each person in his own way, although not as a whole, and one seldom or never risks any discussions, or otherwise one would encounter harshnesses; in Jena, though, everything is still "clad in desert dust (where they have led Moses through)," one has always to be afraid of the first shaking off there; and you feel, that this would be the most unpleasant thing, and you are afraid of this; what one if afraid of, of this one thinks a lot, without conscious intention by the object, that is giving us this fear. Well, *bon soir*.[11]

With the writing of her letters, Rahel tries to give evidence for her individuality. To be able to leave "the nation," however, and be able to strive for that individuality, Rahel would have to give up what has already defined her as a "unique person." Predictably, Rahel is not alone with her paradoxical misfortune. Her brother Ludwig Robert writes to her, a year after his own conversion to Christianity:

That one has to live apart, is truly a great misfortune; and it writes [*schreibt*] its origin from the great deep birth defect, not to have a fatherland; but if one does not have it, only climate, area, and mainly the *strange country* [*Fremde*] must be sufficient;

because to feel like a stranger at home, this is the homelessness which is really [*eigentlich*] unbearable. Because of this—and because I feel financially poor in Berlin —I cannot stand being there. But as everything—even misfortune—has its good side, this birth defect does again prove to be the basis of my individuality; and I cannot ignore it [*wegdenken*] therefore, or even miss it, without destroying myself. This was the content of the talk that I just had with [Eduard] Gans; and we thought that the baptized Jews' hatred of the non-baptized Jews was abominable . . .[12]

IV

Jews have to be individualized. The fate that Judaism confers, however, is precisely that of belonging to a group as well as of individualization. This is already obvious in Rahel's early fantasy of her birth. But Rahel, telling her own paradoxical story of misfortune, does not end with her birth. She continues her letter to Veit, and borrows his name in doing so. The change from heart to foot proceeds in Veit's words, who is made to comment on the extraterrestrial's sentence and its connection to the suffering of the lame foot:

You may smile, or feel the tears from pity, but I can derive each evil, each harm, each trouble for you from t h e r e: and it does not bother me to become ridiculous in the eyes of another person. This opinion is my being [*Wesen*]; and I have to give you clear evidence of this, before I die. This satisfaction I cannot deny myself. I will answer myself in your name, and let reason speak from your lips. "Yes," you would say, "the greatest misfortune has happened to you, that could only meet you, you are lame: but you should hear, you should see, you should taste, if you are always looking at your foot, you are yourself the one who is making you lame." (134)

This time, Rahel does not have to repeat the extraterrestrial's words. It is David Veit, her correspondent, who leads her pen and dictates the words which he will later read. Rahel, the individual born, is in need of the dialogue to make any sense of her birth. Veit's lesson, as set forth by his student Rahel, insists again on a forgetfulness. There are other senses, Veit reminds her: hearing, sight, and taste. Authoring Veit's words, Rahel redirects the cause of her misfortune in the other's name and to her own person; she herself may be the author of her fate. By not concentrating on the sense of sight, Rahel sees what should remain unnoticed. It is her attention to her foot that makes her lame.

Rahel's lame foot becomes her birth defect, and it is this foot—and not her birth—that may be the origin of her trouble.[13] If she would hold it forth like a limb that is not an essential part of herself, her averted glance could prevent a conscious transport. In telling the story of her truth, however, Rahel can also tell the story of her essential being (*Wesen*). In contrast to Veit, her being is and claims another opinion: the knowledge of the origin, the statement of birth itself. By naming this birth, Rahel turns the scene into a theatrical, a comedy or tragedy, and it may elicit smiles or tears. For the author, however, there is only one effect to be derived from it: satisfaction.

This satisfaction cannot deny her body. Veit's words are therefore spoken as a piece of advice to be rejected: "Yes, if I could live outside the world, without customs, without relationships [circumstances, *Verhältnisse*], diligently in a village"(134). Rahel, however, is not the extraterrestrial of her fantasy, but the Berlin Jewess. Continuing with her rhetorical exercise, she echoes the "yes" and generalizes her truth beyond her individual self. Any lame person could speak and put Veit in his place:

Yes, the lame person would say, if it would not be necessary for me to walk; but I do not have it to live, and each step, that I want to make, and cannot make, does not remind me of the general calamity of men, against which I want to take steps, but I feel my special misfortune still, and twice and ten times, and one is always heightening the other. How ugly am I not at this; is the world clever then, one says then: "The poor one is lame, let's meet him with this, ah, how burdensome each step must be for him, one can see it!"(134)

The general response, the dialogue within her letter, moves from the physical step to those steps a person has to take. The difficulty of action in general must be visible, but to presuppose this visibility would mean to follow a mistake. "Ugliness" is pushed aside not by the averted glance, but by the incapacity and unwillingness to repeat its causes. The lame foot cannot convey the difficulties of stepping out; it cannot be read as a sign of furious madness. The foot elicits a general response, the individual fate becomes a parable to which anyone could supply the second, reacting voice. At the same time, the "I" changes, the lame person in this generalization becomes a man and is of Veit's rather than of Rahel's gender: "let's meet him with this." Is it Rahel now who can look upon a lame foot with the distance of a different sex? Can she, a woman who has always been powerless and "lame," know the proper walk at all, know it otherwise than by looking on, comparing her own weakness with the other image?

The owner of the lame foot and the voyeur looking at it share no common experience. Sight records the visible and remains blind. Rahel, however, was sentenced with special sensations, the ambivalent price of Judaism. The wound of Judaism cannot be separated from the wound caused by the special sight. Here, she takes up again her individual plight:

No; they do not notice his steps, because they do not make them, they find them ugly, because they see them, and they do not meet him with anything, because his efforts do not hurt them, and their own effort is awful to them. And the lame, forced to walk, should not be unhappy? (134)

The onlookers, meanwhile, turn into a group. Fixed in their own bodies, they see without the wish to slip into the lame person's role. Following the description of her individual fate with this generalization, Rahel, ironically, has reached again the desert's dust. Her question, forceful and poignant, echoes the tone of the Bible: "And if ye offer the blind for sacrifice, is it not evil? and if ye offer the lame and sick, is it not evil? offer it now unto thy governor; will he be pleased with thee, or accept thy person? saith the Lord of hosts" (Malachi 1:8). Sacrifice and satisfaction: putting forth the immobility of her lame foot, Rahel gives evidence for both.

V

But can Rahel's story be understood without the translation of the eye into life, into the common experience that the lame person demanded? Again, Rahel returns to the rhetorical figure, the metaphor, the simile, the image, the picture to be translated. Her story, taken as such, is lame itself, she claims. Her lines cannot be put into life: "If I have ever seen a lame parable [likeness, Gleichnis], this is it; it limps so much, that one would not be able to recognize [ersehen] my misfortune in it in the least, unless one would know it" (134–135).

To be able to see something truly, to see what it is about [ersehen], personal knowledge is required. Individuals need to recognize each other. Any move outside one's own experience is treacherous. In regard to another, more desirable nation, Rahel is, for example, able to interrupt her text to Veit to let her thoughts be known, and report what she can see and hear: "Apropos, this comes to my mind: I like Livonians, they always have blue eyes, are blond, have good teeth, look clean, and have very beautiful language."[14] In regard to the Jews, however, perhaps silence would be the best. In another letter to Veit, Rahel silences herself on the topic of Jews, diverts her language to the image, where likeness is, again, at stake:

I would still be able to tell you something about Jews, but to be silent about it is much nicer. We have Schiller's copper engraving here; people who know him say that there is an extraordinary likeness, and I trust especially Mad. Unzelmann in this, who has confirmed it to me: I, however, have the misfortune to find in it a resemblance with the dancing master Meyer, and with Herrn Salomon's Attaché Moses, who must have travelled with you, and nobody who knows both has denied this yet. He may w e l l look quite weak there. B u t, he can still look t o t a l l y different; and the copper can be very accurate [well met, *getroffen*].[15]

Rahel replaces her silenced thoughts on the Jewish nation with reflections on a clearly non-Jewish individual. By taking Germans one-by-one, Rahel repeats the tactics described for the acceptability of Berlin Jews. In judging Schiller's likeness, however, Rahel encounters another misfortune. The individualization leads uncannily to recognition: the German poet himself does not avoid the desert dust. The single engraving cannot meet the image of its proper nation. Comparing the engraving seen with people known to her, Rahel remembers her acquaintances Meyer and Moses. Even the actress Madame Unzelmann, practiced in *Darstellung*, has to relate Schiller's portrait to these inappropriate lives, and Veit confirms her sentence:

Schiller's copper engraving looks like Moses; with the dancing master I cannot find any resemblance. It is very much like him, I have seen him since. He has himself some resemblance in the lower part of his face (around mouth and chin) of [sic: *von*] Moses. Don't you mean these lines [features, *Züge*]?[16]

Describing Schiller's face, Veit's own German grammar slips. Is it this "sprain," these lines, that Rahel means?

To save Schiller from any negative judgment and visible weakness, Rahel has to separate the portrait from the person, and establish a difference between the accuracy of the line and his true looks: "But, he can still look totally different; and the engraving can be very accurate." Looking at what she perceives as a physical "ugliness," Schiller's weak features, Rahel is eager to dissociate them from any further handicap. It may be of no consequence: picture and life may match in difference. A weak chin, moreover, is not a lame foot; only for Jews, sight and sentence meet, their bodily ailments signify their experience. If the portrait meets him (*treffen*), it cannot hit him with a dagger. The treacherousness of the line—the portrait, the letter—applies to Jews and gentiles in a different way. To salvage a difference of birth, only the knowledge of the possibility of difference is needed. Rahel's misfortune here does not lie in remembering her own different, ailing body, but in recognizing another's likeness while having to forget it.

Recognizing and forgetting: individualization and the division into nations work against each other. Individualization and separation are, however, bound together in the story told by the term "nation" itself. It is this problematic crossing that defies Arendt's concept of the utopia of individuality, exemplified by Rahel Varnhagen's person and exemplified by her salon, while, at the same time, insisting on Arendt's general argument. Describing a scene of birth, Rahel recognizes this crossing with her fantasy. Still, turning against blind viewers as well as the blinding desert dust, she understands this insight itself as her individual misfortune. But her description of her scene of birth points also to the argument that will be taken to transcend her individual fate: even if the term *antisemitism* is not born yet.

Notes

1. Hannah Arendt, *Antisemitism, Part One of The Origins of Totalitarianism* (San Diego: Harcourt Brace Jovanovich, 1985), p. vii.
2. *Rahel Varnhagen: The Life of a Jewish Woman* (New York: Harcourt Brace Jovanovich, 1957). Arendt began to write this book in the thirties; it was first published in the English version. The *Origins of Totalitarianism* appeared first in 1951.
3. See the essays in the collection *The Jews as Pariah: Jewish Identity and Politics in the Modern Age*, ed. Ron H. Feldman (New York: Grove Press, 1978).
4. See for example Reinhard Rührup, "Judenemanzipation und bürgerliche Gesellschaft in Deutschland" (1968), in *Emanzipation und Antisemitismus: Studien zur "Judenfrage" der bürgerlichen Gesellschaft*, ed. Reinhard Rührup (Göttingen: Vandenhoeck und Ruprecht, 1975), pp. 11–36, 134–35; and Arno Herzig, "Das Problem der jüdischen Identität in der deutschen bürgerlichen Gesellschaft," *Deutsche Aufklärung und Judenemanzipation*, ed. Walter Grab, *Jahrbuch des Institutes für deutsche Geschichte* Beiheft 3 (Tel Aviv: Institut für deutsche Geschichte, 1980), pp. 243–62.
5. Arendt, "The Jew as Pariah: A Hidden Tradition" (1944), in *The Jew as Pariah*, p. 68.
6. Letter to David Veit, February 16, 1805. *Rahel, Ein Buch des Andenkens für ihre Freunde* I, ed. Karl August von Varnhagen (Berlin: Duncker und Humblot, 1834), p. 264. A reprint issue of the published collections of Rahel Varnhagen's letters was edited by Konrad Feilchenfeldt, Uwe Schweikert, and Rahel E. Steiner, *Rahel-Bibliothek* (Munich: Matthes & Seitz, 1983). The translations here and elsewhere are mine.
7. Theodor Zondek offers a short biographical sketch of David Veit (1771–1814) in the *Leo Baeck Institute Bulletin* 15, Neue Folge (1976): 49–77.
8. Letter to David Veit, March 22, 1795. *Buch des Andenkens* I, p. 133.
9. Letter to Karl August von Varnhagen, February 19, 1809. *Buch des Andenkens* I, pp. 400–401.

10. Letter to David Veit, October 31, 1794. *Briefwechsel zwischen Rahel und David Veit* I ed. Karl August von Varnhagen (Leipzig: F. A. Brockhaus, 1861), p. 263.

11. Letter to David Veit, November 16, 1794. *Briefwechsel zwischen Rahel und David Veit* II, pp. 15–16.

12. Letter to Rahel Varnhagen, May 27, 1820 [?], reprinted in Miriam Sambursky (ed.), "Ludwig Roberts Lebensgang/Die Briefe," *Leo Baeck Institute Bulletin* 15, Neue Folge (1976), p. 41. Ludwig Robert (1778–1832) was a writer, primarily of plays and opera libretti. Eduard Gans (1797–1839), a law scholar specializing in comparative and property law, was president of the Association for the Culture and Science of the Jews (*Cultur und Wissenschaft des Judentums*). He converted to Christianity in 1825.

13. Moshe Lazar is currently working on a book on the conflation of the images of the Jew and the devil in Europe since the tenth century (see Chapter 2 of the present book). Within this context, Rahel's "limping" gait takes special significance: she is taking up, and playing with—and quite literally affected by—a description given to the Jew. The question of Rahel's gender is, of course, involved here as well.

14. Letter to David Veit, December 12, 1794. *Buch des Andenkens* I, p. 126.

15. Letter to David Veit, November 17, 1794 (continuation of the letter written on November 16). *Briefwechsel zwischen Rahel und David Veit* II, p. 16.

16. Letter to Rahel Varnhagen, December 1, 1774. Ibid., p. 25.

[7]

Dualistic Thinking and the Rise of Ontological Antisemitism in Nineteenth-Century Germany: From Schiller's Franz Moor to Wilhelm Raabe's Moses Freudenstein

Walter H. Sokel

By "ontological antisemitism" I understand hostility toward the Jews that concentrates on their being rather than their religion or economic practices, or any one particular attribute.[1] For ontological antisemitism conversion cannot save the Jew since it is unable to change his nature. The old anti-Judaism of the Christian churches was directed against Judaism. The Jewishness of the Jew resided for it in his religion. His stigma could be wiped out by baptism. The newer phenomenon of antisemitism paradoxically focuses its main attack upon the Jews' attempted emancipation from Judaism. It is less anti-Jewish than anti-modern insofar as Jewish assimilation to the mainstream of Western society signifies secular modernity. It directs its particular venom against the most radical form of Jewish assimilation—baptism. Richard Wagner, who, after Fichte and Schopenhauer, can be considered one of the founders of ontological antisemitism, as I understand it here, exemplifies this attitude most clearly. In his essay, "Jewry in Music," of 1850 Wagner writes:

This paper was first published in the Summer 1987 issue of *Shofar*.

In our time the cultured Jew emerges in society. We have to observe precisely wherein he differs from the common run of uneducated Jews. The cultured [or educated] Jew has made every conceivable effort to shake off the striking peculiarities of his lowly co-religionists. In numerous instances he has even deemed it useful to camouflage all traces of his origin by conversion to Christianity. However, his zeal has never allowed him to reap the hoped-for rewards. It has merely led to his total isolation and has succeeded in making him the most heartless of all human beings to a degree that we have been led to lose our former sympathy for the tragic fate of his race.[2]

The work with which I shall mainly deal here, Wilhelm Raabe's novel *The Hunger Pastor* (1864), reads like a fictional illustration of Wagner's statement.

According to Wagner's reasoning, the Jew can never become like the gentiles, no matter how hard he may try. It is not his religion that separates him from the rest of humanity. It is something much deeper, something omnipotent, an inborn fate, an unalterable essence. Subsequently it became identified with blood or race.

Ontological antisemitism is difficult to distinguish from racial antisemitism; they overlap in many ways. Yet, it seems to me, there are important differences. While racist antisemitism might see the Jews as one race among other inferior or noxious ones, ontological antisemitism descries in the Jew the principle of evil in the universe. Furthermore, ontological antisemitism is less biologically deterministic and naturalistic than metaphysical and moral. For it, the evil in the Jew is an evil will endowed with the freedom to choose evil. This makes the Jew successor to the devil. Indeed the Jewish villain of Raabe's novel appears, in a feverish vision of his gentile friend, as the devil incarnate. Thinking in such terms reveals, of course, the theological root of ontological antisemitism which it shares with traditional Christian hatred of the infidel Jew. However, its special virulence derives from extremely dualistic habits of thought imported into Western monotheism from Zoroastrianism and Manichaeism. The Jew of the antisemite is a nineteenth- and twentieth-century embodiment of the power of darkness constantly conspiring against the principle of light. Antisemitism receives its militancy from this warlike pattern of religious thought.

Yet, ontological antisemitism does not make its appearance until that moment in history when the dogmatic content of Christianity, including of course its belief in Satan, has given, or is giving, way to secularization. Ontological antisemitism pretends to have gone through the school of the Enlightenment and freed itself from medieval superstition. It considers the religious issue of Christian anti-Judaism closed. It can tolerate Jewish religion, but it cannot tolerate Jews. It represents an incomplete stage of secularization. It appears when secularization has dissolved the dogmatic literalism of Christian faith, but has not advanced far enough to dispose of the need for inherited theological patterns of feeling as distinguished from doctrinal belief.

Ontological antisemitism was particularly deep-seated and virulent in Germany where emotional secularization was greatly retarded. The long-delayed and frustrated development of modern political and economic institutions helped to postpone and pervert the rise of a robust civic and economic self-confidence in the German middle class. The absence of stable self-assurance of individual and group intensified the need for dependence not only in political, economic, and social, but also in spiritual terms. A strong craving for emotional support from religious or quasi-religious consolation proved, on the whole, more enduring in Germany than in Western Europe and created a hostile atmosphere for modernity which was felt as a threat to desperately needed faith. The secularization of Christian dogma took place in Germany as elsewhere. However, it tended to be deflected, more than elsewhere, to the search for substitutes. Mental attitudes inherited from Lutheranism tended to be preserved in more or less transmuted forms. Pietism which, as is well known, played an enormous role for German culture and thought in the eighteenth and nineteenth centuries greatly facilitated a blending of emancipation from Christian dogma and retention of emotional patterns shaped by it. Loosening the fetters of orthodoxy, Pietism had shifted Protestant emphasis from intellectual belief to intensity of feeling—culminating in Schleiermacher's famous equation of religion with the *feeling* of dependency *per se.* A new dualism sprang up which was not one of right and wrong belief, but between strong and lukewarm, or sincere and inauthentic, feeling. A great liberator from the tyranny of dogma, Pietism inspired a new kind of intolerance, or at least suspicion, of those who could not share its fervor.[3] Enthusiasm for God, and subsequently for His works, was a sign of grace, cool rationality a likely token of damnation.

In slightly secularized form this kind of dualism meets us in Schiller's drama *The Robbers* (1781). It appears in the radical contrast between the two brothers Karl and Franz Moor. Karl, fiery, passionate, generous, and warm, is pitted against the cold, rational, diabolically calculating Franz. Written in the heart of Swabian Pietism, which pervaded the atmosphere in which Schiller grew up,[4] his youthful melodrama presents in Franz the mortal threat which the radical atheistic Enlightenment, imported from France, represented to a Pietistically influenced sensibility even when, as in Schiller's case, it was emancipated from the doctrinal ground of its cult of enthusiastic feeling.[5] Schiller's villain Franz Moor is the forerunner of the emancipated Jew of ontological antisemitism. It is, of course, highly significant that Schiller's drama includes a second villain, Spiegelberg, who is of Jewish birth. He functions as a parallel to Franz Moor insofar as he offers, within Karl's band of outlaws, the same kind of contrast to the hero that Franz represents within the family plot. As Karl's treacherous rival, the "circumcised" Spiegelberg constitutes a variation of Karl's envious and coldly scheming brother.

Already in Wagner's essay "Jewry in Music," it is indeed his cold intellectuality that marks the Jew's forever alien nature. The "cold heart" of Moses Freudenstein forms a *leit-motif* in Wilhelm Raabe's novel which, like Schiller's drama, was written in Stuttgart, capital of South German Pietism. The contrast between Moses and his "Aryan" childhood friend Hans Unwirrsch echoes in many essential respects the polarity presented in *The Robbers*. The brothers in Schiller become the inseparable childhood friends in Raabe, and Hans indeed spends a good many hours of his formative years in the subterranean dwelling of the Freudensteins like a brother of Moses being brought up in the same household. As the model of his villain, Schiller obviously has the French-style court intriguer and petty despot of Germany's tiny principalities in mind. It was not difficult to transfer the model of negativity from him to the newly emancipated Jew of nineteenth-century Germany. In fact, courtier and Jew had historically been united in the court financier Süss Oppenheimer who practically ruled Württemberg in the early eighteenth century and, the target of most intense popular hatred, ended by being hanged in public.[6]

I have chosen Raabe's *Hunger Pastor* for a close discussion because it illuminates, with great clarity, the nature of ontological antisemitism as a secularized form of metaphysical and theological dualism. Historically the novel is located between the first beginnings of ontological antisemitism in Fichte,[7] Schopenhauer, and Wagner, and its systematic elaboration as a *Weltanschauung* by Wilhelm Marr, Eugen Dühring, Paul de Lagarde, and Houston Stewart Chamberlain in the last three decades of the nineteenth century. *The Hunger Pastor* was written at the height of the liberal period of German history by a liberal democrat, a man who professed to be free of anti-Jewish bias and shared the ethos of the Enlightenment.[8] Even in this novel in which, as I shall try to show, Jewishness itself stands accused, antisemitism stands in a complex relationship to philosemitic tendencies,[9] which makes for the particular interest of this novel for our present purposes here. For it shows a peculiar rhetoric of ontological antisemitism which initially builds up pro-Jewish sympathies not only the more effectively to destroy them, but also to vindicate hatred of the Jews to a modern consciousness that feels accountable to the humanitarian ethos of the Enlightenment and claims to stand above medieval prejudice. It seeks to demonstrate that hatred of the Jew arises necessarily from original friendship with and love for him. The close friendship between the gentile Hans, who becomes the poverty-stricken pastor of the title, and the Jewish junk dealer's son, Moses, who will become a brilliantly successful intellectual and, after conversion to Christianity, privy councillor and police informer, represents the German-Jewish symbiosis which began in the Enlightenment with the archetypal friendship of Lessing and Moses Mendelssohn. (The villain's first name Moses alludes to the latter.) By describing the genesis, history, and catastrophic consequences of this friendship, the plot of the novel tends to disprove the possibility of German-Jewish community. The novel had an enormous impact in Germany and enjoyed long-lasting popularity, particularly after 1900. Its prestige understandably reached its apogee in the Nazi period when it was praised as a pioneering and prophetic work. Since the Second World War its reputation has plummeted and has remained low ever since.

Time does not permit me to draw, in some detail, the fascinating parallels between Schiller's late eighteenth-century drama and Raabe's nineteenth-century novel. Such a comparison would show how Raabe's antisemitic portrait of the Jew fits into an already existing stereotype of the diabolical materialist who threatens faith in the meaning of life. It would show ontological antisemitism to be the continuation of a process of Satanization of the critical spirit of modernity, which is the other face of the modernization or secularization of Satan.

Before turning to the discussion of *The Hunger Pastor*, I shall, however, point out one further example of dualistic thinking which proves to be of very great significance for the understanding not only of the typology of Raabe's novel, but also of the relationship between antisemitism and the philosophy of German Idealism. The founder of German Idealism, Fichte, took consistent stands against the Jews. He claimed that one could free them of their Jewish ideas and "give them citizenship" only by cutting off their heads in the same night.[10] However, I shall focus here on a less obvious link between German Idealism and the type of thinking that tried to make modern antisemitism intellectually respectable.

In the preface to the second edition of his *Wissenschaftslehre* (1796), Fichte posits two types of thinkers totally opposite each other. Referring to Kant's critiques of reason, he calls one the critical, the other the dogmatic thinker. The critical thinker, by whom he understands the Idealist, sees the world ultimately as a creation of mind. Thought or knowledge for him is a projecting, organizing, productive, and creative power. The dogmatist, on the other hand, assumes the given existence of an objective reality, entirely external to and independent of mind, which is a mere derivation from it. Mind for him is a passive receptacle of external influence, and knowledge is the mere gathering of facts. It is obvious that dogmatism includes for Fichte the general tendency of modern West European thought, from French materialism to British empiricism, and that it, as we might add, will lead to positivism. It is the foundation on which the triumphal march of modern science has been based. Fichte holds that the dogmatist can never understand the critical thinker. By his very nature he is condemned to be blind to the Idealist vision of the truth. No amount of argument can convert him, since his mentality, being totally different, must stay forever inaccessible to the insight of the other type. By positing within human thought a dichotomy so absolute, Fichte implicitly removes any possibility of argument appealing to rational and universally valid evidence. He despairs of the persuasiveness of reason and abandons the possibility of truth being demonstrable to all. By the same token he removes the basis for any belief in the essential oneness of humanity. Fichte's absolute dualism of human types opens a gulf within mankind that cannot be bridged. His thought points in two historical directions. On the one hand, it harks back to the Protestant division between predestined grace and damnation. On the other hand, it points ahead to the theory of unbridgeable difference between groups of human beings—the basis of racism. It lays the theoretical foundation on which ontological antisemitism can build. For Fichte divides mankind into two camps—one of which is incomparably superior to the other. Between them there can be no real communication, no ultimate understanding, no genuine meeting of minds.

If we substitute gentile or Aryan—the term is already used by Raabe— for critical thinker, and Jew for dogmatist, we arrive at the ontological antisemitism of *The Hunger Pastor*. Raabe's protagonist, Hans Unwirrsch, conforms, by his imaginative inwardness and idealistic disposition, to Fichte's subjective Idealist, while his Jewish antagonist, his childhood friend Moses Freudenstein, corresponds to Fichte's dogmatic type.[11]

In explicit terms, Raabe's novel is indebted to German Mysticism. Jakob Böhme, for whom dualism resided in the Godhead Himself, is its inspiration. He is, as it were, the patron saint of the protagonist.[12] The protagonist's father, a shoemaker like Böhme, looks to him as to his model. Both father and son are aware of an inner light, a spark within the soul which, at the same time, is also the gate to the transcendent and divine. A multicolored globe over the shoemaker's lamp symbolizes this source of all light. It serves as a sign of something akin to Fichte's "productive power of the imagination" and transforms the earthly light of "the poor lamp" (499)[13] into a radiance that transmutes and recreates all objects it illuminates. This mysterious glow raises Hans above his wretched poverty-stricken circumstances. Compared to Don Quixote, Hans in his poor attic, is "happy ruler in the kingdom of his dreams" (569). Their imagination transports the Unwirrsches always far away from their physical surroundings. Hans moves sometimes as in a thick fog which, while hiding the real world, allows the imagination to see things in it of which the intellect can never be certain. Fog—one of Hans Unwirrsch's favorite weather conditions—requires the highest virtue—faith.

The drawback of this mystical enchantment of the world is the risk of losing one's place in the struggle for mundane existence. Happily immersed in "golden dreams," mastercraftsman Anton fails to procure real gold in his trade, as illuminating trances frequently distract him from his work. In wordly terms, he is no success, and upon his death can leave very little to his widow. To support her small son, Frau Unwirrsch has to take work as a washerwoman. Hans too will never be successful in terms of the world. He feels too deeply, and is assailed by too many thoughts at once, to be articulate. In him inwardness exceeds the possibilities of verbal language. This puts him at a disadvantage in the scramble for worldly honors and rewards. He fails to be successful at any of the three tutorial positions he occupies and ends as a wretchedly poor clergyman—the hunger pastor of the title—in an out-of-the-way fishing village on the Baltic coast. The world would consider him a failure.

Hans's lack of practical wordliness makes the Jew a challenge to him which he cannot meet. The Jew appears in every respect as the absolute opposite, the true countertype, of the emotional, idealistic, spiritual German. He is richly gifted with worldly capacities and goods, but has no part of the kingdom of spirit. The junk dealer Samuel Freudenstein, Moses' father, has incomparably more money to throw onto the scales of fortune for his son than the poor widow Unwirrsch has for hers. And yet, the narrator tells us,

around the head of the widow and her child stood a spirit which kept better watch than all the armed might of Israel. (558)

The narrator excludes the Jew from the spiritual realm. All the Jew has are earthly treasures and earthly weapons. Therefore, for all his advantages of wealth and intellectual brilliance, Moses must be the loser in the end.

In Hans and Moses, Raabe draws the contrast between spirit and mere intellect. As in Schiller's portrayal of Franz Moor, rational intellect receives an absolutely negative evaluation. Moses is brilliant, while Hans is dumb in the original sense of speechless. He is overwhelmed by emotion and always too far ahead imaginatively to be able to present a clear and tidy sequence of ideas. The Jew, by contrast, ever wholly present in the situation at hand, expresses himself astutely and with perfect clarity. In competing with the Jew, inwardness is a handicap. Try as he may, Hans cannot hope to match Moses and become the first in his class. The first is always "naturally" Moses. However, Moses' advantage is purchased at a price ultimately much heavier than the one Hans has to pay. Moses completely lacks Hans's warm feelings and enchanting imagination. Even in his childhood, Moses, who is said to have never been a real child, seems to channel all emotional response immediately into cerebral speculation (*grübeln* is the term used by Raabe). The narrator shows this by one of those juxtapositions within a common situation in which his dualistic technique resides.

The childhood friends are losing their little girl friend Sophie to a fatal illness. Hans is overcome by grief. But Moses, quite cool and composed, reacts speculatively. Where will she be going now, he wants to know. He inquires into the precise locality of her future whereabouts. His intellectual curiosity absorbs all feeling of loss. Intellect takes the place of emotion. Moses is literal-minded, oriented toward what is present both in the spatial and temporal sense. His mind does not venture into the invisible and merely possible. It does not project; it does not conjure what is not evident to the senses. What he tries to picture to himself about Sophie's journey after death is determined by what he sees at the moment. It happens to be a cold rainy day. While Hans, nourished by his Christian faith, defies the gloomy actuality and projects a blue sky where Sophie will join "the dear Lord and the angels" (538), Moses registers only the dreary rain of the real day and ignores his friend's cheerful and consoling interpretation of events. Fixed only on what he can see with his physical sight, Moses rejects the glad tidings offered by an imagination that superimposes its wishful vision upon the world. Moses rejects comfort and hope in favor of the visible. "Oi," he states, "she will have a bad trip! She will be freezing on the way!" (539).

In this scene, Raabe contrasts the dogmatism—in Fichte's sense—of the Jew with the religiously formed imagination of the Christian. He shows Christian upbringing helping the imaginative power of the child, aiding it to soar above the given and ignore it in favor of creating a world amenable to human needs and desires. Hans, too, the text tells us, sees the rain running down "the dreary window" and his body freezes as much as Moses'; but faith in the unseen makes him project a better world. Thus the Christian reveals a "critical"—again in Fichte's sense—mentality. "The Productive power of imagination"—Fichte's *produktive Einbildungskraft*—lifts him above the here and now.

The contrast between the two friends is founded on a—hardly secularized —theology. The Christian's readiness to transcend the limitation of circumstance and to project unseen states of being derives from Protestant Christianity's prime commandment: faith—which must always be faith in the unseen. The Jew's insistence on sensory evidence constitutes a rejection of this message of faith. Thus the Jew repeats the original act which set Jewry apart from Christianity.

The narrator indicates that Moses was not born bereft of the productive imagination; but he has deliberately repressed it because he cannot "use" it (609). His one-sided reliance on reasoning and his skeptical distrust of any imaginative leap result from the rigorous training he has imposed on himself. To be unmoved is the program by which he lives. His coldness increases in the course of the story in direct ratio to his advance in knowledge and sophistication. "With sneering mockery he strangled the last remnant of warm imagination that had still remained in him" (571). His hypertrophied intellect and his atrophied emotions are self-inflicted mutilations—sins against his own soul. In an analogous way, his father Samuel had shut out from his dark dank cellar the light of the day—the sunlight and fresh air of the street. He had deliberately chosen darkness as his dwelling. In the eternal war between darkness and light, "Schiwa and Wischnu, destruction and preservation" (491), to which the narrator alludes in the opening paragraph of the novel, Samuel symbolically enlists on the side of darkness. "Woe to him," the narrator exclaims in regard to Samuel's choice. Samuel rejects the gifts of nature. He shuts his door on them as the Eternal Jew shut his heart to Christ. He prefers seclusion with his treasures to the light of the world. He thus repeats toward God's creation the original sin of his people toward God's son. The narrator holds the "sins" of the Jewish people—their own and their forefathers'—responsible for their sufferings (543). Here the theo- logical substratum of the antisemitic attitude becomes transparent. In con- trast to the Freudensteins, the Unwirrsches—father and son—show by the faithfulness to the light that shines through Böhme's globe that faith which bespeaks ultimate grace.

Samuel's rejection of the light, which alludes to the Jew's rejection of Christ, also implies his rejection of humanity, i.e., the life of the streets. Itanticipates Moses' rejection of the glad tidings which feeling and imagina- tion bring. Rejection of the gifts bestowed by nature and by faith in the unseen illuminate the relationship between predestined character and re- sponsible will. To be sure, his inborn nature predisposes the Jew to his merely earthly vision. Yet, insofar as he makes his inborn tendency deliber- ately into his whole being, eliminating in himself all vestiges of the other side of the duality between flesh or matter and spirit or imagination, he damns himself. He becomes responsible for his mentality. The eradication of his emotional and imaginative humanity is the work of his own will, and thus his sin. It is in this moral dimension that ontological antisemitism differs from its racist variant.

By his self-imprisonment in physical reality, Moses deprives himself of the joys of the imagination. Creation and recreation as empathetic projec- tion into the other, the non-self—whether it be another world or another person's feeling—are closed to him. While Hans, during a lesson on Thu- cydides, feasts on the sight of the Athenian sails sparkling in the Greek sun of two thousand years ago, but misses the cue as the teacher calls on him to recite, Moses sees nothing but the words on the page and hears nothing but the teacher's voice calling out names. Thus his grades will surely surpass those of Hans; but he will be the poorer for shutting out the invisible world to which words refer and which they are able to conjure for Hans who is always ready to look for meaning. The driving force of Moses' intellectuality is the will to power which his father had inculcated into him. Samuel Freudenstein had unobtrusively amassed a fortune which is to serve the education of his only son. Samuel's paternal love, which is certainly an endearing feature, is perverted by his intention to use his son as an instrument for the vicarious satisfaction of his vindictive desire to humble the gentiles and pay them back the insults and persecutions he and his race have had to endure at their hands. Through his son's ascent to glory and power, he will experience the gratification of vengeance. He craves to see the gentiles enslaved to a scion of his despised race. "I shall live to see the day when the *goyim* will bow down before him; God of Abraham, I shall sit in the darkness, but my heart shall laugh and rejoice!" (571). Samuel has not repressed his imagination; he has twisted it into an instrument of negation and destruction. He perverts an originally fine moral quality—self-sacrificing solicitude for his child's future—into an evil. This evil is twofold. He not only indulges in lust for vengeance, instead of forgiving his former enemies; what is worse, he abuses his son, degrading him to be a tool in his vendetta against the *goyim*. As the sinners in Dante's *Inferno*, his punishment is meted out in the coin of his sin. Moses' brutal callousness toward his aged father, as soon as he realizes what riches his father has amassed for him, induces the stroke that kills the old man.

In his portrait of Samuel Freudenstein, Raabe employs cliché ideas about the Jew as stock villain of traditional Christianity. Moses is the modernized version. He is the new Jew as bearer of subversive modernity. The book is to show the metamorphosis of old-time Jewry into this modern variant and to make clear the underlying eternal continuity of evil in the two—very much in accord with the profoundly ahistorical vision of dualism announced in the opening paragraph of the book. The opposition between the two antagonistic principles involved here, "Schiwa and Wishnu, destruction and preservation," will always exist; it will continue "until the end of the world" (491). This division is found within the central symbol itself—hunger— which occurs in the title. Hunger is present in both—the gentile and the Jew. Like Schopenhauer's Will, it is the monistic power that forms and moves the universe. But it has two aspects: one constructive-creative, the other destructive-annihilating. The Will builds worlds; the Will also destroys them. The constructive-creative aspect lives, yearns, aspires, hopes, and believes in the gentile. It is the hunger for the light symbolized by Jakob Böhme's reflecting lamp, the hunger for insight, the striving for love.

The destructive aspect connives in the Jew. It is the hunger for material riches and earthly power. In this scheme, love is the close sibling of the imagination, and both together mark the creative Will whose innate tendency is to unite the fragments left by the destructive aspect and build them into ever larger unities, eventually realizing the oneness of all. However, the destructive aspect of the Will always seeks to prevent it from coming about. The destructive, disuniting aspect of the Will is embodied in the Jew. The destructive purpose can be accomplished only by the analytic procedures of abstract intellect. Jewish intellect represented by Moses takes apart what gentile imagination tried to connect and see as one. Thus analytic rationality appears as guilt toward life. By analyzing it, Moses is said to dissolve "the colorful variety of life" and to subject it to the pigeonholing of "a merciless logic" (571). But the analytic intellect is merely *one* aspect of that same fragmenting of the divine unity which, on a social and moral level, we find as the principle of egotism. The analytic logician is in the realm of intellect what the egotist is in the realm of daily life. Both substitute the fragment for the whole. Both are seen to undermine coherence and continuity. What analysis breaks asunder in the mental sphere, egotism subverts, disrupts, and smashes in the social sphere. On both counts the supreme agent of such subversion is the Jew—Moses Freudenstein, who significantly begins his career by causing the death of his father.[14] Like Schiller's Franz Moor, Moses is a parricide from colossal selfishness.

However, what Raabe presents as the twin principles of the destructive pole—analysis and egotism—likewise represent the two chief motors of modernity—natural science and the profit motive. In Moses they are combined by his selfishly utilitarian cast of mind which thinks in purely practical and strategic terms. Moses has nothing but contempt for anything he cannot "use," and discards whatever does not advance him toward his goals. He has no need for old books that he will not use again. He has no attachment to memories. He knows no loyalty to persons. He forgets his father totally over his inheritance. During years of separation he does not write a single letter to the close friend of his youth who has ceased to be useful to him. He neglects his wife and mistreats her as soon as she has been disinherited. He abandons his French mistress, who loves him and whom he has persuaded to follow him to Berlin, and puts her out into the street when he no longer needs her services. Nothing holds Moses back from the pursuit of egotistical goals. He is utterly indifferent to nature, finds landscapes "boring," and is impatient to get to his destination. Aesthetic experience *per se* is inaccessible to Moses because it is an end in itself and Moses is interested only in means and strategies. Consequently where, in contrast to aesthetic experience, knowledge about art and critical opinion are concerned, Moses can show admirable sophistication and knowledgeability. He is a highly respected purveyor of taste and propagator of fashion. For to create the impression of being conversant in the aesthetic realm is extremely useful in the high society to which Moses aspires. He makes a name for himself as an art and music critic. Raabe's portrait of the Jew as a skillful disseminator of emerging artistic tastes and fashions echoes Wagner's attack on Jews as mimics rather than creators. Wagner compares Jewish composers to "parrots [that] imitate human words and phrases" and "like those funny birds" are superficially entertaining but "without [true] expression and genuine feeling."[15]

Moses' "Machiavellian" pragmatism—Machiavelli is one of his favorite authors—is ultimately bound up with the diabolical motivation of his thought.[16] A talented pupil of his father, Moses uses his intellect as an instrument of war against mankind. His mind is "not a tool for use and joy to himself and the world; he forged with it only weapons—nothing but weapons against the world" (581). Moses takes up Samuel's hoped-for vendetta against the gentiles. This continuity of hatred is the only bond that unites father and son. Since it also marks the only Jewish characters of importance in the novel, the author suggests the idea that in this will to vengeance, conquest, and power lies the essence of Jewishness. In this quest reason is reduced to mere instrumentality. While hunger for knowledge for its own sake—the Faustian drive for *Erkenntnis*—characterizes the Unwirrsches, the apparently parallel encouragement of learning in the Jewish household actually represents an opposite pole. Samuel too wants his son to subordinate everything to learning and the acquisition of knowledge. "If you are offered the choice between a cake and a book, forget the cake and choose the book," runs Samuel's advice to Moses; and Moses concentrates on his studies with a zeal which would be admirable if used for a beneficent cause. However, here, in the Jewish family, the relentless drive for knowledge is only a tool for a destructive purpose. Old Samuel's crude vindictiveness toward the *goyim* reappears in a modernized, philosophical garb, in Moses' mental sadism toward his German friend. Again and again, Moses delights in puncturing Hans's daydreams, illusions, and reverential enthusiasm for nature and for human beings. He displays a "truly diabolical glee" (604) as he pours "buckets of cold water" (609) on Hans's passionate feelings. Unable to share the worshipful attitude toward being which defines the German partner of this unequal pair, the Jew cannot tolerate it. Resembling a caricature of Heine in this respect,[17] Moses scoffs at the fairy-tale world of German Romanticism in which Hans feels happy and at home. He derives "much pleasure from the pained feelings of his friend" (608). The Jew

assaults the foundations of the gentile's world. He does so from sheer gratui-
tous pleasure in destructiveness in which his diabolical nature emerges.
Those critics who have tried to see "Moses Freudenstein not as a Jew, but as
.the diabolical principle"[18] overlook the importance of seeing that principle
embodied in a Jew and manifested, in different form and degree, in two
successive generations of Jews who also happen to be the only male Jewish
characters presented in the novel.

Of course, Moses does not succeed in causing Hans to lose his faith in the
goodness, beauty, and spirituality of the universe. Yet, the Jew's constant
jabs of aggressive irreverence wound the German's sensibility more and more
profoundly as time goes on. When Moses cynically dissociates himself from
the struggle of the German people for freedom and unity, claiming his—the
chosen—people's privilege to stand aloof from the efforts of those among
whom they live, ready to benefit from their successes and abandon them in
their failures, Hans burns with indignation. He trembles with the desire to
make Moses realize the baseness of his position. However, he proves no
match for the Jew's rhetorical brilliance. The Jew's virtuosity of dialectical
reasoning—Moses writes his doctoral dissertation on Hegelianism—leaves
the German speechless. He must suffer in silence Moses' merciless undermining of the grounds of German self-respect. Moses analyzes the backwardness,
provincialism, and servility of the Germans with a forcefulness and an
insight—again we can detect allusions to Heine in these, perhaps also to
the young Marx—that hits home and leave poors Hans all the more bitterly
outraged at his own lack of ability to refute the Jew.[19]

Since Hans has to keep his anger silent, this only serves to fan its flames
and heighten the violence of his fury when it finally erupts. Certain now
that Moses is his "unappeasable enemy" (758), Hans craves to "seize [him]
with fists and teeth" (757) and "squeeze the soul out of his body" (779).
Strangling the Jew would appear a good deed carried out by Hans's "two
good fists" ("brave Fäuste"). To be sure, Hans's murderous wish is the
temporary product of a feverish state of crisis brought on by Moses' villainies.
Nonetheless, this violent end of the friendship of German and Jew constitutes a disturbing fictional prelude to the terrifying fate which awaited the
German-Jewish symbiosis in our century. Dismissing such a startling connection as "historical nonsense"[20] would seem to bespeak of an amazing underestimation of the significance of symbolic action in and for history.

Yet, Raabe cannot be classed on a par with the Nazis who hailed him as
one of their prophets.[21] A not inconsiderable remainder of enlightened

humaneness, irony, and feeling for complexity separates *The Hunger Pastor* from the advocates of genocide. To be sure, his one-time Jewish friend is dead for Hans; but Hans considers this death a loss—the loss of a dream. He mourns over the unused possibilities the friendship of German and Jew once seemed to hold. The novel ends not with the physical destruction, but with the symbolic reghettoization of the Jew. By his own deeds—culminating in his services as an informer on his fellow exiles—Moses has died in a "bürgerlich," that is, a social sense. He is shunned and despised by all sides, including those he serves. He stands outside society, ostracized. Morally and socially he has been relegated to a ghetto which this time is an invisible one. Emancipation has been revoked, and the Jew alone is to blame for its failure. Society has quarantined him in self-protection. The antisemitism of the plot of *The Hunger Pastor* conforms to what Raul Hilberg calls the second stage in the prehistory of the Holocaust—segregation. It does not yet correspond to the third and final stage—physical extermination.[22] Hans's feverish wish to kill Moses does suggest the "final solution" as the brainchild of a state of fever, no matter how understandable it might be as the anguished reaction to "unbearable" Jewish provocation. A similar dilemma marks the conclusion of another document of nineteenth-century ontological antisemitism— Eugen Dühring's *On the Jewish Question,* written seventeen years after *The Hunger Pastor.*

There is an even deeper and, as it were, "metaphysical" reason that places *The Hunger Pastor* this side of the divide between civilization and the Holocaust. Hans realizes that the difference between him and the Jew pertains to a division within being itself. There is in Raabe a monism overarching his dualism and making it less than absolute. Here, in conclusion, we arrive at the meaning that Arthur Schopenhauer's thought, which appears in Raabe in the guise of Jakob Böhme's, holds for nineteenth-century ontological antisemitism.[23] The ontological antisemite needs to stress two sides about the Jew—both of which are also the essence of modernity. One is positivism—the subordination of mind to matter and idea to fact. The other is egotism—the will to self-assertion. Each has its opposite in Christianity. The Christian opposite of positivism is faith. The Christian opposite of egotism is love. Faith and love—the cardinal Christian virtues—are united through the imagination which, on the one hand, produces the unseen target of faith, and on the other hand, suspends egotism by making the ego lose itself in things envisioned. What characterizes Jewishness for Schopenhauer is reliance on physical phenomena as ultimate reality and on the self-assertion of the Will as embodied in the individual ego. For Schopenhauer, philosophy, such as Spinoza's, is "Jewish," if it optimistically affirms the world of objects as the ultimately real world,[24] and fails to see destructiveness as the eternal other of creation—"Schiwa, the destroyer" as Raabe puts it, as the eternal opposite and counterpart of "Wischnu, the preserver." Blinded by the grasping Will in his ego—symbolized in the jealousy and vengefulness of his Jehovah—the Jew does not see that all particular wills, including his own, are merely ephemeral, ever-emerging, ever-perishing manifestations of one Will.

Thus, unlike the Aryan Indian, the Jew is the exemplary dupe of the Will as he is its crassest embodiment. Like Mephistopheles and like Moses Freudenstein, he is the "poor devil," who always gets cheated in the end. In Raabe's plot, which, in this respect, is closely akin to Schopenhauer's thought, Moses Freudenstein is cheated of the fulfillment of his hopes. His half-aristocratic wife is disinherited for having eloped with him. Deprived of her fortune, for which he had so assiduously schemed and betrayed, he finds himself, in the end, a betrayer betrayed. Unwittingly he repeats the tragic irony of his father's fate. Samuel, who had so fervently craved to triumph through his son, is finally killed by him.

He who has seen through the Will has, according to Schopenhauer, nothing but compassion for all that exists. Revenge, jealousy, and pride which animate "the chosen people" and their God are meaningless to him. For even as he sees the oneness of all existence, he also sees the death sentence that hangs over all its individuated forms. He has nothing but compassion for the frustration, disappointment, and suffering all willing entails. For Schopenhauer, this "Aryan wisdom" of the ancient Hindu lives on in the Christian message of universal love.

Raabe's novel includes the Jew in the compassion with all that is. Even though there can be no understanding of the gentile by the Jew, as matter must always be blind to spirit, spirit *can* condescend to matter and take pity on its unredeemable state. In the end, Hans pities "poor Moses." In this sentimental remnant of humanist universality lies the most essential difference that separates Raabe's ontological antisemitism from the mentality that produced genocide.[25]

Notes

1. Ontological antisemitism is, of course, very close to "metaphysical antisemitism," a term which has been aptly applied to Arthur Schopenhauer's attitude

toward Judaism. (Cf. Henry Walter Braun, *Schopenhauer und das Judentum*. Bonn 1975.) "Metaphysical antisemitism" can be considered a subdivision within the broader concept of "ontological antisemitism." The latter is not restricted to philosophical systems, but describes a widespread climate of thought and sensibility.

2. Richard Wagner, "Das Judentum in der Musik," *Gesammelte Schriften*, ed. by Julius Kapp, vol. XIII: *Der Polemiker*. Leipzig n.d., 7–29, 16. Translation WHS.

3. Cf. Koppel S. Pinson, *Pietism as a Factor in the Rise of German Nationalism*. New York 1934, 44, 50, 52f.

4. Cf. Ernst Benz, "Johann Albrecht Bengel und die Philosophie des Deutschen Idealismus," *Deutsche Vierteljahrsschrift für Literaturwissenschaft und Geistesgeschichte*, vol. XXVII 1953/54, 528–54.

5. For the Pietist influence on young Schiller, cf. Walter Müller-Seidel, "Georg Friedrich Gaus.: Zur religiösen Situation des jungen Schiller," *Deutsche Vierteljahrsschrift für Literaturwissenschaft und Geistesgeschichte*, vol. XXVI 1952/51, 76–79, and 93 in particular; Werner Kohlschmidt, "Schiller und die Reformation" in his volume, *Tradition und Zeitgeist*. Bern, 1965, and particularly Arthur W. McCardle, *Friedrich Schiller and Swabian Pietism*. Bern-Frankfurt 1986.

6. Süss Oppenheimer was the subject of one of the most notorious files of the Nazi period.

7. For the importance of Fichte in the development of modern antisemitism in Germany, see Waldemar Gurian, "Antisemitism in Modern Germany" in *Essays on Antisemitism*, ed. by Koppel S. Pinson, New York Conference on Jewish Relations 1946, 218–66, 222, and Jacob Katz, *From Prejudice to Destruction: Antisemitism 1700–1933*. Cambridge, Mass. 1980.

8. On the strong philosemitic aspects of Raabe, see Marketa Goetz-Stankiewicz, "Die böse Maske Moses Freudensteins. Gedanken zum Hungerpastor", *Jahrbuch der Raabe-Gesellschaft* 1969, 7–32, especially 17, 26. On Raabe's political liberalism, see Jürgen Manthey, "Wilhelm Raabe und das Scheitern des deutschen Liberalismus," *Jahrbuch der Raabe-Gesellschaft* 1976, 69–106.

9. These tendencies are also pointed out by Rudolf Mohr, "Der Hungerpastor— ein Pfarrerroman?" *Jahrbuch der Raabe-Gesellschaft* 1977, 48–85, 63f.

10. See Katz, 57.

11. Raabe's strong affinities with Fichte have been pointed out by Manthey, 82, although in an entirely different context from the one considered here.

12. For the important differences between Böhme's dialectical duality within each person and the crass Manichaean dualism of *The Hunger Pastor*, see Rudi Schweikert's illuminating " 'Vom Hunger will ich handeln.' Überlegungen zur 'Hunger'-Metapher und zum Licht-Dunkel-Gegensatz in Wilhelm Raabes 'Der Hungerpastor,' " *Jahrbuch der Raabe-Gesellschaft* 1978, 78–106, 101–5.

13. All quotations from and references to Raabe's text refer to this edition: Wilhelm Raabe, *Die Chronik der Sperlingsgasse. Unseres Herrgotts Kanzlei. Der Hungerpastor*. Werke in vier Bänden. Herausgegeben von Karl Hoppe nach der von ihm besorgten, im Verlag Vandenhoeck & Ruprecht erscheinenden historisch-kri-

tischen Gesamtausgabe der Werke Raabes. vol. I. Darmstadt 1961. Page numbers are given parenthetically in the text.

14. Cf. also Schweikert, 93.

15. Wagner, 17.

16. Moses has been frequently associated with the diabolical principle, either in its dialectical Mephistophelian form, as in Goethe's *Faust*, or in the traditional sense of the devil as evil incarnate. For the former view, see especially Mohr, 56–62; for the latter view, see Hans Schomerus, "Über die Gestalt des Bösen in den Werken Wilhelm Raabes," *Jahrbuch der Raabe-Gesellschaft* 1962, 32–56, 35, 45.

17. On the relationship of Moses Freudenstein to Heine, see particularly Goetz-Stankiewicz, 17, 28.

18. Friedrich Sengle, "*Der Hungerpastor* (1863/4). Zum Problem der frohen Biedermeiertradition," in *Wilhelm Raabe: Studien zu seinem Leben und Werk*, ed. by Leo A. Lensing and Hans-Werner Peter, Braunschweig 1981, 77–98, 94.

19. Schweikert emphasizes quite correctly Hans's envy of Moses' quickness of mind as an essential motivation. Not Faustian striving for knowledge, but "rivalry with Moses" is "the mainspring of his energy" (89). The pages of *The Hunger Pastor* echo tradition-oriented Germans' deep-seated resentments of the tough competition recently emancipated Jewry posed not only in trade and manufacture, but also in the intellectual professions.

20. Sengle, 94.

21. See Goetz-Stankiewicz, 8.

22. Raul Hilberg, *The Destruction of European Jews*. Chicago 1961, *throughout*.

23. Although Raabe objected to his being classified as a mere Schopenhauerian, his reservations were aimed at his interpreters' ignoring of his personal reasons for leaning toward pessimism. (Cf. Manthey 77.) His protest does not imply that he was not familiar with and sympathetic toward much of Schopenhauer's thought.

24. Cf. Arthur Schopenhauer, *Die Welt als Wille und Vorstellung*, book 4, chapter 50, par. 4.

25. The approach and results of my chapter sharply diverge from Horst Denkler's highly controversial article, "Das 'wirck-liche Juda' und der 'Renegat': Moses Freudenstein als Kronzeuge für Wilhelm Raabes Verhältnis zu Juden und Judentum" (*German Quarterly* 60/61, Winter 1987, 5–18). Denkler's intent is to absolve Raabe of the charge of antisemitism by emphasizing his "unencumbered open-mindedness toward his Jewish contemporaries" (9). What, according to Denkler, Raabe tried to portray in Moses Freudenstein was not the Jew, but the "renegade" as a villain. Moses Freudenstein was not only a religious renegade who forsook the faith of his forbears, but also a political renegade who, for the sake of careerism and financial gain, betrayed the liberal friends of his youth and switched to the reactionary camp where he acted as an informer. For Denkler Raabe's villain is a composite portrait of two historical figures, both converted Jews, who betrayed the liberalism of their youth and became fanatical servants of absolutist monarchy. Denkler's identification attempts are highly speculative and not supported by considering evidence. More disturbing, however, is Denk-

ler's failure to inquire into the textual-structural elements of Raabe's novel which conspired to produce what even Denkler concedes as its "disastrous reception history" (14). Denkler does not consider the extreme "Manichaean" dualism of the novel's structure, its light/darkness symbolism. He does not take account of the contrast between the Jewish-born villain and the gentile German hero—in every respect the dark Jew's shining opposite. Above all he does not mention the negative treatment of Moses' archetypically Jewish father, Samuel Freudenstein, who is not a renegade, and yet hardly less villainous than his son. Samuel Freudenstein is not only his son's victim, but also his model and an embodiment of the traditional topos of the avaricious, scheming, heartless, and power-hungry Jew of anti-Jewish lore. To be sure, one has to agree with Denkler that Raabe himself was certainly not an antisemite. However, as I have tried to show, this particular novel can be read only in terms of an ontological antisemitism; and what is particularly alarming is the fact that it was written by a man rightly known as a liberal.

[8]

The Theme of Anti-Semitism in the Work of Austrian Jews

Ruth Kluger

I propose to sketch the reaction to Austrian anti-Semitism in some significant creative works by Jewish writers from the mid-nineteenth century through the Hitler period. My point of departure is the question: How did Jewish intellectuals feel, think about, fight or succumb to a force whose deadliness none of them could know, while we cannot look back without a terrible hindsight? Austrian anti-Semitism was formative for both Theodor Herzl and for Hitler. That simple consideration alone shows that it was more than a provincial variant of a European disease and highlights Austria's central position in the history of the Diaspora in modern times. All the writers I shall discuss were in varying degrees integrated into the mainstream of Austrian cultural life, were removed from Jewish orthodoxy, and all of them, at least at some point in their lives, considered themselves on the way to further integration, whether they called it assimilation or emancipation. The intensity of their reactions to anti-Semitism is all the more striking.

Probably the first Jewish work on anti-Semitism that had a significant impact on the general public was Hermann Mosenthal's play *Deborah*, written in 1848.[1] This drama achieved an extraordinary international success, though helped no doubt by its conventionally romantic interest. The play is set in 1780 and 1785 in Styria (Steiermark), in an area of Austria where Jews were not permitted to settle. Seventeen-eighty was also the beginning

173

of the independent reign of Joseph II, and in the last act the "merciful emperor," the emperor of emancipation, had given the Jews permission to stay. Thus the play has a highly political frame and background, which remain thought-provoking. The intensely personal action in the foreground, on the other hand, has dated. It involves two strong heroines and a weak hero. The women are cast in fashionable juxtaposition, both humanly appealing as well as romantically attractive, one "wild" and dark and Jewish, the other blond, sweet, domestic and Christian. The weak hero is in love with both of them. His friends and relatives manipulate him into marrying the Christian girl, his original love. They do this by convincing him that the Jewish woman loves only money and can be bought off. Although this charge is slanderous, the author still validates the marriage of the old sweethearts. Intermarriage would have involved the conversion of the Jewish woman, and since her Christianity would have been imposed on her, it would have been in conflict with her roots, her childhood memories. The argument is significant. Mosenthal toys with the possibility of total assimilation and rejects it in the figure of the village schoolmaster. This man is a converted Jew who hides his Jewish past and inveighs against other Jews, until he is found out and admits the error of his ways. Thus emancipation and coexistence emerge as the reasonable solution. Hanna, the Christian girl, represents enlightened religion, and through her the author argues that the New Testament offers ample justification for Christians to treat Jews as brothers.

When the play was first performed some Jews objected to it as anti-Jewish, presumably because of its strong emphasis on the Christian tolerance embodied in Hanna and Deborah's contrasting dreams of revenge, which culminate in a curse on the Christians who have hurt her, a curse that she retracts only near the end. As recently as 1978 one scholar wrote: "Mosenthal has portrayed the Jewish characters in *Deborah* from a Christian standpoint, giving the Christian 'God of love' credit for the eventual reconciliation of all the characters. When closely examined, his portrayals of Jewish characters emerge as unfavorable."[2] This criticism leaves out of account that Mosenthal was writing for a Christian audience: the play is meant for Gentile consumption and therefore tries to appeal to a Christian sense of fairness and generosity. Mosenthal does not gloss over the problems inherent in an ugly situation. He presents homeless Jews, who have escaped from a pogrom in Hungary, and argues for their integration in a tolerant, pluralistic society that would allow them to live their lives in their own way. He does not cover up the murderous potential of village Jew baiting, for the village folk get very close to killing the refugees, and with the exception of the few enlightened Christians they show no sympathy whatever for the outsiders. On the other hand, Deborah's speeches present a good deal of Jewish liturgy and folklore, in an obvious attempt to familiarize an ignorant audience with an attractive aspect of Judaism.

For all its aesthetic flaws, *Deborah* touched on practically all the relevant issues of Jewish-Gentile relations, including Zionism, albeit in its pre-political stage of development. In the fourth act Ruben, a member of an Austrian group of Jewish emigrants, speaks of Jewish attachment to the land of their birth. As he is about to leave for America, he picks up a handful of earth and calls it the earth of the promised land. When Deborah points out that the promised land is Jerusalem, he contradicts her. That idea, he says, is a beautiful fairy tale. Home is the country whose language we speak, where our cradle stood, where our individual lives have their roots. Austria, Ruben claims, is his mother, and it is only his Gentile brothers who are driving him away, while he looks forward to a future recognition of their common family bonds. Ruben thus demonstrates the Jewish capacity for patriotism. In his speech enlightened, that is emancipatory, thinking merges with Romantic attachment to the soil to culminate in the guarded hope that the Diaspora will ultimately accommodate the Jews.

But the play was apparently not always seen in the light of its intellectual substance. Austria's most distinguished playwright and man of letters, Franz Grillparzer, told Mosenthal he should have omitted the Jewish theme altogether, that the play did not need it. A gipsy girl or some other female tramp would have served better than the Jewish Deborah. Mosenthal, who admired Grillparzer but who understandably felt that the old man had missed the point of his play, which was about nothing if not the Jewish problem, expressed his consternation when he recorded this conversation. Grillparzer, it appeared, felt that the Jewish theme got in the way of *das Reinmenschliche* (the purely human).[3] If this conversation took place around 1850 or somewhat later, then Grillparzer was himself working on a "Jewish" subject, his drama *The Jewess of Toledo*, with its problematic fusion of Jewishness and sexuality. The tendency to think that the differentiated treatment of real problems (*das Tendentiöse*, as Grillparzer put it) is too specific to be *reinmenschlich* is not untypical in the reception of other works I shall mention. Most of them are treated cursorily if at all in German literary histories, and the issue of anti-Semitism gets no serious scholarly attention from literary historians in search of the higher values. I am thus, in effect, sketching a lacuna in literary historiography.

Mosenthal, like many artists and writers, was a patient but also a guest of Dr. Johann Schnitzler. In his autobiography *Jugend in Wein*, Arthur Schnitzler recalls that among the many poets and actors who were his father's patients and friends, Hermann Mosenthal stood out for the child, because he gave him the first autographed work for the little library the boy had just started. The work was of course *Deborah*. Schnitzler was pleased with the pretty gray cover as well as the signature.[4] In our context there is a peculiar fitness to this little scene, which not even the adult Schnitzler, recalling it, could have appreciated as we do who know the end of the story. When Mosenthal wrote his play, it was possible to be optimistic about the future of the Jews in Austria. As the second half of the century took its course, Austrian liberalism lost out and anti-Semitism became a party issue and a positive ideal for certain right-wingers. The Austria in which the boy Schnitzler was to be an adult gave far less grounds for optimism. In fact, the problem was assuming new dimensions.

To the Gentile world it simply was not a problem of anti-Semitism, it was the "Jewish" problem. Grillparzer's indifference to the ideological substance of Mosenthal's play continued to be the attitude of well-meaning Gentiles. The most the world was willing to grant the Jews was a half-hearted tolerance, without any comprehension of either the political or the psychological significance of what the Jews were experiencing. For with the defeat of liberalism, anti-Semitism became more than dislike for Jews, a dislike that might have been overcome on better acquaintance, as the Jews kept hoping and as the likes of Mosenthal had suggested. Instead, anti-Semitism was now elevated to an ideal, a rallying cry, that offered Gentiles salvation from hardship and probably absolution from sin as well, if the Jews fulfilled their scapegoat function. Peter Rosegger, an enormously popular Austrian writer who glorified village life, wrote in a letter of March 1889: "Nationalism and anti-Semitism are in and of themselves noble and great because the latter combats evil and the sources of discord [*Zwietrachtstiftendes*], while the former works towards unity and humanism." Rosegger saw himself as a moderate anti-Semite and, turning against more rabid Jew haters than he was, he warned that anti-Semitism must be treated like the high ideal that it is. If it is spoiled through nasty means, it is like a violated woman from whom we naturally (*naturgemäss*) turn away, whom we can pity but no longer love enthusiastically.[5] Note the false morality of the metaphor: anti-Semitism is a pure virgin who must be kept pure and not become the victim of a violence that would render her unworthy of love. He means to say that Jews should be treated badly, but within certain limits. As so often, sentimentality and brutality go hand in hand, with a dash of sexuality for flavor. The level of discourse, elevated kitsch, reveals the imperviousness of popular turn-of-the-century anti-Semitism to rational argument.

It is this upbeat aspect of anti-Semitism that Schnitzler refers to at the beginning of "Leutnant Gustl," where the good Leutnant is uncharacteristically attending a concert and notes the large number of Jews who are also there. He is indignant that they can't be kept out, not here and not even out of the army. He thinks, if I have to put up with this company, what good is anti-Semitism? (The untranslatable original idiom is "Dann pfeif ich auf den ganzen Antisemitismus.")[6] Gustl is disillusioned because anti-Semitism, which he wants to embrace as a positive force, is not pervasive enough to suit his wishes.

Schnitzler, more than any other Jewish author, tried to depict the thoughts and emotions of Gentiles towards Jews from the inside and with objective distance. Yet the story "Leutnant Gustl" is not primarily about anti-Semitism. Its primary target is a benighted and outdated code of honor. Nor is the play *Professor Bernhardi* primarily about anti-Semitism. Its main concern is an individual's struggle for integrity within the ethics and realities of medicine and politics. Yet today the play remains interesting mainly for its account of how the authority of the physician is undermined when he belongs to a minority. Schnitzler's late novella "Fräulein Else," about a young girl's suicide, does not even deal directly with Jewishness. But when we find out that Else is in fact Jewish and worried about whether she looks it or not, her despair acquires an added dimension.[7] And the novel *Der Weg ins Freie (The Road to the Open)* of 1908 is at first glance primarily the story of an artist's development. In other words, Schnitzler never gave the "Jewish problem" or anti-Semitism, a central place in any of his works. And yet, more than any other writer, he has preserved and interpreted for us the last generation of Viennese Jews that were unaffected by the Nazis.

Why did he not write a play or a story where this subject, which was evidently of burning interest to him, was central and not overshadowed by some other? One must assume that even *he* thought it was not in and of itself important enough. While anti-Semitism is a recurrent theme in the autobiography, it never becomes dominant, and there is some evidence that Schnitzler thought the problem would ultimately take care of itself. But where his imagination was his guide, in his fiction, there is no such optimism. There he shows that being Jewish is not only a serious liability in one's public and professional life, but that anti-Semitism even poisons the relations of Jews among each other and of Jews and their non-Jewish friends. And he shows the situation to be hopeless. His characters try every conceivable alternative, the whole gamut from assimilation to Zionism, yet the best of the non-Jews, like Wergenthin in *The Road to the Open*, have nothing better to offer than tolerance, and are essentially repelled when they have to confront psychological pain.

Though told in the third person, the novel's point of view is almost exclusively that of its non-Jewish hero, Georg von Wergenthin, an aristocratic budding composer who moves in Jewish circles. It is customary to say that the Wergenthin-artist theme is unconnected with the Jewish theme of the novel. I believe this is not so. Wergenthin's personal life and his indifference to others, his need to keep a distance, even from the woman he loves, mirror and complement his distasteful withdrawal from the social problems with which his Jewish friends are struggling. As I read it, it is Wergenthin's unwillingness to engage himself, if only through a word of sympathy, an outburst of anger against injustice, that ultimately, if only indirectly, seals the fate of these Jews. When the novel ends, they are essentially left in their limbo. The road to the open is only there for the non-Jew.

More than any other writer, Schnitzler has given us a picture of Jewish life in Vienna at a time when anti-Semitism was on the rise but Jews also had opportunities to make a good living and contributed importantly to the city's intellectual productivity. If the plot is mainly about Wergenthin, the background is an intense and rich picture of Jewish reaction to discrimination, seen through the eyes of a man who couldn't care less. Georg likes his Jewish friends as long as they amuse him, feed his ego and contribute to Vienna's artistic ambience. But he wishes they wouldn't carry on so. They embarrass him when they tell him what they have to put up with. It doesn't occur to him to show sympathy, to ask questions, in a word, to treat them as true equals. Ultimately he treats the "Jewish problem" as he treats the problem of having a mistress whom he dearly loves but whom he doesn't want to marry. It is in his detachment that the two parts of the novel intersect. If the Jews have no better friends than the likes of Wergenthin, then their situation is hopeless enough, whether they convert to Christianity, go to jail for the Socialists or give money to the Zionist cause. Schnitzler's own attitude, as we know, and as the book suggests, was oddly close to Mosenthal's, a kind of middle-of-the-road assimilationism, a secular Jewishness of the garden variety. But this is not to say that he felt more Austrian than Jewish. He was an Austrian Jew, and the two elements could not be separated. Nor can they be separated for any of his Jewish characters: the great merit of the novel is that it presents us with the many but futile attempts at escaping from the dilemma.

We cannot help but read Schnitzler with hindsight. More, it is reductive to try not to read him with hindsight. *The Road to the Open* begins during the year after the first Zionist Congress in 1897. The young people in the book, the ones who are still unmarried and do a lot of partying, are the generation of my grandparents. In old age their counterparts in the real world, and the children of these counterparts, would be forced into emigration or into the gas chambers. As we read about them, they represent to us a doomed society, though Schnitzler did not know it. But Schnitzler did know that their situation was not trivial and that the problem was not ephemeral. *We* know that it was far more urgent than he could have dreamed, and for that very reason his book is spellbinding today. What were the Jews of Vienna thinking in those days when Hitler learned his anti-Semitism in that city? We are only a few years off when we say that this was Hitler's Vienna. Could they do nothing, did they see nothing? Schnitzler's answer is, they saw everything, and they did everything. They invented Zionism, they tried to make the public aware of their plight, and they desperately tried to be like everyone else. Nothing that they did could prevent what was coming. With this reflection we engage the characters somewhat differently from the way the author intended, as we read the diary of Anne Frank differently from the way she wrote it, out of our knowledge that her shelter was not safe.

Reading Schnitzler today, we feel that the characters who are most obsessed with their Jewishness, the ones who are closest to despair, are the ones who have the right outlook. Schnitzler in any case gave us the whole spectrum, though he did not set the accents quite where we do. Thus the angry old man of the novel, the successful businessman Mr. Ehrenberg, who feels that the Jews have been betrayed by all parties and have nothing to expect of the Gentile world, seems a kind of prophet in retrospect. We feel with him when a younger man coolly remarks that Ehrenberg lacks "desirable objectivity" and Ehrenberg, shaking with rage, asks him whether he is baptized, whereupon the young intellectual replies haughtily that he is neither a Christian nor a Jew, that he is *konfessionslos* (without religion, in Austria a legal status) "for the simple reason that I never felt Jewish." And Ehrenberg replies, "You'll feel Jewish alright when you get beaten up downtown on account, you should pardon the expression, you have a somewhat Jewish nose."[8]

And we feel the shallowness of the Gentile Wergenthin, when he tells a Jewish friend that he had thought him to be above *(erhaben über)* anti-Semitic insults.[9] Reading the passage eighty years after it was written it reminds me of Elie Wiesel's father, who put on the yellow star with a shrug and said, "The yellow star? Oh well, what of it? You don't die of it." His son comments, "Poor father, of what then did you die?"[10] In other words, the intervening history has sharpened the issues in this novel, but not so that we have become more expert at what Schnitzler describes. We have to provide the comments, but he remains one of the best guides to Jewish minds and the Jewish malaise in the period that culminated in the Holocaust.

A less gifted playwright but more famous contemporary of Schnitzler's did handle the Jewish problem outright in a play which premiered in Vienna in 1898. The Dreyfus affair may have been crucial in Theodor Herzl's intellectual development, but ultimately it was Vienna that shaped his perceptions. His novel *Altneuland* starts in a Viennese coffee house, where unemployed and overeducated Jews waste their time because as Jews they can't get into the civil service and their fathers don't want them to be shopkeepers. Herzl's drama, *Das neue Ghetto,* now virtually forgotten, deals with the same Jewish community as *Der Weg ins Freie. The New Ghetto* was written in 1894 before the first Zionist Congress and premiered shortly after that Congress, in 1898. The new ghetto of the title is one of moral and spiritual isolation, the world of the new secular Jews. The protagonist is an idealistic young Jewish lawyer who works without fee for the underprivileged and exploited, specifically mine workers, and whose sense of honor forces him to fight a duel in which he is killed. Herzl lacks the complex irony with which Schnitzler or, for that matter, Arthur Koestler, in his autobiography *Arrow in the Blue,* treat the subject of duelling. In Herzl's play the duel is a meaningful assertion of Jewish masculinity. Jakob, the good lawyer, is surrounded by relatives and others who conform to the world's picture of the money Jew, the *Geldjude.* Although these characters are unattractive and have no higher goals and ideals, they are shown to be trapped by circumstances that have made them materialistic. The Gentile world despises them when they are poor and takes advantage of them when they have money to spend. That attitude extends from the Gentile servants to the aristocracy. In comparison with the new ghetto, the old one, the actual *Judenstrasse*, fostered certain familial virtues, as the rabbi in the play points out, and these virtues are now threatened with extinction. The Jews have wandered from one ghetto into a worse one, and their contacts with the Gentile world are too fragile to lend them support. Jakob has a Gentile friend who deserts him for political reasons and because he feels repelled by Jakob's relatives. He only returns when Jakob "redeems" himself by fighting his duel. Jakob's parents cling to their old-fashioned virtues, but still lose their only son. Another alternative is conversion, which is sympathetically presented, as a possible, though not a foolproof, way out of the "new ghetto." The Jews' concern with money is not for money's sake but yet another attempt to escape. The implication is that none of them succeed. Jakob's last words are: "Jews, my brothers, we'll be allowed to live only if you . . . Why do you hold me back? . . . I want out. Out of the ghetto."[11] Since the play is by Herzl, we think we know what the solution should be. But the play does not touch on Zionism; it confines itself to presenting the situation in which the Jews are caught.

I have tried to show how this pre-Nazi literature is inevitably read in the light of subsequent persecution, hence within a wider context than it provides. That context was catching up with the next generation of Jewish-Austrian authors, among them Hermann Broch. Broch did not write directly about anti-Semitism, yet during the early Hitler years he did write a symbolic novel in which there are Jewish surrogates. I mean *Die Verzauberung (The Bewitchment)*, also known as *Der Versucher (The Tempter)* or *Bergroman (Mountain Novel)*. Here Broch attempts to interpret the psychological lure of fascism. A village in the Austrian mountains succumbs to the enticement of a newcomer who promises a kind of political-religious salvation. The "Jews" in this story are the Wetchys, a family of Protestant sectarians, whose customs differ from those of the local Catholic population. They are further set off from their peasant neighbors because they are perceived as belonging to a hostile commercial world. Father Wetchy sells agricultural machinery, radios and insurance policies, items that the villagers need or crave but that they come to reject under the influence of Marius, the charismatic would-be savior. The Wetchy family, branded as outsiders, are finally forced to leave the village and return to the city. Before they take this step, a crowd of drunk young villagers tie up and torture Mr. Wetchy.

In a final confrontation between Wetchy and Marius, the fascist "tempter," Marius promulgates a *Blut-und-Boden* philosophy and expresses his contempt for city people who are removed from the soil and therefore responsible for wars. The city makes men greedy and ungodly as well as unmanly, he claims. Wetchy counters persuasively that greed is quite prevalent in the village, too, and insists on his faith in the human soul and in God. For his part, he proffers a value system that is based on invisible qualities and not on a person's occupation. And he shows that his faith in the invisible is tied to his love for his family.[12]

It is obvious that a conventional Jewish life and faith is implied in all this. But by making Wetchy a sectarian Christian Broch widens the scope of the problem and universalizes it. The shift allows him to concentrate on the specific qualities of *modern* prejudice against minorities and to omit traditional Christian prejudice against Jews. In other words, it allows Broch to zero in on the new elements he sees emerging in the thirties, on the subversive or revolutionary aspects of fascism. Perhaps the most revealing aspect of the Wetchy episode is the narrator's attitude. The narrator is a country doctor who does not succumb to the tempter yet understands him and sympathizes with some of his demands. And to him Wetchy is a pathetic individual who inspires pity but no respect, even when he sides with him. The narrator saves Wetchy from his tormentors but feels no indignation. On the contrary, he exonerates them. "They were not bad, none of them, just hideously drunk."[13] Broch builds up this scene so that at first we only know that the villagers are slapping Wetchy's face. Only later, as the doctor examines him, do we learn the full extent of the physical damage he has undergone. He has lost a tooth, has a broken rib and has been kicked in the groin. By that time we, as readers, have already absorbed the narrator's basic indifference to the victim. And the narrator's attitude does not change as he finds out how severely his patient has been maltreated: it remains essentially an attitude of exasperation. He wants the situation solved by the removal of the Wetchy family, even though, or perhaps because, he identifies with them, since he, too, is a man from the city.

Thus, the narrator's sympathies remain with the villagers, even when he is critical of them. Like Schnitzler's Wergenthin, Broch's doctor does not want to get involved with the minority beyond certain limits. He is clearly not a reliable witness, unless we assume that Broch, a Jewish author writing in the thirties, could look on gang violence and the torture of defenseless victims with the same cool detachment as his narrator. But neither is he wholly unreliable. To be sure, his view of the Wetchys shows up his own shortcomings and those of the majority to whom he belongs. On the other hand, the Wetchy family, even as they are victimized, remain pathetic, ridden by fears and anxieties, and slightly ludicrous with their illnesses, their small size, their petty bourgeois family life and their insistence on religious customs that have no particular relevance. They are ultimately incidental to the upheavals that Marius is causing in the village. Thus their role is far smaller than that of the Jews in Nazi ideology. But Broch may have had fascist models other than Hitler in mind for his Marius Ratti, most obviously Mussolini. In any case, the author's attitude to his family of outsiders remains ambiguous and somewhat puzzling. It is not quite the narrator's but neither is it diametrically opposed to that of the narrator. To themselves as to their enemies the Jews of Austria were neither a tragic nor a noble people. They understood all too well how the rest of the world perceived them, and their empathy with those who hated them left its mark on their self-portraits.

That is the stuff of Werfel's comedy, *Jacobowsky und der Oberst* (*Jacobowsky and the Colonel*) of 1943. It is a kind of apotheosis of the comical/heroic Jew, pitted against his counterpart, the military hero, who is stupid, athletic, romantic and conventionally brave. The play was a success, not only on stage as adapted by S. N. Behrmann, but also on screen as late as 1958 with the title *Me and the Colonel* and Danny Kaye as the lead. It was *the* comedy of refugees. Reading it today, it retains much of its wit and charm, but at the same time it appears dubious in its basic assumptions. And these have to do with the depiction of anti-Semitism. The scene is France in 1940, as the Germans are occupying the country. The three main characters are the Jewish intellectual, born in Poland, raised in Germany, exiled in Austria and then in France, in search of a new place of refuge; secondly the anti-Semitic Polish colonel Stjerbinski, chivalrous and poetic, who despises the Jew; and thirdly Marianne, the colonel's beloved, who is willing to flee with him to England. The colonel has to smuggle military secrets across the Channel and is singularly unsuited for this task. He needs someone who has a quick mind to help him, while Jacobowsky needs someone who knows how to drive the car he has bought. As Jacobowsky makes himself increasingly useful in the course of their common journey, he finds more and more favor in Marianne's eyes, and in the last scene she gives up her place on the boat to him. This triangle and the ambience of some crucial scenes, especially the final, leave-taking scene, is in some ways reminiscent of the film *Casablanca*. There is a dishonest wish fulfillment of immediate audience appeal in both. As we watch the world fall apart, a soothing voice seems to reassure us, "All shall be well in the end" because of basic human decency. There is no sense that something irrevocable was happening in this war, that the wound would not heal seamlessly, that the world would not be the same as before. In Werfel's case, the note of optimism goes beyond the hope for an allied victory and includes an optimistic outlook on anti-Semitism. The play is dated because it does not convey a sense of the unprecedented dimensions of the Holocaust. Its humor is upbeat. A comedy on this subject has to be a black comedy.

The colonel's anti-Jewish barbs are as blunt as the Jew's repartees are sharp. Werfel recreates the stuff of real viciousness but makes it enjoyable through Jacobowsky's witty triumphs. These are not only verbal, for Jacobowsky's cleverness, coupled with altruism, win over Marianne and help the whole party survive and escape. Ultimately the two antagonists are joined in mutual respect and even friendship of a sort. The play's message runs something like this: although the Nazis cannot be swayed and must be defeated, apart from them anti-Semites can be accommodated, can be won over, through words and deeds. Even when they won't cease being anti-Semites, we can live with them.

Werfel meant his work to carry a message and his characters represent more than themselves. The colonel's beloved, as her name implies, is the embodiment of the spirit of France. In a non-realistic analogy to the main theme, the Wandering Jew and St. Francis bicycle in tandem through France on their way to America.[14] Now while Jacobowsky can stand identification with the Wandering Jew, the colonel is no St. Francis. It is a constellation that gives too much credit to the anti-Semite. For all his prejudices, the nobility of Stjerbinski's character is validated by Marianne's love for him. He is a worthy liberator of France. It is true that Jacobowsky once tells him that he could easily become a Hitler. But the action of the play softens that accusation so that a reconciliation between the two can take place. The tension between them is subsumed in a dialectic of eternal opposites that can be synthesized. But the abstraction does not fit the case: because Jacobowsky always wins out in the battle of wits, we forget that he is nevertheless the victim and the colonel is the victimizer. To make them equals in an eternal duel of archetypes amounts almost to a vindication of anti-Semitism.

In this presentation the danger is confined to the Nazis. If they can be defeated, the rest of mankind, no matter how prejudiced, will live happily together. Jews can be friends with those who despise them, even those who will not change their minds. This view is not new. Nicholas de Lange shows in chapter 1 of this volume that what he calls the eternal anti-Semitism theory was popular into the fifties. Werfel's play may be taken as an illustration of this theory. Werfel builds a false analogy between being Jewish and being anti-Semitic: for one may be born a Jew, but anti-Semitism is an acquired taste. No one is born hating Jews.

Moreover, the mental furniture of the play takes us back to pre-Holocaust times and has not been adjusted to the new realities. Nazi anti-Semitism is neatly separated from, say, the Slavic kind. And French anti-Semitism does not exist at all. There are three French characters: Jacobowsky's landlady in the first act, Marianne, and a French policeman who enforces the law only during working hours and proves helpful to the refugees once he is off duty. All are kindly disposed towards Jacobowsky and show no trace of hostility towards Jews in general. This popular comedy, then, simplifies matters far more than Schnitzler in his excellent novel and Herzl in his second-rate play had done. And I am afraid it is precisely the simplification that made for its success. Anti-Semitism, after the war, was not a phenomenon one wanted to face once more. Stjerbinski as the eternal complementary figure to the Eternal Jew: they combine to a suggestion that what happened under Hitler has no significance beyond itself, and that it does not require a new context or new terms of discussion.

If Werfel's play is the comedy of emigration and escape by cunning adults who know how to help themselves, Ilse Aichinger's novel *Die grössere Hoffnung* ("The greater hope" but translated as *Herod's Children*), is about the children they left behind in a limbo of a fatherland. Born in 1921, some thirty years after Werfel, Aichinger tells the story of a child in a city much like Vienna who lives with her grandmother after her Jewish mother has had to leave. The father, who is Aryan, has been drafted and has abandoned his family. It is a tale of a circumscribed, limited universe, which has some elements of fantasy, but these arise simply out of the extreme alienation of the children who are its protagonists. The book opens as Ellen, the heroine, has fallen asleep in the consul's office and dreams of the world's homeless children who are trying to escape from Europe. Ellen has come to beg for a visa. Her playmates are a group of Jewish and partly Jewish children who are not allowed to use the playgrounds of their city, who have to wear the yellow star and who, like Ellen, dream only of leaving their hometown. Every place outside the city is marvelous and has a fairy-tale quality, while the city itself has acquired the tinge of nightmare. Aichinger consistently maintains the child's point of view. The book is historically very exact in its use of actual restrictions that affected children and is in that sense realistic. But its realities are transformed into the complexities of a child's inner world. All the details of persecution become internalized and assume a different value as the children cope with them.

One evening Ellen meets her father. He is an officer who officially asks her and her friends whether they have the right to sit on a public bench. (Jews didn't.) Aichinger's style and method lend a surrealistic quality to the absurdity of a grown man in uniform asking the city's children for legal proof that they may sit on the city's benches. Of course, they cannot produce the "correct" ID cards. "Are you Aryans?" the officer asks. At this point his daughter steps forward with the simple words, "That's for you to say, father."[15] She then embraces him to keep him away from her Jewish friends, simultaneously kissing and biting him in a desperate ambivalence that reflects more than one child's love-hate relationship with a parent. As he sends her home to her Jewish grandmother, she is once again rejected by the father who wears the uniform of authority and prevents her from being at home where she was born. In this book Austria has shrunk to a Jewish child's private hell. No longer a place where a minority seeks equal rights, it is now a place where a child grasps at straws on her way to death, her mother in exile, her father an enemy.

Earlier on I mentioned a somewhat unctuous speech which Mosenthal puts into the mouth of one of his minor characters. Ruben, in the process of emigrating, would like to stay in Austria and says that he and the other Jews are at home in the land of their birth and upbringing and not in some remote biblical homeland. With Aichinger we have come full circle. The child who stumbles blindly through these pages and who desperately wants a visa, wants to leave, is nevertheless nowhere else at home but where she is most despised. Anti-Semitism has been brought to a last level of intimacy: the anti-Semite is no longer the host who ejects the guest but instead the father who turns from his child. Ellen belongs where she is least wanted and the choice is not up to her: for no child can change its father. The girl who dies in this book, after the other Jews have emigrated, is part of the culture that kills her. In the other works I mentioned the degree of the Jews' outsiderdom was precisely the question under debate. With Aichinger the boundaries between insider and outsider have collapsed, as has the boundary between inner and outer reality. The image that lingers is not of a country casting out a minority but one of Austria abandoning and devouring its own children.

Notes

1. S. H. Mosenthal, *Gesammelte Werke*, 6 vols. (Stuttgart & Leipzig: Hallberger, 1878), vol. 2, pp. 1–87.

2. Charlene A. Lea, *Emancipation, Assimilation and Stereotype: The Image of the Jew in German and Austrian Drama (1800–1850)* (Bonn: Bouvier, 1978), p. 68.

3. Mosenthal, "Miniaturbilder: Grillparzer," *Gesammelte Werke*, vol. 1, p. 280. For an account of the success of *Deborah*, see vol. 6, "Lebensbild" by Josef Weilen, pp. 33–38.

4. Arthur Schnitzler, *Jugend in Wien. Eine Autobiographie* (Vienna-Munich: Verlag Fritz Molden, 1968), p. 31.

5. Quoted by Guy Stern, "Präfaschismus und die respektable Literatur," *Der deutsche Roman und seine historischen und politischen Bedingungen,* ed. Wolfgang Paulsen (Bern: Francke Verlag, 1977), p. 113.

6. Arthur Schnitzler, *Die erzählenden Schriften* (Frankfurt: S. Fischer Verlag, 1961), vol. 1, pp. 338–39.

7. Ibid., vol. 2, p. 333.

8. Ibid., vol. 1, p. 689.

9. Ibid., p. 670.

10. Elie Wiesel, *Night* (New York: Avon, 1969), p. 20.

11. Theodor Herzl, *Gesammelte Zionistische Werke* (Berlin: Jüdischer Verlag, 1935), vol. 5, p. 124.

12. Hermann Broch, *Die Verzauberung*, ed. Paul M. Lützeler (Kommentierte Werkausgabe Hermann Broch, vol. 3, Frankfurt: Suhrkamp, 1976), pp. 340ff.

13. "Sie waren ja schließlich alle nicht schlecht, sie waren nur stinkbesoffen." Broch. p. 289.

14. Franz Werfel, *Gesammelte Werke. Die Dramen* (Frankfurt: S. Fischer Verlag, 1959), vol. 2, pp. 302–5. English adaptation by S. N. Behrmann, *Jacobowsky and the Colonel* (New York: Random House, 1944). Behrmann omitted St. Francis and the Wandering Jew but added a little boy for Marianne to hold as the boat leaves for England.

15. Ilse Aichinger, *Die größere Hoffnung* (Frankfurt: S. Fischer Verlag, 1966), p. 41. The English version is *Herod's Children*, transl. Cornelia Schaeffer (New York: Atheneum, 1964). See also Dagmar C. G. Lorenz, *Ilse Aichinger* (Königstein: Athenäum, 1981), pp. 60–76.

[9]

The Modern Character of Nineteenth-Century Russian Antisemitism

Alexander Orbach

Political, literary and popular forms of antisemitism surfaced in a number of countries in the last quarter of the nineteenth century. Beginning with a definition of the Jews as a people substantially different from those around them, the advocates of these forms of antisemitism did not address themselves to abstract theological issues, nor, for that matter, did they criticize traditional, or even contemporary, Jewish ritual and practice. Furthermore, unlike the medieval opponents of the Jews who were interested in converting Jews to Christianity, the modernists, instead, sought to effect a legal and even physical separation of the Jews from the non-Jewish societies in which they found themselves. Thus, the modern antisemite defined the Jewish Question as the need to circumscribe contemporary Jewish activity in order to resolve the new political, economic and, most important of all, cultural problems that had emerged as a consequence of the development of the new nation-state with its emancipated citizenry.

Antisemites emphasized two themes. First, they contended that the extension of full rights to Jews, a people with a history and culture all of their own, had destroyed the concept of an organic nation-state, an entity which, in their view, was intended to link together all like-minded souls living in a particular location. Antisemites stressed that membership in the nation should not be open to all, but should, instead, be restricted to those who qualified on the bases of the newly evolving national and ethnic categories. Therefore, they rejected as completely unacceptable the concept of naturalized citizenship, based on a vision of universal humanity with inalienable rights for individuals.

Second, beyond this theoretical stance, the antisemites insisted that the emancipation of the Jews had been a grave mistake on practical grounds, too. They claimed that once set free, Jews immediately rushed to the center of national life, and because of the skills that they had developed over the centuries during their isolation from western society, they were then able to impose their world views on the newly emerging states and their unsophisticated residents. Antisemites charged that the new state had become "judaized" and that restrictions and regulations governing Jewish participation in civic life were now necessary in order to return the polity to the "people" and to protect the majority population from being both dominated and tyrannized by the Jewish minority. Hence, the earlier ghettoization of the Jew was now interpreted as a protective measure intended to secure the continuity of Western civilization against an ever present and powerful threat committed to its eventual destruction. It follows then that, for such people, the immediate steps toward the ultimate resolution of the Jewish Question entailed the liberation of their states from the alien and pernicious Jewish yoke. Once that had been accomplished, those states could be rebuilt on the bases of true, nativist values and traditions. This new antisemitism was thus racist rather than religious in nature, and was linked directly to the depiction of the Jew as an unassimilable entity, undeserving of both the rights and privileges of full citizenship in the modern state. Such rights were to be reserved only for true members of the nation.[1] The first expressions of this antisemitism then came to be directed against the dual ideas of Jewish emancipation and Jewish integration.

In developing their analyses of modern antisemitism, some scholars have argued that the movement really represented an expression of hostility to nineteenth-century liberalism with its insistence on individual autonomy and the extension of legal and political rights to all, independent of religious and ethnic background. These new rights and liberties, exchanged for obligations and duties, came to be embodied in legal agreements, constitutions, adopted by all of the new nation-states appearing at this time. In this way, modern antisemitism has been explained as an indirect attack on the new political order by a coalition of groups dissatisfied with the existing state of affairs but still not strong enough to challenge the new liberal and constitutional governments directly. Therefore, without real strength to overthrow the system, the opponents of parliamentary democracy, finance capitalism and individual liberty focused their criticism and launched their attacks against that one group against whom negative residual attitudes still persisted in the popular culture, and who appeared to be the principal beneficiaries of the new state of affairs, that is, the Jews.[2]

However, the problem with this analysis is that it must be restricted to such states as Austria, France and Germany that were created as a consequence of the overthrow of traditional polities. Only in those locations where constitutional guarantees came to be introduced and Jews were emancipated can the argument be advanced that the local antisemitic movements reflected a profound unhappiness with the new political order and its consequences. Hence, this approach cannot be employed successfully in assessing expressions of antisemitism in those parts of the world where either such political developments did not take place, or where emancipation and constitutionalism served as the points of departure for the subsequent history of that society. For instance, manifestations of modern antisemitism in such disparate locations as the Russian Empire in the nineteenth century and the United States in the 1920s and 1930s cannot be viewed as displaced attacks against liberalism and constitutionalism. In the case of Russia, antisemitism of a public and even political sort emerged long before the emancipation of the Jews, while in the case of the United States, one can say that its history only begins with the Declaration of Independence (1776) and the ensuing Revolutionary War culminating in the Constitution (1787). Therefore, the American antisemite really had no pre-emancipatory period to refer back to, while his Russian counterpart of the pre-Soviet era was still living in his "golden age."

In order to explore this problem more fully, a focus on antisemitism in Russia at the close of the nineteenth century becomes an important test case. Such an analysis will serve at least two purposes. First, an examination of the nature of those developments will help to decide if the Russian experience should be included within the larger framework of modern antisemitism and thereby cease to restrict that discussion to western and central Europe only.[3] If we conclude that nineteenth-century Russian antisemitism is truly modern, then we should explore its roots carefully and compare them to those identified with the Western expressions of the same phenomenon. Second, if we are able to identify certain features common to both the

Russian and Western expressions, we will then be able to comment more precisely on the forces at work in generating this form of anti-Jewish hatred.

I

Without doubt the most widely known and discussed eruptions of anti-Jewish behavior in the last quarter of the nineteenth century occurred in Tsarist Russia. There, a series of riots, some quite major in scope, spread through the southern sections of the Empire in the years 1881–82. Unlike earlier pogroms in Tsarist Russia, the riots of 1881–82 were not isolated events, localized and contained within a particular geographical region. The disturbances flared up in over two hundred different Jewish settlements, including the cities of Kiev, Odessa and Warsaw.[4] These riots were not directed against recent political gains and were not motivated by any recognizable political ideology. Rather, the unleashing of violence and destruction in April 1881 reflected a popular antisemitism that was not at all modern in either its character or form of expression. In fact, recent scholarship has emphasized the spontaneous nature of these disturbances and has verified the absence of any organized conspiracy to touch off the riots or to direct them once they did break out.[5]

In a careful assessment of the pogroms, Michael Aronson has demonstrated how the immediate background to those riots resembled that often found at the time of earlier popular attacks against Jews. On the one hand, difficult economic conditions had produced a larger than usual group of unemployed migrant laborers in the spring of 1881. On the other, an unsettled political situation had emerged in the aftermath of the recent (March) assassination of Tsar Alexander II. Finally, an increase in the public anti-Jewish agitation in the press at the time tied Jews to both the complex economic difficulties as well as the assassination. These developments together contributed to fashioning a volatile climate of opinion that contributed to sparking the pogroms.[6]

Yet, in spite of these predictors, the riots were still unexpected. Trends in Russian-Jewish life since the late 1860s reflected recent tendencies toward Russification, as measured by increased Jewish enrollment in Russian schools, circulation of Russian-language periodicals within the Jewish community and the emergence of societies created for the promotion of Russian culture among Jews. Such developments pointed to the growing acculturation of the community. An optimistic faith in the Russian government's ultimate good will and positive approach to the Jews of the realm had overshadowed the danger signals of 1881. Thus, the pogroms and the ensuing hostile governmental response fell as an unexpected thunderclap upon the Jewish community.[7]

In response to the pogroms, the government convened a number of commissions of inquiry to determine the causes of the riots. Fearful that these disturbances were linked to the recent assassination and were part of the revolutionary movement's assault against the government, the administration of Alexander III was eager to get a clearer picture of what had happened. The initial investigations soon led to a series of new laws whose immediate effect was to restrict even further the limits of Jewish opportunity within the Pale. Called the Provisional Laws, these harsh regulations of May 1882 remained in force through the remainder of the tsarist period.[8] With these enactments, the government moved on two fronts. First, contending that Jewish interactions with the local peasant population had generated the anger that led to the riots, the government reduced sharply Jewish rights to create new settlements in rural areas of the Pale. Second, claiming that Jewish commercial activities on Christian feast days were offensive to the Russian people, the government reduced the number of market days available to Jewish merchants by prohibiting trade on a designated number of Christian holy days.[9] As a consequence, the Jews of Russia, already beset by serious economic difficulties at a time when the Russian economy was itself in the process of a major transformation, now found themselves even more adversely affected as these laws served to reduce their economic opportunities even more.[10] Thus, Russian Jews had not only suffered physically at the hands of the pogromists; they had also come to be blamed by the government for being the cause of that very violence which had been unleashed against them. Unlike the expressions of antisemitism in central and western Europe then, the events in Russia featured a popular campaign against Jews that was not only *not* a displaced attack against the government, but rather was exploited by the authorities in order to launch an even more devastating assault against the local Jewish community.

After 1882, no one could argue that the government was positively predisposed toward the Jews of the realm. Rather, the May Laws marked the beginning of a concerted governmental campaign carried out over the next two and one-half decades against Russian Jewry. For instance, in the more liberal atmosphere of the 1860s, the government of Alexander II permitted Jewish graduates of institutes of higher learning to breech the boundaries of the Pale and take up residence in the interior of the Empire, including the capital cities, Moscow and St. Petersburg. This policy was introduced as part of an overall campaign intent on modernizing Russia; and it was thought that by offering opportunities to educated and technically trained Jews, both they and Russia would derive concrete benefits. A quarter of a century later, the administration of Alexander III, fearful that modern education had not only failed to inculcate patriotic feelings within the Jewish community, but that it had contributed significantly to the dissemination of revolutionary views among Jewish youth, introduced a quota system in the school, restricting Jewish enrollment. This legislation effectively eliminated the most important avenue of escape for many young Jews eager to quit the Pale of Settlement and make a career for themselves in Russia.[11]

In the same period, other enactments further reduced the size of the Pale by introducing additional residential restrictions in that zone. Additionally, in the 1890s, efforts to expel Jews from areas recently opened to them outside of the Pale were also undertaken. The most brutal of these expulsions occurred in the spring of 1891 when twenty thousand Jews, or nearly two-thirds of the community, were driven out of Moscow by the local authorities.[12] Finally, Jewish professional attainments were also curtailed by decisions of tsarist policy makers. For instance, Jews found that not only was it more difficult to gain admission to law schools, but that once trained, they were subject to legislation that sharply curtailed their right to practice law.[13] Needless to say, each step in this bureaucratic offensive contributed substantially to the growing pauperization of the Jewish community and consequently to the rising rate of Jewish emigration from Tsarist Russia after 1881.

The Russian experience thus witnessed both a popular assault against the Jews, as well as a state campaign against the community. This two-pronged approach clearly distinguished this experience from contemporary developments elsewhere in Europe. There, as will be recalled, the antisemites identified the Jews with the new power structure and raised their voices against such changes which had equalized the status of the Jews. In Russia, on the other hand, the government not only did not defend the Jews against their enemies, but jumped into the fray with its own assault against them. Hence, the character of antisemitism in Russia at the close of the nineteenth century did not conform in its critical aspects to contemporary developments in the West. Yet, in spite of these distinctions, Russian antisemitism did possess a number of modern features or characteristics which should be explored more fully.

The strong anti-capitalist and anti-urban elements within the antisemitic expressions and actions of both the masses and the government certainly gave the movement the vocabulary of modern antisemitism. In Russia, too, Jews were associated with the market economy, and those well-to-do Jews who had left the Pale in the 1860s, especially for St. Petersburg, were highly visible in the emerging Russian credit and banking fields. Furthermore, Jewish urban concentrations within the Pale resulted in economic and social confrontations with both peasants and workers as the latter began to move into the cities in order to participate in the industrialization of the country which was proceeding rapidly in the 1880s. In addition, the use of the full power of the state against the Jews immediately brings to mind the later experience in the 1930s when the Nazi government also used legislative, judicial and, finally, physical force against the Jews of Germany. Parallel restrictions on Jewish mobility, economic opportunity and, ultimately, the denial of legal equality stand out sharply in the comparison between Russia of the 1890s and Germany of the 1930s.[14] While it is true that similar restrictions against Jewish life can be discerned in the pre-modern era too, the chief characteristics of nineteenth- and twentieth-century antisemitism, the use of state power through bureaucratic machinery and the ever-present threat of physical violence employed either by the mob or the organs of the state, distinguish these later movements from pre-modern campaigns against the Jews. In fact, an even more direct relationship exists between tsarist antisemitism and the Nazi movement, and that is to be found in their respective presentations of a fully developed, worldwide Jewish conspiracy thesis.

While the idea of Jews conspiring surreptitiously in order to dominate the world is not novel, the notion of a specific organization created in order to implement such an objective does have modern roots and is to be found in both nineteenth-century Tsarist Russia and twentieth-century Nazi Germany. Jacob Brafman, an apostate, working as both a censor of Jewish written works and adviser on Jewish affairs in the office of the governor of the Vilna district in the 1860s, published a series of articles later collected in book form in which he alleged the existence of secret and illegal Jewish communal boards that governed the Jews of Russia. These boards, known as *kehillot* and officially disbanded by Nicholas I in 1844, yet still in existence according to Brafman, not only controlled the behavior of Russian Jewry, but also served as the local arm of the worldwide Jewish government centered in Paris in the Alliance Israélite Universelle.[15]

Russian Judeophobes eagerly repeated Brafman's charges during the decade of the 1870s and disseminated them widely to the Russian reading public through the periodical press of the day.[16] Latent suspicions about the sincerity of Jewish commitments to Russia now came to be verbalized openly, especially in the aftermath of the Polish rebellion in 1863 and the attempt on the tsar's life in 1866. Hence, the groundwork was already prepared for the later publication (1903–5) of Serge Nilus's *The Great and the Small* which contained the full concretization of the Jewish conspiracy thesis wherein revolutionaries were themselves in the pay of Jewish capitalists and worked toward a common objective, that being the overthrow of the established Christian world order.[17]

Fabricated by the tsarist secret police, this text was intended to discredit the revolutionary movement at the turn of the century by intimating that it was a tool of the Jews, used by them as part of their effort to gain dominion first over Russia and then over the whole of the earth. We are offered here the picture of naive and innocent Russian youth being manipulated by treacherous Jewish rhetoricians able to cast their spell over youngsters with noble sentiments but poor political judgment. This association of Jews with revolutionary activity in Russia had become so complete by the turn of the century that pogroms in 1905–6 were now explained by their makers and by other right-wing elements as legitimate efforts aimed at defeating the revolution and defending the true nature of Russia.

Unlike the earlier pogroms, those of 1905–6 were politically motivated.[18] They were part of the effort to defeat the coalition of workers, peasants, conscience-stricken gentry, urban *intelligenty* and national minority groups who had come together in a loose alliance to contest the legitimacy of absolutist tsarist power over the Empire. The upholders of autocracy unleashed their fury against the Jewish community in a series of murderous assaults. The Odessa pogrom of October 1905, which claimed over three hundred Jewish lives, erupted almost immediately after the promulgation of the October Manifesto establishing a parliament (Duma) to be elected by the Russian people, including the Jews of the realm.[19]

This theme of the Jews as revolutionaries or as supporters of political revolution repeated itself in the Ukraine in 1919–20 as anti-Bolshevik nationalist groups identified local Jews as aliens with a pro-Soviet stance, interested only in defeating the national independence movement and bringing the Ukraine under Soviet control.[20] However, the most brutal and destructive expression and implementation of this perspective came with the Nazi invasion of the USSR in June 19441. At that time, the Einsatzgruppen, commissioned to murder all communists as part of the German military campaign against guerrilla warfare, began their work by fanning the flame of popular, nationalist antisemitism in the occupied areas of the USSR. Chiefly, by re-affirming the image of the Jew as an internationalist or as a Bolshevik sympathizer in support of the Soviet takeover of the Baltic Republics in 1940 and of the Ukraine during the Civil War, these German antisemites appealed to long-standing stereotypes that they shared with a sizable portion of the local population. This incitement to pogrom-like activity made it easier for the Einsatzgruppen to concentrate the Jews in German hands and to proceed with their own policy of systematic mass murder.[21]

The similarities and the ties between Russian antisemitism and contemporary western manifestations are unmistakable. Even though some differences remain, the common features whereby Jews are defined in collective and cultural, rather than in religious terms and the close connection, even collaboration of the Jews with the forces of change, be they economic, social or political, overshadow the differences in the two movements. The fact that antisemitism in Russia was not used against liberalism and constitutionalism becomes less important when one realizes that, in the Russian context, these ideas were replaced with other variants of political modernism: socialism and anarchism. And, in Russia, these latter revolutionary movements were clearly identified with the Jews. In both eastern and western Europe then, Jews were seen as agents of change, as the creators of forces intended to uproot the idyllic world of the past. It is true that in Russia, antisemitism never assumed the overtly biological and racial tendencies that it did in the West. However, in the multi-national empire of the tsars, the concept of race and purity of race could never be as widely popular in its political appeal as it was in the West where societies were so much more homogeneous. What remains then is the need for a closer assessment of the modern ideological roots of antisemitism in Russia with the expectation that such an exercise will help to shed light on those shared beliefs or views that surfaced there as well as in Germany, France and Austria.

II

Just as central and west European writers struggled with the issues of personal identity and national community, so, too, did their Russian counterparts. That Russians did so was a curious, even surprising development. It is understandable that such topics should bubble to the surface in the West. After all, in the aftermath of the French Revolution and the destruction of the *ancien régime*, new political realities emerged as new relationships between citizen/subject and state authorities developed. Most important of all, the concept of sovereignty was being redefined and expanded, as power, previously narrowly circumscribed, came now to be extended to wider sections of the population. However, it was not only the case that there was a shift in political philosophy taking place, as larger numbers of people were brought into decision making, but the very geographical boundaries of the state were also recast significantly. Old dynastic borders came to be replaced by new demarcations reflecting the dominant national and ethnic identities of the population residing within the territory in question.

However, such changes did not take place in Russia. It is true that Russian expansion at the end of the eighteenth century to the west, at the expense of Poland and Lithuania, and to the south, at the expense of Turkey, added significant territories and peoples of different ethnic and religious background, including nearly three-quarters of a million Jews, to the population under tsarist rule. However, territorial expansion did not bring with it an expansion of the political rights enjoyed either by the Russian population or the newly added peoples now brought into the Empire. Thus, while Russia participated actively in the Napoleonic Wars and even endured occupation by French forces, the funnel cloud of political upheaval associated with the Revolution and its bearers did not transform the tsarist state. Nevertheless, Russian thinkers of the 1830s and 1840s still found themselves grappling with many of the same issues of identity and community that their western counterparts were struggling with at the same time. However, in Russia those discussions were much more theoretical and abstract than they had been and continued to be in the West.

In those years, two major schools of Russian thought emerged prominently. The Westernizers were identified with the circle around the literary critic Vissarion Belinsky. They insisted that Russia, even though she had not experienced the seminal events or movements associated with western history, such as the Renaissance and Reformation, nor participated in the exploration of the New World nor shared in the scientific and technological revolution of the seventeenth century, had, since the days of Peter the Great, been joined to western life and culture and as such could not escape the impact of recent trends. Accordingly, the Westernizers argued that rather than allow Russia to be overwhelmed by those forces, the country's leadership should prepare for the inevitable and work actively to assimilate the contemporary forces of change constructively into the fabric of Russian life.

Concretely, the Westernizers called upon Russian officials to pursue a course of economic modernization that would stimulate capitalistic development as a means of achieving rapid economic growth, thereby enabling Russia to participate fully and competitively in the new world then dawning in the nineteenth century. Consequently, they believed that the expansion of urban life would lead to the growth of a native commercial and entrepreneurial class which would, in turn, become the foundation upon which a political effort advocating increased individual freedom and liberty for the Russian people could be built. In time, they hoped that this process would transform the Russian political system so that it would become more responsive to and representative of the population of the Empire. According to this view, even though Russia was presently considered "backward," the country was still in an advantageous position. Because she lagged behind the West in development and because she was destined to follow that same path that her neighbors had taken, Russia had the luxury of being able to skip whole stages in the historical process. Rather than expend the effort or the resources needed in research and development, Russia would be able to adapt both modern technology and technique quickly so as to stand alongside her western neighbors in the new world. And, being aware of the problems already experienced by the trailblazers, Russia and her leaders would be in the favorable position of being able either to sidestep troublesome obstacles altogether, or to deal with them before they became too problematic. So it was with a sense of real optimism that these "prophets" looked to the future.[22]

The Westernizers never addressed themselves explicitly to the question of Russia's growing Jewish population. In fact, they did not give very much serious thought to any of the non-Russian people living under tsarism. In this, they conveniently overlooked the very real differences between the multi-national Russian Empire and the more homogeneous nation-states of western Europe. However, since they were liberal-minded and generally sensitive to foreign models and experiences, their approach to the question of the Jews and their future in the society can be readily adduced. As emancipationists and cultural accommodationists committed to the ideas of general societal improvement, these writers would have supported the general theme of Jewish liberation, provided that the Jews then went on to integrate themselves socially and culturally into Russian life.

Because the Westernizers were liberals does not mean that their opposite number, the Slavophiles, were reactionaries. In fact, the Slavophiles were perceived by the government as being equally as dangerous to the autocracy as were the liberals. Thus, the Slavophiles, too, came to be placed under similar conditions of surveillance and harassment. Slavophile publications were subjected to rigorous censorship, and Slavophile meetings and discussions were closely monitored by the government of Nicholas I.

The Slavophile position began with an affirmation of the non-western origins of Russian life and culture.[23] Arguing that Russia, and the rest of the Slavic world, for that matter, had been shaped by the Greek rather than the Roman experience, Slavophiles rejected the validity of the Roman-German model as the appropriate one for future Russian development. Instead, the major Slavophile thinkers, Ivan Kireevsky,[24] Alexei Khomiakov and Constantine Aksakov,[25] insisted on the uniqueness of the Russian experience and sought to delineate a future path for Russia that would not only be independent of the western course, but would also stand in clear opposition to it, as the true means for building a deeply rooted and just society in the modern world.

The Slavophiles began their critique from a religious perspective. They condemned the rationalism they found in the western religious tradition, both in Roman Catholicism and in Protestantism, and saw modern individualism as a false value stemming from this rationalistic worldview. Furthermore, they contended that the infusion of Roman legalism into western religion further undermined the spirituality and the communality of western Christianity. Thus, flawed at its very core, the West, in the teachings of the Slavophiles, was doomed.[26]

Meanwhile, the principal Slavophile writers spoke of true Christianity, as captured in its eastern traditions, in near mystical terms. They emphasized Christianity's role in bringing people together in communities linked by bonds that transcended rational and legal understanding. Slavophile writers stressed the concepts of harmony and human togetherness and saw these values as being the true bases upon which to build the Russian community.

Such harmony always began with a focus on the land as the source for authentic human values. In language borrowed from German romanticism, the Slavophiles stressed the mystical ties that bound a people to the soil of a particular region. This mystical soil/soul connection dominated the formation and character of the community, the folk, and was to serve as the true basis of the ensuing political entity. The first unity was thus that of true Christian fellowship, while the second one was the natural link between a people and its own land. Therefore, based on authentic and natural principles, as understood by the Slavophiles, the Russian community would not later be beset by those internal conflicts that would ultimately tear apart western society because it had been based on inappropriate and unnatural legal agreements. Slavophile thinkers contended that, by following the logic of its cultural and philosophical underpinnings, Westerners had been forced to reduce to contractual terms those relationships and understandings which should have long ago been internalized by the people so as to become the bases of their social and communal life.

As part of their critique, the Slavophiles spared neither the Russian autocracy nor the contemporary Orthodox establishment. In their view, the true Russian state should be the cap on a structure that united the Russian people organically and not administratively. Looking to the past, the Slavophiles focused on the medieval institution of the *zemsky sobor*, a consultative assembly in which the rulers and the ruled both participated, as the authentic basis for the governance of the Russian people. Hence, they dismissed as artificial the prevailing ideology of Nicholas I's Russia, Official Nationalism, even though it was based on the triad of Church, Throne and Russian nationality.[27] From the Slavophile perspective, those official formulations were not authentic expressions of those concepts; rather, they had been fabricated in order to serve political objectives and to justify an oppressive authoritarianism. Thus, even though they opposed western liberalism and its attendant values, Slavophiles did not support the existing form of Russian autocracy either. As a consequence, they, too, came to be subjected to the government's system of police surveillance and literary censorship.

Even though the Jewish community, which had not been permitted to live on Russian lands before the Polish Partitions of the last quarter of the eighteenth century, was now growing larger and larger in both its size and visibility, the Slavophiles did not especially focus on it or its overall relationship to Russia. Yet, at those times when they did have something explicit to say about Jews or Judaism, the Slavophiles did so in hostile terms.[28] For example, on a number of occasions, A. S. Khomiakov termed Judaism the antithesis to true Christianity and he criticized it as being superficial and devoid of true spirituality. Furthermore, he took special pains to attack the seventeenth-century Jewish philosopher Baruch Spinoza as the promulgator of a Jewish materialist worldview that had had a wide-ranging influence upon western intellectuals in the eighteenth century.[29]

Of much greater significance than such comments, though, or other indirect references to Judaism were the implications of the general Slavophile ideology for the future of Jewish life in Russian lands. The fundamental focus within Slavophilism on the Russian people and the assertion that an existing authentic community built on the pillars of land and faith should be the basis for the future Russian state denied to Jews any meaningful place in that picture. The anti-western thrust of Slavophile thought that included the rejection of individualism and the dismissal of the pattern of modern economic and political development as being irrelevant for Russia was a serious obstacle when considering the question of on what foundations the future Jewish equality in Russia could be based. That Slavophiles rejected individualism, western capitalism and political liberalism meant that they had closed off completely the three paths used by the Jews in the West in order to attain full equality. Hence, for Jews to be accorded full status in a Slavophile Russia, an alternative historical path would have to be developed. Clearly, though, Slavophiles were not prepared to find such a path for a community that had always remained alien and outside of the frame of the idealized Slav world.

By focusing on the themes of community and the unique character of Russian history, both the Westernizers and the Slavophiles formulated approaches to the fundamental questions of Russian life that neglected altogether the multi-national character of the existing state. It is true that within the Westernizer position there did exist the possibility of integrating such diverse groups within the larger frame, provided such entities linked their fate to that of the Russian people and accepted the primacy of Russian rule and culture within the state. Of course, this was essentially the *quid pro quo* of emancipation in the West, as well. However, the multi-national character of the Russian Empire made such an equation much more difficult to implement there than it had been in the West. On the other hand, even a theoretical acceptance of the equality of diverse groups was not forthcoming from the Slavophiles. With their point of departure being the people, the folk, and its welfare, they were totally committed to a mythic Russian ideal which focused exclusively on one group, its culture and its ties to that land. The Slavophiles juxtaposed those idealist images and values to both the existing authoritarian tsarist structures as well as to the western models developing beyond Russia's borders, and they found both of those systems wanting.

The bases for an ideological antisemitism in Tsarist Russia in the nineteenth century emerged as a consequence of the visions and approaches adopted by contemporary Russian Slavophiles in their articulation of a Russian path of development. While these visions were intended to be liberating and were to serve as the foundations for the model Russian community of the future, they defined that community in especially narrow terms, thereby denying access to those who did not share its particular cultural or historical heritage. Therefore, the Jews, who in the nineteenth century had, for the first time, become visible within the Empire, now confronted a nativist worldview which denied to them all hopes of ever attaining a status of legal equality or of developing any type of relationship with the Russian people based on mutual respect and acceptance. The commitment to preserving an unsullied Russian state, devoid of alien influences, had maneuvered the Slavophiles into a position of having to assume a stance of enmity toward the Jews. On the bases of their theoretical framework, the Slavophiles had come to identify the Jews as the vanguard of a movement that they rejected categorically. Upon examining their views then, it is fair to say that the very presence of the Jews in Russian lands would be seen as threatening to the future of the true Russian state. Without explicitly making such a statement, the Slavophiles were able to communicate such sentiments clearly to both their readers and admirers.

How then does a movement associated with a limited number of writers restricted to obscure journals, and focused mainly on esoteric philosophical or literary issues become the starting point for that ideological and bureaucratic antisemitism that emerged in the 1880s? In fact, the visions and teachings of Khomiakov, Kireevsky and Aksakov were not encapsulated by the censors or the secret police of the Third Department. The Slavophile heritage was absorbed, popularized and then widely transmitted, especially by Russian Panslavism in the era of Alexander II (1856–1881). While Slavophile ideas were recast in a way that their originators would probably have found objectionable, the fundamental insights and perspectives of Slavophilism, nevertheless, reached sectors of the Russian reading public far beyond those addressed by their originators in their own day. As Michael B. Petrovich, the historian of Russian Panslavism, has written:

The Slavophiles formulated nearly every basic tenet of the Russian Panslavic ideology. It was the Slavophiles who transmitted to the Panslavists the theory of the chosen peoples succeeding each other to primacy in world history—an idea that later Panslavists . . . were to attempt to invest with the authority of scientific truth. Probably the main contribution which Slavophilism made to Panslavism was its division of mankind by cultures and its postulate of a Slavic culture—original, independent and self-contained—whose basic principles were not only distinct from, but opposed to, the basic principles of the Romano-Germanic culture. Slavophile doctrine provided the Panslavists with a delineation of a Slavic way of life which they were to use in judging their brethren abroad.[30]

Panslavism emerged in the public arena during the reign of Alexander II, a time when censorship and police intrusion were considerably relaxed and when Russia embarked on a rapid program of economic development in the aftermath of the disastrous Crimean campaign. While not an original thinker, Ivan Aksakov, brother of Constantine, emerged as the principal disseminator of Panslavist ideologies in the 1860s.[31]

Associated with the four most important Panslavist periodicals of the decade, notably *Parus* (1859), *Den'* (1861–65), *Moskva* (1867) and *Moskvich* (1867–68),[32] Aksakov was both the link to the earlier ideology and its popularizer for his generation. Through his journalistic skills, Aksakov focused the attention of his Russian readers on the larger Slavic world and on Russia's hereditary leadership role in that realm. While it is impossible to measure definitively either the qualitative or even the quantitative input of these publicistic efforts, it is still fair to say that the Russian reading public, whether supportive or even sympathetic to the Panslavist point of view, came to be sensitized to the idea of Slavism through the journalistic efforts of the Panslavists.

Slavic identity and the cause of the oppressed Slavs in the Balkans or under Hapsburg rule were given even greater recognition with the establishment in the 1860s of a number of public benevolent committees formed in order to give humanitarian aid to fellow Slavs. Furthermore, the Moscow Slav Conference of 1867, held in conjunction with an ethnographic exhibition focused on the peoples living on Russian lands, brought delegates to that city from all Slavic areas, with the exception of Poland, in a public celebration of Slavic identity and culture that further stimulated Slavic self-consciousness. While overstated, Ivan Aksakov's immediate assessment of the Slav Conference did convey the importance of that event for Panslavists as part of their effort to shape contemporary Russian consciousness. He concluded, "The greatest, the best result of the Slav visit is that the Slavic Question has penetrated the mind and consciousness of Russian society. It has passed from abstraction to active reality; it has passed from the realm of books into life."[33]

In spite of some indifference to and even official displeasure with Panslavism, especially within the Ministry of Foreign Affairs where the Panslavists were thought to be a nuisance intruding into the foreign policy of the state, the ideas of the movement had gone beyond closed circles of intellectuals and had attained a public dimension that continued to develop over the years. Through Panslavism, both Slavic identity and Slavic culture were being extolled publicly, while other peoples and their cultures were being continuously denigrated and even villified.

Unlike Slavophilism, Russian Panslavism did not have a consistent and clear ideology. When reduced to essentials, however, its attitudes were neither irrelevant nor benign. They were instead the expressions of a Russian cultural and even political imperialism. For some, Russian Panslavism became a narrow, xenophobic articulation of hostility to all ethnic groups different from the idealized Slavic world dominated by Russia. For others, both in and out of government, Russian Panslavism came to mean a heightened form of Russian nationalist chauvinism directed against both external and internal enemies. Unlike Slavophilism, though, Panslavism was never a threat to the existing government. It never challenged the principle of autocracy and never made any serious demands for any form of popular participation in decision making. On the contrary, Russian Panslavists were consistently in favor of a strong central government that would pursue an aggressive foreign policy on behalf of the Slavic people.

The real public impact of Russian Panslavism manifested itself in the 1870s. In the middle of the decade, Panslavists played a crucial role in mobilizing public opinion, such as it was in nineteenth-century Russia, in favor of tsarist intervention in the Balkans on behalf of the Bulgarians and Serbians against the Turks.[34] Raising money, organizing the dispatch of volunteers to the Balkans and pressing the government to be more active diplomatically, and if need be, militarily on behalf of fellow Slavs, the Panslavists were successful in gaining the support of both the Empress and the heir to the throne for their cause during the crisis of 1876. Large sums of

Russian money and numbers of volunteers began to move south in what was almost a crusade-like atmosphere in the summer and fall of 1876. Finally, manipulated by its Panslavist ambassador in Constantinople, N. P. Ignatiev, the man who served as Minister of the Interior in 1882 when the May Laws were introduced, and by feverish propagandistic activity orchestrated by the Panslavists at home, the government of Alexander II went to war against Turkey in the spring of 1877, ostensibly on behalf of the Christian victims of Turkish atrocities.[35] Panslavism had reached the pinnacle of its influence and power.

A recounting of these developments enables us to go beyond the immediate circumstances of 1881 as described by both Aronson and Berk in their studies of the pogroms. We can now establish the mood of the period immediately preceding the pogroms and see the structures out of which those attitudes emerged. As seen, the violence of 1881 cannot be solely attributed to recent economic dislocation and urban unrest or to political instability. Such assessments restrict discussion of anti-Jewish attitudes to local developments only or tie them to cyclical economic trends. In addition, such approaches do not adequately explain the three and a half decades of uninterrupted antisemitism that followed the riots of 1881. Furthermore, explaining governmental antisemitism by focusing on political machinations in the last years of tsarism, or on particular governmental officials, or even aspects of macroeconomics neglects the cultural dimension that seems to transcend time and place, economics and politics, and even personality.[36]

In Russia, the popularization of the Slavophile ideology, mainly through Panslavism, and that movement's success in the 1870s as a disseminator of a national chauvinism, contributed significantly to exciting a Russian national consciousness directed against aliens. These developments were not sudden. They were the end product of decades of thought and discussion, private and public, focused on the nature of Russia and her ultimate future. Now, in the aftermath of a major military campaign fought as a holy crusade, at a time when economic and social change began to be felt by wider and wider segments of the population, and in the immediate wake of the assassination of the Emperor, these developments climaxed with a major eruption directed against the Jews of the realm. While the assault was initiated by the mob, it was followed up immediately by the official authorities who had also come to see the Jews as a threat to the true nature of Russia. Long associated with change, and alien in all categories of classification, the Jews of Russia suffered the full impact of the explosion. The attitudes and emotions associated with an intensified national self-awareness permeated Russian life in the southern part of the Pale to such an extent that even members of the Jewish community came to be influenced by them. However, rather than moving toward despair or self-hate, this heightened sense of national distinctiveness led such Jews to formulate a new theory of Jewish identity based on Jewish nationhood. Thus, one of the initial, and more significant, Jewish responses to the pogroms of 1881, the affirmation of a Jewish national identity with its ensuing call for a Jewish nation-state in order to "normalize" the Jewish community, should also be placed and understood within the context of the modern Russian, including secularized Jewish intelligentsia's search for an authentic national identity in this period.[37]

This highly developed sense of national self penetrated the popular consciousness and reinforced existing stereotypical depictions of the Jew. Heretofore alien on account of his religion, the Jew had now become a cultural alien, too. Thus, the former religious enemy had now been transformed into a political enemy whose own vision of a future Russia, constitutional and built on western models, diverged sharply from the nativist ideology. Thus, the political and material developments of the spring of 1881 were the sparks that set off the kindling already fully prepared to be ignited. And, because the ideology of national exclusivity had penetrated the popular consciousness so thoroughly and because the alternative positions, those espoused by the liberals, were themselves so weak on this question, the effort to stop the blaze was one limited to containment rather than extinguishment.

III

We are now in a position to isolate those critical factors that were truly common to modern antisemitism in Russia and the West. From this discussion, it is clear that neither political nor economic developments were the principal variables. Rather, the issue that really counted was that of "belongingness," of cultural unity and the threat that the Jew posed to it. The fundamental question of the day was that of membership in the new entity, the nation-state. Who may join it? On what terms and conditions and with what consequences? These matters took on the highest priority for ideologues struggling with this new frame within which modern life was to be developed. Directly related to these issues were the next set of problems. These touched on the following: What would the culture of the nation be?

Who would shape its social and political character, and what notions of the past would provide the unifying myths of the present and the future?

Since the nation-state, from the time of its initial appearance, had no commonly agreed-upon boundaries or definitions, the issue of inclusion was always open to debate. When definitions determining membership were narrowly drawn, such as those offered by racists in the West and Slavophiles in Russia, then the possibility of integrating diverse peoples within the group was ruled out. By stressing the cultural development of the historic community, rather than amalgamating all residents into a common union, an exclusionist society was envisioned. This would-be state was not only surrounded by potential foreign foes, but in those lands with a heterogeneous population, the state, it was thought, had serious internal enemies as well. Foreigners might be able to defeat the nation through force of arms. However, the alien, who lived within the organism was even more dangerous because he undermined the very foundation of the group and thereby rendered it defenseless against the outside threat. Hence, the strength of the nation-state was perceived as being related directly to its ability to build a deep and solid structure based upon its own, native community and its authentic way of life.

The development of modern antisemitism, therefore, is directly related to the evolution of a mystical and xenophobic cultural nationalism. In declaring the Jew to be the unassimilable alien, and attributing to him all of the characteristics deemed threatening to the native group, the proponents of such ideologies shared a common worldview: the need to build the nation-state of the future on a firm and authentic foundation. For them, authenticity was to be based on historical roots and not on contractual relationships. Such antisemitism was genuine rather than functional. It was not the case that they used the presence of the Jew in order to attack a particular vision of the state. Instead, in their view, it was the very existence of the Jew within their society that precluded that entity from becoming the kind of genuine organism that would be truly reflective of the idealized folk community that they had envisioned. While related to earlier expressions of anti-Jewish behavior and certainly built upon existing stereotypes, this modern form of antisemitism is significantly different from those previous episodes. Because it denies the possibility of any Jewish integration into the group, modern antisemitism stands apart from any religiously based system of exclusion. After all, in all religious systems, possibilities for conversion are clearly spelled out and are usually encouraged. Conversion brings with it renewal, rebirth and removal of all previous identities or characteristics. Cultural exclusivity, on the other hand, is built on romantic conceptions of intra-human relationships of blood and extra-human relationships of shared cultural values engendered by a mystical interaction with a particular cosmos, the geographical setting in which the people are to be found. This form of cultural nationalism denies the universality of human nature and thus the possibility of any form of conversion or naturalization process that will permit outsiders to enter the inner circle.

The appeals to national character, to a national consciousness and heritage, or to the restoration of authenticity based on national values became the first arguments used by cultural exclusionists in their effort to restrict access to the state. Such phrases surfaced in Russia in the second half of the nineteenth century, just as they did in central and western Europe at that very same time. The search in both locations for that specific group identity upon which the new community in this new age would be built was the common characteristic that prepared the ground for those subsequent anti-semitic convulsions that so shaped our contemporary world.

Notes

A grant from the Faculty of Arts and Sciences Third Term Grants Committee at the University of Pittsburgh facilitated the research for this study. I am most grateful to the members of that committee for their support.

1. Notable practitioners of this antisemitism included Edouard Drumont in France, Wilhelm Marr in Germany and Georg von Schönerer in Austria. Biographies of each are available. See Fredrick Busi, *The Pope of Antisemitism: The Career and Legacy of Edouard A. Drumont* (Lanham, Md., 1986); Andrew G. Whiteside, *The Socialism of Fools: Georg Ritter von Schönerer and Austrian Pan Germanism* (Berkeley, California, 1975); and, Moshe Zimmerman, *Wilhelm Marr, the Patriarch of Antisemitism* (Oxford, 1987). George Mosse's analysis of European racism in the nineteenth century has been especially influential in the development of this essay. See G. L. Mosse, *Toward the Final Solution. A History of European Racism* (Madison, Wis., 1985) [originally 1978].

2. This is the approach developed by Hannah Arendt, *Origins of Totalitarianism* (Cleveland, Ohio, 1958) and continued by other writers including James Parkes, *Antisemitism: A Concise World History* (Chicago, 1963) and P. G. J. Pulzer, *The Rise of Political Antisemitism in Germany and Austria* (New York, 1984).

    This approach could lead some readers to the conclusion that for its practitioners, antisemitism was functional in that it served as the most convenient means to attack the real target, the modern state. Such readers would then argue that if that were the case, then there is no reason to take manifestations of antisemitism and especially its ideology seriously. However, the truth is that for Marr, Drumont, von Schönerer and the other ideologues of antisemitism, the place of the Jew in modern society was the critical issue. In their view then, the Jewish Question was first on the list of concerns that had to be addressed in the transformation of the modern state. Radical antisemites were totally committed to the resolution of what they considered to be the Jewish Question rather than to its mere exploitation.

3. That is exactly what Jacob Katz does in his study *From Prejudice to Destruction: Antisemitism, 1700–1933* (Cambridge, Mass., 1980). Either Katz's approach does not allow him to treat developments in Russia at that time, or he does not deem them worthy of assessment. In either case there is a glaring omission here that makes the title of his work problematic.

4. A convenient summary of the events of 1881 is offered by Steven Berk, *Year of Crisis, Year of Hope: Russian Jewry and the Pogroms of 1881–82* (Westport, Conn., 1985). For readers of Russian, the primary source material has been collected by G. Ia. Krasnyi-Admoni (ed.), *Materialy dlia istorii antievreiskikh pogromov v Rossii* (Petrograd, 1923).

5. I. Michael Aronson has prepared a book-length manuscript "Troubled Waters: The Origins of the 1881 Anti-Jewish Pogroms in Russia," wherein he refutes the thesis that the pogroms were a product of a larger governmental or extra-governmental conspiracy.

6. See I. Michael Aronson, "Geographical and Socioeconomic Factors in the 1881 Anti-Jewish Pogroms in Russia," *Russian Review*, 39 (1980), pp. 18–31. On the role of the contemporary Russian press in the spring of 1881, see John D. Klier, "The *Times* of London, the Russian Press and the Pogroms of 1881–82." *Carl Beck Papers in Russian and East European Studies*, no. 308 (1984).

7. Louis Greenberg, *The Jews in Russia: The Struggle for Emancipation*, vol. 1 (New Haven, Conn., 1944), pp. 73–101.

8. On the commissions, see I. Michael Aronson, "Russian Commissions on the Jewish Question in the 1880's," *East European Quarterly*, 14 (1980), pp. 59–74. Also, see B. Z. Dinur "*Tokhniyotov shel Ignatiev . . .*" [Hebrew], *Heavar*, 10 (1963), pp. 5–12 for a discussion of Minister of the Interior N. P. Ignatiev's approach to the Jewish community in the immediate aftermath of the pogroms.

9. Greenberg reviews the impact of the May Laws in his survey of Russian Jewry. *Jews in Russia*, vol. 2, pp. 30–32.

10. I. M. Dijur, "Jews in the Russian Economy," in G. Aronson (ed.), *Russian Jewry 1860–1917* (New York, 1966), pp. 120–143. See also Arcadius Kahan, *Essays in Jewish Social and Economic History* (Chicago, 1986), pp. 1–70, for a thorough review of the economic and demographic aspects of Russian-Jewish life at the turn of the twentieth century.

11. Greenberg, *Jews in Russia*, vol. 2, pp. 34–38.

12. That expulsion was vividly described by Harold Frederic, *The New Exodus: A Study of Israel in Russia* (London, 1892).

13. Greenberg, *Jews in Russia*, vol. 2, p. 38. Also, see Leo Errera, *The Russian Jews: Extermination or Emancipation?* (London, 1894).
14. Mindful of the Nazi experience, Hans Rogger has assessed the Russian right at the turn of the century in two articles which have been republished in his *Jewish Policies and Right Wing Politics in Imperial Russia* (Berkeley, Calif., 1986), "The Formation of the Russian Right," and "Was There a Russian Fascism? The Union of the Russian People."
15. I. A. Brafman, *Kniga kagala* (Vilna, 1869).
16. John D. Klier, "Iakov Brafman's *Book of the Kahal* and its Enemies," (forthcoming). I thank Professor Klier for sharing an early draft of this article with me.
17. Norman Cohn, *Warrant for Genocide* (New York, 1966), pp. 67–69.
18. E. Semenoff, *The Russian Government and the Massacres. A Page of the Russian Counter Revolution* (Westport, Conn., 1972) [originally, London, 1907].
19. Sidney Harcave has studied Jewish participation in both the election campaign and the subsequent Duma. See his articles: "The Jews and the First Russian National Elections (1905)," *American Slavic and East European Review*, 9 (1950), pp. 33–41 and "The Jewish Question in the First Duma," *Jewish Social Studies*, 6 (1944), pp. 155–76.
20. Peter Kenez, *Civil War in South Russia, 1919–1920* (Berkeley, Calif., 1977). Also, E. Tcherikower, *Antisemitizm un pogromen in Ukraine* [Yiddish] (Berlin, 1923) as well as his larger study, in Hebrew, *Yehudim be ittot ha mahapekhah* [Jews in revolutionary periods] (Tel Aviv, 1957).
21. Wila Orbach, "The Destruction of the Jews in the Nazi-Occupied territories of the U.S.S.R.," *Soviet Jewish Affairs*, 6 (1976), pp. 14–31.
22. This summary reflects a distillation of a number of studies. Most influential have been Richard Hare, *Pioneers of Russian Social Thought* (New York, 1964), pp. 3–83; and Andrzej Walicki, *The Slavophile Controversy* (Oxford, 1975).
23. Hare, *Pioneers*, pp. 83–122 and Walicki, *Slavophile Controversy*, pp. 287–335.
24. On Kireevsky, see the fine biography prepared by Abbott Gleason, *European and Muscovite: Ivan Kireevsky and the Origins of Slavophilism* (Cambridge, Mass., 1972).
25. Walicki's thorough assessment of the three Slavophiles, in *Slavophile Controversy*, pp. 121–283, should be the starting point for all subsequent discussions of Slavophilism.
26. Ibid., pp. 394–455.
27. Nicholas V. Riasonovsky, *Nicholas I and Official Nationality in Russia* (Berkeley, Calif., 1961).
28. The contention that the ideological roots of modern Russian antisemitism are to be found in Slavophilism was developed by Shmuel Ettinger, "*Hareka haidiologi . . .*" [The ideological background . . .] [Hebrew], *Ziyon*, 35(1970), pp. 193–223.
29. See Ettinger's discussion of Khomiakov in "*Hareka . . . .*" pp. 195–96.
30. Michael B. Petrovich, *The Emergence of Russian Panslavism, 1856–1870* (New York, 1956), p. 35.

31. See Stephen Lukashevich, *Ivan Aksakov, 1823–1886: A Study in Russian Thought and Politics* (Cambridge, Mass., 1965).

32. Petrovich, *The Emergence,* pp. 114–15.

33. Quoted by Petrovich from Aksakov's *Moskva* (July 1, 1967) in *The Emergence,* p. 235.

34. B. H. Sumner, *Russia and the Balkans, 1870–1880* (Oxford, 1937), pp. 56–80.

35. William L. Langer, *European Alliances and Alignments, 1871–1890* (New York, 1950) [originally New York, 1931] pp. 66–69, 91, and 111–27.

36. The most recent investigations of Russian antisemitism focus on those political, economic and personal themes. See Heinz-Dietrich Löwe, *Antisemitismus und reaktionäre Utopie: Russischer Konservatismus im Kampf gegen der Wandel von Staat und Gesellschaft, 1890–1917* (Hamburg, 1978), and the work of Hans Rogger in his collection *Jewish Policies and Right Wing Politics in Imperial Russia* (Berkeley, Calif., 1986). See especially the article entitled "Russian Ministers and the Jewish Question."

37. Pinsker's statement, "O grant us only what you granted the Serbians and Romanians, the advantage of a free national existence," in his pamphlet *Autoemancipation* (1882) written in the aftermath of the pogroms, has clearly been influenced by the heightened Panslavic agitation in Southern Russia in the 1870s and the recently concluded Russo-Turkish War.

[10]

Antisemitism in Crisis Times in the United States: The 1920s and 1930s

Leonard Dinnerstein

The worst period of American antisemitism was sandwiched between the ends of World War I and World War II. Societal changes in the 1920s, the Great Depression of the 1930s, and the anxieties during the Second World War intensified and exacerbated attitudes that had already manifested themselves earlier. These hostile feelings coalesced from the 1920s through 1945 at such an accelerated pace, however, that many Jews thought that what happened in Hitler's Germany might very well occur in the United States as well. Though preposterous, such fantasies fueled fear and the increased incidents of bigotry and discrimination whipped the Jewish people in America into a frenzy of panic. Some chose to deal with the problem by changing their names and trying by other means to hide their origins; others believed that the best policy was to "lie low" and not be "too Jewish" in public; but the overwhelming majority of Jews in America in those years were East European Jewish immigrants and their children who could not disguise themselves, whose children were still in school, and who struggled mightily to earn a living and get through their day-to-day lives.

Jews living through the 1920s and 1930s may not have been able to step back and analyze their situation in the context of societal change. But when one looks at the various indications of discontent during the period it is easy to see that antisemitism, a problem by itself, was also one aspect of the

212

intolerance Americans showed in the decades after World War I. Dissent and difference were to be shunned and suppressed. All of the following smacked of bigotry and intolerance: Prohibition, the Red Scare, the outrageous nature of the trial of Sacco and Vanzetti, the Palmer Raids, the prevalence of the Ku Klux Klan, the rigidities of the Fundamentalists as expressed in the Scopes trial, the Immigration Restriction Acts of 1921 and 1924 designed to curb entry, especially of East European Jews and Southern Italians, and the election campaign of 1928 in which fantastic rumors circulated that, if elected President, Al Smith would hold a daily mass on the White House lawn and that a tunnel would be built between the Vatican and Washington and the Pope would bicycle back and forth. Antisemitism was part and parcel of these expressions of hostility toward the foreigner and the outcast. But it was something more as well. Jews were much more upwardly mobile than any of the other European immigrant groups who had come to the United States in the late nineteenth and early twentieth centuries. They were seen as parvenus who really might take over businesses, country clubs, residential areas, and universities if not reined in. There was a measure of jealousy in both WASP attitudes and expressions by other immigrants whose lives had not fared as well as those of the Jews.

Since the Colonial era Americans had always displayed a cultural schizophrenia toward the Jews. Welcomed because white people were needed to help build a society in the wilderness, Jews were also scorned for having denied the truthfulness of Christian teachings. Centuries of indoctrination convinced most other white Americans that Jews were not only rejectors of the Savior but usurers concerned primarily with money who were willing to take their "pound of flesh." The Shylock image of the economic exploiter came along with the Christian one. (A politician in Tucson recently told me that he had grown up in a small town in Indiana and before going to college all he ever knew about Jews was that they had killed Christ.) But Colonial America needed people, and so in most of the colonies Jews may have been distrusted and regarded as a people apart, and precluded in some colonies from pursuing the professions of medicine and law or voting in public elections, but they were not otherwise handicapped. In fact, on occasion they participated fully in society and voted where the laws specifically stipulated that only Christians were entitled to the franchise. Even after the American Revolution an oath indicating belief in the divinity of Christ prohibited Jews from voting in Maryland until 1826, in Rhode Island until 1842, and in New Hampshire until 1877.

Tolerance and acceptance of diversity are also part of the American creed but not always part of individuals' experiences in this country. Although Americans have often waxed eloquently about freedom of religion, and neither state nor federal laws have ever stipulated otherwise, Mormons and Catholics, among others, were often victimized by bullies and ruffians who did not want them in their midst. Jews, on the other hand, were never as a group manhandled before the late nineteenth century. To be sure, several Christian societies wanted to convert them, politicians and Justices of the Supreme Court spoke out frequently about the United States being a Christian nation, and credit bureaus gave Jews low ratings simply because of their religion, but on the whole Jews prospered, remained among themselves when they lived in cities in appreciable numbers, and both intermingled and intermarried with Christians where their numbers were slight. (Both the first and second wave of Jewish immigrants to Richmond, Virginia, in the eighteenth and nineteenth centuries witnessed the disappearance of their groups as children remained single or married Christians.)

Not until the Civil War were there major outbursts against Jews in this country. But then, in both North and South, Jews served as convenient scapegoats for the frustrations of others. General Ulysses S. Grant at one point expelled all Jews from western Tennessee (the order was later rescinded by President Abraham Lincoln) and in the South, Confederate Attorney-General Judah P. Benjamin was often attacked as being responsible for the problems in the Confederacy.

In the late nineteenth and early twentieth centuries the increased numbers of immigrants and the rapid industrial changes combined to frighten Americans into thinking that their way of life was being significantly changed by societal forces beyond their control. Jews loomed large as one of those groups Americans reacted most strongly against. By the 1920s, Jews were feared as both capitalists determined to take over control of the economic system and communists who wanted to undermine American values.

Manifestations of these prejudices were seen first in exclusion from social and patriotic organizations (like New York's Union Club or Pittsburgh's Duquesne Club; the Sons of the American Revolution and the Daughters of the American Revolution), in exclusion from resort areas, and in physical attacks upon Jews in various parts of the country. The former practices affected the middle and upper classes, the latter mostly the immigrants. But as the newcomers began to move from the bottom of the social classes into the middle levels of society, prejudice and discrimination became much more apparent and quotas became customary after World War I in some of the areas where the immigrants and their children were likely to appear in numbers viewed too close for comfort: pleasant residential areas, country clubs, desirable employment fields, and many of the northeastern universities.

President A. Lawrence Lowell of Harvard, an early supporter of the Immigration Restriction League and its Vice President since 1912, brought the issue of university restrictions to public attention in 1922 when he advocated limits upon the enrollment of students who were not the social peers of those young men who usually attended the school. A significant number of students and faculty agreed with his position because they feared a "New Jerusalem" and an undermining of Anglo-Saxon tradition might result if scholarship alone became the criterion for admission. Many WASPS complained about the Jews, who spoke with foreign accents, had "unpleasant personalities," or undermined the "social prestige" of their universities. As one articulate alumnus explained, "so far as the classroom is concerned, Jewish students are one thing; but at the 'prom,' or the class-day tea, the presence of Jews and their relatives ruins the tone which must be maintained if social standing is not to collapse." Another WASP expressed the same sentiment somewhat differently: "The Jew sends his children to college a generation or two sooner than other stocks, and as a result there are in fact more dirty Jews and tactless Jews in college than dirty and tactless Italians or Armenians or Slovaks."[1]

Regardless of the words or phrases used, what most of the elite universities seemed to fear in the 1920s was that the "pushy" Jews, who "had little training in the amenities and delicacies of civilized existence," might inundate their schools. As a result, throughout the country rigid quotas were established to prevent these institutions from being overrun by people these universities considered undesirable, and this led to a steep decline in the percentage of Jews attending private colleges and universities. While this made less difference, in the long run, at the undergraduate level, it created severe hardships when these restraints were applied to the professional schools: Jews constituted 46.92 percent of the student body at Columbia's College of Physicians and Surgeons in 1920; they totaled only 8 percent in 1940. Other medical and dental schools showed similar declines. The percentage of CCNY graduates who applied, and were admitted, to medical schools throughout the country fell from 58.4 percent in 1925 to 15 percent in 1939. In 1930 fewer than 20 percent of CCNY's Jewish graduates who applied, but

75 percent of the Gentiles, were accepted into medical school. By 1945, 75 percent of Gentile applicants, but only one in thirteen Jewish applicants were accepted into United States medical colleges.[2]

It was also during the 1920s that Henry Ford's *Dearborn Independent* began its crusade against the "International Jew" with the publication of the "Protocols of the Elders of Zion." According to the "Protocols" Jews had an affinity for Bolshevism, manipulated economic and political power, and were determined to undermine the world order. They allegedly favored alcoholism, spread pornography, subverted Christian principles, and would no doubt take over American government and society if allowed to do so. Jews constituted, according to the *Dearborn Independent*, the "world's foremost problem." For more than six years Ford's publication railed against the alleged vices of the avaricious and scheming Jews and probably would not have relented even later in the decade had it not been for the adverse fortunes of the Ford Motor Company which experienced severe business losses as a consequence of Ford's antisemitism. Ford then sent his representatives to New York to find out with whom he could negotiate in order to retract his bigoted remarks and was put in touch with Louis Marshall, President of the American Jewish Committee. Marshall dictated the nature of the apology desired, Ford complied, and the *Dearborn Independent* ceased its diatribes against the Jews. But the apology could not erase the years of attacks and the ceaseless tirades, as Leo Ribuffo reminds us, "spread the notion that Jews menaced the United States."[3]

The 1920s also witnessed outbursts of antisemitism from other extremists and respectable members of society alike. Jews were looked upon as "a group apart . . . perennial strangers"[4] and therefore legitimate scapegoats for the frustrations and prejudices of a wide variety of Americans. Moreover, the sharply nationalistic focus of the United States in the decade after World War I had no tolerance for deviants of any kind and Jews were simply not Christians. When a Jewish student at the University of Illinois requested permission to use the school's athletic fields which were closed on Sundays the Dean of Men informed him, in 1920, that "this is a Christian country established upon Christian traditions and this is an institution backed largely by Christian communities"[5] and for those reasons the field would remain closed. A minister told the Presbyterian Ministers Association meeting in Philadelphia in 1922, that Jews and Roman Catholics were plotting to do away with Bible reading in the schools.[6] In Pocatello, Idaho, a Klan leader openly threatened to expel Jews and Catholics from the city while in Denver, Klansmen proclaimed that Jews could never be real Americans.[7] Employment agencies carefully screened non-Protestant applicants, while one factory owner informed a survey taker: "We try to have only white American Christians in our factory regardless of religion."[8] The savagery of extant feelings may have been summed up by H. L. Mencken, who expressed his own opinion that "the Jews could be put down very plausibly as the most unpleasant race ever heard of. As commonly encountered they lack many of the qualities that mark the civilized man: courage, dignity, incorruptibility, ease, confidence. They have vanity without pride, voluptuousness without taste, and learning without wisdom. Their fortitude, such as it is, is wasted upon puerile objects, and their charity is mainly a form of display."[9]

The 1920s, however, were only a warm-up for the next decade when an "ominous new wave of anti-Semitism" occurred. Antisemites "everywhere went on the offensive" Henry Feingold tells us, and "Christian" campaigns, physical attacks on Jews, and violent propaganda advocating force and violence ran rampant. The hysteria against Jews spread from society to schools to offices to shops and to factories. Exclusion of Jews from privileges and communal enterprises became even more intense and the professions of banking, engineering, and even teaching were "closed to all but a few." "According to the records compiled from twenty-seven thousand cases by a Christian placement specialist, ninety out of each hundred Jewish applicants to the employment agencies are disqualified by their Jewishness without regard to their other qualifications." In 1936, *Fortune* magazine observed that "leading members of the Jewish community in the United States—men who had previously looked to the future with confidence—have been shocked into fear. The apprehensiveness of American Jews has become one of the important influences in the social life of our time." Three years later, *Time* commented "that talk about anti-Semitism has grown like a weed in the U.S. during the last decade is a fact that no well-informed U.S. citizen can truthfully deny. Yet the U.S. press has for the most part studiously, purposefully and almost universally ignored the subject." And a year later, in 1940, the American Jewish *Congress Bulletin* indicated that "at no time in American history has anti-Semitism been as strong as it is today."[10]

The reasons for the increased antipathy toward Jews in the United States may be attributed both to the economic depression of the decade and the propaganda spread by Hitler and the Nazis, but one must not ignore those other forces that had coalesced after World War I ended—the intensification of immigration restrictions, the so-called scientific proofs of Anglo-

Saxon superiority as expressed in the writings of Madison Grant, Theodore Stoddard, and Kenneth Roberts, and the increased associations of the Jews with radicalism in general and communism in particular. Furthermore, the depth of antisemitic feelings came not only from the ravings of the lunatic fringe, but with the voices of respectability like publications representing the Protestant and Catholic churches. [11]

Both Protestants and Catholics were united in their antisemitic feelings in the 1930s as they had never been before. Antisemitism became "no more unfashionable than white racism," employers routinely refused to hire Jews, and a Christian New Englander confessed that although he had lived for "over forty years in a country where 'something would have to be done about the Jews'" and had "been surrounded by and part of a passive anti-Semitic multitude of Christians," only in the 1930s did a concerted effort arise to do something about it. A liberal Protestant journal, *The Christian Century*, also embarked upon a campaign to do something about the Jews. It ran a series of essays castigating them in the 1930s and in one, in 1937, an editorial read: "We hold that the Jew himself" is responsible for the Jewish problem. "The first step toward its recognition is to discern that his determination to maintain a permanent racial strain is incompatible with democracy." Jews lived under an "illusion," the writer continued, that they "are the object of the special favor of God." "If this racial group feels that way about itself," the editorial went on, "and insists upon living apart in biological and cultural, as well as religious, aloofness, let it take the consequences." [12] (It is noteworthy that in the 1930s Jews were still regarded as a separate race.)

Catholics, too, showed no love for the Jews. They condemned them for supporting the Republicans in Spain, favoring liberal causes, and for supposedly being rich. The *Catholic Transcript* of Hartford, Connecticut, wrote in 1937, "The Jews . . . are hated because they are too prosperous, too successfully grasping. . . . They are the richest men in the world." The notorious Catholic priest, Charles E. Coughlin, advised followers that "the 'sons of Jewry' wielded great influence in every walk of life . . . particularly in all fields of communication," and Catholics were also told "to avoid exposure to the Jewish dominated newspapers and to avail themselves exclusively of Catholic newspapers." Coughlin would later reprint the "Protocols of the Elders of Zion" in his *Social Justice* (July 1938) and in a November 1938 radio address "launched a slashing, full-scale, anti-Semitic crusade, accusing the Jews not only of devising Communism but also of imposing it on Russia, and excusing Nazism as an understandable effort to block the Jewish-Com-

munist Plan for subjugating Germany." Such bigotry as expressed by Coughlin and other Catholics resulted in the formation of the Christian Front
organization in the big cities of the East and also in the assault of Jewish
youth by Irish toughs in the late 1930s and early 1940s in cities like Boston
and New York.[13] It also led to a rebuke by the Unitarian *Christian Register*
which observed, "The Roman Catholic Church represents the most powerful
organization of bias anywhere to be found."[14]

Not to be ignored, either, in contributing to American antisemitism was
the rise of Nazism in Germany. Although Hitler may have been unpopular
in the United States, his views of Jews were not. And whereas before 1933
there were no official antisemitic organizations in this country, by 1939 over
one hundred existed, including the German-American Bund, the Silver
Shirts, the National Union for Social Justice, the Knights of the White
Camellia, and the Christian Front. "It was in the extremist groups openly
aping the Nazis," historian Melvin Urofsky later observed, "that the anti-
Semitism of the 1930s found its most sensational expression."[15]

The depth of the depression also permitted employers to discriminate in
their hiring practices to an extent that had never been done before. To be
sure, Jews had difficulty in finding some types of jobs earlier, but with the
advent of large numbers of well-educated Jewish professionals barriers were
more firmly erected in the academic, legal and medical fields. In addition,
the major industries just about cut Jews out entirely from the upper echelons
of the corporate structure. Despite these facts, however, *Fortune* magazine
still felt it necessary to publish a major article showing that Jews did not
monopolize economic opportunity in the United States.[16] As usual, people
with prejudices did not allow facts to disturb their opinions. A 68-year-old
retired rubber worker in Akron, Ohio, admitted to an interviewer, "I don't
know what's the matter with me, but I hate the sight of a Jew. They control
the money of the United States." And *The Nation* reported: "an important
businessman with a reputation for liberalism said recently: 'The Jews are the
cause of all our troubles in this country and I wish that every one of them
could be deported.'"[17]

Perhaps the most obvious indication of antisemitism is the denunciation
of President Franklin D. Roosevelt's program as the "Jew Deal." Over and
over again, in a variety of contexts, political opponents of the President
linked his administration with some kind of nefarious Jewish conspiracy and
even where accusations were totally without foundation, nonetheless continued to spout forth their uninformed opinions. One outstanding example of

this was the denunciation of the President himself as having "Jewish blood." An article entitled, "Roosevelt's Jewish Ancestry," stated that the President was descended from Rosenbergs, Rosenbaums, Rosenblums, Rosenvelts, and Rosenthals. "Not infrequently," Marquis Childs later wrote, "the Roosevelt phobia is linked with anti-Semitism and an anti-labor attitude. 'The President has brought a lot of radical Jews to Washington and they're running the government.'" Thus those uncomfortable with the new labor policies and a liberal woman in the Cabinet, who could not be attacked directly because of her sex, stooped to condemning her alleged Jewish origins. The Secretary of Labor, Frances Perkins, tried to handle the charges with aplomb. "If I were a Jew," she announced publicly, "I would make no secret of it. On the contrary, I would acknowledge it."[18]

But Roosevelt and Perkins were not the only targets. Those who opposed the New Deal often condemned the President for being guided by Jewish liberals who formulated and executed administration policies. Lewis Douglas, for example, Roosevelt's first Director of the Budget Bureau, attributed the flaws in the early New Deal to the "Hebraic influence" in the administration. "Most of the bad things which it has done can be traced to it. As a race they seem to lack the quality of facing an issue squarely."[19] The names of Felix Frankfurter and Benjamin V. Cohen, both close associates who had the President's ear, were cited as proof of Jewish control. These accusations, slurs about Jews in government, and condemnation of Jewish professionals were found among every class of the population and in all sections of the country. Father Coughlin may have complained about "the Tugwells, the Frankfurters and the rest of the Jews who surrounded the President," but others found the large numbers of Jewish lawyers disconcerting. One person told an interviewer, "You can't find an official in the whole [government] who hasn't got a damn Jew lawyer sitting by him at his desk." W. M. Kiplinger, in a special article on the subject, agreed that "men who are Jews occupy very influential positions" in Washington but he quickly acknowledged that "there is no such thing as a 'Jewish influence' in Washington." Nonetheless he argued for a reduction in the proportion of Jews who were working in government because 4 percent of the federal employees were Jewish yet they constituted only 3 percent of the nation's population. "Inherently it may not be wrong," Kiplinger argued, "but it looks wrong to have any public offices manned by people of any particular group."[20]

Public opinion polls had already underscored what Kiplinger discussed. Jews were believed to be too powerful and adding to their existing "power."

Americans viewed Jews both as controlling and as being unfair and dishonest in business, of having too much money, of being too grasping, having bad manners, being clannish, aggressive, overbearing, noisy, and generally unpleasant. To the question, "Do you think Jews have too much power in the United States?" asked regularly by poll takers in the 1930s and 1940s, those answering affirmatively increased from 41 percent in March 1938, to 55 percent in February 1946.[21]

To his credit, the President went against popular prejudices and made his appointments to office based on skills and talents that he thought he needed. To be sure, the overwhelming number of his appointees to all offices were Protestants, but unlike his predecessors he did not shun Catholics and Jews and members of both of those groups found greater opportunities in his administration than they had ever before known in Washington. Furthermore, many of the most visible of his associates, Samuel Rosenman, Felix Frankfurter, Ben Cohen, and Secretary of the Treasury Henry Morgenthau, Jr., were also Jewish. American Jews appreciated these open associations and revered Roosevelt for his apparent lack of bigotry and willingness to stand by them when no other leader was willing to do so. (His attitudes and policies toward Jewish immigrants and Holocaust victims is another question which did not surface in the United States until 1967 when Arthur Morse published his book, *While Six Million Died.*)[22]

But no prominent business, religious, or government officials spoke out strongly against the enormous amount of antisemitic fervor in this country. To be sure, Secretaries of Labor and the Interior, Frances Perkins and Harold Ickes, respectively, surrounded themselves with Jewish subordinates in policy-making positions, but neither one took anywhere near as much heat as Roosevelt who was extremely sensitive to the accusations of presiding over a "Jew Deal," but who could not respond to the charges directly.

Jews in the United States may have loved Roosevelt for appointing coreligionists to office and not yielding to the nation's bigots, but they were also increasingly frightened by the animus they saw all about them. Many of their leaders thought that if Jews shed their foreign characteristics and appeared indistinguishable from other Americans, Christians might think more highly of them. Their hopes were in vain but their efforts, in retrospect, appear pathetic. They ceased publishing statistics on how much money they raised for Jewish charities and talked endlessly with one another on how to end the existing prejudices and rumors and that there was a Jewish-communist plot to overthrow the government. They made every effort to disassociate themselves from foreign groups and causes, including those Jews being persecuted in Germany. Efforts were made to promote ethical conduct among other Jews, to encourage non-citizens to become citizens, to discourage their brethren from engaging in left-wing politics, and to promote brotherhood and understanding among all faiths. In Indianapolis, also, some Jews even petitioned the Dean of the Indiana University Medical School to recommend fewer Jews for internships so that there should not even be the slightest indication that Jews might be favored over Christians. (To his credit the Dean turned down such a preposterous suggestion.) [23]

On the eve of America's entry into the Second World War, Judge Jerome Frank, one of Roosevelt's appointees to the Federal courts, wrote an embarrassing article for the *Saturday Evening Post* in which he tried to disassociate most Jews from things Jewish. "American Jews," he told readers, "voice the same opinions as their non-Jewish neighbors, see the same movies and root for the same ball teams. Cultural assimilation, through the adoption of non-Jewish ways of thinking, feeling and acting, is then, developing rapidly, despite the existence of persons and groups identifiable as Jewish." He claimed that "the majority of those American Jews who are not immigrants have rejected all or most of the old Jewish customs" and labeled those who supported the idea of a Jewish state in Palestine as "a small group of fanatic Jewish nationalists." Frank claimed that for those who chose the path of Reform Judaism, "what remains of the historic Jewish religion consists principally of some noble ethical principles and spiritual values . . . to call them 'Jewish' is to be a pedantic antiquarian." He was proud, he noted, that "his religion is actually closer to liberal Protestantism than to Jewish orthodoxy," and he wanted to share with *Post* readers the fact that "in virtually all respects" the life of the "Reformed" Jew "follows the same pattern as that of his next-door Christian neighbor." [24] Frank's revealing analysis of how many Reform Jews felt received hardly any attention because the day after publication the Japanese attacked Pearl Harbor and Americans of all stripes had totally different subjects with which to concern themselves.

The question must be asked now, as I summarize my observations, why antisemitism surfaced as it did between the two world wars. I think there are several reasons. As I pointed out at the beginning of this chapter, the climate of opinion that developed after World War I was extremely hostile to foreign radicals and non-WASPs. The Bolshevik Revolution in Russia frightened Americans and created a heightened sensitivity to anyone suspected of too liberal a bent. Jews were one of those groups most closely linked with liberalism and radicalism even while they were still being denounced as capitalist manipulators. The 1920s also saw the coming to maturity of many of the children of turn-of-the-century East European immigrants who sought educations in prestigious schools and jobs in prominent firms. People who always used to be on the other side of the tracks were now competing, in large numbers, for places that had traditionally been reserved for scions of the WASPs.

Early religious training about Jews being Christ-killers also came to the fore and extremists denounced New Deal programs as radical and Jewish at the same time. Furthermore, there were more articles and comments critical of Jews in respectable Protestant and Catholic periodicals than had ever before appeared in such numbers. Hitlerism also came to America in the 1930s. What the Nazi bunds were saying was quite similar to the expressions of *The Christian Century* and the diatribes of Father Coughlin and other Catholics. Thus the voices of Nazism found congenial soil and a not hostile response for their message. Still another point that needs to be gone over is that many of the non-Jewish immigrants to the country who arrived in the late nineteenth and early twentieth centuries, as well as those who had come to this country earlier, possessed strong antisemitic feelings of their own. The American climate in the 1930s encouraged the expression of these feelings. And, finally, the depths of the Depression created such havoc and hopelessness that the presence of Jews, both in and out of government, provided the spark necessary to ignite a desperate people in search of a villain. As one prescient commentator observed at the beginning of the New Deal years, the nation was "undergoing the worst economic crisis in the history of the United States. To paraphrase Voltaire, if there were no Jews, it would be necessary to create them in order to have a scapegoat for the desire of the masses to vent an impotent rage against bad times."[25]

By the end of the New Deal years, just before the beginning of World War II, an astute reporter wrote, "the conviction is growing in Washington that an organized campaign of intimidation and terror has been undertaken in America against the Jews."[26] No responsible observer at the time would have disputed the remark.

The war interrupted the worst attacks on Jews, though they certainly continued into the early 1940s. But the decision of American Jewry to organize and strike back, made in 1943 and 1944, combined with a changed postwar atmosphere, resulted in a reversal of the antisemitic attitudes and policies that only a decade earlier had many Jews believing that "it can happen here."

Notes

1. Morton Rosenstock, "Are There Too Many Jews at Harvard?," in Leonard Dinnerstein, ed., *Antisemitism in the United States* (New York: Holt, Rinehart & Winston, 1971), pp. 102, 103; "May Jews Go to College?" *The Nation*, 114 (June 14, 1922), 708; Ralph Philip Boas, "Who Shall Go to College?" *Atlantic Monthly*, 130 (1922), 446; Stephen Steinberg, "How Jewish Quotas Began," *Commentary*, 52 (September, 1971), 74; Henry Feingold, *Zion in America* (New York: Hippocrene Books, 1974), p. 266.

2. Steinberg, "How Jewish Quotas Began," pp. 72–74; "Anti-Semitism at Dartmouth," *New Republic*, 113 (August 20, 1945), 208; Frank Kingdom "Discrimination in Medical Colleges," *American Mercury*, 61 (October, 1945), 392, 394, 395; Morris Freedman, "The Jewish College Student: 1951 Model," *Commentary*, 12 (October, 1951), 311; Dan W. Dodson, "College Quotas and American Democracy," *American Scholar*, 15 (July, 1946), 269; M. F. Ashley Montague, "Anti-Semitism in the Academic World," *Chicago Jewish Forum*, 4 (Summer, 1946), 221–22; Alfred L. Shapiro, "Racial Discrimination in Medicine," *Jewish Social Studies*, 10 (April, 1948), 134; Lawrence Bloomgarden, "Medical School Quotas and National Health," *Commentary*, 15 (January, 1953), 31.

3. Leo P. Ribuffo, *The Old Christian Right* (Philadelphia: Temple University Press, 1983), pp. 10–11; anonymous source; Ribuffo, "Henry Ford and the International Jew," *American Jewish History*, 69 (June, 1980), 437.

4. Bruno Lasker, "Jewish Handicaps in the Employment Market," *Jewish Social Service Quarterly*, 2 (March, 1926), 174.

5. Quoted in Jacob M. Sable, "Some American Jewish Organizational Efforts to Combat Anti-Semitism" (Unpublished Ph.D. dissertation, Yeshiva University, 1964), p. 55.

6. Minutes of the American Jewish Committee's Executive Committee, 4, Part 3, (1923), p. 1044.

7. Ibid., (May 27, 1923), p. 1099; Feingold, *Zion in America*, p. 2170; Ribuffo, *The Old Christian Right*, p. 12; Michael W. Rubinoff, "Rabbi in a Progressive Era: C. E. H. Kaiwan of Denver," *The Colorado Magazine*, 54 (Summer, 1977), 234, 236.

8. Quoted in Lasker, "Jewish Handicaps in the Employment Market," p. 171.

9. Quoted in Heywood Broun and George Britt, *Christians Only* (New York: The Vanguard Press, 1931), pp. 276–77.

10. Feingold, *Zion in America*, p. 270; Johan J. Smertenko, "Hitlerism Comes to America," *Harper's Magazine*, 167 (November, 1933), 661; Editors of Fortune,

"Jews in America," reprinted in Leonard Dinnerstein and F. C. Jaher, eds., *The Aliens* (New York: Appleton-Century-Crofts, 1970), p. 230; "Hush-Hush Ends," *Time*, 33 (May 8, 1939), 52; David Brody, "American Jewry, the Refugees and Immigration Restriction (1932–1941)," in Abraham J. Karp, ed., *The Jewish Experience in America* (5 volumes; Waltham, Mass.: American Jewish Historical Society, 1969), vol. 5, p. 336.

11. Ribuffo, *The Old Christian Right*, p. 9; Feingold, *Zion in America*, p. 266.

12. William Manchester, *The Glory and the Dream* (Boston: Little, Brown, 1974), p. 8; "The Shadow of Anti-Semitism," *The American Magazine*, 128 (November, 1939), 92; "Jewry and Democracy," *Christian Century*, 54 (June 9, 1937), 735; Smertenko, "Hitlerism Comes to America," p. 661; *Newsweek*, 13 (January 19, 1939), 13–14; Feingold, *Zion in America*, p. 266.

13. J. David Valaik, "In the Days before Ecumenism: American Catholics, Anti-Semitism, and the Spanish Civil War," *Journal of Church and State*, 13 (Autumn, 1971), 468, 473; *Catholic Transcript* quoted in Oswald Garrison Villard, "Issues and Men," *The Nation*, 148 (April 22, 1939), 470; Melvin I. Urofsky, *American Zionism: From Herzl to the Holocaust* (Garden City, N.Y.: Anchor Press/Doubleday, 1976), pp. 373–74; David H. Bennett, *Demagogues in the Depression* (New Brunswick: Rutgers University Press, 1969), pp. 279, 280.

14. Quoted in *Time*, 31 (June 13, 1938), 55.

15. Norton Belth, "Problems of Anti-Semitism in the United States," *Contemporary Jewish Record*, 2 (May–June, 1939), 9; Urofsky, *American Zionism*, p. 374.

16. Feingold, *Zion in America*, p. 266; Myron I. Scholnick, "The New Deal and Anti-Semitism in America," (Unpublished Ph.D. dissertation, Department of History, University of Maryland, 1971), p. 27; Smertenko, "Hitlerism Comes to America," p. 661; *Newsweek*, 13 (January 19, 1939), 13–14; Editors of Fortune, "Jews in America," pp. 229–47.

17. Alfred Winslow Jones, *Life, Liberty, and Property* (Philadelphia: J. B. Lippincott, 1941), p. 274; "Anti-Semitism Is Here," *The Nation*, 147 (August 20, 1938), 167.

18. "Anti-Semitism Is Here," p. 167; Richard Yaffe, "The Roosevelt Magic," *The National Jewish Monthly*, 87 (October, 1972), 31; George Wolfskill and John A. Hudson, *All But the People* (New York: Macmillan, 1969), chapter three; Scholnick, "The New Deal and Anti-Semitism in America," pp. 83–84; Paul W. Ward, "Washington Weekly," *The Nation*, 143 (November 7, 1936), 540; Marquis W. Childs, "They Still Hate Roosevelt," *The New Republic*, 96 (September 14, 1938), 148; Benjamin Stolberg, "Madame Secretary," *Saturday Evening Post*, 213 (July 27, 1940), 10; George Martin, *Madame Secretary* (Boston: Houghton Mifflin, 1976), 399.

19. Quoted in Robert P. Browder and Thomas G. Smith, *Independent: A Biography of Lewis W. Douglas* (New York: Alfred A. Knopf, 1986), p. 111.

20. T. R. B., "Washington Notes," *The New Republic* (January 10, 1934), 250; E. Digby Baltzell, *The Protestant Establishment: Aristocracy and Caste in America* (New York: Random House, 1964), p. 248; Scholnick, "The New Deal and Anti-Semitism in America," pp. 76–77; "Anti-Semitism Is Here," p. 167;

Wolfskill and Hudson, *All But the People,* p. 86; *The New Dealers by an Unofficial Observer* (New York: The Literary Guild, 1934), p. 322; Michael R. Beschloss, *Kennedy and Roosevelt* (New York: W. W. Norton, 1980), p. 120; Albert Jay Nock, "The Jewish Problem in America. II," *The Atlantic Monthly,* 168 (July, 1941), 74; W. M. Kiplinger, "The Facts about Jews in Washington," *Reader's Digest,* 41 (September, 1942), 2–3.

21. "The Fortune Survey: XX," *Fortune,* 19 (April, 1939), 104; "Confidential Report on Investigation of Anti-Semitism in the United States in the Spring of 1938," pp. 12, 13, 28, 38, American Jewish Committee Archives, New York City; Leonard Dinnerstein, "Anti-Semitism Exposed and Attacked, 1945–1950," *American Jewish History,* 71 (September, 1981), 135.

22. Leonard Dinnerstein, "Jews and the New Deal," *American Jewish History,* 72 (June, 1983), 475; Arthur D. Morse, *While Six Million Died* (New York: Random House, 1967).

23. Minutes of the American Jewish Committee's Executive Committee, 7 (June 2, 1939), 128; Brody, "American Jewry, the Refugees and Immigration," pp. 342, 344, 347; Judith E. Endelman, *The Jewish Community of Indianapolis* (Bloomington: Indiana University Press, 1984), pp. 173, 174, 175.

24. Jerome Frank, "Red White and Blue Herring," *Saturday Evening Post,* 214 (December 6, 1941), 83, 85.

25. Smertenko, "Hitlerism Comes to America," p. 662.

26. Michael Straight, "The Anti-Semitic Conspiracy," *The New Republic,* 105 (September 22, 1941), 362.

1918 and After: The Role of Racial Antisemitism in the Nazi Analysis of the Weimar Republic

Steven T. Katz

Post-1918 Europe was a breeding ground for conditions in which racial theory and political reality converged. The final coalescence of these two vectors after 1933 was neither "fore-ordained" nor "historically inevitable," but rather, one of the fecund possibilities that a traumatized and exhausted post-war Europe generated. The forces and personalities that could have acted to prevent this victory, that could have brought about some other scenario, failed the test, leaving Nazism, and its phantasmagoric racial doctrines, victorious.[1] The causes of this devastating eventuality lie inherent in the fact that from 1918 to the *NSDAP* seizure of power, German political and social life was caught up in a series of crises and contradictions, eight general elections between June 6, 1920 and March 5, 1933[2] being symptomatic of the instability that plagued Weimar and from which it could never extricate itself. The consequence of these unsettled circumstances was the radicalization of German life in all its public modalities, necessarily including those affecting the Jewish community,[3] and not least the formulation and articulation of various types of antisemitism. The conservative and more restrained style of the Wilhelmine period now gave way to an era of unbridled polarization of expression and action on both the left, e.g., Eisner's revolution,[4] and the right, e.g., the Kapp Putsch of 1920,[5] and again Hitler's failed 1923 Putsch. In this environment racial antisemitism, in particular, was given a new and uncontrolled life.[6] And it is with its character and manifestation that we shall concern ourselves for the remainder of this chapter.

To advance our understanding of this obscene, yet powerful, phenomenon, it is essential to analyze four repercussive historical *topoi*. They are: (a) the defeat of 1918 and Jewish behavior in World War I; (b) the Versailles Treaty and the conditions of peace; (c) the stereotype of the Jew as revolutionary; and (d) the caricature of the Jew as supranational capitalist.[7] On the face of it this limited but inclusive list, except for those particulars created by the war, contains a by-now standard conservative indictment of "the Jews." However, in the transformed context of 1918 and after, each of these polemical elements stands under the ominous shadow of an ever more virulent racialism. "Blood mixture and the resultant drop in the racial level," Hitler would write in the 1920s, "is the sole cause of the dying out of cultures; for men do not perish as a result of lost wars, but by the loss of that force of resistance which is contained only in pure blood."[8]

I

The Defeat of 1918. A large segment of German society, especially among those who had fought in the war, could not assimilate the stark reality of defeat.[9] German national chauvinism, allied with individual and class egotism, made it impossible for considerable sectors of the populace to admit that weakness which the defeat represented.[10] Therefore, to account for the disaster that had occurred, this community required another, alternative explanation, and they found one readily at hand.[11] The nation had been betrayed from within by leftists,[12] unpatriotic profiteers, pacifists and, above all (and overlapping with the other categories), the Jews.[13] It was the Jews, the disloyal aliens *par excellence*, who, with the aid of their corrupt leftist puppets, had consciously administered the fateful "stab in the back" which had undermined Germany's ability to wage a successful war.[14] This despite the remarkable, even disproportionate enthusiasm German Jews had showed for the war, and their major participation in it. Eighty thousand Jews had served in the Kaiser's army, a tremendous patriotic effort given the size of the total German Jewish population which numbered just over 500,000.[15] Moreover, of those who served, 12,000 had died and no fewer than 35,000 had been decorated,[16] while at home Jews like Rathenau and Haber played major roles in the organization of the war economy. Yet all this was forgotten, even impugned. A German soldier reports his quite typical view of the reasons for the defeat:

The way the war ended we simply could not understand. I was resigned to the disloyalty of the Poles (which I had encountered during the war) but could never grasp how Germans could let us down. Today I know better. There were people who once called themselves Germans and now pledge loyalty to another people if necessary. They taught our German brothers lies and hatred. They stabbed our soldiers in the back. The German Siegfried found his murderer . . .

Captivity [in a POW camp] is death and freedom means life, or so I thought in those days. But I soon noticed the chains slung around our poor people and recognized our slave-masters. The first official to meet me at home was a Jew who talked very fast and praised the blessings of the revolution. I replied with hard and bitter words but was not yet completely aware of the role of the Jews. Years of observation and, at last, reading my "Führer's" book *Mein Kampf* fully opened my understanding for the fateful mole-like activity of these corrupters of the earth.[17]

. The terms of the Peace following upon this humiliating defeat saddled the Weimar Republic with a burden it could not carry, not least a "guilt by association" in the minds of many who, illogically, held the Republic to be the result of the war betrayal and its aftermath. According to this logic, the Republic was the creation of those same leftists[18] and Jews[19] who acted with nefarious intent in 1918 and before. As a consequence, the post-war leadership inherited a political debt which eventually helped overwhelm it, while making it vulnerable almost from its inception. Over and over, every national issue became a "Jewish" issue, every motion or proposal, especially if prompted by actions taken by the allies, became an act of "International Jewry." For example, when the Dawes Plan was accepted by the Reichstag with the support of President Ebert, Ludendorff railed: "This is a disgrace to Germany. Ten years ago I won at Tannenberg. Today they [the Weimar liberals and allies] have won a *Jewish Tannenberg*."[20] This cant was symptomatic of the politics of the anti-republican camp. All right-wing parties, i.e., from the *Deutschnationale Volkspartei*[21] rightwards, would exploit this putative Jewish connection, this vulnerable element within the immature democratic structure, until Weimar's final collapse. As early as 1919, the *Deutschnationale Volkspartei* had called for the rejection of "the predominance of Jewry in government and public life, which since the revolution [of 1918] has become increasingly ominous. The influx of aliens [eastern Jews] across our border is to be cut off."[22] In exploiting this sensitive issue, however, no one was as strident or as successful as Hitler. For him, while the German army and the Kaiser had made specific tactical errors, the real cause of the defeat of 1918 lay in the racial degeneracy that overtook the Kaiserreich in its final phase.

> The deepest and the ultimate cause for the ruin of the old Reich was found in the non-recognition of the race problem and its importance for the historical develop-ment of the people. For events in the lives of the nations are not expressions of chance, but, by the laws of nature, happenings of the urge of self-preservation and propagation of species and race, even if the people are not conscious of the inner reasons for their activity . . . .
>
> If we let all the causes of the German collapse pass before our eyes, there remains as the ultimate and decisive cause the non-recognition of the race problem and especially of the Jewish danger.
>
> The defeats in the battlefield of August, 1918, would have been easily bearable. They were out of proportion to the victories of our people. Not the defeats have overthrown us, but we were overthrown by that power which prepared these defeats by robbing our people systematically, for many decades, of its political and moral instincts and forces which alone enable and entitle peoples to exist in this world.
>
> The old Reich, by inattentively passing by the question of the preservation of the racial foundations of our nationality, disregarded also the sole right which alone gives life in this world. Peoples which bastardize themselves, or permit themselves to be bastardized, sin against the will of eternal Providence, and their ruin by the hand of a stronger nation is consequently not an injustice that is done to them, but only the restoration of right. If a people no longer wants to respect the qualities which Nature has given it and which root in its blood, then it has no longer the right to complain about the loss of its worldly existence . . . .
>
> All really important symptoms of decay of the pre-War time ultimately go back to racial causes.[23]

It is imperative to understand Hitler's argument correctly, to locate his perversion of the truth properly. For his biocentric contention embodies and gives voice to not only or even primarily a radical political critique of Weimar and the traitorous clique of 1918 peacemakers, but rather and more elementally expresses his primordial conviction that political behavior was an epiphenomenal manifestation of one's racial nature. The disaster of 1918 was not properly analyzed as a political error or as the effect of a failure of national will, but rather as the "catastrophic consequence of a moral and ethical poisoning."[24] The language of deconstruction is not social and polit-ical, nor again economic and class directed, but biological.[25] Race, "blood," was the decisive arbiter. "Heroically our people won the war," Hitler de-claims. "It took four and a half years to poison our people to the point that it defeated itself." And again, "How could a people that waged such heroic battles lose its national spirit all at once? Through moral contamination by the Jews."[26] It was in this sense that he saw himself as a "servant of the German people against the mortal enemies of our people, against Jewish blood—and race poisoning."[27] He declared that "to dispose of the evil mushroom [Jewry] . . . the evil must be grasped by its root." That is, "solving the Jewish problem is for us National Socialists the core problem. This problem cannot be settled by tenderness, but in view of the enemy's fearful weapons only by brachial violence."[28]

> If at the beginning of the war and during the war, twelve or fifteen thousand of these Hebraic corrupters of the nation had been subjected to poison gas such as had been endured in the field by hundreds of thousands of our very best German workers of all classes and professions, then the sacrifice of millions at the front would not have been in vain. On the contrary, twelve thousand scoundrels eliminated at the right moment and a million orderly, worth-while Germans might perhaps have been saved for the future.[29]

It was only thus that Germany could "efface the poison outside and inside of us" which would make recovery possible.[30] This racial analysis was believed by its proponents to explain the present malaise and the source of national humiliation as could no other. Still more importantly, having revealed the nature of the disease only the Nazi party could propose the correct therapy.[31]

II

The Versailles Treaty. The Versailles Treaty, whether rightly or wrongly, was an unexpectedly harsh blow to Germany. "No subject," Gordon Craig has correctly observed,

> agitated the textbook writers more or gave them a better excuse for oblique attacks upon the Republic than the Versailles Treaty. This was inevitable, for there were few Germans who were not left aghast when its terms were revealed. Having placed their faith in the American President and convinced themselves, by an extraordinary feat of wishful thinking, that the decisions made at Paris would be guided by the spirit of reconciliation that he had expressed in the speech announcing the Fourteen Points, they were outraged to discover that the victors intended to apply that older principle of settlement, *vae victis*. Most indignant, naturally, were those who had least cause to complain, the people who had luxuriated in the most grandiose dreams of conquest and material acquisition during the war. But even more reasonable persons, who had expected the terms to be severe and had even believed that their country deserved to be punished, were shocked by what appeared to them to be the Entente's flagrant violation of their own declarations (for example, in their plundering of Germany's colonial empire), of the facts of history (in their attribution of

exclusive responsibility for the war to Germany and its allies), and of the rules of economic reason (in the horrendous load of reparations that the war-guilt clause was intended to justify), and were left incredulous by their apparent lack of interest in the question whether Germany was to become a viable democracy or not (else why would they heap these indignities upon the new Republic?).[32]

And, of course, in the treaty conditions[33] lay many, though by no means all, of the difficulties never overcome by the Republic.[34] How could such a monstrous, purposely demeaning[35] treaty, unconnected with the real military situation, have been negotiated? Who would have accepted such a "syphilitic peace?"[36] Certainly not a "true German." Again it was the *Dolchstoss*[37]—the betrayal. Candidates for this role were not hard to conjure; a familiar list was paraded out with "the Jews" at the top, cited especially as manipulators of the Republic and as its chief beneficiaries. Indeed, this contended linkage, this putative Jewish influence, even domination, was fatal for the Republic. Already as early as the election of 1920 this association began to take its negative toll, with the right-wing parties successfully exploiting it in their campaign rhetoric to undermine the electoral support of the three pro-Weimar parties whose share of the vote fell to that of a minority position with only 43.6% and 206 out of 459 parliamentary seats. By contrast, the right-wing, anti-Republican parties gained 33% of the vote and 157 seats and the anti-Republican left 20% of the vote and 87 seats.[38] This lamentable outcome provided a deeply wounded basis for Republican government.[39]

Once the Church had used "the Jews" as the symbol of antithesis and negativity; now this was the fashion of all segments of German society opposed to the treaty. Typical is this description of events given by a German soldier returning home:

The partisan squabbles took an even greater hold of the people. The Jews had laid such a foundation and they had managed to prepare all this inner corruption behind the facades. Wherever you looked, wherever you went to talk to people, you found Jews in the leading positions.

And so I was seized by such a tremendous hatred that once, in 1922 at a war invalids' meeting, I launched into the open struggle against the Jews without realizing in my innermost mind the consequences to which their regime would take us. I began to search. I bought books that threw some light on the Jewish way of life and its goals. I studied Freemasonry and discovered that, according to the documents handed down, this terrible war had long been prepared and planned. Although they tried to tell us that the war was our fault, I suddenly realized that it was all a game of intrigues, a net of lies without equal in world history.[40]

Still more significant, Hitler never forgot nor forgave the signing of the Versailles Treaty. Paradigmatic of his unwavering feelings in this regard is his *völkisch* commentary of 1923: "The Versailles dictate is the death sentence for Germany as an independent state and as a *Volk*."[41] And again in *Mein Kampf*:

While the international world Jewry slowly but surely strangles us, our so-called patriots shouted against a man and a system which dared, in one corner of the earth at least, to free themselves from Jewish-Masonic world embrace and oppose a nationalistic resistance to this international world poisoning . . .[42]

By this last phrase—"international world poisoning"—Hitler means to refer to "Jewish control" over Britain, Europe, Russia of course, and even America—except for "a single great man, [Henry] Ford"[43] (at least in the first edition of *Mein Kampf*, before Ford recanted his antisemitic nonsense in the face of a Jewish boycott of his Model T).[44] A control must be especially exercised along racial lines:

[One] *must open their eyes on the subject of foreign nations and must remind them again and again of the true enemy of our present-day world. In place of hatred against Aryans, from whom almost everything may separate us, but with whom we are bound by common blood . . . it must call external wrath upon the head of the foul [Jewish] enemy of mankind as the real originator of our sufferings. It must make certain that in our country, at least, the mortal enemy is recognized and the fight against him a gleaming symbol of brighter days, to show other nations the way to salvation of an embattled Aryan humanity.*[45]

The Treaty of Versailles is seen, as is here evident, not as a political contract between nations, but as a declaration of racial war by Jews against Aryans. To evade its deadly intent, to overturn its funereal ambition, mere political transformations are inadequate; only a racial revolution will suffice. *"Today it is not princes and princes' mistresses who haggle and bargain over state borders,"* i.e., it is not a simple national struggle but rather, *"it is the inexorable Jew who struggles for his domination over the nations."*[46] This biological line of thought, this racial meditation on the rise and fall of nations, of mastery and servitude, is again clearly expressed in *The Secret Book* of 1928. There, reflecting on the implications of the Versailles Treaty, Hitler observes:

in opposition to the present bourgeois conception that the Treaty of Versailles has deprived our people of arms I can reply only that the real lack of weapons lies in our pacifistic-democratic poisoning, as well as our internationalism, which destroys and poisons our people's highest source of power. For the *source of a people's whole power does not lie in its possession of weapons or in the organization of its army, but in its inner value which is represented through its racial significance, that is the racial value of a people as such.*[47]

And the unmistakable meaning of this genetic-normative axiom is this:

Blood mixing and lowering of the race are then the consequences which, to be sure, at the beginning are not seldom introduced through a so-called predilection for things foreign, which in reality is an underestimation of one's own cultural values as against alien peoples. Once a people no longer appreciates the cultural expression of its own spiritual life conditioned through its blood, or even begins to feel ashamed of it, in order to turn its attention to alien expressions of life, it renounces the strength which lies in the harmony of its blood and the cultural life which has sprung from it. It becomes torn apart, unsure in its judgment of the world picture and its expressions, loses the perception and the feeling for its own purposes, and in place of this it sinks into a confusion of international ideas, conceptions, and the cultural hodge-podge springing from them. Then the Jew can make his entry in any form, and this master of international poisoning and race corruption will not rest until he has thoroughly uprooted and thereby corrupted such a people. The end is then the loss of a definite unitary race value and as a result, the final decline.[48]

Fate played a cruel trick on the Jewish people in this unhappy circumstance; it placed Walter Rathenau, self-hating Jew yet Jew nonetheless to all the antisemites,[49] in the position of German Foreign Minister in 1922, decisive "evidence" that Weimar was a *Judenrepublik*. ("The sudden outbreak of *Judenkoller* tends to occur," Peter Merkl's study shows, "most often among respondents complaining about the new Weimar leaders or about social disintegration in 1918.")[50] Whether rightly[51] or wrongly,[52] Rathenau felt himself honor bound, on behalf of Germany, to abide by the terms of the treaty:

We Germans are obligated by our signature, by the honor of our name that we have placed under the treaties. We will fulfill and we will go to the limit of our ability in order to preserve the honor of our name, which stands affixed to the treaties, and we recognize their binding character even though they do not express our wishes.[53]

This support of the agreement was held as little short of treasonous by the vocal antisemitic nationalist and rightist groups both within and without the Reichstag. General von Rabenau would express this broadly when, after Rathenau's murder, he wrote "The nomination of this ethnic alien [was] a sharp challenge to those Germans mindful of their race."[54] The assassination of Rathenau[55] would not, of course, prevent the French from occupying the Ruhr in 1923[56] as a consequence of Germany's failure to abide by its treaty obligations,[57] but it could be manipulated to keep alive the myth of betrayal.

And why were the Jews so inclined to betray Germany? Because of Jewry's racially motivated supranational, conspiratorial loyalties, of which more below, bred of biological rather than national allegiance. The truth, of course, was decidedly otherwise. Jews in the disputed territories in the east, assigned to Poland, and in the west assigned to France, continued their fierce loyalty to Germany. In the eastern districts in particular, Jews spared no efforts in order to maintain their connection to Germany, including joining in the underground free-corps units that fought to keep these areas German. When polled in the League of Nations plebiscites they overwhelmingly voted to remain part of Germany, and when this did not happen many, at great personal cost, emigrated to German territory.[58] In this behavior, it should be added, they replicated a by-now nearly century-old pattern according to which Jews tended to favor Prussian rather than Polish rule. For example, after the 1848 revolution Jews in Poznan and related regions, mindful of Polish antisemitism, pogroms and the exploitive nature of the *szlachter* (Polish aristocracy), sided with the pro-German nationalists.[59] Tragically, all these, and other, profound and purely motivated expressions of that German-Jewish symbiosis[60] so real to most German Jews were ignored, and then ploughed under by the racialist bands that eventually won the day.

III

Jews as Revolutionaries, Marxists and Bolsheviks. Closely allied to the charge of Jewish defeatism and disloyalty was the accusation that Jews were revolutionaries of one left-wing variety or another whose sworn purpose was to undermine the established order and its values, replacing them, in turn, with a "Jewish" form of government which would invert the economic and power relations between Aryans and Semites. The significance of this issue was made real by the revolutionary events in Bavaria in November 1918, the leaders of which would forever be known as the "November Criminals" in the jargon of the right, and credited with the defeat of 1918 and much more. Begun in naval circles in Kiel,[61] the revolutionary mood spread to Munich, where a coalition of left-wing groups, led by the socialist Kurt Eisner, took power on November 8, and to Berlin, where a national republic was declared on November 10, and an armistice with France agreed on November 10 and signed on the eleventh.[62] This, in turn, unleashed a civil war between factions of the extreme Communist[63] left and a coalition of the republican right,[64] finally resolved with the defeat of the Communists in

1919, that radicalized and divided German society along political lines as never before.[65] In the eyes of those on the right, this division was the work of the Marxists and Jews (the two being more often than not interchangeable) who were intent on destroying German culture as they knew it.

This stereotypical reaction reflected a peculiar amalgam of empirical evidence and paranoia. The hard data were supplied by the reality of events in 1918–1919 Germany as well as the legitimate fears generated by the Bolshevik revolution[66] of 1917. For, was not Eisner a Jew, Liebknecht and Rosa Luxemburg Jews, Landauer and Kautsky Jews?[67] Again was not Zinoviev, Trotsky, and for many Lenin, a Jew? One of the Abel interviewees reports: "When in 1918 the Marxist revolution broke out . . . the Spartakists dressed as sailors, raged and destroyed everything . . . they were headed by Jews."[68] Paranoia was sparked off because the Eisner-Spartakist action was seen as conforming to, and confirming, a mythic paradigm of Jewish-Marxist world revolution and eventual domination. In this Eisner and his colleagues supposedly mirrored and replicated the age-old pattern of Jewish revolutionary behavior.[69] Hitler's fantasies on this score, indebted as they were to Rosenberg and Eckart, and the *Protocols of the Elders of Zion*, knew no bounds. For example, his account of the Exodus from Egypt was based on the notion that the Jews were expelled for preaching revolution, while the Jew Paul "virtually invented Christianity in order to undermine the Roman Empire . . ." Likewise, Hitler argued, "the Old Testament already provided the pattern of the Jewish assault upon the superior, creative race, a pattern repeated again and again down the ages."[70] With this ancient, inherent design revealed, the racial critics argued, the November revolutionaries were now unmasked, their eternal, undeviating nature and their degenerative purpose exposed. And Hitler's rancid imaginings were not his alone. Eckart could refer assuredly to "the Christian-Kosher-butchering dictatorship of the Jewish world savior Lenin";[71] the *Deutsche Völkischer Schutz-und-Trutz Bund* could disseminate in good conscience a German translation of the *Protocols*, resuscitate charges of ritual murder, and reissue Rohling's slanderous *Talmudjude;*[72] popular novelists like Arthur Dinter and Gustav Freytag[73] could become wealthy exploiting the theme of Jewish racial-sexual pollution of Aryan women; and Theodore Fritsch could continue to issue ever-new editions of his rabidly antisemitic *Handbook*. At the same time, the police, courts,[74] army,[75] schools, churches and universities[76] could all fall back on the idiom of racially inspired subversion. Consonant with this shrill racist mythology the *Münchener Beobachter* of October 4, 1919, in rhetoric now

typical of the extreme right-wing press, could report on contemporary revolutionary events as follows:

[These are] dreadful times in which Christian-hating, circumcised Asiatics everywhere are raising their bloodstained hands to strangle us in droves! The butcheries of
Christians by the Jew Issachar Zederblum, alias Lenin, would have made even a
Genghis Khan blush. In Hungary his pupil Cohn, alias Bela Kun, marched through
the unhappy land with a band of Jewish terrorists schooled in murder and robbery, to
set up, among brutal gallows, a mobile machine gallows and execute middle-class
citizens and peasants on it. A splendidly equipped harem served him, in his stolen
royal train, to rape and defile honorable Christian virgins by the dozen. His lieutenant Samuely has had sixty priests cruelly butchered in a single underground room.
Their bellies are ripped open, their corpses mutilated, after they have been plundered
to their blood-drenched skin. In the case of eight murdered priests it has been
established that they were first crucified on the doors of their own churches! The
very same atrocious scenes are . . . now reported from Munich.[77]

Revolution and the chaos it unleashed were uniquely the work of the
Jews. Hitler, employing this explanatory archetype, perceived the Russian
revolutionary situation and its immensely destructive consequences wholly
in racial terms. "Here Fate itself seems desirous of giving us a sign," he
writes.

By handing Russia to Bolshevism, it robbed the Russian nation of that intelligentsia
which previously brought about and guaranteed its existence as a state. For the
organization of a Russian state was not the result of the political abilities of the Slavs
in Russia, but only a wonderful example of the state-forming efficacy of the German
element in an inferior race. . . . For centuries Russia drew nourishment from this
Germanic nucleus of its upper leading strata. Today it can be regarded as almost
totally exterminated and extinguished. It has been replaced by the Jew. Impossible as
it is for the Russian by himself to shake off the yoke of the Jew by his own resources,
it is equally impossible for the Jew to maintain the mighty empire forever. He himself
is no element of organization, but a ferment of decomposition. The giant empire in
the east is ripe for collapse. And the end of Jewish rule in Russia will also be the end
of Russia as a state. We have been chosen by fate as witnesses of a catastrophe which
will be the mightiest confirmation of the soundness of the folkish theory.[78]

Still more generally, writing in 1928, Hitler declaims, "The economic conquest of Europe by the Jew was pretty much completed around the turn of
the century, and now he began to safeguard it politically." This means,
according to the governing biocentric logic, the "attempt to extirpate the
national intelligentsia . . . in the form of revolution." Everywhere in Europe, beginning with his successful campaign in Russia, the Jew has the same
subversive design, assisted by "Marxism, democracy and the so-called Chris-

tian center" which are, in reality, only the Jew's "shock troops"[79] in this struggle for domination. Given this awesome association of Jews, Bolshevism, and left-wing revolution, Hitler's description of the meaning of National Socialism is apt and chilling: "[The aim of National Socialism] is very brief: Annihilation and extermination of the Marxist worldview."[80] A prescription which for Hitler meant, certainly, the Marxist-Jewish worldview. Should there be any doubt about this intimate, inseparable association in his perverted deciphering of world events, I recall, from many possible examples, his continuous, and for him necessary and inescapable, linkage of Jews and Marxism. Thus in his rabid remarks in *The Secret Book* regarding "the Marxist defilers of culture . . . in the South Tyrol . . . [who] have let the theater sink to the level of a brothel, into sites of demonstrated race defilement . . . [who] let German literature sink into mud and filth," he concludes his diatribe by suggesting that these Marxist culture corrupters have "surrender[ed] the whole intellectual life of our people to international Jewry."[81] Similarly, in *Mein Kampf* he moves effortlessly from "the Social Democratic Press . . . directed predominantly by Jews" to "this type of Marxist press production";[82] while again in *The Secret Book* the fateful connection is drawn: "The end of the Jewish world struggle . . . will always be a bloody Bolshevization."[83] Ever and again in his rhetoric it is the fault of the Jewish-Marxists, the "Jewish-God-denying Marxists,"[84] and their subservient minions.

The real as well as distorted association of Jews with the extreme revolutionary left was enough to poison the more authentic collaboration of Jews with moderate socialist parties such as the *SDP* (*Sozialdemokratische Partei Deutschlands*) in which they did play a considerable role. It is estimated that 10% of the *SDP* Reichstag representatives during the Weimar period were Jews.[85] To the antisemite, however, such nuanced distinctions regarding alternative and quite varied socialist affiliations were irrelevant, while to the mass of uninformed citizens the connection of Jews and Marxism was only further reinforced by the perception of Jewish involvement in socialist politics. It should, however, be noted that, in contradistinction to this prejudiced construal, the actual reality was that Jews as a group overwhelmingly voted for centrist parties.[86] Even during and after the Depression this pattern, in general, remained constant.

Yet, truth aside, the grotesque stereotype of the revolutionary Jew was fixed: he was the embodiment of negativity, he destroyed the political order, exploitatively manipulated the world economy for selfish gain, eroded the foundations of true morality, opposed God and His Church, sexually corrupted all peoples, created internal social strife and caused civil war, worked to invert the natural order, sought to impose the base on the noble, the ignominious on the ideal and above all attempted to racially poison the nations of the world, thereby guaranteeing his own victory. Should he triumph, however, his conquest would be illusory for, given his parasitic and necessarily destructive nature, ultimately he must consume even himself. "If with the help of his Marxist creed," the future Führer tells his Weimar audience, "the Jew is victorious over the peoples of the world, his crown will be the funeral wreath of humanity and this planet will, as it did millions of years ago, move through the ether devoid of men."[87]

IV

The "Supranational" Jew. The putative racial distinctiveness of the Jew, given the governing and immutable postulates of the racial analysis of nationality and national history, made it impossible for the Jew to be seen as a loyal, integrated member of any state. His racial destiny, the genetic and meta-genetic imperatives to which he was subordinate, demanded his transcendence, or subscendence, of national parameters at the same time that they required that he work for the exploitation of all political entities in his own self-interest. In this ontological necessity rooted in blood lies the ground of his alliance with revolutionaries and revolution, though it extends even beyond the Marxist-Revolutionary category. For according to the logic of extreme racial antisemitism, the Jew's meta-political nature is a telling symptom of his normative standing outside the ordinary universe of obligations and rights normally imposed by national criteria and definition. Not belonging to any polity (other than that of the Jewish people), the Jew feels no obligations to any civic morality, and thus, conversely, he exists outside the accepted realm of human rights. Accordingly, the human transactions between the Jew and others are ethically anachronistic, with the consequence that the juridical and ethical premises that otherwise apply to intergroup relations do not obtain in the case of political relations with Jews and the Jewish community. Recognizing this, the Jew-hater seeks to reverse the entire process of emancipation that has occurred since the French Revolution, the erroneous axiomatic basis of which is the human equality, the fundamental anthropological sameness, of the Jew. "A rational antisemitism," Hitler would therefore write, "must lead to the systematic legal fight against and the elimination of the prerogatives of the Jew. . . . Its ultimate goal, however, must unalterably be the elimination of the Jews."[88]

This call for disemancipation was, of course, not invented in its generality by the antisemites of the Weimar era. What the post-1918 generation did witness, however, was a deepening of the political exclusiveness envisioned by such a program as a consequence of the new emphasis on the racial nature of this heretofore largely socio-political question. When the *Judenfrage* was thus transformed into a meta-biological issue, its very character was transmogrified to such an extent that it eventually fed, after many unexpected and unpredictable turns, a genocidal rather than a national-exclusivist (i.e., one that favored disenfranchisement and expulsion) teleology. Ahaseurus, according to classical Christian anti-Judaism, had to wander, had to be made to wander, but his life was inviolate and his journey could end through his adoption of the true faith. By contrast, Hitler and the racial ideologues of the right after 1918 spoke in a new and different idiom. On the one hand they repeated the slogans about legal disenfranchisement, e.g., the *NSDAP* Party Program of February 24, 1920 called for the end of all Jewish gains in civil status achieved since Emancipation as well as the deportation of the Jews under certain conditions, while, on the other hand, they also spoke far more ominously about "eliminating the Jews altogether."[89] This extremism found voice because Jewish racial corruption could not be warded off simply by keeping it at arm's length, or even by some mysterious process of "conversion," for race, especially the assault of microbial racial infection, could not be neutralized by expulsion nor rendered harmless by dunkings in the baptismal font. "With the Jews there can be no bargaining, but only the hard either-or."[90]

Above all, it needs to be understood that, from the Hitlerian perspective, the Jewish assault on the nations of Europe was racial rather than national in character and victory came not through conquest but through pollution. A polluted people becomes weakened and thereby enslaved, genes not armies decide the fate of the world. In this light

the highest purpose of the folkish state is its care for the preservation of those racial primal elements which, by providing culture, create the beauty and dignity of a higher humanity. We, as Aryans, are therefore able to imagine a state only as the living organism of a people [*Volkstum*] which not only safeguards the preservation of that people, but which by a further training of its spiritual and ideal abilities, leads it to the highest freedom.[91]

In speaking here of freedom Hitler, as ever, is not referring to the freedom of the individual but rather to that of the state and to its primordial basis the *Volk*. Understanding this, one is able to comprehend the pseudo-organic meaning he attributes to the state: "The German Reich, as a State, should include all Germans; it has not only the task of collecting from the people the most valuable stocks of racially primal elements and preserving them, but also to lead them, gradually and safely, to a dominating position."[92] By comparison, "the final goal," Hitler writes of Jewish racial supranationalism, "is denationalization, is sowing confusion by the bastardization of other nations, lowering the racial level of the highest, and dominating this racial stew by exterminating the folkish intelligentsias and replacing them by members of his own race."[93]

Going still further, it must be understood that for Hitler, and here we summarize a more complex conceptual deconstruction of the metaphysical dogmatics of Nazism,[94] the Jews are not merely human enemies, but incarnations of the principles of darkness and chaos that transcend all that is human and virtuous and thus their transcendence of the nation, that structure through which men give form to their lives and through which they protect their racial purity, is in keeping with their inner and essential nature. As such, their supranationalism, their "internationalism," is reflective of the metaphysical *Kampf* between the "human," the racially pure, most authentically represented by the Aryan, humanity's highest fruit, and the non-human Jew. "If our people and our state become victims of these bloodthirsty and avaricious Jewish tyrants of nations, the whole earth will sink into the snares of this octopus."[95] The Jew is external, systematically and naturally alien, not only to Germany or France, to this nation or that, but to all nations, all units of human fellowship, all circles of noble and "pure" blood. It is for this reason, predicated on this ontological decipherment of Jewish supranationalism, that the stakes are so high in the Aryan-Semite encounter: "if Germany frees herself from this embrace [of the octopus], this greatest of dangers to man may be regarded as broken for the whole world."[96] Israel is not only another human competitor and her potential victory means not only economic exploitation, colonial oppression and political domination; rather, and far more serious, with all the gravity of a pathogenic catastrophe: "Judah is the plague of the world."[97] And why is Jewry such a dire threat? Because she encourages in her own self-interest "Blood mixing and lowering of the race. . . . For this reason internationalmindedness [read Jews] is to be regarded as the mortal enemy of these [noble racial] values."[98] Or put differently, the nation ideally emerges from the *Volk,* while the Jew, in the name of the nation, would destroy the *Volk* through miscegenation.

In pursuit of his ends the Jew's assault on nations [and *Volk*] takes, in addition to the manifestations of revolution and induced chaos, two additional, significant forms. The first is as economic exploiter, a theme with particular resonance in inflation-ridden and then depression-bound Weimar. The second is as degenerator of culture, the all-powerful destroyer of the virtuous and sublime. The theme of economic corruption needs little elaboration; its untruth has been made a cliché, but it is no less decisively destructive for that. Neither did it matter that in fact the German Jewish community was seriously impoverished by the same economic gyrations that caused havoc within the population at large. The number of upper-middle-class Jews, for example, judging by the tax register, dropped nearly 50% during the 1920s. In 1912, 10.6% of Berlin Jews earned over 5,000 marks a year; in 1924 this number had fallen to 5.8%, while the number of Jews with incomes under 1,200 marks jumped from 73.3% of the Jewish population to 83.6%. In addition, the Berlin Jewish community alone was forced to open nineteen soup kitchens and seven shelters for the homeless.[99] Donald Niewyk has also pointed out that "signs of [economic] decline within the Jewish middle class were by no means confined to the years of inflation and depression" but continued throughout the later years of the Weimar era.[100]

Nonetheless, though the hyperinflation destroyed the lives of Jews and non-Jews alike, this indiscriminate economic victimization proved an enormously effective tool for antisemitic propagandists. Both in 1923 and then even more importantly after 1930, inflation, wedded to the other deep civic and political dislocations of the Weimar era, caused a social vertigo in which people lost their sense of place and order, finding eventual re-equilibrium only in Nazism's preachments about righting the existing economic and related wrongs. The national trauma of defeat and Versailles, the sense of shame and national weakness exposed and betrayed by "the Jew," were the enemy that Nazism, above all other parties, consistently attacked with unsparing, single-minded vehemence. Where inflation generated uncertainty, Hitler promised fiscal and political certainty; where economic chaos threatened all security, Hitler pledged to solve the economic crisis and provide security; where society appeared to be devolving, Hitler spoke of social coherence; where Weimar was the new, the urban, the "un-German," Hitler promoted the old, conservative virtues (or so it appeared), the agrarian-*völkisch* style, the true Germanic manner; where a near-chiliastic sense of doom, even annihilation settled over large segments of the populace as their financial independence and life-long savings eroded, Hitler appeared as a savior possessed of heavenly secrets through which the kingdom could be achieved;[101] where Germany was passive before its enemies, Hitler encouraged direct action; where 1918 and after were the fault of the new exploitative master-class, the Jews, Hitler made a commitment to return things to their proper order—Aryans on top, Jews on the bottom. Anomie,[102] individual and collective, monetary and normative, was the consequence of this many-sided disarray, while National Socialism believed itself, and made others believe, it was the re-integrative antidote.

It is not accidental that Nazi electoral popularity was directly related to the degree of economic uncertainty felt among Weimar's citizenry. Between 1924 and 1928, relatively prosperous and secure years for the Republic, the Nazis' share of the vote, as that of right-wing parties in general, continually diminished while the Social Democratic Party, the party most deeply committed to the Weimar Republic, prospered. In 1928 the *SDP* elected its first Chancellor in eight years and saw its popular vote increase by over one million, while the *NSDAP* saw its share of the electorate drop to 810,000 votes, a mere 2.6% of the vote.[103] In contrast, the Depression reversed this trend, pushing the Nazi vote to unprecedented heights. In the election of September 1930 they gained 107 seats, 6,410,000 votes, or 18.3% of the vote, and this count rose to 230 seats in the July 1932 elections. Alternatively, as the economy improved in the fall of 1932 Nazi popularity declined and by November 1932, they had lost two million votes and 34 seats,[104] a negative trend that continued through the remainder of 1932.[105]

According to Nazism's sovereign mythology, international Jewry manipulated the economies of countries for their own gain, while they avoided the pain associated with local economic catastrophes by being supranationalists. That the real causes of German economic disarray lay elsewhere, namely in the vast governmental overexpenditures that exceeded government income by over thirty million reichmarks[106] between 1920 and 1923 was of no consequence, for the republican leadership was, in any case, Jewish. But if the Nazis' explanation of the inflation was altogether deficient, it nevertheless had the "positive" virtue that it seemed to make the crisis less the consequence of large and impersonal forces and more the product of intelligible and manageable elements, "The Jews," that every person could understand. It also made for a simple cure: eliminate the Jews. The immediate

244 Steven T. Katz

concrete expression of this rationalization, of this diagnosis, was the large "pogrom" in the Jewish quarter of Berlin on November 5–6, 1923. The same (il)logic applied during the Great Depression, only more so.[107] In this series of crises the eternal semitic enemy stood ready as a convenient explanation.[108]

The second meaningful aspect of the Jew's supranationalism, his corrosive impact on culture, though less significant to the average German, was also trumpeted across the land. The fluid, often vibrant and creative, certainly original, culture of Weimar was seen as shockingly debased and "un-German" by the cultural mandarins of the right.[109] To them, its experimentation and novelty were a sign of moral[110] and aesthetic decay. And the role of the Jews in the ferment was not lost on friends and foe alike. Walter Laqueur's summary of Jewish participation is succinct as well as accurate:

Without the Jews there would have been no "Weimar culture"—to this extent the claims of the antisemites, who detested that culture, were justified. They were in the forefront of every new, daring, revolutionary movement. They were prominent among Expressionist poets, among the novelists of the 1920s, among the theatrical producers and, for a while, among the leading figures in the cinema. They owned the leading liberal newspapers such as the *Berliner Tageblatt*, the *Vossische Zeitung* and the *Frankfurter Zeitung*, and many editors were Jews too. Many leading liberal and avant-garde publishing houses were in Jewish hands (S. Fischer, Kurt Wolff, the Cassirers, Georg Bondi, Erich Reiss, the Malik Verlag). Many leading theatre critics were Jews, and they dominated light entertainment.[111]

Rather than appreciating this creativity, the despisers of Weimar culture viewed all these developments with genuine alarm. To the antisemites they represented another form of the Jewish virus, of the Jewish racial attack on all that was orderly, vigorous and healthy in traditional German life. "The metropolis began its race-annihilation work. . . . A race chaos of Germans, Jews, and anti-natural street races was abroad. The result was mongrel art."[112] As a being devoid of the higher human characteristics, certainly barren of desirous virtues, the Jew is incapable of producing authentic, ennobling spiritual products. "Culturally," Hitler argues, the Jews' "activity consists in bowdlerizing art, literature, and the theatre, holding the expressions of national sentiment up to scorn, overturning concepts of the sublime and beautiful, the worthy and the good, finally dragging the people to the level of his own low mentality."[113] At the same time, this materialistic racial shallowness makes him envious of the high innovativeness of others. He is therefore the enemy of all aesthetic and cultural greatness. And this negative vulgarizing proclivity has its roots in racial soil: "to turn upside down the most natural hygienic rules of a race. The Jew makes night into day; he stages the notorious night life and knows quite well that it will slowly but surely destroy . . .";[114] and again, "Blood mixture and the resultant drop in the racial level is the sole cause of the dying out of old cultures."[115]

With this contention the biological circle comes full: every decrepitude, every vice, every degeneracy political, economic, and cultural has one cause, racial decay, one causal agent: "The Jews." And this in a period of political fluidity when the *NSDAP* was still a minority party, distant from the mechanisms of power, those mechanisms which when controlled in totalitarian fashion drive the ideological to become still more absolute and extreme in the absence of sufficient resistance. Fed by the reality of power, the theoretical becomes more, not less extreme in the actuality of its implementation.[116] This is true not only of Nazism, but also of Stalinism, Maoism, Castroism and the Cambodian regime of Pol Pot, among many possible examples. For us this means that racial antisemitism, raised to previously unprecedented heights in Weimar, would know still more unrestrained expression and incomparable genocidal reality in the years of Nazi political control. And even before this final, deadly transformation of the political landscape of Germany and her allies, this racial perspective would have scored a notable success in setting a good deal of the political agenda—even for those in the political center and left. The universally heightened sensitivity to Jewish issues caused by the unrelenting propaganda of the extreme right forced the shape of political debate into contours constructed out of, even if opposed to, this racial program. In this way the racists of the Weimar era can already be seen to have achieved a lasting victory, for they had succeeded in undermining the *givenness* of Jewish emancipation and Jewry's collective participation in a modern pluralistic Europe.[117]

Notes

1. It needs to be emphasized that in the discussion that follows, the focus is on a typological account of the roots and nature of Weimar and more specifically Hitlerian antisemitism. As such, it over-emphasizes this factor in Weimar life to a certain degree. To correct this historical distortion, i.e., to properly situate our analysis in its historical context, it must be noted that the outright antisemitic parties never garnered more than 8% of the total vote during the life of the Weimar Republic prior to 1930.

2. Koppel Pinson, *Modern Germany* (New York, 1955), p. 419.

3. On the demographic profile of Weimar Jewry, see Eric Rosenthal, "Trends in Jewish Population in Germany, 1910–1939," *Jewish Social Studies*, Vol. 6 (1944), pp. 233–74; Esra Bennathan's essay on "Die demographische und wirtschaftliche Struktur der Juden," in Werner E. Mosse and Arnold Paucker (eds.), *Entscheidungsjahr 1932: Zur Judenfrage in der Endphase der Weimarer Republik* (Tübingen, 1966²), pp. 87–131; and Donald L. Niewyk, *The Jews in Weimar Germany* (Baton Rouge, 1980), pp. 11–42. Peter Gay, *Freud, Jews and Other Germans* (New York, 1978), calls attention to the demographic growth of the Ostjuden in Germany in the first quarter of the twentieth century. In 1900 there were approximately 11,000 Ostjuden in Berlin out of a total Jewish population of 92,000. This figure increased fourfold in absolute terms and doubled in percentage terms by 1925 when Ostjuden numbered 43,000 out of a Berlin Jewish population of 172,000 or 25.4% (p. 172).

4. R. H. Lutz, *The German Revolution, 1918–1919* (Stanford, 1922). Gerhard A. Ritter and Susanne Miller (eds.), *Die deutsche Revolution 1918–1919* (Frankfurt a. M., 1968); Allan Mitchell, *Revolution in Bavaria, 1918–1919: The Eisner Regime and the Soviet Republic* (Princeton, 1965); Gordon Craig, *Germany 1866–1945* (New York, 1978), pp. 396–414; and David W. Morgan, *The Socialist Left and the German Revolution: A History of the German Independent Social Democratic Party, 1917–1922* (Ithaca, 1975).

5. Robert Waite, *Vanguard of Nazism: The Free Corps Movement in Germany, 1918–1923* (Cambridge, 1952); Johannes Erger, *Der Kapp-Lüttwitz Putsch. Ein Beitrag zur deutschen Innenpolitik 1919–20* (Düsseldorf, 1967); G. Craig, *Germany*, pp. 429–32; and John W. Wheeler-Bennett, *The Nemesis of Power: The Army in Politics, 1918–1945* (London, 1953), pp. 60–82.

6. There are a number of valuable narrative histories of this era from which I have benefited: Gordon Craig, *Germany 1866–1945*; Koppel Pinson, *Modern Germany* (New York, 1955); Erich Eyck, *A History of the Weimar Republic*, 2 Vols. (Cambridge, 1962–1965); Albert Schwartz, *Die Weimarer Republik* (Konstanz, 1958); Hajo Holborn, *A History of Modern Germany* (New York, 1969); Donald L. Niewyk, *Jews in Weimar*; and Ferdinand Friedensburg, *Die Weimarer Republik* (Berlin, 1946).

7. Of course, for racist thinkers like Hitler all these, and many other phenomena, are just the outward expression of more deeply rooted racial laws.

8. Adolf Hitler, *Mein Kampf* (German edition, Munich, 1941), p. 296.

9. P. Merkl's evidence, based on the Abel interviews (see Theodore Abel, *The Nazi Movement: Why Hitler Came to Power* [New York, 1966]), puts this figure at 46% of veterans, *Political Violence under the Swastika* (Princeton, 1975).

10. K. Pinson, *Modern Germany*, p. 414, notes that "not a single school text in Weimar Germany presented the true story of German defeat in 1918." As a consequence, this resentment at Allied and "fifth columnist" behavior, as well as at the Weimar Republic for "agreeing" to exist on such terms, was passed on to successive generations of young Germans which in turn made "high school and universities . . . focal centers for the rightist nationalist movements" among

both students and faculty. On education in Weimar, see also G. Craig, *Germany,* pp. 421–24. This issue has been helpfully analyzed in the important works of Wolfgang Kreutzberger, *Studenten und Politik 1918–1933: Der Fall Freiburg-im-Breisgau* (Göttingen, 1972); and R. H. Samuel and R. H. Thomas, *Education and Society in Modern Germany* (London, 1949). The importance of these facts is brought home by the Abel interviews which reveal that 50% of politicized activist Nazi youth in the 1920s reported "having had a völkisch or Nazi teacher or conflict with Jewish fellow students" at school. P. Merkl, *Political Violence,* p. 277. On the opposition to Weimar in the universities, see W. Laqueur, *Weimar: A Cultural History 1918–1933* (London, 1974), pp. 183–223. Laqueur describes the majority of professors "as reactionary *tout court,* the minority was *vernunftre-publikanisch,* pro-republican because they accepted it as a political necessity, rather than out of instinct or deep moral conviction" (p. 184).

11. See the responses of early Nazis to the defeat as reported in P. Merkl, *Political Violence,* pp. 144–88.

12. It should be noted that the German Communist Party also railed against the "chains of Versailles"; see K. Pinson, *Modern Germany,* p. 417.

13. Jews were already singled out in this respect by the 1916 War Ministry census carried out in order to check on the rate of German participation in the war. On this issue, see the early study by Franz Oppenheimer, *Die Judenstatistik des Preussischen Kriegsministeriums* (Munich, 1922); Egmont Zechlin, *Die deutsche Politik und die Judem im ersten Weltkrieg* (Göttingen, 1969), pp. 524–37; and Werner Angress, "Das deutsche Militär und die Juden im Ersten Weltkrieg," in *Militärgeschichtliche Mitteilungen,* Vol. 19 (1976), pp. 77–146. In respect of this issue it is surely ironic, as Robert Waite points out, that Hitler's Iron Cross First and Second Class, earned during the war, was only granted to him as a consequence of the strenuous effort made on his behalf by his adjutant, Hugo Gutmann, who was Jewish. See R. Waite, "Hitler's Antisemitism," in B. Wolman (ed.), *The Psychoanalytic Interpretation of History* (New York, 1971), p. 195.

14. See P. Merkl's *Political Violence,* p. 169; see also pp. 213–14.

15. The official German count gives 539,000 Jews in Germany in 1910, 0.92% of the population.

16. Figures given in Hugo Valentin, *Antisemitism: Historically and Critically Examined* (New York, 1936), p. 109.

17. P. Merkl, *Political Violence,* p. 166.

18. I purposely use this general and vague term, rather than identifying specific left-of-center political parties, because this is how Hitler and the right-wing parties used it. The unspecific abstraction served better.

19. Peter Gay calls this connection to the fore by reminding us that "Hugo Preuss, the architect of the Weimar constitution, was a symbol of revolution; as a Jew and a left-wing democrat, he had been kept out of the university establishment for all his merits, and now he, the outsider, gave shape to the new republic, *his* Republic." *Weimar Culture* (New York, 1968), p. 17. Then again, the flag of the Republic was accused by nationalists of containing "the yellow stripe of Jewry." Cited in E. Eyck, *History of Weimar,* Vol. 1, p. 190.

20. Cited by E. Eyck, *History of Weimar*, Vol. 1, p. 315.

21. On the *Deutschnationale Volkspartei*, see the monograph by that title by Werner Liebe (Düsseldorf, 1956).

22. Quoted in W. Liebe, *Deutschnationale Volkspartei*, p. 115.

23. *Mein Kampf*, pp. 388 and 452–53.

24. *Mein Kampf*, p. 252.

25. E. Jäckal observed this same phenomenon in *Mein Kampf*:

    In the antisemitic passages one is struck, first of all, by a very peculiar vocabulary. Here is a catalogue from Volume One of *Mein Kampf* as it appears there in the sequence of pages: The Jew is a maggot in a rotting corpse; he is a plague worse than the Black Death of former times; a germ carrier of the worst sort; mankind's eternal germ of disunion; the drone which insinuates its way into the rest of mankind; the spider that slowly sucks the people's blood out of its pores; the pack of rats fighting bloodily among themselves; the parasite in the body of other peoples; the typical parasite; a sponger who like a harmful bacillus, continues to spread; the eternal bloodsucker; the peoples' parasite; the peoples' vampire. Almost all of these expressions derive from the realm of parasitology; the Jew was isolated from the rest of human society, and the use of language suggests the methods of his elimination. (Jäckal, *Hitler's Weltanschauung, A Blueprint for Power* [Middletown, 1972], pp. 58–59)

26. Cited by R. Binion, *Hitler among the Germans* (New York, 1976), pp. 36 and 39. This theme was an *idée fixe* of Hitler's which never changed. Thus in 1941, in his table talk with Himmler, he reminded him "that race of criminals [Jews] has on its conscience the two million [German] dead of the first world war and now hundreds of thousands more" (p. 87).

27. Cited by R. Binion, *Hitler among the Germans*, p. 24.

28. In *Mein Kampf* (English edition, trans. R. Manheim [Boston, 1943]; henceforth cited as E.T., p. 800), he would demand that "some day a German national court will have to sentence and to execute some ten thousand of the organizing and thus responsible criminals of the November treason."

29. *Mein Kampf* (E.T.), p. 984.

30. Cited by R. Binion, *Hitler among the Germans*, pp. 26, 27, 28.

31. Hitler's extremism was, of course, not yet acceptable generally and would also have to wait its turn, which was not too long coming.

32. G. Craig, *Germany*, pp. 424–25.

33. These are well summarized by K. Pinson:

    For the average German, irrespective of political party, and reconciled though he might have become to the restoration of Alsace-Lorraine to France and Eupen and Malmédy to Belgium, the Treaty of Versailles was an "instrument of subjugation." It had turned over German territory and German population in the east to Poland, a nation traditionally regarded by Germans as beneath contempt; it créated the "impossible" Polish corridor which divided the German Reich in two and cut off the "hallowed" soil of East Prussia from the rest of the Reich. Measured in terms of the resources of Germany before the war, the treaty meant the loss of 13 per cent of its territory, 10 per cent of its population, 100 per cent of its colonial domain, about 15 per cent of its arable land, 74.5 per cent of its iron ore, 26 per cent of its hard coal assets, 68 per cent of its zinc, 17 per cent of its potato yield, 16 per cent of its rye, and 13 per cent of its wheat. To top all that, the Treaty of Versailles meant the complete demilitarization of Germany and the military occupation by the Allied powers of 6 per cent of its remaining domain. (K. Pinson, *Modern Germany*, pp. 424–25)

34. This was argued very strongly, for example, by Ludwig Zimmermann, *Deutsche Aussenpolitik* (Göttingen, 1958), pp. 474f. But cf. the useful review of the evidence by Erich Matthias, "The Influence of the Versailles Treaty on the Internal Development of the Weimar Republic," in Anthony Nicholls and Erich Matthias (eds.), *German Democracy and the Triumph of Hitler* (New York, 1971), pp. 13–28. See also E. Eyck, *History of Weimar*, Vol. 1, pp. 80–128.

35. It was not accidental that the peace conference began on January 18, the anniversary of the founding of the German Empire, in the same Hall of Mirrors where the victorious Germans had issued the proclamation of Empire fifty years earlier, while June 28, the signing date, was the date of Archduke Ferdinand's assassination. J. Fest, *Hitler* (New York, 1973), p. 82.

36. *Völkische Beobachter*, April 6, 1920.

37. In addition to the recurrence of this theme in *Mein Kampf* and Hitler's early *Reden*, see also Hermann Göring, *Germany Reborn* (London, 1934), pp. 19–20; the interviews in T. Abel, *The Nazi Movement*; and P. Merkl's two volumes, *Political Violence*, already cited and *The Making of a Stormtrooper* (Princeton, 1980).

38. Electoral figures summarized from V. R. Berghahn, *Modern Germany* (Cambridge [England], 1982), p. 74. See also on the entire question, Karl Bracher, *Die Auflösung der Weimarer Republik* (Villingen, 1960³). The results of the Weimar elections are closely analyzed by Alfred Milatz, *Wähler und Wahlen in der Weimarer Republik* (Bonn, 1965). For the election of 1920, see pp. 29–39.

39. For more on the lasting effects of the defeat of 1918 on Nazi ideology and practice, see the interesting essay by Tim Mason, "The Legacy of 1918 for National Socialism," in A. Nicholls and E. Matthias (eds.), *German Democracy and the Triumph of Hitler*, pp. 215–39.

40. P. Merkl, *Political Violence*, pp. 511–12. See also, as a related indicator of such sentiment, Joseph Goebbels, *Der Angriff* (Munich, 1935), and again Hermann Göring, "Wahrt das Recht des Volkes," *Völkischer Beobachter*, Sept. 11/12, 1932. Göring laments: "The destruction of Carthage was as nothing compared to the shameful peace of Versailles."

41. *Mein Kampf*, p. 454.

42. Ibid., p. 465.

43. Ibid., p. 639.

44. Henry Ford's antisemitism is intelligently and fairly discussed by Leo Ribuffo, "Henry Ford and *The International Jew*," *American Jewish History*, Vol. 69 (June, 1980), pp. 437–77.

45. *Mein Kampf*, p. 640. Emphasis in original.

46. Ibid., p. 651. Emphasis in original.

47. Adolf Hitler, *The Secret Book* (New York, 1983), pp. 27–28. Emphasis in original.

48. *The Secret Book*, pp. 28–29.

49. See G. Craig's description of the role Rathenau's Jewishness played, *Germany*, pp. 441–42. Also, for more on this issue, see sources listed in Craig, *Germany*, pp. 441–42, note 18.

50. The objective truth was vastly different. Jews were still approximately 1% of the total population, in 1925 there were 568,000 Jews out of a total population of 63,181,000, or 0.90%. Intermarriage was rampant, reaching 24% in 1929. Economically Jews were overwhelmingly middle-class, only 2% were, despite antisemitic propaganda, bankers or stockbrokers. For the detailed breakdown of Jewish demographic and economic life in Weimar, see Esra Bennathan, "Die demographische und wirtschaftliche Struktur der Juden," in Werner E. Mosse (ed.), *Entscheidungsjahr 1932, zur Judenfrage in der Endphase der Weimarer Republik*, pp. 87–131. They were considerably overrepresented in the white-collar professions; 16% of Germany's lawyers, 10% of her doctors, 3% of her university teachers, 5% of her journalists and 4% of her creative artists were Jews. I summarize here the discussion of Karl A. Schleunes, *The Twisted Road to Auschwitz* (Urbana, 1970), pp. 38–41. In addition, and very important, Jews did not "control" the press, over 50% of which was owned by Alfred Hugenberg, chairman of the right-wing *DNVP*, Hitler's coalition partner in 1933. The quote from Peter Merkl's work is from his *Political Violence*, p. 559.

51. K. Pinson defends the Versailles Treaty as being as good as could be expected under the circumstances and not unduly harsh by prevailing standards, e.g., the German treaty of Brest-Litovsk with Russia, *Modern Germany*, p. 423.

52. See Arno J. Mayer, *Politics and Diplomacy of Peacemaking: Containment and Counter-Revolution at Versailles, 1918–1919* (New York, 1967); G. Craig, *Germany*, pp. 424ff.

53. Cited in K. Pinson, *Modern Germany*, p. 429. See also on this entire issue, David Adler, *Walter Rathenau and the Weimar Republic: The Politics of Reparations* (Baltimore, 1971). It is also not irrelevant to this matter that Alfred Rosenberg had publicly linked Rathenau to Bolshevism and Bolshevism to World Jewish power in his 1922 pamphlet *Pest in Russland.*

54. Cited by E. Eyck, *History of Weimar*, Vol. 1, p. 215.

55. G. Craig, *Germany*, p. 444, note 27, censures David Adler, *Walter Rathenau and the Weimar Republic*, for "over-emphasizing" antisemitism as the motive for Rathenau's murder. It appears to me that Craig is wrong in this judgment, given the virulent attack upon Rathenau *qua* Jew. After all, the right had cried, "Knallt ab den Juden Rathenau/die Gottverdammte Judensau," while right-wing groups sang "Schlagt tot den Walter Rathenau / Die gottverfluchte Judenau." Cf. also E. Eyck, *History of Weimar*, Vol. 1, pp. 211f. Consider also as paradigmatic here, i.e., the turning against the Jews as traitors who could become "scapegoats" for Germany's defeat, Ludendorff's memoirs, *Kriegsführung und Politik* (Berlin, 1922), in which he decries "the Supreme Government of the Jewish People who work hand and hand with France and England." The role of the *Protocols of the Elders of Zion* in the thinking of Rathenau's murderers, i.e., of Rathenau as one of these Elders, as described by them at their trial, also

strongly suggests that Rathenau's Jewishness was central to his assassination. See the important discussion of this connection in Norman Cohn, *Warrant for Genocide* (New York, 1969), pp. 141–48 and 178–79. For details, see also Eyck's summary, *History of Weimar*, Vol. 1, p. 214. The political careers of Helferding and Heilmann, two Jewish ministers in later Weimar governments, are also instructive on this point. Recently, Henry Pachter, "Walter Rathenau: Musil's Arnheim or Mann's Naphta?" in his *Weimar Studies* (New York, 1982), pp. 171–88, also called attention to the ironic role the *Protocols* played among those who wanted Rathenau to serve as Foreign Minister, hoping that as one of the *Elders* he could influence the reparations treaty, p. 171. Pachter also writes (p. 186) "He was murdered not because of what he stood for but because of what he was—for being Jewish." Alternatively, one must acknowledge how common political murder in early Weimar was. One fair estimate suggests that there were 376 political murders between 1919 and 1922, 354 committed by the right. See George Mosse, *The Final Solution* (New York, 1978), p. 183.

56. G. Mosse, *Final Solution*, pp. 175–76, calls attention to the importance of the use of black troops in the 1919–1920 French occupation and the role they played in enflaming racial concerns and hatreds in Weimar Germany. The Jews, not unexpectedly, were accused by the right, of causing this "disgrace," of waging a "Negro-Jewish" war on Germany. This issue is also explored in more detail in Keith L. Nelson, "The Black Horror on the Rhine: Race as a Factor in Post-War I Diplomacy," *Journal of Modern History*, Vol. 42, No. 4 (December, 1970), pp. 606–28. The French were careful *not* to repeat this experiment in 1923 when no black soldiers served in the occupation of the Ruhr.

57. Such obligations were continually attacked by the right as turning Germany into little more than a slave-labor colony for the victorious allies. See, e.g., Hitler's remarks in his *Reden* (Würzburg, 1962–63), Vol. 1, pp. 7–8, (ed.) M. Domarus; and Alfred Rosenberg, *Der Mythus des 20. Jahrhunderts* (Munich, 1930), p. 1, for the repetition and exploitation of this theme.

58. These events are described more fully in D. Niewyk, *Jews in Weimar*, pp. 109–10.

59. On these events, and the circumstances surrounding them, see Hans Schmidt, *Die polnische Revolution des Jahres 1848 im Grossherzogtum Posen* (Weimar, 1912), pp. 150–52; on the Jewish issues, see A. Heppner and J. Herzberg, *Aus Vergangenheit und Gegenwart der Juden und der jüdischen Gemeinden in den Posener Landen* (Koschmen-Bromberg, 1909), pp. 851–52. A useful review of the nationality question in Poland is now available in William W. Hagen's, *Germans, Poles and Jews: The Nationality Conflict in the Prussian East, 1772–1914* (Chicago, 1980), pp. 109, 116–17.

60. For a classic defense of this thesis, see Hermann Cohen, "Deutschtum und Judentum," in his *Jüdische Schriften*, 2 Vols. (Berlin, 1924). The classic critique of this position has been offered by Gershom Scholem in his essay, "Wider den Mythos vom deutsch-jüdischen Gespräch," in his collected essays, *Judaica*, Vol. 2 (Frankfurt, 1970), pp. 7ff.

61. For the events leading up to this rebellion, see Daniel Horn, *The German Naval Mutinies of World War I* (New Brunswick, 1969), and in more summary fashion by G. Craig, *Germany*, pp. 398–400; and K. Pinson, *Modern Germany*, pp. 355–57.

62. For a full review see A. Mitchell, *Revolution in Bavaria*; and G. Ritter and S. Miller, *Die deutsche Revolution*; briefer reviews are found in G. Craig, *Germany*, pp. 400–402; and K. Pinson, *Modern Germany*, pp. 357–65.

63. Cf. Eric Waldman, *The Spartacist Uprising of 1919 and the Crisis of the German Socialist Movement* (Milwaukee, 1958).

64. On this coalition, see Harold Gordon, *The Reichswehr and the German Republic 1919–1926* (Princeton, 1957); G. Waite, *Vanguard of Nazism*; G. Craig, *Germany*, pp. 402–12; K. Pinson, *Modern Germany*, pp. 366–91; and F. L. Carsten, *The Reichswehr and Politics, 1918–1933* (Oxford, 1966).

65. For a description of the major political groupings and their views on the *Judenfrage* and relationship to antisemitism, see D. Niewyk, *Jews in Weimar*, p. 43–81.

66. "In Russian Bolshevism we must see the attempt undertaken by the Jews in the twentieth century to achieve world domination," *Mein Kampf*, p. 960.

67. See Hitler's speech of November 1928 on the "November Criminals"; "The Jewess Rosa Luxemburg"; and "The Jew Kurt Eisner." The Jewish presence in revolutionary councils was, of course, a reality. See, e.g., on Ludwig Marum and Ludwig Haas, two Jews in the Baden revolutionary government of 1918, John Peter Grill, *The Nazi Movement in Baden, 1920–1945* (Chapel Hill, 1983), p. 30. One should also recall the role of Paul Hirsch in the Prussian revolutionary government and that of George Gridnauer in Saxony, while the role of Luxemburg, Liebknecht and Eisner requires no further comment. For a detailed biography of Luxemburg, see Gilbert Badia, *Rosa Luxemburg, Journaliste, polémiste, révolutionnaire* (Paris, 1975); while on Liebknecht, see Helmut Trotnow, "The Misunderstood Karl Liebknecht," *European Studies Review*, Vol. 5, No. 2 (1975), pp. 171–91; and Enzo Collotti, "Karl Liebknecht e il Problema della Rivoluzione Socialista in Germania," *Ann. dell'Instituto Giangiacomo Feltrinelli*, Vol. 15 (1973), pp. 326–43. See also the reporting of these events in serious papers such as the *Augsburger Postzeitung* and the *Münchener Neueste Nachrichten*, not to mention the gutter journals of the extreme right. On the entire issue, see Werner Angress, "Juden im politischen Leben der Revolutionszeit," in W. Mosse and A. Paucker (eds.), *Deutsche Judentum in Kreig und Revolution* (Tübingen, 1971), pp. 137–315.

68. P. Merkl, *Political Violence*, p. 146. See also Merkl's statistical breakdown on the attribution of "causes" of the revolution to specific groups, p. 289.

69. The role of the *Protocols of the Elders of Zion* is very important here.

70. J. Fest, *Hitler*, p. 211, based on Hitler's remarks to Dietrich Eckart while in Landsberg Prison.

71. Cited in J. Fest, *Hitler*, p. 132.

72. G. Mosse, *Final Solution*, pp. 182–83. On the circulation of the *Protocols* in post-1918 Germany, see N. Cohn, *Warrant*, pp. 130ff. See also on the Schutz-

und-Trutz Bund, Uwe Lohalm, *Völkischer Radicalismus: Die Geschichte des Deutschvölkischen Schutz-und-Trutz-Bundes* (Hamburg, 1970), throughout.

73. The irony here is notable in that it was Freytag who, in 1869, defended Jews against Wagner's attack in the journal *Die Grenzboten*. In reply to Wagner's antisemitic call, Freytag wrote of the Jews that "in no area are they predominantly representatives of a trend which we must hold socially injurious." "Der Streit über das Judentum in der Musik," *Die Grenzboten*, No. 22 (1869), reprinted in G. Freytag's *Gesammelte Werke*, Vol. 16 (Leipzig, 1898), pp. 321–26. Quoted from Alfred D. Low, *Jews in the Eyes of the Germans: From the Enlightenment to Imperial Germany* (Philadelphia, 1979), p. 338. See his entire discussion of "Freytag vs. Wagner," pp. 338–39. In the *Mitteilungen des Vereins zur Abwehr des Antisemitismus* for 1895, a letter is recorded from 1892 indicating that Freytag married a Jewess and even supported her son's (his stepson's) Hebrew instruction at home.

74. See D. Niewyk's careful study of Weimar courts. He reminds us that, of course, not all, or even most courts were under the sway of radical antisemitism. However, such attitudes did exist, and were both actualized in specific instances, and agitated for all the time by the racial antisemites. For a full discussion, see D. Niewyk, "Jews and the Courts in Weimar Germany," *Jewish Social Studies*, Vol. 37 (1975), pp. 99–113; and his summary in idem, *Jews in Weimar*, pp. 74–77. See also Thilo Ramm (ed.), *Die Justiz in der Weimarer Republik: Eine Chronik* (Neuwied and Berlin, 1968); Ambrose Dozkow and Sidney Jacoby, "Anti-Semitism and the Law in Pre-Nazi Germany," *Contemporary Jewish Record*, Vol. 3, No. 5, (1940), pp. 498–509; and Heinrich Hannover-Druck, *Politische Justiz 1918–1933* (Frankfurt a. M., 1966), pp. 263–73. An indictment of the right-wing sympathies of the courts is provided by P. Gay, *Weimar Culture*, pp. 20–21.

75. The character and significance of antisemitism in the German army during the Weimar era has been briefly summarized by D. Niewyk, *Jews in Weimar*, pp. 77–78.

76. See on the issue of the enormous rise in student antisemitism, Hans Peter Bleuel and Ernst Klinnert, *Deutsche Studenten auf dem Weg ins Dritte Reich* (Gütersloh, 1967); Michael H. Kater, *Studentschaft und Rechtsradikalismus in Deutschland 1918–1933* (Hamburg, 1975); W. Kreutzberger, *Studenten und Politik 1918–1933*; Jürgen Schwarz, *Studenten in der Weimarer Republik* (Berlin, 1971); and Michael S. Steinberg, *Sabers and Brown Shirts: The German Students' Path to National Socialism, 1918–1935* (Chicago, 1973).

77. Cited in J. Fest, *Hitler*, p. 95.

78. *Mein Kampf*, pp. 654ff.

79. The material quoted and the two lines quoted above are from *The Secret Book*, pp. 214–15. See also Hitler's views on Bolshevist Jewry vs. England, pp. 158–59 and 175 of *The Secret Book*.

80. Cited in J. Fest, *Hitler*, p. 92. See also the role the "Jewish Conspiracy Theory" played in the maturing thought of Himmler in Bradley F. Smith, *Heinrich Himmler* (Stanford, 1971), pp. 74–75.

81. *The Secret Book*, pp. 185–86.
82. *Mein Kampf*, p. 61.
83. *The Secret Book*, p. 213.
84. Ibid., p. 58.
85. See on the *SDP* D. Niewyk, *Socialist, Anti-semite, and Jew* (Baton Rouge, 1971); and idem, *Jews in Weimar*, pp. 25–27.
86. See P. B. Weiner, "Die Parteien der Mitte," in W. Mosse and A. Paucker (eds.), *Entscheidungsjahr 1932*, pp. 289–321.
87. *Mein Kampf*, p. 249 (E.T., p. 269).
88. Hitler's memo of Sept. 16, 1919, Ernst Deuerlein (ed.), "Hitler's Eintritt in die Politik und die Reichswehr," in *Vierteljahrssheft für Zeitgeschichte*, Vol. 7 (1959), p. 204.
89. However, one must not read full-blown genocidal intentions into these early post-war phrases.
90. *Mein Kampf* (E.T.), p. 269.
91. Ibid., p. 595.
92. Ibid.
93. Ibid., p. 325.
94. See, as a very preliminary study, my essay, "Hitler's 'Jew': On Microbes and Manicheanism," *Proceedings of the Ninth World Congress of Jewish Studies* (Jerusalem, 1986), Vol. 3, pp. 165–72.
95. See *Mein Kampf* (E.T., pp. 324–27). Of course, Hitler's use of traditional theological notions was only propaganda.
96. See Hitler's remarks on Jewish influence in Britain and Italy in *Mein Kampf* (E.T.), pp. 622ff. Thus he continually ascribed British opposition to "Jewish influence," e.g., late in the war he "confessed": "I myself have underrated one thing: the extent of Jewish influence on Churchill's Englishmen." H. R. Trevor-Roper (ed.), *The Testament of Hitler* (London, 1960), p. 30f. Reading Bernard Wasserstein's indictment of British action (and inaction) during the Sho'ah, *Britain and the Jews of Europe* (New York, 1976), makes one realize how preposterous this notion is.
97. *Mein Kampf* (E.T.), p. 906.
98. Cited by E. Jäekal, *Hitler's Weltanschauung*, p. 57.
99. Cited from D. Niewyk, *Jews in Weimar*, p. 18.
100. Ibid., p. 19.
101. P. Merkl, *Political Violence*, pp. 498ff. calls this "Adolf Hitler's Big Lie." Alternatively, James Rhodes, *The Hitler Movement: A Modern Millenarian Revolution* (Stanford, 1980), has elaborated on this theme at length under the term, borrowed from Michael Barkum, *Disaster and the Millennium* (New York, 1974), "The Disaster Syndrome," pp. 31–42.
102. See the important observations of William Kornhauser, *The Politics of Mass Society* (Glencoe, Ill., 1959).
103. These figures are provided by Fred Weinstein, *Dynamics of Nazism* (New York, 1980), p. 60; and J. Fest, *Hitler*, pp. 259–332.
104. See G. Craig, *Germany*, pp. 562–63.

105. Goebbels thus wrote in late 1932: "The year 1932 was one long succession of bad luck. . . . The past was difficult, and the future looks dark and troubled; all prospects and hopes have vanished." Quoted by F. Weinstein, *Dynamics of Nazism*, p. 62.

106. See for details Gustav Stolper, *German Economy, 1870–1940* (New York, 1940), pp. 81ff. The details are also clearly summarized by G. Craig, *Germany*, pp. 448–56. See also K. Laursen and J. Pederson, *The German Inflation of 1923* (New York, 1969); and R. J. Schmidt, *Versailles and the Ruhr* (London, 1968).

107. On the impact of the Depression on German Jewry, see Ernst Hamburger, "One Hundred Years of Emancipation," *Leo Baeck Yearbook*, Vol. 15 (1970), p. 32; D. Niewyk, *Jews in Weimar*, pp. 18–19; and Hans Joachim Bieber, "Anti-Semitism as a Reflection of Social, Economic and Political Tension in Germany, 1880–1933," in David Bronson (ed.), *Jews and Germans from 1860 to 1933* (Heidelberg, 1979), pp. 33–77.

108. And there was much to explain when, e.g., unemployment moved from 1,899,000 in 1929 to 3,076,000 in 1930, 14% of the work force, and then to over 5.4 million by February 1932, 10% of the total population. For more on these economic conditions, see G. D. Feldman, *Iron and Steel in the German Inflation* (Princeton, 1977); A. Ferguson, *When Money Dies* (London, 1975); F. Graham, *Exchanges, Prices, and Production in Hyperinflation Germany* (Princeton, 1930); and L. E. Jones, "Inflation, Revaluation and the Crisis of Middle-Class Politics," *Central European History*, Vol. 7 (1974), pp. 143–68.

109. For the manifestation of this same sort of sentiment among the common folk, see P. Merkl, *Political Violence*, p. 173.

110. For a more detailed excursus on the Nazis' claimed moral decline in Germany after the war, and the Jews' central role in it, see James M. Rhodes, *Hitler Movement*, pp. 92–95.

111. W. Laqueur, *Weimar; A Cultural History*, p. 73. See also, on the Jewish involvement in Weimar cultural and artistic life, Istvan Deak, *Weimar Germany's Leftwing Intellectuals* (Berkeley, 1968); K. Pinson, *Modern Germany*, pp. 457–66; P. Gay, *Weimar Culture*; K. Bullivant (ed.), *Culture and Society in the Weimar Republic* (Manchester, 1978); Wolfgang Rothe (ed.), *Die deutsche Literatur der Weimarer Republik* (Stuttgart, 1974); and Walter Fahnders and Martin Rector, *Linksradikalismus und Literatur: Untersuchungen zur Geschichte der sozialistichen Literatur in der Weimarer Republik*, (Hamburg, 1974), 2 Vols. Also of interest in this connection is the role of the Jews in left-wing intellectual circles, e.g., Walter Benjamin, Georg Lukács, and the various members and activities of the *Institut für Sozialforschung*, begun in Frankfurt in 1923. For more details on Lukács, see Istvan Meszaros, *Lukács' Concept of Dialectic* (London, 1972); and for the Frankfurt school, see Martin Jay, *The Dialectical Imagination: A History of the Frankfurt School and the Institute of Social Research 1923–1950* (Boston, 1973), and Susanne Petra Schad, *Empirical Social Research in Weimar Germany* (Paris, 1972), pp. 76–96.

112. A. Rosenberg, *Mythus*, cited in Robert Pois (ed.), *Race and Race History and Other Essays* (New York, 1970), p. 149.

113. *Mein Kampf,* pp. 273–74.
114. See Hitler's entire bizarre discussion of the "ills" that plague German society and the role of the Jews in this crisis. *Mein Kampf* (E.T.), pp. 327–64.
115. Cited in J. Fest, *Hitler,* pp. 140 and 210. Hitler here tapped a deep feeling among Germans, and especially those who joined the *NSDAP,* as is clear from the Abel data.
116. Herein lies the fallacy of so many, both inside and outside Germany, who thought once Hitler came to power, "reality" would force him to moderate his "rhetoric," which was no rhetoric but his deepest belief, on the *Judenfrage.*
117. This is increasingly true even for left-wing parties. On this issue, see G. Mosse, "German Socialists and the Jewish Question in the Weimar Republic," *Leo Baeck Yearbook,* Vol. 16 (1971), pp. 123–34; Bela Vago, "The Attitude towards the Jews as a Criterion of the Left-Right Concept," in B. Vago and G. Mosse (eds.), *Jews and Non-Jews in Eastern Europe* (New York, 1974), pp. 21–50; and G. Mosse, *Final Solution,* pp. 185–88.

[12]

Anti-Semitism and the Killing of Latvia's Jews

Andrew Ezergailis

In this chapter I want to enter the realm of speculation about the causes and motives that made so many Latvians participate in the gruesome killings of Latvia's Jews. After having examined the record of Latvian/Jewish relations, I began to suspect anti-Semitism as a sufficient cause for Latvian participation in the killings. Though anti-Semitism existed in Latvia, especially in the social realm of the cities, it is difficult to construct connections that would transpose this social anti-Semitism into a cause for murders.

The Jews of Latvia were killed in two waves: the first one lasted from June 23 to October 15, 1941, and was perpetrated by Einsatzgruppe A, commanded by General Walter Stahlecker. In it about 35,000 people were killed. The second one covered the period from October 15, 1941, to January 1, 1942, when, under the leadership of Gen. Friedrich Jeckeln, the Higher SS- and Polizei Leader of Russia's North and of Ostland, about 30,000 men, women, and children were eliminated. There was also a third wave of killings, that of foreign Jews, brought in from Germany and other European countries, when another 20,000 people were killed during the first half of 1942. Latvians participated in all of these killings, but the nature of the participation differed from wave to wave. Some Latvian SD (*Sicherheits-dienst,*) units were also shipped out to Belorussia and other neighboring countries to take part in killings there, but evidence about those activities is less reliable. The Latvian participants in the killings were organized in SD *Sonderkommandos* (the smaller units were sometimes referred to as *Wachkom-*

mandos or *Schiesskommandos*). The most important of these was led by Viktors Arājs.[1]

Why did the Latvians participate in these killings? For the purposes of this article, I want to exclude from the discussion the German organizational efforts in creating the Latvian *Sonderkommandos*, important, even indispensable, as the connection was. There is no doubt that if, instead of the men of Himmler and Heydrich, Poles or Lithuanians had entered the territory of Latvia, Latvia's Jews would still be alive. But that is only one side of the story. The Latvian *Sonderkommandos* were organized, and they did extend significant help to the German Security Police and SD forces. The Latvian kommandos were organized more or less on the German Einsatzgruppen pattern: they were small and mobile. The Arājs kommando used Rīga city buses to get around in Latvia. Though it was the Germans who organized the kommandos and installed their commanders, it is also clear that nobody was coerced into participation[2] in the killing kommandos and the killings themselves.

In explaining Latvian participation in Himmler's actions, there are two schools of thought: 1. That Latvians were motivated by a deep-seated anti-Semitism; and 2. that the participation was a revenge for Jewish "crimes" against the Latvians during the Soviet occupation of Latvia in 1940/41.

Dissimilar as these two explanations sound, there is also a basic agreement between them—the second being a specific case of the first. The first view is taken mostly by Jewish writers and the second by Latvians, mostly those in emigration (public opinion being mute in Soviet Latvia).[3] The first is a charge of anti-Semitism, the second, an acceptance of the charge. These arguments originated in an emotional state of affairs, during the period of the trauma or soon thereafter, and for that reason alone they should perhaps be rejected as sufficient explanations for the Latvian involvement with the Security Police and SD designs. They may provide plausible explanations, but neither can withstand a full analysis. Neither of the two schools of opinion has received a thorough scholarly analysis.

For a good part of this chapter I shall be examining these two theories, and then I shall construct my own explanation.

I

I shall take up the second theory first. There are two issues connected with the "revenge theory": 1. How much historical truth is there to the Jewish

domination, the Jewish-Bolshevik nexus, of Latvia during the Soviet occupation, and 2. who believed it, and when did that explanation come into
currency?

To begin with, the "revenge theory" should be rejected because it is based
on a historical falsehood, no documentary evidence has been adduced, and,
it is ethically reprehensible, because in arguing it, one ends up blaming the
victim, the murdered Jews, for being murdered. It is an unreconstructed
restatement of a variety of anti-Semitism that the Germans brought along
when entering Latvia. There is no reason to assume that the Latvian beliefs
(regardless of how widely or narrowly one defines Latvian) about the Jews
would have so closely coincided with those of the Nazis. Throughout the
1930s there was a strong anti-German feeling in Latvia, and it is not likely
that many Latvians would have regarded Hitler's ravings with great seriousness.[4] The revenge theory should also be rejected because it accepts the
principle of collective guilt—Jewish guilt and Latvian guilt.

This theory was also promoted by the Soviet propaganda agencies, although not quite in such a blatant manner as that of the Nazis. As early as
June 17, 1940, when the Soviets entered Latvia, their approach to the
population was calculated to create maximum friction among nationalities,
especially between the Jews and Latvians. The Soviets did not install any
Jews in the highest ranks of the puppet government, as they did in post-war
Poland, but they did agitate among Jews, especially the youth, to make their
presence felt on the street. They engaged in Latvian-baiting in the Jewish
press, by repeatedly writing stories about Latvian anti-Semitism and about
the dangers that the Jews might expect from Latvians.[5]

To add to the Latvian/Jewish tension, Soviets mandated that Jews from
there on, must be referred as *ēbrejs* in place of the traditional Latvian word
žīds.[6]. The word *ēbrejs* was annoying to the Latvians because it was associated
with the Soviet occupation. The implication was that the word *žīds* con-
noted anti-Semitism, that the Latvian republic had been anti-Semitic, and
that the Jews had suffered under the Latvian state. (The Jewish situation in
Latvia during its statehood will be discussed below.) This linguistic fiat,
perhaps more than anything else, made many Latvians think that the Jews
were especially favored by the Soviets, and, when the Germans entered
Latvia, this vague feeling made it much easier for Goebbels' agents to
interpret the Soviet occupation as one in which the Jews had ruled.

It is not clear when the belief that the Jews were responsible for the
Bolsheviks entered Latvia, but, though held by certain anti-Semites during

the 1920s, it does not appear to have had much popular currency until 1941. There is no question that this view did gain popularity among the Latvians in 1941 and in emigrations has grown ever since. Until the 1940s Latvia was generally free from this belief because the Latvians themselves had a deep involvement with the Bolshevik revolution,[7] and because Latvia during the period of its Republic had a strong Social Democratic component. It is a matter of historical record that Jews had very little to do with the Latvian Communist movement.[8] During the 1930s more Jews seemed to enter the Communist underground, but even then, when Soviets occupied Latvia in 1940, the Jews were in a small minority within the Latvian Party. The truth or falsity of the Jewish/Bolshevik connection, then, as far as Latvians are concerned, rests on whether or not Jews had much to do with the Soviets during the 1940/41 occupation of Latvia.

Though it would not be wrong to say that a certain number of Jews, local Latvian ones and those who arrived as Soviet functionaries, were active on a variety of administrative levels, it is an absolute falsehood for anyone to maintain that the Soviet power in Latvia rested on the Jewish presence. Of all those who worked in the Soviet apparatus, the number of Jews was small, perhaps not even exceeding 5%, comparable to the proportion of Jews in the population. For one, Jews were practically absent from the administration of Latvia's countryside, which means that for about 70% of Latvia's population there were no objective grounds for associating the Communist rule with Jews,[9] and there is no reason to think that the country people, prior to the Nazi occupation, ever did so. It must be noted that just about every Latvian had a Communist in the family background, perhaps even one living in the USSR.

If, on the one hand, there were very few Jews within the administrative structure of the countryside, at the same time it also must be said that at the very top of the Latvian SSR government there were likewise no Jews.[10]

If there were Communist activist Jews, they must have been on the middle level of administration and mostly in the cities and towns. And only in those cities in which there was a substantial Jewish population. That would exclude most towns in Vidzeme (Livonia) because in that northern province the Jewish population was very sparse.[11] To what degree the city people thought of the Jews as Communists is of course also problematic, because there was Social Democratic strength in the cities. And even if the city people knew some Communist Jews, they certainly would and did know conservative Jews, as well as Jews who suffered under the Communist regime.

Those who argue for Jewish domination of Latvia during the Soviet occupation usually say that there were more than a proportionate number of Jews in the judicial system, the Party, and the Cheka.[12] But, as far as I have been able to ascertain, these statements are bald assertions, without statistical analysis of numbers or lists, not unlike those that Nazi propagandists made during the occupation of Latvia. During the occupation, an Institute of Anti-Semitism was established in Rīga that was to study the relationship of Jews to Bolshevism. To my knowledge this Institute did not come up with any findings. A Latvian sociologist Alfreds Ceichners published a remarkable book in 1943, under the Nazi occupation, one that, though not completely free of anti-Semitism, is not blaming Jews for the Soviet occupation of Latvia. In his opinion, it was the Russians who welcomed the Red Army: "A large number of Russians thought of the smashing of the Latvian state and the arrival of the Red Army not as a victory for Bolshevism, but as a triumph of the Russian State and of the Russian people."

As far as the Jews' welcome of the Soviets in Latvia is concerned, Ceichners sees it in a historical context of hard choices between Hitlerism and Stalinism, a view that many Latvian Jews share.

Even happier [than Russians] about the arrival of the Red Army were the Jews. They did not expect material benefits (more likely losses, because Jews were mostly prosperous merchants and also industrialists), but they feared Germany's expansionism in Eastern Europe and eventual occupation of Latvia by the German Army, which would mean the destruction of Jewish wealth and prosperity in Latvia.[13]

By saying this, I do not want to imply that Jews did not serve in the Communist apparatus of 1940/41; the "truth" of this has been so frequently proclaimed by men of no evil intent, including Jews, that a certain credence must be given to the fact that indeed numerous Jews served in the Soviet apparatus. But, even if we grant that 10% of judges and Cheka operatives were Jewish, it would fail to prove that the Jews dominated Latvia under the Soviets.[14] It is difficult to deal with this question in a concrete way because the proponents of the Jewish/Bolshevik conspiracy theory have not come up with any data to analyze. That is a minimum that could be expected, especially from those who were using those grounds for justifying the killing of Jews in Latvia.

It must, however, be said that the Soviet regime did open up the administrative ranks to Jews, as they had not been open for the duration of Latvia's republic. Consequently, we may assume, and there is eyewitness evidence to the effect, that, with the arrival of the Soviets, Jews entered Latvia's administration. Considering that prior to occupation there were practically no Jews in administrative jobs, a certain impression of Jewish "domination" might have arisen in the minds of some, especially the urban Latvians. To what extent the Jews who made their presence felt were Latvian Jews rather than imports from the Soviet Union is yet another contentious question.

Those Latvians who argue for the Bolshevik/Jewish nexus have a special point to make about Jewish youth. The argument runs that the young Jews, upon the entrance of Soviet tanks into Latvia, showed an unseemly glee about the arrival of the Red Army. I have heard stories, mostly originating from Rīga, of Jews kissing Soviet tanks and dancing the *Hora* around them. This then is couched in the context of Jewish ingratitude for the freedoms that were theirs to enjoy under the government of the free state of Latvia. Apropos of these stories, there are the following points to be made: they deal in general impressions; none of the narrators—the one who told me about the kissing of the tanks, or the one who saw the Jews dancing the *Hora*— were closer to the scene of the happening than 100 meters. In general, the observers of the happenings on the streets of Rīga on June 17 and subsequent days have told us that the groups of people rejoicing at the arrival of the Red Army were small, and that some cobblestone throwing took place on the streets of Rīga among rival groups. What the composition of these "well wishers" who heaved the stones for the Soviet side was has never been established, but, even if young Jews were among them, these groups were by no means limited to Jews. Russians were certainly heavily represented in those groups. These were staged events. It is even thought that the crowds on the streets of Rīga were inflated by people brought in from the USSR. In any case, the staged nature of the crowds does lessen the sincerity and spontaneous nature of the greetings. In any event, it was not people carrying flowers who decided the issue of power, but tanks.[15]

I do not want to gloss over the moments of tension, especially among urban Latvian Jewish youth within the schools and at times on the streets. Later in the year the Jewish *Komsomols* seem to have attracted hostility from Latvian youngsters.[16]

The Latvians who tell these stories and talk about Jewish ingratitude, however, have not taken into consideration one historical fact: the Latvia that was occupied by the Soviet tanks on June 17, 1940, was no longer a

Republic of Latvia, but had become a dictatorship. Benign as the Ulmanis regime might have been in comparison with other dictatorships of the period, Ulmanis had established it by military force—civil rights were suspended, the free press became non-existent, and a lot of arm twisting of leftists had taken place. The use of force in politics is a dangerous thing, for its consequences can never be anticipated. A tyrant had fallen. That numerous people, including Jews, rejoiced on June 17, 1940, at the fall of a "tyrant" is not, from a historical viewpoint, all that unpredictable or strange: a government that comes into being by force must be prepared to die by force.[17] That some young people of Rīga and Liepāja greeted the tanks of a dictatorship that was incomparably more repressive and vicious than that of Ulmanis may testify to the foolishness of the young people, not necessarily to their ingratitude.[18]

The deportations of June 14, 1941, are the next most important example that is invoked by Latvians who promote the Jewish/Bolshevik nexus theory. Many Latvians in emigration testify that this is an important juncture in the development of Latvian attitudes towards Jews. This view implies the hidden assumption that the Jewish Bolsheviks were not only harmful to the nation in a general way, but that the deportations proved that the Jews were actual murderers of Latvians. This is high anti-Semitism. What is the proof for this view? Upon analysis, there is less reason for saying that Jews abetted the deportations that there is for saying that they danced around the Soviet tanks. A great deal is made of the fact that an NKVD agent S. Šustin was a Jew. That Šustin was a high NKVD agent in Latvia can not be doubted— his signature is even attached to a document ordering the killing of 78 Latvians in June 1941. The first problem is that Šustin's name cannot, in a documentary way, be tied to the deportations. This is not the place to engage in any detailed analysis of the deportations; suffice it to say that nobody has tried to find out how good a Jew Šustin was. It is unlikely that he was a practicing religious Jew. How many Jews were direct participants in the deportations nobody knows. If they were present at the deportation of Latvians, they must have been present at the deportation of Jews, too.[19] The assertion of Jewish complicity in the deportations is so spurious that it hardly requires any refutation. Nobody has even attempted an approximate count of them. No Jewish names are tied to the deportations. The deportations were a major Soviet administrative/military enterprise and so, by necessity, some Jew must have taken part in them.[20] There is no reason to assume that the Jews participated in the deportations in any larger proportion than they did in Latvia's administration. Most likely the largest number of people participating in the deportations were Latvians, followed by Russians. Jews were perhaps the third most numerous nationality group.

In unraveling the whole Jewish/Bolshevik syndrome, more important than names or numbers of any group participating is to assess the "when." When did the Latvians, in any sizable numbers, come to believe in this Jewish/Bolshevik conspiracy? Did the Latvians, on June 15, 1941, come to the conclusion that it was the Jews who had deported their relatives to Siberia? There is not an iota of evidence that Latvians drew that conclusion at the time. Did the Latvians believe that on June 22? There is no evidence for that either. It must be noted that between the deportations and the German occupation there was nobody to make the case for that "truth" known. The Latvians, most certainly the country people, did not believe in this Jewish conspiracy because it was absurd. The neighbors of the deported Latvians saw who manned the trucks. But, within about two weeks after June 14, the German forces occupied Latvia, and their propaganda apparatus relentlessly, by word of mouth, in print, and over the air, told Latvians about the "Jewish murderers." With the first hours of the war the Latvians began to be bombarded with Nazi propaganda over the airwaves from Kön-igsberg. Upon entrance in Latvia, the Einsatzgruppen leaders began to orga-nize the digging up of burial sites of Communist victims, and the pictures of the decomposing corpses were displayed in the newspapers. The propaganda drum was beating, and it announced that it was the Jews who were responsi-ble for the twisted, half-decomposed bodies. Did the Latvians succumb to this propaganda? When did the view of the Jews as Bolsheviks, the killers of Latvians, finally take hold? There is no doubt that the feelings against the Jews, especially among many urban Latvians, were heightened by this drum-beat. But, at the same time, my interviews reveal that the Latvians at large resisted this propaganda absurdity. There is no reason to think that a major-ity of Latvians ever came to believe the Nazi assertions. There is even a question, one that I shall raise later in this chapter, whether at the outset the men who joined the killing kommandos believed in the Jewish conspir-acy with the fervor that the Germans desired. In other words, it is highly doubtful that this most vicious propaganda was a motive for the Latvians to do the bidding of the Germans. It is true that, in due time, during the occupation, more and more people came to be persuaded of the idea; cer-tainly the members of the killing kommandos became anti-Semitic. During the occupation in Latvia, a Latvian infrastructure developed that was thoroughly Nazified, consisting of people who believed in Hitlerism to the last, of the kind that not only pursued Jews and Communists, but also Latvians who listened to the BBC.

But the specific idea that the killing of Jews was justified as a revenge for victimized Latvians perhaps did not harden until emigration. As amazing as it may sound, an idea first implanted in Latvia by Himmler's men flourished among numerous Latvian emigrants, long after the perpetrators of the idea were defeated, punished, and dead. But the biological anti-Semitism that was Hitler's major rationale for the killing of Jews never had any echoes among Latvians.

Next I want to consider anti-Semitism as such in Latvia, prior to the Soviet and German occupations. In that discussion, I shall show that anti-Semitism in Latvia was not deep-seated—that there was very little prior to the outbreak of World War II, that anticipated the tragedy of 1941.

II

Before World War II Latvia was not a society saturated with anti-Semitism. While the independence of Latvia lasted, there were no anti-Jewish laws, and up to the last, Jews from Europe found refuge in Latvia.

One problem with the concept of anti-Semitism is the unclarity of its meaning, or the multiplicity of meanings that the concept can have. At times it may mean just a recognition of an ethnic difference between the Jews and gentiles. At other times anti-Semitism is a racial theory, of which hatred is an important component. Then there is the whole matter of Jews as Bolsheviks, discussed above, and Jews as shameless capitalists. Hitler promoted biological (he called it scientific) anti-Semitism, one that grew out of nineteenth-century anthropological theories. In his mind Jews became defilers of the Aryan/Nordic peoples.

When does anti-Semitism become a motive for murder? And what kind of anti-Semitism does it take to start killing Jews? There is no doubt that Hitler and his minions had crossed the line. The question is: did the Latvians who participated in the murder of Jews do it because of anti-Semitism? In this section of the chapter I want to review the history of Latvian/Jewish relations prior to the tragedy of 1941.

The history of Latvian Jews is complicated by the fact that prior to 1918 there were three provinces of Latvians—Kurzeme (Kurland), Vidzeme (Livonia), and Latgale (also known as Polish Livonia, which in the nineteenth century was part of Vitebsk gubernia). Jews in these three territories had different traditions and origins.[21] Jews arrived in Latvia through Poland and settled first in the Polish-ruled territories, Latgale and Kurzeme. The census of 1897 registered 142,315 Jews in Latvia, but due to the chaos of war and forced deportations their numbers dropped to 79,368 in the 1920 census. By 1925 the numbers had climbed back to 95,474, but then by 1935 decreased to 93,479, below 5% of the total population. According to Nazi statistics in 1941, at the time of occupation there were 70,000 Jews in Latvia, of whom all but about 2,000 were killed.

Our knowledge of Latvian/Jewish relations prior to 1900 is fragmentary. The historical record reveals no pogroms within the territories inhabited by Latvians. Traditionally, the Latvian country people encountered the Jew in two capacities: as a peddler, and on the market days as a buyers of crops and livestock. Latvian literature and theater especially celebrates the peddler and the itinerant tailor. The buyer has not found much room in the Latvian collective memory.[22]

One source for traditional Latvian attitudes towards Jews can be found in Latvian folk songs. Out of twelve volumes of folk songs there are about 150 four-line stanzas that mention Jews.[23] To assess the folk song attitudes towards the Jews would take more space than available in this chapter, for to do so fully, one would need to enter into an analysis of the Latvian folk song genre, linguistic and thematic. On the surface the Latvian folk songs give a chaotic impression, for they exist as individual four-line stanzas, descriptive or lyrical, sometimes depicting social, class, and ethnic (also sexual) relationships, sometimes containing an epigrammatic piece of wisdom or advice, and sometimes having no other purpose than alliterative joy for word play. Within the social genre, one encounters a lot of grotesqueries, ridicule, satire, and skewering of pomposities. The Jewish songs cover a spectrum of attitudes. There is no one single attitude towards Jews: in the post-Holocaust context some of them may even be taken as anti-Semitic. If in general the Jew is treated as a stranger, then there are also many verses that point to intimate social relationships. The celebration of nuptials with Jews is frequently encountered. If the folk songs are any indication, then intermarriage with Jews was not an infrequent occurrence. Fear or hatred of the Jew is not encountered in the songs. Of negative attitudes, perhaps caricaturing and indifference are the most frequently encountered ones. And of the positive ones: sympathy and charity.[24]

The portrayal of Jews in Latvian literature, though lacking in the spectrum of attitudes and feelings of the folk songs, is more positive towards the Jews. In Latvian literature of the first quarter of this century the Jew is a not infrequent subsidiary character. K. Tolmans has anthologized and translated into Hebrew a volume of stories, *The Jew in Latvian Literature* (1938).[25] The stories deal almost exclusively with the itinerant Jew within the peasant context, and, with one exception, they would not be judged anti-Semitic even today.[26] The feeling in these stories, though at times one of condescension, is also one of sympathy, frequently of pity, for the loners of the road who are condemned to live a life away from family and their people. Some of the stories have a comic premise, and that approach makes it more difficult to evaluate them for their philo- or anti-Semitic content. The most fully developed description of Jewish social life is found in J. Janševskis novels, *Dzimtene*, (Fatherland), *Mežvidus ļaudis* (People of the Woodland) and *Bandava* (Cornfield). The itinerant Jew is also treated frequently in Latvian drama, especially in the plays of Rūdolfs Blaumanis, the turn-of-the-century master of Latvian theater. The Jew in his plays is usually introduced to add to the merriment of the show, although not infrequently the Jew is also present to add a more somber note, to communicate some deep human truths. The comic elements, when they are present in these stories, are ones of gesture and accent.

One hostile portrait of the Jew, anti-Semitic almost in a medieval mold, is to be found in Andrievs Niedra's novel, *Kad mēness dilst* (When the Moon is Waning), published in 1902. In the novel Niedra depicts an old bearded Jew who, to avenge wrongs committed against him and his sons, engages in ritualistic if not ritual murder of Christians.[27] How much influence that kind of portrayal, by a writer very popular at the time, would have had, is difficult to assess. Niedra is a forbidden author in Soviet Latvia, as he was also under Ulmanis' regime.

From 1900 to 1917 Latvians were engaged in revolutionary struggle, and in history books, especially those with Social Democratic leanings, this period is portrayed as one of fraternal Latvian/Jewish struggle against the autocracy. A stormier era in Latvian/Jewish relations was 1918–21, the period of Latvia's War of Independence. The tension, even street violence, between Latvians and Jews in this period has been noted by both parties. Prof. Laserson says that "minor" assaults had occurred in Bastejkalns Park, and in the provinces, "particularly in Rezhitza (Rēzekne)."[28] Frida Michelsons, writing about her Holocaust experiences, has a more violent incident to recollect. She notes that her relatives from Varaklāni, a town in Latgale inhabited by Jews, experienced a pogrom at the hands of Latvian soldiers in 1919: "We still remembered the atrocities of 1919 after the occupation of Varaklāni when the Latvian soldiers were given thirty minutes to do as they pleased. Murder, rape, and robbery reigned for those thirty unforgettable minutes."[29]

Some violence was perpetrated by a company of soldiers on relief from the Eastern front in a Rīga park in 1920. The soldiers, for no apparent reason, had begun chasing Jews out of a park, shoving some into the canal. The violence was of short duration, and it was resolved by the prompt appearance of Minister President Ulmanis and the Minister of War Balodis in the regimental headquarters: the offending company was ordered back to the front.[30]

However many of these incidents there were, we may suppose that they were not widespread because, if they had been, we would know about them. The government of Latvia was operating under democratic procedures, and it was mindful of Latvia's international position because a full diplomatic recognition had not been obtained. The Social Democrats too, who considered the leftist Jews their allies, would not have countenanced such activities. And the Jewish deputies in the Constituent Assembly would not have been quiet about them.

If, on the one hand, during the early years of Latvia's republic the Jewish/Latvian relationship can be described as tense, then also during these same years the Constitution of Latvia's republic, adapted in 1922, was written. It was a unique document because it not only conferred a full spectrum of civil rights on all citizens, it also conferred rights on minorities. Each minority was sovereign and autonomous within the Latvian republic. Prof. Laserson, who was a participant of the Latvia's Constituent Assembly, wrote about it thus: "The fact that these minority rights were conferred not upon the individual members, but on the nationality as a whole is particularly noteworthy in view of the fact that Latvia was the first European state to adopt such a law after the World War."[31]

In practical terms, these ethnic autonomous rights meant that Jews could pursue their cultural life in a free and uninhibited manner, the state of Latvia guaranteeing schools in their own language (both Hebrew and Yiddish),[32] not to mention religious rights,[33] and those of free press and assembly. There is no Jewish writer to be found who thinks Latvia's Constitution was deficient or prejudicial to them.[34] This latitudinarianism was, and still is, unique in the world, peculiar to the constitutions of the three Baltic

States. This extended internal autonomy had no Western models but was an outgrowth of the Russian Revolutionary experience.[35]

It must also be noted that Jews fought in the Latvian War of Independence against the Bolsheviks and Germans, some earning the *Lāčplēsis* medal, the highest Latvian award for valor.[36] There existed an Association of Jewish War Veterans, and the First Foreign Minister of Latvia's republic was a half-Jew, Zigfrīds Meirovics. To what degree Jews shared in the land reforms of Latvia is not so clear, but at least to the war veterans, land was distributed without prejudice.[37]

When a more detailed history of Jewish/Latvian relations gets to be written, then indeed one may discover some yet unperceived perilous underwater rock that would explain the tragedy of 1941. But so far, the Jewish and Latvian writers have portrayed those relations as tending more towards the idyllic than to the menacing.[38]

If, in a general way, the period of the republic from 1919 to 1934 could be characterized as philo-Semitic, then it must also be said that hostile voices made their occasional appearance in Latvia's press and Saeima (Parliament).[39] The first anti-Semitic organization entitled *Nacionālais klubs* (The National Club) made its appearance in the early years of the republic.[40] And a party with a strong anti-Semitic undertone, the National Peasant Society led by Reinhardts, had a voice in the Saeima.[41] A Jewish writer saw this appearance of anti-Semitism as originating in the insecurity of the Latvian intellectuals during the period of the early republic that subsided in the mid-twenties. In general, we can follow Laserson's conclusion that, within the Saeima, Jews as such never became a major issue. In the conflicts between the Latvian majority and minorities, the Germans took the heat of it.[42]

In the late twenties, with the rise of fascism in Europe, a more clearly articulated anti-Semitism reared its head, this time under the name of *Ugunskrusts* (Firecross), later to become *Pērkoṇkrusts* (Thundercross). This organization was the one to introduce the slogan LATVIA FOR LATVIANS, thus placing itself at odds with the multiethnic nature of Latvia as defined by the Constitution of 1922.

Anti-Semitism in Latvia was found almost exclusively among the intellectuals, and though Pērkoṇkrusts was small in membership, it is said to have exercised considerable influence among university students and especially fraternity circles.[43] Pērkoṇkrusts was not an electoral success. Pērkoṇkrusts was an anti-Semitic organization, but anti-Semitism was not its exclusive preoccupation: it was even more vociferous about the Germans. In the early

1930s, when Nazi sympathies began to make their appearance among the Baltic Germans, this anti-German aspect of their ideology attracted even greater attention than their anti-Semitism. [44]

In 1934 Ulmanis outlawed Pērkoņkrusts, imprisoning many of its leaders. Thereafter Pērkoņkrusts operated as an underground organization, but it atrophied in influence and membership. In 1937 its leader Gustavs Celmiņš was exiled. Pērkoņkrusts still had its final hour during the early weeks of German occupation in July/August 1941. In terms of 1941, it is not easy to assess the influence of Pērkoņkrusts. No group of Latvians has been mentioned with greater frequency as being the main participants in the Holocaust killings than the Pērkoņkrusts. The truth of the matter, however, is, and here I am at pains to disagree with numerous Holocaust survivor writings, that the participation of the Pērkoņkrusts in the killings was only peripheral. There is no doubt that some Pērkoņkrusts members belonged to the killing troops, but they were only few among many. The Pērkoņkrusts member with the highest standing in the SD apparatus was Rikards, but his assignment was to keep a file on Latvians, not to participate in the killing of Jews. The Pērkoņkrusts responsibility in the Holocaust is an indirect one, in providing a background of anti-Semitism in Latvia, and giving it an intellectual and social respectability. Their educational efforts, educating the educated youth, cannot be underestimated. It is also true that, upon German entrance in Latvia, they hoped to play a major role. But it turned out that the Germans only used them, gave them promises that were not meant. They failed not for lack of trying but rather because they were Latvian nationalists and because the memories of the Nazified Baltic Germans went back to the early thirties when Pērkoņkrusts ridiculed the Nazis. It was not part of the German plan to allow the Latvian organization to establish a network of loyalties, and it is not surprising at all that Pērkoņkrusts was banned again. Thereafter individual Pērkoņkrusts members were still among the Nazi favorites, but the organization ceased to exist, except for one branch that was led by Gustavs Celmiņš into the underground. In 1943 Celmiņš was arrested, to end up in a KZ Lager in Germany. [45]

The reason why many Latvians and Jews overestimate Pērkoņkrusts' role in the atrocities is not hard to find. In the attempt of Latvians, especially in the post-Holocaust years, to find a culprit, there is some party infighting between the Ulmanis men and Pērkoņkrusts. On the part of Jews it is a question of being perplexed, in trying to find a reason for the brutalities that they suffered at Latvian hands. They clutched into the only accessible answer: since Pērkoņkrusts was anti-Semitic—it must have done the killing of Jews. The most incriminating aspect of the Pērkoņkrusts was their insignia, the swastika (and although it differed from the Nazi one, by bending the other way, visually the difference was not easily detectable). For the first few weeks of July 1941, Pērkoņkrusts was able to create the impression that it was the Party of the future, and many careerists, among them Arājs, rushed to join the organization.[46]

What of anti-Semitism under Ulmanis? Ulmanis, as previously noted, was not an anti-Semite, and no Jews who knew his policies have ever called him an anti-Semite. And yet there are certain ambiguities about his rule. It is true that Ulmanis prohibited anti-Semitic writings. "With the strengthening of the Ulmanis regime this kind of publication disappeared," writes an unknown Jewish author.[47] Whatever one can say about the causes of Latvian participation in the killing of the Jews, one cannot ascribe it to the presence of anti-Semitic literature.[48]

Anti-Semitism, of course, could exist without being overt and without being fostered by the state. If we look deeper into the problem, indeed one can make the case that there was a lot of social/private and institutional anti-Semitism, as we would put it today. In the civil service Jews would have had a hard time getting a job. In Latvian student fraternities Jews could pledge, but not gain full membership. In the military academy, it would have been difficult to gain entrance. The University was opened to the Jews, but in some departments there might have been unofficial quotas. Entrance into the University was based on tough competitive examinations which the Jews had no problem passing so that their percentage in the University was much larger than their proportion in the population.[49] At the same time it must also be said that the Latvian institutions of higher learning were not always first-priority institutions for the Jewish students, who, if they could afford it, would go to universities in Germany, France, and England.

The situation of the Jew under Ulmanis was far from simple. If we can say that under Ulmanis there was no overt anti-Semitism, and that no anti-Jewish legislation was passed, it still does not mean that Ulmanis did not create a situation that set the Jews on edge, making them angry and fearful for their future. After all, Ulmanis did create a dictatorship, disbanded political parties, and prohibited the free press. Certainly no leftist or Social Democrat had any reason to like Ulmanis, for their parties were banned and some of their leadership incarcerated.[50] Since the ascension of Stalin, especially since the purges, Communism among Latvians and in Latvia was on the wane, but Ulmanis in his anti-parliamentary, anti-socialist putsch came to be the biggest Communist-maker in Latvia since Pobedonestsev and Plehve, the Great Russian russifiers. Ulmanis drove all of the leftists of Latvia—Latvian, Jewish, or Russian, into the arms of communism.[51]

Conservative/religious Jews liked Ulmanis. The social, educational, and religious privileges that the 1922 Constitution guaranteed to Latvia's minorities were in general preserved by him, but they were preserved in an altered form. The Aguda party was the big winner. "With the advent of the authoritarian regime, which turned over the Jewish schools system to the Aguda, religious observance was definitely encouraged by the state, whereas pronounced anti-religiosity was bound to be considered characteristic of leftism."[52] Ulmanis purported to be the great unifier of Latvia, but it was only a surface unity; everyone of leftist leanings, including Jews, had a good reason to dislike Ulmanis. This fact, perhaps more than any other, may explain the joy that many young Jews might have felt about the Soviet deposition of Ulmanis in June 1940.

If Ulmanis' political and social policies alienated the leftist Jews, then his economic policy antagonized the propertied Jews. After placing the Pērkoņkrusts leaders in jail Ulmanis adopted the Pērkoņkrusts slogan: LATVIA FOR LATVIANS. Whether or not he meant by it the same thing as had Pērkoņkrusts is not so clear. Ulmanis was mainly thinking about the control of industry and commerce in Latvia. He wanted to Latviniaize Latvia's economy, and that brought him in conflict with Jewish capitalists. Ulmanis, inspired by Mussolini's state-directed economic policies, began to squeeze out, not to say nationalize, numerous commercial and industrial enterprises, absorbing them under the auspices of the state.[53] Though this policy was not specifically directed against the Jews, the Jews whose properties and profits were threatened had no reason to like Ulmanis. Although it was not Jewish businessmen alone who had reason to fear Ulmanis policies (German capitalists and some Latvian ones were equally harmed), the Jews were correct in interpreting that the intent behind this anti-capitalist line, was, among others, limitation of Jewish influence on Latvia's economic life. Ulmanis was especially concerned about banking and credit institutions in Latvia. The Jewish emigration from Latvia that we see in the late 1930s must in part be attributed to Ulmanis' economic policy. The intricacies of Ulmanis' economics are perhaps even more complicated than those of his cultural politics, and this is not the time to delve into them, suffice it say that Ulmanis, in his six short years of power, without being anti-Semitic, in fact, being personally friendly to Jews, did manage, on the eve of happenings fateful to both peoples, to poison Latvian/Jewish relations. Ulmanis' slogan LATVIA FOR LATVIANS, which might have had an idyllic pastoral meaning in the 1930s, in the era to come, under the German occupation, was twisted out of shape and filled with a content that no user of that slogan in the 1920s or thirties had anticipated.

But the slogans may not have been the worst of Ulmanis' policies; his ideological indoctrination, installing a blind hatred for leftism in the minds of the youth of the 1930s, and an inability to separate a Communist from other leftist variants, reaped a much more gruesome harvest. As the German occupation shows, Ulmanis' notion of *vadonība*, the Latvian version of the Führer principle, must have robbed a lot of people of the ability to make independent judgments. The most fateful of all of Ulmanis' policies was the smothering of the press. For some falsely conceived foreign policy reason, Ulmanis' censors had taken the attitude that newspapers in Latvia should tread carefully on the sensibilities of Stalin and Hitler. Consequently, the Latvians had no good way of learning about the impending dangers, either the full truth about the Winter War in Finland, or about the German atrocities in Poland. Numerous Poles were crossing the frontier into Latvia and brought along with them atrocity stories about the Einsatzgruppen activities there. But none of the news ever surfaced in the pages of the press. To some degree, the Jews of Latvia knew more about German atrocities than did the Latvians, due to their family contacts with Poland.

The meaning of historical responsibility is elusive, and seldom can we be sure that we can make a solid case for it. In Ulmanis' case, however, unintended as the consequences might have been, his regime, pastorally moderate in comparison to the other dictators of the 1930s, did, in part, prepare the way for the tragedy to follow in 1941. In fairness to Ulmanis it must be said that until the very last he kept the door open to Jewish refugees from Germany and Austria, even after numerous other European countries, including Sweden, had ceased to do so.[54]

So far this chapter has considered Latvian/Jewish relations up to spring 1941. Perhaps there has been too much emphasis on the positive. When a more detailed history of the problem is written, an underwater rock may be discovered that will show that Latvian/Jewish attitudes were full of hatred, envy, and murderous intent all along. But an undogmatic approach to the evidence, as we have it today, testifies to a high degree of tolerance. Nothing had occurred in Latvia that in any way could anticipate the Latvian participation in the murder of Latvia's Jews.

Latvians have never spoken with one voice, and, as Dov Levin shows in his article, if it is possible, the Jews of Latvia had even more discordances amongst them than did Latvians. Ulmanis is a controversial figure even among Latvians—many dinner parties have broken up over Ulmanis. At the Arājs trial, numerous Latvian Jews, all survivors of the Holocaust, were asked whether or not they thought Latvia had been a hostile, anti-Semitic country before the Nazi occupations: none answered the question in the affirmative. But there is no reason to make the relationship too idyllic: there was little interaction between the two peoples; they lived like oil and water separated by tradition, religion, and language. The 1922 Constitution, though embodying a high ethical standard, a respect for human diversity that perhaps the larger democratic states ought to try out, at the same time fossilized the relationship into separate compartments to assure that one was prohibited from seeing the other otherwise than "other."

Next I want to construct an explanation for the Latvian collaboration with the Nazi killing kommandos that does not rely exclusively on anti-Semitism as a necessary cause.

III

At the outset of the Barbarossa Plan, Latvia was in a chaotic condition. This is not the place to give the whole sociological background of Latvia before and during the occupation, but an enumeration of those "realities" that created the chaos is in order.

1. Just one year before, Latvia had undergone a Soviet occupation—the Red Army, on June 17, 1940, invaded Latvia.

2. The Soviet occupation activated a major population exodus from Latvia to Germany: the major migration consisted of Baltic Germans who, as a consequence of the Molotov-Ribbentrop pact, were given the privilege to repatriate to Germany. There were two waves of these repatriations: the first in the winter of 1940, the second in the winter of 1941. At the time of the second repatriation, the Barbarossa Plan was on the drawing board. In addition to the Baltic Germans, a smaller wave of Latvians also emigrated or fled the country. It is a matter of record that from these groups the Wehrmacht, the Abwehr, the civilian administration, and the Security Police

forces recruited hundreds of their personnel. The Latvian refugee recruits were assigned only the lower-level jobs, mostly in the Abwehr to obtain intelligence.[55] The psychology of the Baltic Germans, one of whom, Rosenberg, had made it to the very top of Nazidom, was a complicated one, fiercely anti-Bolshevik and, with few exceptions, hostile to the Latvians. Returning to Latvia in their military or police uniforms, the Baltic Germans carried along anger and grudges that dated back to the 1905 revolution, not to mention the land expropriations of the 1920s. For them the Festigung Deutschtums im Osten took on a meaning that even Himmler, Heydrich, and Hitler had no way of comprehending. In their attitudes towards the Bolsheviks and the peoples of the East, they out-Nazied the Reich Nazis. The Latvian "Bolshevik" past of 1917 and 1919 was not forgotten by them.[56]

3. Latvia had undergone a Stalinist revolution. In fact, when the Germans arrived, it was still going on. The salient features of this "revolution" were: (a) the social infrastructure which had made Latvia a stable society from 1920 to 1940 was destroyed, and (b) class and ethnic antagonisms were intensified. The Stalinization was most intensely felt in Latvia's countryside. The Communists had replaced the *pagasts (township) councils* with *executive committees* consisting of the "landless" representatives of the *pagasts,* and dispossessed the landed farmers of their lands in excess of 30 hectares. These confiscated lands were distributed in ten-hectare parcels to the erstwhile landless farmhands.[57] A whole new population subgroup, the "ten-hectare people" *(desmithektarnieki)* was created, a group which, though not by and large Communist, came to be suspected as Communist collaborators after the German occupation. Among all Latvian subgroups, save for the Communists, this group suffered most under the Nazis. They comprised the core of the Latvian prison population during the years of occupation and many of them, along with Jews, became victims in the first wave of the so-called "self-cleansing" pogroms.

4. On the eve of the German occupation, June 14, the Communists had transported about 15,000 Latvian citizens to Siberia. These deportees consisted mostly of the "stable" Latvian classes, the large landowners, the erstwhile leaders of the pagasts in the countryside, the intelligentsia, and the economic/political/social leadership in the cities. Among the deported were about 4,000 to 5,000 Latvian Jews.[58] Latvia's Jewish community, too, was in a highly disorganized state when the Nazis arrived. It is significant to note that the Jews proportionately suffered more than the Latvians under the Communists in 1940/41.

5. A counterwave to those Latvian citizens, Baltic Germans and others who were returning with the German forces, was composed of Latvians fleeing towards the Soviet interior. Among these there were perhaps as many as 15,000 Latvian Jews. The number would have been larger had the Soviets opened the frontier between Latvia and the USSR (sometimes referred to as the old frontier) earlier and had there been sufficient means of transportation towards the East.[59] The frontier opened up during the final days before occupation, but by that time many Jews had given up any hope of escaping.[60]

6. All laws, rules, and social/political organizations that had survived the Soviet occupations were suspended and dispersed by the German occupiers. Though nominally Latvia was turned over to a German civilian administration in about two months after the occupation, as far as the Latvian population was concerned, martial law was never lifted.

7. Since 1934 there had not been a free press in Latvia. Under Ulmanis it was moderately censored, while under the Soviets and the Nazis news was distorted and fabricated.

These social disruptions and transformations made Latvia, along with the other two Baltic countries, Lithuania and Estonia, unique among all Nazi-occupied lands. Czechoslovakia and France were allowed a number of autonomies, and Denmark was left its royalty. The closest to the kind of occupation that was imposed on the Baltic countries was Poland, but Poland, with the exception of its eastern part, had not undergone a double occupation. Its intellectuals and leadership were killed by Nazis, not Soviets.

The policies and assumptions with which the Germans entered Latvia need not detain us here. Initially they did not intend to grant any concessions to Latvian nationalism. Latvia was to undergo a precipitous Germanization, a refeudalization of the land, with German palatial estates studding the countryside.[61] The German setbacks in the East, starting with Moscow, made the Germans postpone their plans.

But the Germans were not the only ones to occupy Latvia; alongside of the Wehrmacht and the Security Police, the land was also invaded by at least 300 Latvians[62] and numberless Latvian-speaking Baltic Germans. Though most of the 300 appear to have been connected with the *Abwehr*, many were also attached to the Security Police and SD organization. In terms of propaganda effectiveness, no doubt the most pernicious and effective were the Latvian-speaking returnees. They possessed a certainty and authority that the Reich Germans did not have. Those who were not trained for SD work were chosen for their ideological beliefs—they had to be avowed anti-

Semites and believers in the "new Europe." From the very early moments of occupation, the German Security Police created a network of agents that fanned out throughout the countryside agitating, and more than agitating, looking for accomplices in the killing of Communists and Jews.

The propaganda that these agents brought along had two purposes: to create an impression of German invincibility and to enrage the populace against the "Jewish/Bolsheviks." But here is one important point to note: the propaganda never spoke of killing the Jews—the emphasis was on killing Communists. This is a fiction that all Nazi war criminals have maintained, and, on a certain level, at least for the initial stages of the killings, it is true. Dissimulations and lies were very much part of the Einsatzgruppen operations. Even Stahlecker, the leader of the EG A, when recruiting Latvians for the killing operations did not speak of killing the Jews.[63]

At first the Einsatzgruppen planned to liquidate Jews by spontaneous pogroms that they thought could be easily induced among the "liberated" natives. The Einsatzkommandos' endeavors to set that plan in motion were unsuccessful,[64] notwithstanding witnesses (Max Kaufman is especially to be noted) who have left testimonials to the contrary. The judgment against Grauel in the Landgericht Hanover speaks most forthrightly on this point:

The court could not establish that wide circles of Latvian people harbored hatred towards the Jews, such as was planned by the National Socialist leadership. . . . Wider circles of Latvians, however, did direct their hatred and repugnance towards those Jews whom they saw as collaborators with the hated Communist system, but not against their Jewish fellow citizen, with whom they lived together in towns and villages, and who like them earned his bread as craftsman or merchant, except for radical elements that are always around.[65]

Another piece in the puzzle speaks to the same point. At the moment of Nazi entrance in Rīga on July 1, one issue of an uncensored newspaper *Brīvā Zeme* managed to appear. This single side of newsprint, though it already ·glorifies Hitler, does have a ring of a Latvian voice, a voice of experience, one that welcomes peace. The Latvians are asked to be generous in victory:

Give welcome to the heroic German Army which has smashed our biggest enemy and has driven out the inhuman Communist looting gangs. This army, pitiful and defeated, now flees in panic from our land. Latvians, do not kill these pitiful people, disarm them, and take them prisoner, and only in cases when you find resistance, be quick to avert it.[66]

The writer of this editorial, who is thought to have been Arturs Kroders,[67] a veteran of the revolutions and a rightist journalist, had not heard of the "commissar order." Though he is full of hate for communism he discourages his countrymen from killing anyone. There is no mention of a pogrom. Since Gen. Stahlecker forbade all Latvian spontaneous activities, he also made sure that a second issue of the newspaper would not see the light of day.[68]

What were the motives of the Latvians in joining the killing kommandos? How significant was anti-Semitism?

There are no sociological studies available about the participants in these kommandos. In the Arājs trial files there are about 36 depositions from Rīga by participants in the kommando. *Though under the conditions they would not be expected to, none of them testify to anti-Semitism as a motive for joining the kommando.* They were young men, some of them soldiers, others students and workers, with time on their hands. An unusual number of athletes appear to have participated in the killings.[69] It was a time when a lot of men were on the loose, people who had lost their jobs and their social moorings. Arājs appears not to have had any difficulties in attracting captains and lieutenants to his unit. But, at the same time, a number of working-class people, looking for a better-paying job, also joined it. It is wrong to think, as has been said at times, that social outcasts manned the killing kommandos. Although it is unlikely that individuals with jobs and well-established life goals entered the group,[70] the reverse conclusion, that it was the Latvian riffraff that did so, is equally wrong. Arājs himself, at the age of 30, had still not finalized his career ambitions. In 1932 he had entered the University of Latvia in the pursuit of a law degree, but simultaneously, to make a living, he was working as a policeman. Under the Communists in 1941 he obtained a degree in law.

The original Arājs gang consisted of a group of anti-Communist partisans who, on July 1, met Gen. Stahlecker in the prefecture of Riga. The most frequent reason that the depositions give for joining was meeting a friend who told about the job. Some of the men had been out of work for an extended period of time. None say that they did it because they hated Jews.

In the pretrial interrogation, Arājs said that he did not claim to have been a friend of Jews, and that during the first few days of occupation there was a mass "psychosis": "I do not believe," he averred, "that Jews were murdered for racist purposes then."[71]

Even if anti-Semitism can be established as a motive for the young Latvians joining the kommandos, it can only be one of the motives, insufficient for a complete understanding of the problem. The motives for murder can be complex or simple, but here, in the biggest murder story of history, we have a social situation, many individuals participating in the act.

To begin with, we cannot eliminate the classical motives for murder: *greed, ambition,* and *power.*

Foremost it was greed that corrupted the Latvians. The Himmler/Heydrich plan was to kill the Jews and have their property taken to Germany. (One of the sobriquets for Nazi Party Germans in Rīga was *Teppich Roller.*) However, it seems that Stahlecker very quickly modified this rule. He allowed, even encouraged, the Latvians to loot. To the degree that pogroms existed, they were looting pogroms. Appropriation of Jewish goods took place both in provincial cities and in Rīga. We can assume that looting was a preamble for participation in the killings.[72] The "sharing" of Jewish property with Latvians was one way that the Germans involved the locals, though indirectly, in the murder of Jews. In many small towns the less desirable goods were given away gratis.[73]

Ambition and power as motives for joining the killing kommandos are more difficult to pinpoint. But especially the unemployed army officers might have been attracted to SD work for those purposes. Upon the arrival of the Germans in Latvia, the hope of the Latvian military men was to organize a national army and to rush off to the front to fight the Communists. Several recruiting stations were signing up volunteers hand over fist. But Gen. Stahlecker dashed the hopes for a Latvian Army. The Latvian officers were stranded with no income and no purpose. The alternative to SD work was to be a policeman. There is no doubt that Arājs himself saw a career opportunity in the job.[74]

Power has many disguises, psychological and social, from sadism to masochism. Seen from the outside and in retrospect, those Latvians who joined the killing forces surrendered their will to the Germans. But at the time the participants must have felt an illusion of freedom, and perhaps an intoxication with their power over life and death.[75]

Among the miasma of motives there were also *patriotism, resistance to tyranny* (in terms of 1941 anticommunism), *duty,* and *loyalty.* Since the Greeks, these have been upheld as the noblest of values, and so it was for the young Latvians, especially those who came to maturity after the independence of Latvia. And in this connection we must pay attention to a historical turn that a non-Latvian may have difficulty understanding. On the one hand, the defense of the homeland was upheld as the noblest of values, especially under the Ulmanis regime, and yet in June 1940, when confronted with a Soviet ultimatum, Ulmanis made the "prudent" decision not to resist the Soviet tanks. The young, the officers of the Latvian Army, were not given an opportunity to resist tyranny. The young were frustrated and chafing at the bit. The Nazi invasion, especially in view of Stalin's crimes in Latvia, gave an opportunity to the young Latvians to avenge the "enemy," as Ulmanis had not done. Stahlecker's men succeeded in narrowing Latvian patriotism, rechanneling it as anti-communism. Anti-Semitism in itself failed to arouse pogroms in Latvia, but in the guise of anti-communism intermixed with patriotism, it succeeded. Difficult as it is today to imagine, patriotism, loyalty, and duty were factors that drove young Latvians into the killing kommandos.[76]

The impact of *propaganda* and *lies*[77] cannot be overstated in any assessment. The Nazi system lived on lies: they lied to themselves and everybody who came in contact with them. Without the propaganda the German occupation would not have been what it was. The big lies the Nazis brought into Latvia that concerned the Jews were: 1. the lie of the Jewish/Bolshevik nexus; 2. the assertion that Jews were guilty for Stalin's atrocities; 3. and one falsehood that concerns the members of the killing kommandos particularly, that the executions that were taking place were of Communists and not of Jews. This dissimulation did not work for long, but it played a role in getting the killing procedures going, long enough to corrupt the participants and get them used to the job. In the beginning, to keep up the disguise, the Germans were careful to include some Communists with the Jews. Another factor in the success of the dissimulation was that in the beginning only men were killed.[78]

Part of the propaganda was the creation of a desire for *revenge*. This meant revenge in the general sense against the Communists, but a special effort was made by Stahlecker's men to enlist relatives of victims of communism in the killing teams.[79] For this purpose the propaganda apparatus was mobilized and agents were sent out to the countryside to find the kinsmen and cajole them into killing actions. The German agents used the grief of these men for their anti-Semitic purposes. To escalate the sense for revenge, the Einsatzgruppen leaders sought out the grave sites of Communist victims as soon as they arrived in a locale; then they dug them up and displayed the rotting corpses to the public. Digging up graves was the major news during the initial stage of the occupation. An especially gruesome tale of an exhumation of bodies comes from Rēzekne, as told by A. J. Bērziņš. A week after the German arrival the SD men assembled all Latvian local police guards at the edge of a grave site, and local Jews were made to dig up the pit. They dug up about 30 half-rotted corpses.

The day was hot, the corpses had been under for at least a week and they exhumed intolerable stench. I had never seen such horror before or since; I vomited from the stench and the sight. . . . The purpose of this display was to create hatred against the Communists, which we Latvians did not need any more, although I had imagined nothing like it. By making the Jews do the digging up of the tortured, the Germans wanted to underscore that the torturers and the killers had been Jews.[80]

The killing kommandos represented a special form of *male bonding*. To understand the kommandos, we must understand their social context. Homophilia (not homosexuality) is one of the bonding elements. It was the ultimate male society. It consisted of men who liked the companionship of other men. The core of the membership of the Arājs kommando were men of homophilic associations: soldiers, athletes, and fraternity brothers.[81] In the very early stages of the formation of the unit, Arājs used his social contacts, especially within the student fraternity circles. As already noted, membership in the kommando was solicited by word of mouth, from friend to friend. The athletes seem to have pulled each other into the kommandos. As time went on, as the kommando began to be involved in the killing activities, the contacts without, the society at large, began to dissolve, so that the kommando became a society in itself, close-knit and bonded by its secret work. There was nobody but themselves with whom to share their experiences. They ostracized themselves from the society outside, and in turn they were ostracized.[82]

Alcohol was the lubricant of kommando life. It was used before and after the killings. In the Liepāja actions, in the dunes of the Baltic Sea, a milkcan of rum was placed near the killing pits. One can even postulate that without alcohol there would not have been a Holocaust. One can say with assurance that there would not have been an Arājs kommando. It was alcohol that broke down the inhibitions of the young men and enabled them to perform the act for the first time,[83] and it was alcohol that brought them back to the killing pits. After the killing jobs the men drank themselves into a stupor. For those who did the shooting, a bottle of clear spirits was handed out immediately and consumed at the jobsite. And that was only the beginning. All recollections, all literary portraits, of the Latvian Jew-killers are placed in an alcohol-drenched context.[84]

In the context of the other factors discussed above, the *avoidance of military duties* was perhaps not a very strong motive for initially joining an

SD kommando, but this factor was a powerful inducement to continue serving in one.[85]

The problem of assigning causes to any historical act is complicated, perhaps even impossible. The assignment of causes is tied to one's ideological predilections and weighed down by emotions. In this chapter I have sketched in a multicausal or shotgun approach to the problem of the motives of Latvian participants in the killing actions. To say that Jews were killed because of anti-Semitism sounds plausible, even obvious. If anything is the ultimate prejudicial act, it is killing. And that is where the thinking of scholars dealing with anti-Semitism has stopped by and large. Is there another way of looking at the problem? In this study, I have taken the case of Latvia and argued that there is. The problem with the proposition that anti-Semitism kills lies not in itself, not in the idea, because during the course of history anti-Semitism has indeed killed, but it needs revision when it becomes a blanket explanation, when it is applied to all historical eras and social situations, and has become a substitute for study and thought. Analogy is a good way to start an argument, but it has not been much of an argument if at the finish it still holds its power over us. "Anti-Semitism kills" is a proposition true enough, but people are killed for many other causes, sometimes epic, sometimes petty—a handful of change, a cigarette, an insult, or a drink. I have argued in this study that, in the hierarchy of causes that led the Latvians to the killing of the Jews, anti-Semitism played a subsidiary part.

Notes

1. Viktors Arājs was tried and convicted in Landgericht Hamburg in 1978 for his crimes during the German occupation in Latvia. He died in Kassel prison on January 13, 1988. There were various phases in the development of Arājs' kommando, and at its peak it had about 1,100 men, but during the killing period of 1941 it had no more than 300.

2. In general it is true that no one was coerced into joining the kommandos. The exception is some men who in some ways were tainted by collaboration with the Soviets: one hears frequent stories that on occasion they were coerced into joining this or that police kommando. Eduards Freimanis portrays one such case in his novel *Ticība* (The Faith), 1978.

3. To assess the Latvian opinion in Latvia even at this stage of glasnost is not possible, although for the first time since the war, the killing of Jews has been ever so gently raised there.

4. Ernests Blanks, who in the twenties was known for anti-Semitic remarks, ridicules Hitler and his anti-Semitism in a pamphlet written in 1933, *Hitlers, žīdi un Latvija*. Also see Šilde's views in *Latvijas vēsture, 1914–1940*, Stockholm, 1976, p. 568.

5. Dov Levin, "The Jews and the Sovietisation of Latvia, 1940–41, *Soviet Jewish Affairs*, Vol. 5, No. 1, 1975, pp. 40–42. I have tried to check on the incidents that Levin reports finding in the Soviet Jewish press of 1940, but have found no substantiation from the Latvian side. Of course, there may be a kernel of truth behind the incidents, as there usually is, but in general they strike me as propaganda exaggeration.

6. The English equivalents of the two words are "Hebrew" and "Jew."

7. See A. Ezergailis, *The Latvian Impact on the Bolshevik Revolution*, New York, 1983.

8. There was much Jewish/Latvian cooperation during the time of 1905 and 1917 Revolutions, but the leadership of the Latvian revolutionary parties was always in Latvian hands. Semyon Nachimson, a Jew from Liepāja, was the only Jew who played an important leadership role in the Latvian Bolshevik Party in 1917.

9. J. Pētersons, "Mans Dzimtais Pagasts," in *Kosa, Novads un Ļaudis*, A. Plaudis, ed., Melbourne, 1982, tells how power was transferred in his *pagasts*. Right after the occupation, a certain Broms arrived in his *pagasts* and called an assembly of its citizens. When asked on what basis he had called the meeting, he answered that he called it in the name of the Party. When challenged that under democratic rules the leadership of the assembly must be elected, he pointed with his thumb behind a curtain, saying that the Red Army stood behind him. "Then the curtain opened revealing a couple of Red Army men with machine guns at the ready. A few others appeared and stationed themselves at the door" (pp. 18–19). There were no Jews to be found. During the course of the year, Pētersons traveled to his district town Cēsis, and also to Rīga on business. In the course of his engagements at a variety of administrative instances, he had to go all the way to Rīga to encounter a "young, slight Jewish girl, who spoke to him with a Jewish accent, serving in a low administrative post" (p. 23). Pētersons' example certainly does not prove, although it is his purpose to do so, that Latvia's administration was saturated by Jews.

10. For the most credible account of Jewish "power" under the Soviets in 1940, see Dov Levin, op. cit. p. 49.

11. V. Pelēcis, in a letter of 1/22/85, reports that in Alūksne the only Jewish functionaries were three Truman brothers, two of whom served as members of the militia and one as a director of a cooperative store.

12. According to Levin, op. cit. pp. 49–50, Jews were heavily represented in the Workers' Guard which was set up along military lines. Although initially intended as a police auxiliary, after the outbreak of the war they entered the Red Army and fought bravely against the Nazis. In certain locations, such as Liepāja, the Workers' Guard comprised a significant part of the resistance. Many Latvians from Liepāja believe that it was the Jews who were the last ones to give up the struggle against the invading forces.

13. Alfreds Ceichners in *Latvijas Bolševizācija, 1940–1941* (The Bolshevization of Latvia), first published under the Nazis in 1944 (reprinted by Gauja, 1986), pp. 143–44. Ceichners' book can also serve as evidence that, under German occupation, the information about the supposed Jewish/Bolshevik nexus, which the Anti-Semitic Institute purported to study, was not available.

14. It is very likely that Latvians confused the Workers' Guards with Chekists.

15. Edgars Andersons, in his *Latvijas Vēstures Ārpolītika, 1920–1940*, Stockholm, 1984, describes the crowd (about 1,500 to 2,000) on the square by the railroad station as consisting of Jews and Russians. The analysis of the crowd on June 17 requires further study.

16. Georgs Alchimovičs (letter 4/29/85) writes that the first conflict with Jews in Sarkandaugava, a multi-ethnic, highly integrated part of Rīga, occurred during the Soviet occupation: " . . . when, under the Russian occupation, there appeared a group of Jewish *Komsomols*, who were giving us the lip. We boys declared a war on them and we fought with rocks and mud pies. There were a few bumps on the head, but otherwise nobody won." This "war" could as well have been with gangs from Čiekurkalns, Kundziņsala, or Milgrāvis. At the same time it must be noted that there was no separate *Komsomol* organization for Jews. Mirdza Viil in a letter in *Juanā Gaita*, No. 155, 1985, p. 60, writes: "At the time I went to the gymnasium. I remember well that all Jewish children came to school with red scarves around their necks, and they were watching other students. For example, when other kids did not want to sing Communist songs, they made them do it."

17. Ceichners grudgingly admits that, in the beginning some Latvians, Marxistically attuned workers, also rejoiced about the fall of the old government," op. cit. p. 151.

18. Levin's article must be consulted for the variety of tensions within the Jewish community during the course of the year. Op. cit. pp. 48–51.

19. It is usually believed that about 5,000 Jews were deported to Siberia on June 14. If that is the correct number, then it must be concluded that proportionately more Jews suffered from communism than did the Latvians at large, as the figure for Latvians deported and killed during the Soviet occupation is pegged at about 35,000.

20. The anti-Semitic Latvians have been hard to put to name names of Jews in the Soviet NKVD apparatus. The highest number that has ever been named is six, and that includes Noviks, a Latvian from Rēzekne, who was the head of the Latvian NKVD. As one example, see *We Accuse the East—We Warn the West*, Germany, 1948, pp. 22–23.

21. For the most accessible history of the Jews of Latvia, see M. Bobe et al., *The Jews in Latvia*, Tel Aviv 1971, especially the chapter by Mendel Bobe, "Four Hundred Years of the Jews in Latvia," pp. 21–77. For statistical information about Jews in Latvia, see M. Skujenieks, *Latvija, Zeme un Iedzīvotāji, (Latvia, Land and People)*, Rīga, 1927, pp. 307–312 and J. Rutkis, *Latvijas Ģeogrāfija (Latvia's Geography)*, Stockholm, 1960, pp. 448–451.

22. H. Biezais, *Saki tā kā tas ir*, *(Say It, the Way It Is)*, (Lansing, Mich.) 1985, remembers the buyer negatively.
23. There is a lot of repetition in Latvian folk songs, so in reality out of the 150 there may only be about 40 original ones.
24. Imants Freibergs from Montreal supplied me with a printout of Jewish folk songs, for which I am grateful. Latvian folk songs are untranslatable, but as an example I shall give the following:

Rīga Rīga, tāla Rīga,
Labāk šē Jelgavā;
Labāk šē Jelgavā
Pie skaistiem žīdiņiem.

(Rīga, Rīga faraway Rīga,
It's better here in Jelgava;
It's better here in Jelgava
With the beautiful Jews.)

25. See a reportage about this book in *Atbalss*, No. 3, 1985, p. 3.
26. The exception is a story "Mūžīgais žīds" (The Eternal Jew) by Jānis Poruks.
27. Andrievs Niedra, *Kad mēness dilst (When the Moon is Waning)*, 1955.
28. Max Matatyahu Laserson, "The Jews and the Latvian Parliament, 1918–1934," Bobe, op. cit. p. 119.
29. Frida Michelson, *I Survived Rumuļi*, Holocaust Library, New York, 1979, p. 31. Her story is the most extreme on the record, and inasmuch as she only heard it from her relatives, the part of murder and extensive rapings may be an exaggeration.
30. This story is told by my father in a collection of his writings, *Ezergaiļla Grāmata*, Ithaca, N.Y., 1988.
31. Prof. M. Laserson in *Jewish Social Studies*, Vol. 14, No. 3, 1941, p. 276. As quoted in Charles Collins (Kārlis Kalniņš) *Latvian-Jewish Relations: The Tragic Plight of Latvians and Jews under Nazi Occupation of Latvia*, Esslingen, 1949.
32. For a history of Jewish schools in the free state of Latvia, see Z. Michaeli, "Jewish Cultural Autonomy and the Jewish School System," Bobe (ed.), op. cit. pp. 186–216.
33. Abraham Godin, "Jewish Traditional and Religious Life in the Latvian Communities," Bobe (ed.), op. cit. pp. 217–229.
34. Laserson, "The Jews and the Latvian Parliament," pp. 94–185.
35. Karl Aun, "The 1917 Revolution and the Idea of the State of Estonia," A. Ezergailis and G. von Pistohlkors (eds.), *Die Baltischen Provinzen Russlands zwischen den Revolutionen von 1905 and 1917*, Cologne, 1982, pp. 287–294.
36. Edgars Andersons, "Trīs Bezvalsts Tautas Latvijā," *Treji Vārti*, No. 94, 1983, p. 11.
37. Laserson, *Jewish Social Studies*, op. cit. p. 280. Laserson, who was to become a professor at Columbia University, was a member of the Central Land Distribu-

tion Committee, and consequently he speaks on the matter with authority. It must however be noted that only 2% of Jews lived in the country.

38. A franker assessment of the Jewish situation during the democratic period is to be found in Yivo archives, Baltic Countries folder, 1.17, p. 39–2:

    There is little to be said about the attitudes of the Latvian government towards the Jews before the establishment of the authoritarian regime. The government scrupulously fulfilled its obligations as to maintaining the Jewish schools. No limitations were imposed upon the Jews in the political field, for that matter, in the field of free business enterprise. There were limitations, to be sure, as to Jewish participation in officialdom and as to government orders to private business firms. Even more restricted was the admission of Jews to the Latvian University where rigorous entrance tests in the Lettish language were used to keep away a considerable portion of Jewish applicants. As to Jewish professors, only two were admitted to the faculty of the university during the whole time of Latvian independence.

39. The history of the Saeima, especially from the viewpoint of the minority inter-relationship, has not yet been written. Some of the conflicts can be seen in Bobe, op. cit. pp. 62–71. A. Šilde, *Latvijas vēsture, 1917–1940*, Stockholm, 1976. For some of the tensions and conflicts, also see Andersons, op. cit.

40. Brief descriptions of the Nacionālais klubs and other nationalistic organizations and their contacts with European fascists, can be found in Andersons, *Latvijas Vēstures* Vol. I, pp. 395–432, especially footnote 1 of the chapter.

41. Laserson, op. cit. p. 125.

42. Ibid., p. 124.

43. See Šilde's discussion of *Pērkoņkrusts*, Ādolfs Šilde, *Latvijas Vēsture, 1914–1940*, Stockholm, 1976, pp. 562–564. The circulation of *Pērkoņkrusts* newspaper at times reached 15,000 copies, which for an upstart party was considered very high.

44. *Pērkoņkrusts* weekly publication, *Ugunskrusts*, which was not available to me, is indispensable for writing the history of the movement in general and of anti-Semitism in Latvia in particular. In the early thirties the Latvian Nationalist-Socialist Party, which cleaved close to Hitler's Nazis, came ito existence. It had only 80 members. Šilde, op. cit. p. 564.

45. Gustavs Celmiņš, *Eiropas Krustceļos*, Esslingen 1947.

46. See Šilde's deposition in Arājs trial documents, p. 2060.

47. Yivo archives, Baltic Countries folder 1.17, p. 38-1a.

48. The last anti-Semitic pamphlets in Latvia in the early thirties were written, translated, and published by a certain J. Davis. For a review of anti-Semitic literature in Latvia, see Yivo Archives, Baltic Countries folder 1.17, p. 38-1a.

49. In folk stories, on the anecdotal level, there exists the Jew who could not be kept out of the university, regardless of the barriers that guardians of "high standards" might construct against him. If flunked once, this mythic Jew would tenaciously return for the second or third attempt to gain admittance. One mythic professor in the Latvian Language Department had a method whose success in flunking a Jew was foolproof. After the Jew has successfully navigated through all of the subsurface perils of morphology, syntax, and conjugations, the professor would get the candidate on pronunciation, by asking the Jew to

pronounce the name of a literary character: "Biezum Bozums." This Cerberus of Latvian linguistic purity in the anecdote would triumph because supposedly no Jew could ever have mastered the falling, rising, and inflecting intonations of the word.

50. Bobe, op. cit. p. 72.

51. This is very powerfully demonstrated by K. Siljakov in *Mana Atbilde, Vol. II,* East Lansing, Mich., 1985.

52. Yivo Archives, Baltic Countries folder 1.17, p. 30.

53. The policy differed from an outright nationalization inasmuch as it was a gradual one, the state buying out the owners of the firms. See Arnolds Aizsilnieks, *Latvijas Saimniecības Vēsture,* Stockholm, 1968, pp. 606–611. The retail trade, in which more Jews made their living than in any other area, was not interfered with by the state.

54. See Yivo Archives, Baltic Countries folder 1.17, pp. 39-2 and -3. The author of the manuscript attributes this generosity to the influence of Mordecai Dubin, the Aguda leader, with whom Ulmanis had a close relationship. According to this author, visas to Polish Jews, however, were not issued by Latvian consulates.

55. Haralds Biezais' book on the topic is forthcoming. Among his articles on the topic is "Nacionālie partizāni," and "Vācu okupācijas priekšvakarā," *Kara Invalīds,* No. 29, 1984, pp. 12–22 and No. 30, 1985, pp. 21–30. Also Jānis Dzintars, "Ar Kāškrusta zīmi," *Literatūra un Māksla,* Nos. 27–29, 1986.

56. The Nazi roots in the Baltic are traced out in a seminal work by Robert George L. Waite, *Vanguard of Nazism. The Free Corps Movement in Postwar Germany 1918–1923,* Cambridge, Mass., 1952. Without the Baltic connection, the Nazis would not have known what communism was.

57. Aizsilnieks, op. cit. p. 862.

58. From the statistics available, it is not clear whether the 5,000 deported Jews were part of the 15,000 or in addition to them. *Latvijas Enciklopēdija 1962–1982,* Sej. I, 1983, p. 318. Altogether perhaps as many as 32,000 Latvian citizens were deported or killed by the Communist regime of 1940/41. The German security forces in 1941 prohibited counting Jewish victims under the Soviets. Interview with A. Šilde 6/85. Five thousand is the estimate that Max Kaufmann uses, op. cit. pp. 44–45, and it is accepted by Levin, op. cit. pp. 52 and 56. Levin also tells us about 250 Jewish refugees who were arrested and deported to Siberia on June 23 (p. 52). The 5,000 figure is also used by Mavriks Vulfson in his remarkable speech at the plenum of creative societies in Rīga, June 1–2, 1988, *Literatūra un Māskla,* p. 21.

59. Michelson, op. cit., tells about her family's attempt to cross over into the Soviet Union at Zilupe. They were not allowed to do so (op. cit. pp. 30–31). Also Frank Gordon tells of special NKVD troops that barred the entrance of "Western" Jews into the USSR. He and his family escaped from Rīga in a train. "Viņā pusē: bēgšanas," *Laiks,* 1/19/83.

60. The Soviet brutalization of Jews during the occupation, according to Levin's analysis, was another reason why many never even tried to run away. Op. cit.

This especially was the case with those Jews whose properties the Soviets had confiscated.

61. It appears that no single concrete plan had been agreed upon. But numerous memos were circulated and a special planning institute, the *Reichskommissariat für Festigung Deutschen Volkstums im Osten,* was put in place. For Hitler's ideas on the future of the Baltic states, see Bormann's memo in IMT (International Military Tribunal) Vol. XXXVIII, pp. 86–94, document 221 L. Also Seppo Myllyniemi, *Die Neu Ordnung der Baltischen Lander, 1941–1944,* Finnish Historical Society, Helsinki, 1973 and Hans-Heinrich Wilhelm, "Die Einsatzgruppe A der Sicherheitspolizei und des SD 1941/42, Eine exemplarische Studie," in *Die Truppe des Weltanschaungskrieges, Die Einsatzgruppen der Sincherheitspolizei und des SD, 1938–1942,* by Helmut Krausnick and Hans-Heinrich Wilhelm, Deutsche Verdag-Anstalt, Stuttgart, 1981.

62. Sigailis, "Die Vorgeschichte der Entstehung der Lettischen Legion im Zweiten Weltkrieg," *Acta Baltica,* Vol. XXI, 1982, pp. 246–282. Also see O. Freivalds, *Latviešu karavīrs Otrā Pasaules Karā,* Vol. II, 1972, p. 18. Also Dzintars speaks on this matter.

63. I have interviewed a lawyer who spoke with Stahlecker on June 1 and 2 and on several subsequent days, and, according to him, Stahlecker never mentioned Jews in his presence. Interview with T, September 1985. The same is maintained by Arājs in his pretrial interrogation, Landgericht Hamburg, p. 16.

64. For the situation in Rīga, see Stahlecker's Consolidated report, L-180, pp. 22– 23. For Dvinsk, see Ereigniss Meldungen No. 24, July 16, 1941, and the case against Dr. Erich Ehrlinger et al. in the Landgericht Karlruhe, 1961–63, *Justiz und NS-Verbrechen,* Amsterdam, 1978, pp. 66–132. For Liepāja, see the Verdict of Landgericht Hanover of Erhard Grauel et al., 1971. The German court cases against Nazi war criminals concerned with Latvia proceed from the premise that the killings took place as a consequence of planned operations.

65. Landgericht Hanover, Strafurteil gegen Graul u.a. vom 14. Oktober 1971, p. 49.

66. *Brīvā Zeme,* July 1, 1941.

67. Arturs Kroders became a collaborationist after the occupation, and for a very brief period at the beginning, he served as an editor of the SD-controlled *Tēvija.* But the Germans never trusted him.

68. There are only a few Latvian underground publications available, most of them in German translation, that have been found in SD archives. There is a great deal that we can say about those publications, but, in general, to the degree that I have seen them, they seem to be indifferent to the fate of Jews, except for a letter by Pēteris Vilciņš, who charges Hitler with a grave error. See A. Ezergailis, "Pētera Vilciņa padoms", *Saulainā Krasta Vēstis,* No. 1/2, 1986.

69. My article "Arāja komanda," *Akadēmijas Vēstis,* No. 10, 1988.

70. Eriks Pārups, an officer of the Latvian Army who knew many of the people in the kommando, thinks that those officers joined the Arājs ranks who had always dragged behind the exceptional. Conversation on January 5, 1988.

71. Landgericht Hamburg, Arājs pretrial interrogation, p. 16.

72. The actual killers did not even take the bigger cut, if they took any. Especially in Rīga, there was a separation between the looters and the killers. In Rīga the ones who really enriched themselves were not Arājs men but the Rīga city police. It was the city policemen who controlled the Jewish apartments. The biggest opportunity for the Rīga police arose at the time of the ghettoization of the Jews in October 1941. I have obtained especially strong testimony on this matter from Roberts Kalniņš who at that time was with the criminal police division and, on several occasions, had to investigate policemen for having overindulged their acquisitive instincts. Another of my correspondents reported to me that one of her relatives had accumulated a considerable amount of Jewish goods, that in her native town one policeman had been married in a Jewish suit, and that she encountered the wife of Tauriņš, a known SD operative in Viesīte, wearing a fur coat in summertime. Letter T. 6/9/85.

73. In some smaller towns with a large Jewish population, the distribution of property had the potential for corrupting the whole town.

74. The Arājs and other Latvian SD kommandos were organized for a limited purpose and duration to kill Jews and other "enemies." During the mass killing period, July–December 1941, the kommando size was about 300. The kommando expanded to about 1,100 men during 1942, when the war against the partisans began. A. Ezergailis, "Latviešu skaits Sicherheits Dienst kalpībā," *Saulainā Krasta Vēstis*, October 1985, pp. 37–43. Also see Pārups, op. cit.

75. It was the ultimate liberation from taboos. The generation of people who knew the killers, the brothers, the sisters, the cousins, and the lovers, who could impart much psychological insight about the impact of the killing experience to posterity, are passing on. On the folklore level, the Latvian memory of these killers centers mostly on their emotional breakdowns. There are numerous stories of how, over vodka, they begin to weep and confess their crimes, stories about nightmares that they have suffered. There were numerous suicides among the participants in the killing units (still ongoing) and cases of insanity: " . . . the older brother of my friend ran into my father's store, pistol in hand, eyes popped out, incomprehensibly shouting, an open overcoat flapping. He just ran in, went the length of the store, and ran out." Reported by V. Grīnvalds. Those who went insane on the job were killed by the Germans. Parents sometimes received no information about the disappearance of their sons, only a bundle of clothes.

76. In terms of duty and higher orders, it must be noted that it was not Jews alone that the killing Latvians murdered—they also killed the insane and gypsies. They killed anyone that they were ordered to kill. They were also the executioners of the national Latvian resistance members.

77. In the fall of 1941, the SD in Rīga began to look for interpreters, people who knew Russian and German. Two groups of these interpreters were organized, one for potential work in Leningrad, the other for Moscow. The Moscow group was taken to Minsk and eventually used in actions against Jews.

78. Patriotism was the main defense that Arājs made in the trial. Above all, he presented himself as a fighter against communism. As early as 1944 there are indications that Arājs considered himself to have been duped by the Germans.

Prof. Aizsilnieks reports that in a conversation in 1944 Arājs had advised him to stay away from the Germans: "For if you give a German a little finger, he will take all of you, make you do things that you would not want to do" (A. Aizsilnieks, *Dzīves Šūpoles*, Stockholm 1979, p. 158). In the pretrial interrogations Arājs said: "I have hated National Socialism. It has besmirched the Latvians and enticed them into these crimes. At first they sold us to the Russians and later sanctimoniously exploited our national feelings and sense of duty. They came as liberators of our land but broke their promises."

79. The news of the deportations of June 14 were leaked to many individuals. Thinking that families would not be deported, the males alone hid out. It was these stranded males that became special objects of Stahlecker's attention.

80. A. J. Bērziņš, "Tur tālā kaujas laukā," *DV Mēnešraksts*, No. 2, 1973, p. 21. The propaganda gambit worked on the author, not that he became a killer of Jews, but later in the memoirs he tells us that from that time on he swore to take revenge on the Communists and, to do so, looked for opportunities to go the front.

81. U. Ģērmanis, in his novel *Pakapies tornī*, actually makes the Arājs man a homosexual. It would be wrong to generalize from Ģērmanis' portrayal, though he draws his character from real life, to impute homosexuality to the kommando members at large.

82. A person who had an opportunity to meet Arājs' sister in a semi-social situation felt that at that particular gathering this ostracism extended even to her. Conversation with Ms. V. 6.7.86.

83. Valentīna Lasmane reports that the Commander of an SD unit, which was stationed in the agricultural secondary school in Latgale, where she taught, got the boys of the senior class drunk, on an evening in the fall of 1941. Thereafter they participated in the killing of the local Jews. Interview, June 11985.

84. Two novels by E. Freimanis, *Visādi Jēpi* (manuscript) and *Ticība*. The other two authors are Arnolds Apse, *Klostera Kalnā*, pp. 198–200, and U. Ģērmanis, *Pakapies tornī*, serialized in *Laiks*, 4/16/86 to 5/3/86, segments 12–17.

85. The Arājs kommando began to change its character in 1942, when the killings in Latvia were finished. From there on, they did have assignments against partisans, but even so they were considered rear units, meaning that it was safer to serve in the SD than on the front line. The Latvian frontline men referred to the SD as "rear rats."

[13]

The Rhetoric of Anti-Semitism in Postwar American Literature

Guy Stern

A careful, if general, survey by Michael Dobkowski of American anti-Semitism in the nineteenth and early twentieth century, which also includes several sidelong glances at American literature, arrives at the following conclusion:

[Past] theories seem to underestimate the importance of a major source of anti-Semitism—the pervasive negative image of the Jew propagated by the popular culture of the period. The impact of the anti-Jewish thrust, transmitted through flagrant stereotyped expressions that appeared in literature, on stage, and in the press, has not been adequately analyzed. The evidence indicates that even prior to the 1890's many misconceptions and falsehoods circulated in America that had little relation to the agrarian protest or to social claustrophobia. The pervasiveness of this negative imagery is one indication that America was not as tolerant in this fluid and turbulent age as we have been led to believe; it is one more index of the continued presence of anti-Semitism in the American society of that period. Despite all professions of equality, prejudice did persist, and it was expressed, consciously or unconsciously, through the stereotyping of the American Jew.[1]

To update Mr. Dobkowski's conclusion in reference to the literature of our own times, even at this early point in our discussion: Anti-Semitism in contemporary American literature appears less frequently, is usually less blatant, but has forsaken none of the stereotyping images of the past.

It will be the task of this chapter to establish this hypothesis by applying

291

consistent criteria to a set of representative examples, ranging from popular culture to T. S. Eliot. In the past, investigations of literary anti-Semitism, even when comprehensive and insightful, have tended to be impressionistic and emotional, or have tried to defeat the myth of the Jew with the inadequate weapon of Truth.[2] Rabbi David Philipson's classic study *The Jew in English Fiction*, for example, concedes that Jews can be treated in literature, but beyond exposing some of their humorous foibles and vagaries, must be accorded deep respect.[3] Fortunately, an article has appeared in recent months which eschews such subjective judgments and reflects a clear understanding of both sociological and aesthetic methodology. Mark H. Gelber's article, "What Is Literary Antisemitism?" supplemented by a few criteria of other researchers and of my own, has been adapted to serve as the theoretical framework of this investigation. "A cogent, working definition of literary antisemitism," Mr. Gelber argues, "proceeds from literature itself, that is, from texts, but it also takes into account how different readerships have perceived the antisemitic aspects of texts in various ways over the course of time. Basic techniques of literary analysis and character differentiation, and linguistic analysis are central to understanding literary antisemitism."[4]

I

After a lengthy historical survey of Judeophobia, going back to pagan times, Gelber subjects the story of Golgotha to vigorous exegesis and finds, in examples of its literary treatment from the Middle Ages onward, "the aesthetic means . . . [to] implicate the entire Jewish people as responsible for the death of Jesus, including past, present and future generations." Indeed, he adds, the ubiquitous gentile complicity in the Holocaust "is totally incomprehensible without the extensive background . . . of Christian antisemitism."[5] Hence, it follows, as Gelber demonstrates, that all works which emphasize a collective and unexpungeable guilt of all Jews are prejudicial. He is buttressed in this argument by an analysis, also central to this part of my chapter, of the Oberammergau Passion Play. Leonard Swidler and Gerard S. Sloyan deplore the fact that the literary formulations of Oberammergau —such as "the Jews," "the crowd," and "may his blood come over us and our sons and daughters"—encourage Christians to blame all Jews, and for all times.[6]

This animadversion is well timed. Only fifteen years ago Broadway gave birth to a triumphantly successful rock musical, currently the most quintessential form of American theatre, entitled *Jesus Christ Superstar*. "Hailed by *Variety* as 'the biggest all-media parlay in show history,' *Jesus Christ Superstar* started its phenomenal career as a record album with sales soaring into the millions, a subsequent concert attraction, a full-scale stage spectacle, a motion picture, then television presentation, and a theatre piece destined for perennial revivals."[7] Though written by two British-born collaborators, lyricist Tim Rice and composer Andrew Lloyd Webber, the work has found a secure place in popular American literature: It is included in the drama collection *Great Rock Musicals* by the American playright and theatre anthologist, Stanley Richards.[8]

The identical structural elements that were criticized in the Oberammergau Passion Play recur in *Jesus Christ Superstar*. Swidler and Sloyan, the critics of Oberammergau, have advocated that the collective term "the Jews" be replaced by "the leaders of the Jews" or the "adversaries of Jesus," and the inclusive terms "the crowd" or "the people" by something like "the mob."[9] But the following quotations from the play are as all-encompassing in their indictment as Oberammergau:

PILATE: Talk to me, Jesus Christ
You have been brought here—manacled, beaten
By your own people—do you have the first idea why you deserve it?
Listen, King of the Jews
Where is your kingdom?
Look at me—am I a Jew?

Somewhat later in the same scene, "the crowd" answers Pilate:

We have no king but Caesar! Crucify him!

And Pilate retorts:

Well this is new—respect for Caesar
Till now this has been noticeably lacking
Who is this Jesus? Why is he different?
You Jews produce Messiahs by the sackful

To which "the crowd" answers:

We need him crucified
It's all you have to do
We need him crucified
It's all you have to do.[10]

Beyond the inflammatory words, the anti-Semitic message is underscored by the on-beat rhythm of the rock music and the emotion-charged acting on stage. When the musical was filmed by Director Norman Jewsohn—a non-Jew despite his name—two writers on anti-Semitism, Arnold Forster and Benjamin Epstein, were moved to remark, "It is Oberammergau set to music."[11]

II

Mark Gelber, in his historical analysis of literary anti-Semitism, established that the theatre's ongoing evolution towards ever greater individualization of characters to a large extent bypassed Jewish figures: "Jewish stage characters . . . were less successful in breaking out of their customary roles as archvillains."[12] Hence, Gelber argues, the very mention of the Jewish identity of a character in a literary context could be used as a form of opprobrium. And it follows that the villain in a literary work, if identified as a Jew, must be counterbalanced by a more positive figure who is also a Jew, in order to avoid the rhetoric of anti-Semitism. Otherwise the Jew as evil-doer, Mr. Gelber argues, simply reifies ancient prejudices in life and on stage, as projected, for example, in Christopher Marlowe's *The Jew of Malta*. Even many languages, Mr. Gelber observes, have absorbed negative overtones with the noun "Jew" or its verbalized form. Hence, the need for counterbalancing a villain. This balancing act, Mr. Gelber adds, becomes even more complex, if a villain's Jewishness has caused his villainy. Then the more positive and offsetting characters would be perceived as atypical Jews and we can properly perceive such a work as signaling literary anti-Semitism.

As an example of a work featuring a solitary Jew, his detestability stemming from his Jewishness, Katherine Anne Porter's novel, *Ship of Fools*, suggests itself. It will not appear irrelevant that Ms. Porter, some three years after the appearance of her novel, once more and undisguisedly in a 1965 article in *Harper's*, curiously reminiscent of German vilifications of the so-called *Asphalt-literatur*, repeated her slanders:

I am an old American. My people came to Virginia in 1648, so we have had time to become acclimatized. . . . Truly, the South and the West . . . have made and are making American Literature. We are in the direct legitimate line; we are people based in English as our mother tongue, and we do not abuse it or misuse it, and when we speak a word, we know what it means. These others have fallen into a curious kind of argot, more or less originating in New York, a deadly mixture of academic, guttersnipe, gangster, fake-Yiddish, and dull old wornout dirty words—an appalling bankruptcy in language, as if they hate English and are trying to destroy it along with all other living things they touch. [13]

"Fake-Yiddish," but not that phrase alone, is the tell-tale indicator that Jews specifically are the object of her attack. But let us now turn to her novel.

Ship of Fools, published in 1962 (with a few excerpts in magazines preceding the book publication), narrates a journey aboard a German freighter-passenger ship from Vera Cruz to Bremerhaven, with passengers and crew reflecting attitudes—both national and personal—common during the pre-Nazi years. But perhaps the sentiments expressed here are more universal. The author says about her book: "I took for my own this simple, almost universal image of the ship of this world on its voyage to eternity. . . . I am a passenger on this ship." [14]

If so, she has a fellow passenger one Julius Loewenthal, whose ultimate destination is Düsseldorf, where he wishes to pay a visit to his cousin Sarah. He is the only Jew aboard, is not exactly the villain of the voyage—being more sinned against than sinning—but turns out to be a thoroughly unsavory character aboard the ship of fools. Katherine Anne Porter loses no time in pointing out his faith. Except for two Catholic priests, he is the only one who, in a prefatory *dramatis personae*, is identified by his religion, which in turn is immediately set in contrast to his occupation. "Jewish manufacturer and salesman of Catholic Church furnishings . . . " (xi). The author develops this incongruity later in the novel. After a vituperative attack on the Catholic church, a fellow passenger questions Loewenthal's choice of business. "The way I look at it, it's a business. . . . If I don't sell them, somebody else will. So why not I sell them?" (97). His shoddy ethics, it will be noted, are matched by his shoddy English—the same type the author deplored in her article in *Harper's*. His ugliest act, beyond his abhorrence of mixed marriages or even a date with a Gentile, beyond consistently referring to all the other passengers as *goyim* and *shicksahs*, often in connection with other pejoratives, is his intolerance for the religion of others, born directly out of his over-zealous Jewish orthodoxy:

Herr Loewenthal on deck glanced through the window into the small library and saw the Mass going on. He restrained his impulse to spit until he had passed beyond the line of vision of the worshipers; then, his mouth watering with disgust, he moved to the rail and spat like a landlubber into the wind, which blew it back in his face. At his curse being thus returned to his very teeth, his whole body was suffused with superstitious terror, it scurried like mice in his blood, it shook his nerves from head to foot. "God forbid," he said aloud, with true piety. (152)

Scattered over 450-odd pages of text, Julius Loewenthal's "Jewish" appearance emerges with all its presupposed archetypal ugliness. He is short-legged (97), has thick curly lips, heavy-lidded eyes (96), a smooth oily face, chocolate-colored lightless eyes and, for emphasis and variation, once more "unpleasantly thick mobile lips that squirmed as he chewed or talked" (240). Finally, he has the obligatory coarse manners. "[Loewenthal] took half an egg in his mouth, added a heap of cabbage, and chewing awhile, went on [talking]" (241). The depiction of Loewenthal and his actions fits all the components of Gelber's definition of literary anti-Semitism, i.e., that he, a thoroughly unprepossessing character, appears as the only Jew in the novel. True enough, we hear of Jews other than Loewenthal. One of the German Christians has a Jewish wife, whom he loves, even though he believes her blood to be tainted. She is, in the mind of her husband, far superior to Loewenthal, is blond, has an uptilted nose and her mother is so aristocratic that she would set the dogs on the likes of Loewenthal, again on the surmise of Freytag, the equivocal husband and son-in-law (141). But the wife, this alleged paean of Jewish womanhood, is not among the passengers and Loewenthal is left as the lone and unsavory representative of World Jewry.

In one of his final appearances, when his cabin mate and tormentor is carried into their cabin after having been wounded in a barroom fight, Loewenthal breaks out in an entirely justified, Shylock-like burst of self-pity. But he is not allowed even this tiny crumb of self-rehabilitation. The one decent character in the book, the ship's doctor, a German, possibly uniting here with the unidentified authorial voice, condemns him for his burst of self-assertion. "Dr. Schumann [was] deeply repelled by this show of selfishness and bad temper" (257). Katherine Anne Porter, who has told us that she is a fellow passenger on this our common ship of fools, would not, it appears, be an entirely salubrious presence for her Jewish fellow travelers.

III

Examples of the "ugly Jew" could be multiplied. For reasons not otherwise explainable, *the* Jew in the recent opera *Nixon in China*, i.e., Henry Kissinger, is given to sadistic tantrums, unleashed on a Chinese woman.[15] A further criterion of literary anti-Semitism, while my own, grows logically out of the previous postulate. Wherever vilification is coupled with an incitement to pogrom or to genocide, a work harboring such provocations breaks the bounds of aesthetics and becomes, at best, a tract, pamphlet, or broadside. To be sure, revolutionary poetry, in and by itself, is honored by tradition; from the invocation "abreuve nos sillons" in the *Marseillaise* to the German poet Herwegh's exhortation to convert graveyard crosses into swords and to draw them against "tyrants and philistines."[16] But this type of engaged poetry, aimed at specific social or political opponents, stands at a vast remove from enjoining readers to continue the genocide of Auschwitz. Such poems may be found in the lyrics of Amiri Baraka, formerly LeRoi Jones:

Smile, jew. Dance, jew. Tell me you love me, jew. I got something for you now though. I got something for you, like you dig, I got. I got this thing, goes pulsating through black everything universal meaning. I got the extermination blues, jewboys. I got the hitler syndrome figured. What that simpleton meant. He can't stand their desert smell, their closeness to the truth. What Father Moses gave them, and lifted them off their hands. A Magic Charm. A black toe sewn into their throats. To talk, to get up off their hands, and walk, like men (they will tell you). So come for the rent, jewboys, or come ask me for a book, or sit in the courts handing down yer judgments, still I got something for you, gonna give it to my brothers, so they'll know what you whole story is, then one day, jewboys, we all, even my wig wearing mother gonna put it on you all at once.[17]

It seems all too facile to ascribe such lines to black rage or revolutionary fervor. As Irving Howe has put it so well: "When I read LeRoi Jones calling for 'dagger poems in the slimy bellies of their owner jews' . . . then I know I am in the presence of a racist hoodlum, inciting people to blood. And I am not going to be deflected from that perception by talk about rhythm, metaphor, and diction."[18] It should be added, in all fairness, that LeRoi Jones has indirectly repudiated these anti-Semitic remarks in his autobiography and directly in an interview with Tish Dace of *The Village Voice*, where he states: "My whole opposition to white people was based on the fact that they were white, which was incorrect. I've made anti-Semitic remarks in my bourgeois nationalist period, but I'm not anti-Semitic, no, by no means. I'm anti-zionist, Israel is an illegal state but I'm not anti-Jewish. What can I say, I've repudiated those lines. Now I'm a public, identified Communist."[19] Even if one were willing to accept the distinction between the two phobias, it is doubtful that Mr. Jones' retraction can vitiate the effect of his murderous lyrics.

IV

While the literary anti-Semitism in the works of LeRoi Jones and Katherine Anne Porter are still traceable to religious roots—note, for example, the evocation of the Old Testament in Jones' lyrics—the far more frequent brand occurring in American literature is social. Mr. Gelber puts it similarly: "examples of literary antisemitism in the modern period are [even] less concerned with religious aspects of the negative Jewish images" than they are with "other cultural, psychological or biological [racial features]."[20] The Jew in contemporary American society assaults his gentile environment, as Alvin Rosenfeld demonstrates in an article, "as an interloper and corrupter. Someone who tends to mongrelize or defile an earlier or better stock."[21] The stereotype that, in my opinion, has emerged in the American novel as the intruder in this game of socio-cultural anti-Semitism is the social climber. And we can observe his or her transparent machinations in Gore Vidal's novel of wartime America entitled *Washington, D.C.*

Mr. Vidal has voiced his displeasure with interlopers upon the literary scene in a lengthy article entitled "Literary Gangsters," where he deplores Robert Brustein's "lamentations, a sort of Broadway Old Testament prophet, wailing for a Jerusalem that never was."[22] Equally scathing are his words against "the incomplete assimilation of immigrant English into the old language."[23] But one of his characters shows her least offensive trait when she affectedly interlards French phrases into her cocktail party conversation. Irene (she pronounces her name "Irène") Bloch, the nouveau-riche social climber in Gore Vidal's *Washington, D.C.*, is the novel's lone Jewish character. She is immediately identified as a Jew when she initially appears in the novel and a veritable avalanche of pejoratives is quickly unleashed upon her by the other characters—with the authorial voice staying neutral at first:

Peter knew exactly who she was, and realized the significance of her appearance at Laurel House, for his mother was severe to climbers and merciless to Jews, except for a handful of Rothschilds and Warburgs who, she often noted with surprise, were "just like anyone else." Peter's own anti-Semitism had been worn down at the university by his friend the instructor in history, but despite his new liberalism, Peter found himself resenting Irene Bloch in the drawing room at Laurel House. There had to be some standards in society. Jews could be intellectually stimulating but they were not the way people ought to be. They tended to look wrong and behave badly, like Mrs. Bloch, who had got the Poles to bring her to a house where she knew she was not welcome.[24]

As the novel progresses, we hear that Irene Bloch "was a source of constant diversion" (155) to the social elite of Washington, that "her husband—isn't that disgusting—doesn't mind at all who she goes to bed with as long as it is someone important" (155), that "she is everywhere," i.e., where she is not wanted, and even where she knows herself "to be in enemy territory" (163). She, as the wife of a department store owner, is "big as life and twice as rich" (164), and she is willing to spend her money freely to advance socially (202). " 'Mrs. Bloch,' one of the characters remarks, 'will finance us [and our neophyte magazine] for a dinner at Laurel House' " (213). On her first appearance at the exclusive Laurel House, she commits one faux pas after the other; "a new Washington legend has been born," we are told (223). At her husband's funeral, she spreads the information, quite likely false, that he "had always been an Episcopalian" (280). At the end of the novel she marries the ne'er-do-well son of a socially prominent family and buys Laurel House. "She had triumphed," the authorial voice tells us. "No one could ever again overlook or patronize her. With the purchase of Laurel House, her victory was total" (350). But to many of her fellow Washingtonians she remains " 'gruesome' Irene."

As noted before, the savaging of Irene Bloch is, for the most part, accomplished by the characters in the book and could, at first, be attributed to *their* prejudice rather than their creator's. But in various ways, beyond the narrator's description of her triumph, he validates their judgment. Irene does indeed have an affair with a senator, and she does have egregiously bad taste, especially when she furnishes her newly acquired house. "The room was so filled with painting and sculpture that it resembled an art gallery in which guests moved self-consciously from exhibit to exhibit, as though not certain whether or not the objects were on sale" (371f). And then we hear the narrator's perspective, that Irene had indeed been the social climber the others had assumed her to be. "But now that Irene was Mrs. Watress her enthusiasm for anyone celebrated was somewhat breached by her new relations. . . . She tended to save her best hyperbole for the husband of her niece, the First Lady-to-be" (367). Obviously she is, from the narrator's perspective, still climbing upward.

In Gore Vidal's novel, social anti-Semitism has taken the place of its religious predecessor. But the novel is not without its link to that more ideological past. One of the senior characters still nurtures the older brand of anti-Semitism: "Frederika had nothing at all against Irene Bloch. But two thousand years of Christian teaching had done its work. Because Irene Bloch had torn the sacred flesh and smeared herself ecstatically with the blood of the Lamb, she was unclean and ought not to dine at Laurel House" (221).

Having introduced, to be sure with a touch of irony, the hoarier aspects of anti-Semitism, Gore Vidal cannot resist the urge to insert some black concentration camp humor. A woman confined to an insane asylum is visited by her brother with whom she has had an incestuous affair. " 'Welcome,' she said at last, 'to Belsen.' "At least they haven't made you into a lampshade yet.' He kissed her cheek" (269). A novel published in 1967, and set against the backdrop of Washington from the days prior to Pearl Harbor until the Eisenhower era, surely could have included a more suitable reminder of the Holocaust than this sole and grisly repartee.

V

In yet another of his criteria, Mr. Gelber shifts from a thematic approach to considerations of a literary genre: "Satire of Jewish behavior in literature would also be an instance of literary anti-semitism, if no discernible counterbalance to negative Jewish types or pejorative attributions to Jews appear at the same time in a given text."[25] A particularly virulent dramatic satire, this one also by LeRoi Jones, buttresses Gelber's decision to single out satires as a tool with great potential for vituperation. The play, entitled *Jello*, is, in fact, so vicious in its invectives at a public figure, that Mr. Jones' publisher, fearing a libel suit, refused to print it in a volume of his selected dramas.

The play rests on the assumption that the comedian Jack Benny and the cast of his radio show are identical to the personae they represent on the air. One night Rochester, now made into Jack Benny's chauffeur in real life as well as on the radio, revolts. As LeRoi Jones describes it in a note protesting the satire's suppression by his publisher, "the play is about Jack Benny and Rochester and what happens when Rochester digs hisself."[26] By "digs hisself" Mr. Jones appears to mean that he rises from servility to an admirable contemporary Black Robin Hood. He attacks Jack Benny with a switchblade, robs him and other members of the cast of their money, and knocks out Don Wilson, the announcer. Earlier he corners Mary Livingstone, Jack Benny's wife, in order to rape her, but desists when he finds a money bag between her thighs. At the end of the drama he escapes, leaving his former colleagues with the sarcastic farewell wish: "I leave you to your lives."[27]

Anti-Semitic remarks abound from the moment Jack Benny steps on stage. He reveals himself as a convert (11), but is nonetheless referred to as a "little Jewish soul" (12) and "someone with [a] skinny hook nose" (26) by Rochester. Shylock-like, Benny fears more for the loss of his money than his life. When Rochester accuses him of owning a string of price-gouging appliance and butcher stores in Harlem (24), Benny readily admits to these stereotypical slanders. Once attacked, Benny, the supposed Jewish liberal—the likes of which Jones attacks in the above-mentioned protest note—uses every racial slur against his erstwhile friend (e.g., 29 and 31). Finally, to leave out no canard against the Jewish "villain," Rochester discovers a tiara-bedecked human skull in Jack Benny's safe. "You so used to murdering people and cutting their throats for your simple assed pleasure, you don't mind dead people piled up to the ceiling" (24f), Rochester comments.

Satire, it should be conceded, ought to be allowed a wide rein, if it is to be effective at all as a social or political exposé. Such recent American satires as *MacBird* by Barbara Garson[28] or Mark Harris' novel *Mark the Glove Boy; or, The Last Days of Richard Nixon*,[29] each a legitimate voice during national controversies, demonstrate the need for allowing the genre wide latitude. Mr. Gelber comes to a similar conclusion. "To the extent that any general pronouncement or collective criticism concerning a nation of people might be valid or funny, Jews like any other collective are subject to this kind of illogical formulation."[30] Where are we to draw the line? Mr. Gelber only poses the question without, for the time being, providing an answer. I shall attempt one: When satire becomes unspecific, attacking a collective rather than real or purported villains within the targeted group, or when it pillories an individual entirely unconnected with the malfeasance to be exposed, then satire becomes literary genocide or character assassination. Jack Benny, for example, reputed to be a generous and liberal person, was obviously innocent of oppressing black chauffeurs, of being a slum landlord, or a profiteer. Before leaving this point, in the spirit of the above, it must be added that unlike Mr. Jones, many black writers have produced balanced and/or positive portraitures of Jewish characters. But this chapter deals, of course, with the rhetoric of anti-Semitism.

VI

The above yardsticks for satire can readily be applied to two related genres: humor and parody. Curiously enough, examples of literary anti-Semitism in humor are most readily accessible not in humor magazines, but in a recently published scholarly article, written, as the authors assert, with the best possible intentions. Alan Dundes and Thomas Hauschild, in their article "Auschwitz Jokes," for volume 42 (1983) of *Western Folklore*, overstep what is to my mind the boundary of acceptable folkloristic reportage. They begin, to be sure, with perfunctory deferences to the Auschwitz victims. "Nothing is so sacred, so taboo, or so disgusting that it cannot be the subject of humor. . . . In reading the accounts written by survivors, it is hard to imagine that any humor could possibly arise from the mass gassing of thousands of individuals."[31] With this disclaimer and a few misstatements (Dachau was not an extermination camp, the questionable term "half-Jew," without quotes here, certainly does not apply to the fencing champion Helene Mayer), the two authors then proceed to show that the scarcely imaginable is possible after all. The jokes, all of them in egregiously bad taste and, for the most part, collected by Mr. Hauschild in West Berlin in the summer of 1982, must not be dignified here by repetition. They give rise, in the article, to such observations as "[these jokes] suggest that German anti-Semitism is alive and well" (257) and "the Jew–ashes equation turns out to be an all-too-common theme in Auschwitz jokes" (251). The authors also contend as follows: "Whether one finds Auschwitz jokes funny or not is not an issue. This material exists and should be recorded" (250). I believe a demurrer is in order.

Parody as a literary form—the distortion or subversion of an original work's form by applying it to an incommensurate content—has become rare, since the readers of it must be familiar with the lampooned original in order to laugh at the anamorphosis. Yet the genre has flourished by taking aim not at books, but at mass media creations such as popular films or television shows. For that reason parody has become a staple of humor magazines for adolescents or college students. Since this type of pop culture appears to have a wide and lasting appeal, it has also become a subject of scholarly scrutiny. It would be instructive, from the point of view of reception theory, to look here as well for signs of anti-Semitism. Some years ago *Mad*, a magazine for adolescents, lampooned a television series entitled "Hogan's Heroes," which operated on the counter-to-fact assumption that American prisoners of war enjoyed an untrammeled and comfortable life in a German Stalag and were able, from this unlikely base, to sabotage the German war effort. *Mad*'s parody placed the same cast of characters not in a Stalag, but in a luxurious concentration camp and thereby pin-pricked the phantasmagoria of "Hogan's Heroes" through grossest hyperbole. Nonetheless, it must be conceded, the panels contain not a single anti-Semitic reference either in the graphic or the text, though it does identify some of the prisoners as Jews.[32] Yet here we have a case where a parody, aimed at an entirely different target, can unintentionally have a subliminal anti-Semitic effect on the reader. The effect of serious efforts by the American and foreign media—from the series "Holocaust" to the showing of the film *Shoah*—is diminished or vitiated by encouraging laughter at concentration camps. It precipitates the wrong type of catharsis by evoking laughter. Adorno may have been wrong in predicting the impossibility of writing lyrics after Auschwitz; but humor and parody, with Auschwitz the butt of the joke, are not only impossible, but perversions.

VII

Beyond the criteria extrapolated from Mr. Gelber's article, I have distilled an additional one from publications by George Steiner and the British scholar J. A. Morris.[33] I should like to call it the anti-Semitism of silence. It is difficult to define. Gore Vidal's omission of the Holocaust in his novel *Washington, D.C.* may be read as a preliminary definitional example. Some writers, like Ezra Pound and T. S. Eliot, desisted from or attenuated their anti-Semitic rhetoric after World War II. A discussion of the more extreme case of Ezra Pound's personal and literary anti-Semitism can be omitted from this chapter in favor of a recent book-length study by Robert Casillo, which argues that Pound's anti-Semitism is structurally endemic to his poetics.[34] But T. S. Eliot, midway between the wars, suppressed from his poetics jejune lines such as the following, which appear in his lyrica of the early twenties:

> The silent man in mocha brown
> Sprawls at the window-sill and gapes;
> The waiter brings in oranges
> Bananas, figs and hothouse grapes;
> The silent vertebrate in brown
> Contracts and concentrates, withdraws;
> Rachel *née* Rabinovitch
> Tears at the grapes with murderous paws.
>
> (from *Sweeney Among the Nightingales*)[35]

Or, to quote lines in which Eliot, the American expatriate poet, or his poetic alter ego, refers to a Jew of his homeland:

> But this or such was Bleistein's way:
> A saggy bending of the knees
> And elbows, with the palms turned out,
> Chicago Semite Viennese.
>
> (from *Burbank with a Baedeker: Bleistein with a Cigar*)[36]

In commenting on Eliot's subsequent avoidance of overt literary anti-Semitism, J. A. Morris traces it to Eliot's rise in the world of banking and quotes Robert Graves' quip that "Eliot preferred to be penny-wise rather than Pound-foolish."[37] But that is not, of course, a complete explanation. As I have shown elsewhere, T. S. Eliot, editor of the *New Criterion*, struck an entirely cooperative and appreciative stance vis-à-vis Efraim Frisch, the Austrian-Jewish editor and publisher of the *Neue Merkur*, a German intellectual and literary journal.[38] Hence, Eliot's anti-Semitism may have been attenuated through closer associations with capitalists, both Jews and non-Jews.

But if this is an accurate assessment, his literary anti-Semitism, signaled silently through ignoring the Holocaust, becomes all the more unjustifiable. Given the aberrant lines of 1920, was not a literary restitution due to the vilified? George Steiner believes so:

The failure of Eliot's *Notes Towards a Definition of Culture* to face the issue [of the Holocaust or Nazi anti-Semitism], indeed to allude to it in anything but an oddly condescending footnote, is acutely disturbing. How, only three years after the event, after the publication to the world of facts and pictures that have, probably, altered our sense of the limits of human behavior, was it possible to write a book on culture and say nothing?[39]

Silent literary anti-Semitism is therefore—at least to my mind—defined by an omission of a declaration of sympathy for Jewish suffering. The Jewish suffering should at least be mentioned in passages where an omission would strike a neutral reader as a palpable gap in a literary work.

VIII

In his concluding remarks, Mark Gelber argues against past attempts to search for literary anti-Semitism in a work by analyzing the author's attitudes: "The substantial amount of attention devoted in the secondary literature until now in an effort to determine whether a given author might be an antisemite wanes in importance."[40] Instead, Gelber advocates examinations of the effective power of a work upon its readers, but also concludes that "basic techniques of literary criticism, consideration of narrative structures and character differentiation, and linguistic analysis are central to any endeavor to understand literary antisemitism."[41] As a final illustration of the efficacy of a close textual analysis—one which will yield even better results than Vidal's novel—I should like to exhume a work by an obscure novelist, but a well-known, if not notorious, politician. In 1976 Spiro T. Agnew, having resigned from the vice presidency of the United States under the pressure of a bribery charge, wrote a novel, entitled *The Canfield Decision*, which chronicles a global power struggle and exposes the vice president of the U.S. as a treasonous co-conspirator.[42] As the rather simplistic fiction would have it, the People's Republic of China, alarmed at the growing understanding between the U.S. and the Soviet Union, conspires to destroy the existing détente by inciting a confrontation between the two over American military aid to Israel.

One of the agents of the People's Republic, a Persian by the name of Izadi, conspires to manipulate the Jews, generally in favor of better relations between the superpowers, to an armed confrontation. He will mastermind acts of sabotage and assassination and attribute them to Arab terrorists and the Soviets. At a clandestine meeting, he reveals his motives.

You must understand the structure of American politics to see that, . . . American Jews exert an influence on American opinion that is far heavier than their numbers would indicate. They are the strongest single influence in the big media—the media with worldwide impact. They control much of the financial community, and through it, large segments of the academic community. Therefore, they heavily effect, through propaganda, the majority of the Congress. Oh, they scream anti-Semitism whenever anyone mentions their power, but it's true. Look at the tortured differentiations that the intellectuals tried to create between aid to Israel and aid to Vietnam. The Viet Cong were oppressed patriots, but the Palestinians were anarchists. (84)

In further pursuit of gaining support for his plot, Izadi expostulates:

God! What wonderful clay we have to work with. The American Jews are ultrasensitive to persecution. The Anti-Defamation League goes beserk at the slightest criticism of Jews. What do you think they'll do with murders? I'll tell you what—there'll be screams of genocide, and every liberal in the Western world will predict that Israel is in grave danger of attack and needs nuclear defenses. The politicians who like an adoring press will make speeches and the Congress will act to help tiny, courageous Israel endure. (88)

Despite these anti-Semitic slurs—the intimation of a worldwide Jewish conspiracy constitutes one of the worst and most inflammatory canards against the jews—the reader will, at first glance, summarily dismiss these accusations. After all, Izadi is an *agent provocateur* with little credibility and the plot, conceived by himself and the vice president, is ultimately foiled by a patriotic, steadfast, and rational president.

But the novelist Agnew can be as devious as the politician. By various subtle devices he bestows credence on Izadi, a thoroughly tainted source. At first there are a few authorial asides which accomplish this. During a meeting, one of the characters focuses on a map.

He noted that parts of the Sinai, Syria, Jordan and Lebanon were crudely cross-hatched in green crayon to indicate areas still held by the Israeli army in defiance of more than a decade of pitiful United Nations efforts to restore them to their rightful owners. (92)

Then the ambitious, Machiavellian vice president is able to draw on the groundswell of Jewish sentiment that, according to the fiction of the novel, has been unleashed:

The Vice President added earnestly, "But more important than that, my posture has given reassurance and hope to hundreds of humanitarian Jewish organizations which felt that our country was reluctant to state the full implications of its foreign policy on this question—very responsible organizations of impeccable credentials." (129)

In his most private thoughts, Vice President Canfield agrees entirely with Izadi's fanatical belief in a Jewish conspiracy:

He was convinced that Israel was the key to his campaign. He had been the first to recognize the power of the Middle East issue and the hunger of the American Jewish establishment for a foreign policy more visibly supportive of the beleaguered little nation. . . . The American Zionists wanted the American sword to rattle every time a potential attacker made the slightest threat toward their darling. They, who had been the strongest advocates of abandoning Southeast Asia to the communists, were perfectly willing to send war materials, advisors and even armed troops if Israel was attacked. (175)

The vice president's self-serving defense of Israel's military policy is immediately rewarded by a surreptitious visit from an Israeli diplomat, who pledges that "individually we will do all we can to convince our American friends to support your [presidential] candidacy" (216). Then the novel comes forth with other structural signs verifying Izadi's and Vice President Canfield's assumptions. A newspaper, closely resembling the *New York Times*, also in the real world one of the favorite targets of American anti-Semites, endorses offensive weapons for Israel in the precise wording that Izadi had foreseen during his first conspiratorial meeting. "While we do not subscribe to all the strong specifics Mr. Canfield advocates for Israel," the editorial runs, "we are convinced that President Hurley's policy of benign neglect could result in disaster for this small courageous nation" (185). Finally, the Jewish propaganda machine, as the narrative voice informs the reader, swings into high gear:

Sensing a receptive audience the Israelis floated tons of propaganda allegedly documenting plans of an Arab-Soviet attack on them. The plea for IRBM's was intensified, and the American press and public demanded that the Congress and the President of the United States deliver the weapons. . . .

Now the reflective columns and intellectual articles were beginning to appear, pointing out the threat to international stability if America let itself be frightened into abandoning tiny, dependent Israel. The Zionist lobby and the anti-communists of the right wing, unlikely allies, thundered their outrage in concert, and the timid in the government needed no wet fingers to tell them which way the wind was blowing. Indeed, the deluge of one-sided telegrams and letters proved to the sensitive politicians in the nation's capital that it was no ordinary wind, but a veritable hurricane. (245)

At this point Izadi, the unreliable source, stands vindicated. World Jewry, within the structure of the novel, has determined, at least for the moment, American foreign policy. An analysis of the novel, consonant with Mr. Gelber's advocated method, clearly exposes its anti-Semitic thrust.

Also, Spiro Agnew's insipid novel may constitute the last piece of evidence in my attempt to crystallize and test a working definition of literary anti-Semitism. In this effort, my chapter drew on seedbeds as wide apart as pop culture and T. S. Eliot's *Wasteland*. None were drawn from the works of American-Jewish authors; Sander Gilman's masterful analysis of Jewish self-hatred has exhausted any theoretical approach to this demon of the Jewish past for years to come, though new examples of it keep occurring in American life and literature.[43]

It remains the intention of this chapter, as stated at the beginning, to argue for a continued and wider analysis of literary anti-Semitism in American letters and of its potentially corrosive effects.[44] In an earlier study I tried to demonstrate how proto-Fascist, yet respectable writers, became the pacemakers for the National Socialist ideology[45]—stereotyping has a long history.[46] The noted historian George L. Mosse, also taking the spread of German anti-Semitism through popular literature as his point of departure, comes to a similar conclusion:

To be sure, anti-Jewish feeling only acquires particular relevance when it is combined with political issues or when Jewish group interests conflict with other powerful interests, but none of this would be of significance in an age of mass politics without the support and preconditioning of popular culture. That is why we must direct our attention to cultural investigation.[47]

The important phrase "popular culture" in Mosse's exhortation is clearly intended to encompass culture both with a capital and small *c*.

If George Mosse is right, the contributory investigation of *literary* anti-Semitism must survey a nation's literature both with a capital and small *l*. For in all likelihood, to provide a telling example, the size of the audience for the various versions of *Jesus Christ Superstar*—from stage play to video-cassettes of the film—will outstrip many times over the total readership of, say, Ezra Pound's *Cantos*. In short, the toxin of literary anti-Semitism can bubble up from below as well as drip its poison from the heights of Mount Parnassus.

To return to American literature, it has portrayed the Jews of this country, as Lionel Trilling has pointed out, through the traditional admixture of myth and truth, but with some peculiarly American components grafted upon old mythical images. By exposing these myths, we may not be able to neutralize their potentially toxic effects, but we may be able to alert our contemporaries to the danger. To that end we must continue to seek out manifestations of literary anti-Semitism, whether a work was envenomed consciously or subliminally and no matter whether present in subliterary genres or in the canonized body of belles lettres.

Notes

1. Michael N. Dobkowski, "American Antisemitism: A Reinterpretation," *American Quarterly* 29/2 (1977): 166–181, esp. 166–167.
2. Lionel Trilling, "The Changing Myth of the Jew," *Commentary* 66/2 (1978): 24–34. See p. 34 where Trilling discusses the intertwined nature of truth and myth.
3. David Philipson, *The Jew in English Fiction,* 5th ed. (New York: Bloch, 1927) 17–19.
4. Mark H. Gelber, "What Is Literary Antisemitism?" *Jewish Social Studies* 47/1 (1985): 1–20, esp. 1.
5. Gelber 4.
6. Leonard Swidler and Gerard S. Sloyan, *Commentary on the Oberammergau Passionspiel in Regard to its Image of Jews and Judaism* (New York: Anti-Defamation League of B'nai B'rith, 1978).
7. Stanley Richards, "Editor's Notes," 241. (See note 8.)
8. Stanley Richards, ed., *Great Rock Musicals* (New York: Stein and Day, 1979) 246–248.
9. Swidler and Sloyan 17–18.

10. Tim Rice and Andrew Lloyd Webber, *Jesus Christ Superstar*, in Richards 244–288, esp. 283–285.

11. Arnold Forster and Benjamin R. Epstein, *The New Anti-Semitism* (New York: McGraw-Hill, 1974).

12. Gelber 6–7.

13. Katherine Anne Porter, interview by Hank Lopez, "A Country and Some People I Love," *Harper's* September 1965: 58–68, esp. 68.

14. Katherine Anne Porter, *Ship of Fools* (Boston: Little, Brown, 1962) vii. Additional quotations are cited parenthetically in the text.

15. Libretto by Alice Goodman, music by John Adams Electra Nonesuch Records, 1987.

16. George Herwegh, "Aufruf," *Herweghs Werke in drei Teilen*, ed. Hermann Tardel (Stuttgart: Deutsches Verlaghaus, n.d.) 1: 38–39.

17. Imamu Amiri Baraka (LeRoi Jones), *Black Magic: Collected Poetry 1961–1967* (Indianapolis: Bobbs-Merrill, 1969) 154.

18. Irving Howe, *The Critical Point: On Literature and Culture* (New York: Horizon, 1973) 177.

19. Imamu Amiri Baraka (LeRoi Jones), interview by Tish Dace, *The Village Voice*, August 1977.

20. Gelber 7.

21. Alvin H. Rosenfeld, "What to Do about Literary Anti-semitism," *Midstream* 24/10 (1978): 44–50, esp. 47. I am also indebted to Mr. Rosenfeld's article for directing me to several literary works with anti-Semitic content.

22. Gore Vidal, "Literary Gangsters," *Commentary* 49/3 (1970): 61–64, esp. 62.

23. Ibid.

24. Gore Vidal, *Washington, D.C.* (Boston: Little, Brown, 1967), 24. Other quotations cited parenthetically.

25. Gelber 7.

26. Imamu Amiri Baraka (LeRoi Jones), *Jello* (Chicago: Third World Press, 1970). Quotations cited parenthetically.

27. Imamu Amiri Baraka (LeRoi Jones), "Why No J-E-L-L-O?," *Four Black Revolutionary Plays; All Praises to the Black Man* (Indianapolis: Bobbs-Merrill, 1969) 89.

28. Barbara Garson, *MacBird* (New York: Grove Press, 1967).

29. Mark Harris, *Mark the Glove Boy; or, The Last Days of Richard Nixon* (New York: Macmillan, 1964).

30. Gelber 7.

31. Alan Dundes and Thomas Hauschild, "Auschwitz Jokes," *Western Folklore* 42 (1983): 249–259, here: 249. Other quotations cited parenthetically.

32. Despite diligent search, this parody from *Mad Magazine* could not be dated. It was found in the private collection of Mr. Eric Lind, Detroit, Michigan.

33. J. A. Morris, "T. S. Eliot and Antisemitism," *Journal of European Studies* 2, no. 2 (June 1972): 173–182.

34. Robert Casillo, *The Geneaology of Demons: Anti-Semitism, Fascism, and the Myths of Ezra Pound* (Evanston: Northwestern University Press, 1988).

35. T. S. Eliot, "Sweeney Among the Nightingales," *T. S. Eliot: Collected Poems 1909–1935* (New York: Harcourt, Brace, 1936) 65–66.

36. T. S. Eliot, "Burbank with a Baedeker: Bleistein with a Cigar," *Collected Poems* 47.

37. Morris 177.

38. Guy Stern, *War, Weimar, and Literature: The Story of the "Neue Merkur"* (University Park: Pennsylvania State University Press, 1971).

39. George Steiner, *In Bluebeard's Castle* (New Haven: Yale University Press, 1971) 33–34.

40. Gelber 17.

41. Ibid.

42. Spiro T. Agnew, *The Canfield Decision* (Chicago: Playboy Press, 1976). Quotations cited parenthetically.

43. Sander Gilman, *Jewish Self-Hatred: Anti-Semitism and the Hidden Language of the Jews* (Baltimore: Johns Hopkins University Press, 1985).

44. This was also advocated in Dominick LaCapra's response to this paper at the conference on "Anti-Semitism in Times of Crisis," at Cornell University, April 10, 1986.

45. Guy Stern, "Präfaschismus und die respektable Literatur: Deutsche Romanschriftsteller in ihren Selbstzeugnissen und Briefen," *Der deutsche Roman und seine historischen und politischen Bedingungen,* ed. W. Paulsen (Berlin: Francke Verlag, 1977) 107–123.

46. Commenting on "the mechanism of stereotyping," Sander Gilman says "the group defining the Other has projected its own insecurities concerning its potential loss of power onto the world in the shape of that Other through which it imagines itself threatened" (3). Hámida Bosmojian, in *Metaphors of Evil: Contemporary German Literature and the Shadow of Nazism* (Iowa City: University of Iowa Press, 1979), writes in a similar vein. "The human being is bound to accumulate guilt in reality and in fictions about human reality. Usually incapable of loving our neighbor, humankind much more readily loves an ideology or a leader who promises to take care of our collective selves by permitting us to project and unleash our deprivations and anxieties onto a group that has been defined as 'the others' " (9).

47. George L. Mosse, *Germans and Jews: The Right, the Left, and the Search for a "Third Force" in Pre-Nazi Germany* (New York: Howard Fertig, 1970) 76.

Jewish Writers in Contemporary Germany: The Dead Author Speaks

Sander L. Gilman

Toward a Statement of the Problem

In his widely read and often reprinted book of 1970, *Germany without Jews*, Bernt Engelmann, the German newspaperman and former member of the anti-fascist resistance, documented the disappearance of the Jews from Germany[1]—not just their physical absence, but their disappearance from their central, pre-Holocaust role in "Germany's cultural, political, and spiritual development" (4). To do so, Engelmann documents in fastidious detail the role that "Jews" (and his definition is left purposely vague) played in German culture (understood very broadly) from the time of Jewish emancipation in the early nineteenth century through the rise of the Nazis. Engelmann, whom one would not accuse lightly of pro-fascist sentiments, assumes that Jews play no role in contemporary German culture. While he cites a few contemporary examples, they are usually in his view marginal ones, Jews who have allied themselves in the Federal Republic with right-wing causes. For Engelmann, the Jews of the Empire as well as of the Weimar Republic were most often on the side of the angels, and it is the death of this liberal utopia that he mourns. What happens when, in a society, your internalized label for your sense of self becomes taboo? What happens when the category into which you can fit your fictive self becomes invisible?

Other critics who have dealt with the Jew in the contemporary German

311

states have been somewhat more subtle in their analysis. Jack Zipes, whose politics are certainly as "pure" as those of Engelmann, at least sees that Jews exist within the contemporary intellectual life of the Federal Republic but represents them as disaffected and distanced.[2] And he, perhaps more realistically than Engelmann (whose book he nevertheless calls "important"), sees that the so-called "Jewish" presence is much more politically differentiated. But even for Zipes, the presence of Jews in West German culture is marked by their absence. His prime examples of Jewish intellectuals in West Germany are Lea Fleischmann and Henryk Broder, both German-speaking Jews who chose to emigrate from the Federal Republic in the early 1980s. Peter Sichrovsky, in a volume of interviews with young Jews living in contemporary West Germany and Austria, seems to document much the same fact.[3] These Jews are alienated, disaffected, relatively unproductive, and certainly not in the mainstream of (West or East) German or Austrian "Kultur."

The question I wish to address in this chapter is really quite simple: given the fact that there are "Jews" who seem to play a major role in contemporary German "Kultur," at least that narrower definition of culture, meaning the production of cultural artifacts, such as books—a field which, at least for Engelmann, was one of the certain indicators of a Jewish component in prewar German culture—what happened to these "Jews" (or at least the category of the "Jewish writer") in postwar discussions of culture? Or put more simply: who killed the remaining Jews in contemporary German culture and why? Why is it not possible to speak about "German Jews" in the contemporary criticism about German culture? And, more to the point, what is the impact of this denial on those who (quite often ambivalently) see (or have been forced to see) themselves as "Germans" or "Jews," but not as both simultaneously. The cultural difference of German Jews or perhaps better of Jews in the BRD, the difference of having to deal in 1989 with their growing invisibility as well as their past, goes unnoticed. Young (non-Jewish) Germans seem to have no problem dealing with dead Jews, or old Jews, for as Henryk Broder has noted, there seems to be a "incurable love of German intellectuals for dead or half-dead Jews"[4] in the BRD and, one might add, for distant Jews (they had all read Ephron Kishon). But the idea of a negative symbiosis,[5] a need for Jews in the Federal Republic to struggle with their invisibility as living, contributing members of contemporary society, is difficult for them to understand.

Let me begin by doing something that none of the studies I have mentioned risked undertaking and which I, up to now, have done only by inference. Let me define what I mean by a Jew, at least within the confines of my discussion of the role of German Jews in contemporary German literary culture. A Jewish writer is one labeled as a Jew who responds to this labeling in literature, the medium that has the greatest salience for a Jew and a writer. I have documented in great detail in my recent book *Jewish Self-Hatred* how one of the red threads of Christian anti-Semitism has been the view that Jews possess a polluted and polluting discourse.[6] This has formed the theme of a number of the chapters of this present book which have dealt with writers (from Mendelssohn to Broch) who were labeled as "Jews." I have shown how the idea of the special or hidden nature of the Jews' discourse shapes the representation of the self within the text of Jews who respond to such a contextualization of their discourse. And this response takes the form of writing about Jews and attempting to represent their discourse within the confines of the book, the object that not only provides status for the Jew as writer in a society that values writers (such as Germany) but also contains the legend of his or her own inability to ever command the discourse of that culture.

My task in this chapter is therefore twofold. I must be able to show you how, within the confines of postwar culture, in the Federal Republic of Germany, the German Democratic Republic, and Austria, this tradition of representing the Jew as possessing a damaged and damaging discourse maintained itself, in spite of a radical reconstruction of German culture. And I must be able to present to you "Jewish" writers in German who have a broad audience and within whose fictive personalities (and the texts generated by them) the representation of the theme of a "Jewish" discourse plays a major role. If I am lucky I will also find texts in which the reworking of the alienation and isolation appropriate to the fictive personality of writers in the post-Holocaust world reflects constructively upon this problem.

For the first task, I have been helped greatly by Ruth Kluger Angress's exposition of what she calls "A 'Jewish Problem' in German Postwar Fiction."[7] And because she generally limited the parameters of this question to the world of fiction (rather than the stage or lyric poetry), I shall follow her lead while focusing this material for my own purposes. As for the selection of authors—-there are any number of writers who fall into my category of "Jewish" writers, from Wolf Biermann to Günter Kunert, from Stefan Heym to Rosa Ausländer. These are writers who have selected "Jewish" themes and have presented themselves as major figures in the culture life of the state in which they dwell. Some of them returned from exile after 1945, some of them were forced to remain in Germany, either in the camps or in hiding, and some were born after the war. I will discuss in detail two widely read (and filmed) writers, Edgar Hilsenrath, who survived the death camps, emigrated to the United States where he began to write, and then returned to West Germany in the 1960s, and Jurek Becker, whose expulsion from East Berlin in the wake of Wolf Biermann's forced exile was mitigated by the granting of an extended visa to live in the West, ironically because of his status as one "persecuted by the fascist regime." Becker and Hilsenrath are both productive members of the cultural elite, living today in Berlin.

The Representation of the Jew's Discourse in Postwar German Fiction

Ruth Angress illustrates the continuity of stereotypes of the Jew in postwar German fiction (and to a lesser extent in drama) and bases her analyses on clear and close readings of major texts such as Alfred Andersch's subtly slanted portrait of the Jew in *Zanzibar or The Final Reason* (1957). Her essay concludes with the public scandal occasioned by the Frankfurt performance of Rainer Werner Fassbinder's dramatization of Gerhard Zwerenz's novel *The Earth is Uninhabitable like the Moon* (1973) under the title *City, Sewage, Death* (1975), in which a caricature of the Jew as exploiter straight out of *Der Stürmer* (the most rabidly anti-Semitic newspaper of the Weimar and Nazi periods) stands at the center of the work. The fullness of her examples documents the continuity of the image of the Jew after the Holocaust, even in works, such as Andersch's *Zanzibar*, that have an overtly anti-fascist message. Given this context, I will examine the central work of that writer who, at least in the Federal Republic since the 1960s, has stood as the exemplary "liberal" political figure: Günter Grass. Even more than Heinrich Böll, Germany's sole postwar Nobel Prize Winner in Literature, Grass has assumed a major role in defining the idea of the author for the post-Holocaust generation, and more than any other writer of the period, his early work, the so-called Danzig Trilogy, attempted to introduce the image of the Jew into the discourse of literary modernism. Grass's Jews became exemplary Jews, not only for his German-Christian readership but also for his German-Jewish readers, as I shall show.

The figure of Sigismund Markus, the toy dealer in *The Tin Drum* (1958) is, as Ruth Angress observes, "a stereotype with mitigating variations" (222). Let me quote her quite accurate depiction of him:

Markus, like the typical Jew of the Nazi press, is unattractive as a man, though he lusts after an Aryan woman, and ludicrous as an individual, for he acts and looks like a dog. He is a harmless parasite, a Jew without a Jewish community or a family, without a background, or religious affiliation, but with business acumen of sorts, that is, he has the ability "to get it for you wholesale," "it" being cheap stockings for Agnes [the mother of the central figure, Oskar Matzerath]. He has no convictions, has just converted, a pathetic gesture from which he vainly expects to benefit, and seems to have no emotions about the German victory, which he predicts, except that it might help him elope with Agnes to England. (222–23)

However, this is not all. For when we turn to examine the representation of Markus's discourse, how Grass has him speak compared to the other characters in the book, at least up to the point of Grass's *Edelkitsch* (to use Ruth Angress's word) reflection on Markus's death at the end of the first book of the novel, we discover a further characterization of the Jew.

In my study of *Jewish Self-Hatred*, I discussed the use of *mauscheln* or *jüdeln* (speaking with a Jewish accent) as the means by which writers by the end of the nineteenth century characterized the corrupt nature of Jewish discourse. It was not Yiddish, which at least by the close of World War I had come to be recognized in Germany (as well as officially among Yiddish-speaking Jews) as a separate and distinct literary language. For by that point literary works were being translated from Yiddish for the mass German market. Rather, it was *mauscheln*, speaking German with a Yiddish accent, which came to characterize the Jew as parvenu.

When we turn to Markus's language, it is therefore of little surprise, given Angress's thesis, that he speaks in *mauscheln*. Let me quote the conclusion of Markus's address to Oscar Matzerath's mother, Agnes, to whom Angress makes reference in the passage cited above:

All right if you want to bet on Matzerath, what you got him already. Or do me a favor, bet on Markus seeing he's just fresh baptized. We'll go to London, I got friends there and plenty stocks and bonds if you just decide to come, or all right if you won't come with Markus because you despise me, so despise me. But I beg you down on my knees, don't bet no more on Bronski that's meshugge enough to stick by the Polish Post Office when the Poles are pretty soon all washed up when the Germans come.[8]

The quality of Markus's voice can be adduced from the adjectives "supplicating" and "exaggerated," which are used by Agnes to qualify her perception of Markus's message. This, in itself, would prove only that within his fictional recreation of the world of Danzig, Grass selected a specific figure who, with his suicide after his shop is vandalized, represents a sentimentalized type, a so-called "positive" stereotype. But there is much more to it than that. For the opening book of the novel, in which the story of Sigismund Markus's life and death is interwoven, is a world of myriad types, from the peasant grandmother of the central figure, Oskar Matzerath, to the Poles and Danzig-Germans who inhabit his world. No one, however, no matter what their ethnic or linguistic background, speaks in dialect, in a fictionally represented gender-based or class-based idiolect, except Markus, and he does so every time he appears.

Markus is different. His accent marks him as different, but his accent also reveals the nature of his personality. He is both subordinate and aggressive; sexually charged and self-deprecating; a Jew and yet not a Jew. It is the latter, the act of conversion, that reveals the absence of the center signified by the use of *mauscheln.* The speakers of Yiddish (or, indeed, the speakers of German or Hebrew) all have centers to their personalities. They have worlds of culture to which they can relate—books exist in their languages, which mark the boundaries of culture. But speakers who *mauscheln* are between cultures, and individuals represented as moving across boundaries are always understood as polluting and polluted.

One can at least suggest that Grass would have been quite conscious of the implications of his use of *mauscheln.* In the generalized image of the Jew promulgated by the Nazis from the 1920s onward, the image of the *mauschelnd* Jew dominated—for example, in the caricatures in *Der Stürmer.* All Jews were portrayed as *mauschelnd* since the intention of the image was to create the implication that no matter how well Jews spoke German, hidden within them was a *mauschelnd* Jew. In contrast, one can examine a text by Grass's acknowledged literary model, the German-Jewish writer Alfred Döblin, where clearly contrasting images of the discourse of the Jews in Poland can be found.[9] In 1926 Döblin published his *Travels to Poland,* which includes a detailed account of a trip to visit the Jewish section of Warsaw in 1924–25. In this complex text, Döblin critiques the superstitions of the Chassidic community as well as its primitive surroundings. Central to Döblin's image of the Eastern Jew is the image of himself as different, as possessing a secret, hidden language, the language of the Jew, while attempting to be a German liberal writer, that is, a writer without the ideological limitations imposed by any model of race. His image of his mother marks the image of the Jew for Döblin. He remembers her sitting, on religious holidays, "holding one of her books in her hands, and reading in it for a while, in Hebrew and with a half-articulated voice. Sometimes it was only a mumbling. When I think about being Jewish, this image stands before me" (157–58). Yiddish is for Döblin a language not spoken but rather sung, and sung like the sounds of a bird ("sie gurren und singeln jiddisch" [12]). In his description of Yom Kippur, this image of the Jew as possessing only an animalistic mode of discourse repeats itself. The Jews are depicted as "murmeln" and "summen" (92–93), noises associated with animals but also, as will be noted, with Döblin's image of his mother. This overlapping of song and the language of the Jews reflects, as we shall see in Grass's work, a specific inter-textuality. The language of the Jews is literary German, even when the content of their discourse is criticized. Grass consciously chooses the language of one central text used by the anti-Semites of the Weimar period to represent the hidden discourse of the Jews, the sign of the Jews' difference.

In the final volume of the Danzig Triology (following the novella *Cat and Mouse* [1961], which represents a world in which Jews simply do not exist), the massive novel *Dog Years* (1963), Grass thematizes the question of the Jews' discourse and specifies its origin, at least for the German-speaking Jews of the late nineteenth century, in one of its central texts. The plot of *Dog Years* hinges on the complex relationship between a Jew who is not a Jew, Eduard Amsel, and his friend Walter Matern, a German who is not a German. Indeed, this is the complex which Grass wishes to examine in the novel, how the antagonism between two friends mirrors the general dehumanization of both Jews and Germans under the impact of Nazi ideology. Grass locates the conflict within "Eddi" Amsel as resulting from the absence of his Jewish father, killed during World War I, a Jew who responded, within the classic model of self-hatred, to the image of the Jew that dominated his society. And for Reserve Lieutenant Albrecht Amsel, the book that he reads and that shapes his image of the Jew is Otto Weininger's *Sex and Character* (1903). Weininger's work was the classic work of self-hatred of the turn of the century, a work which became notorious in no small degree because of its author's suicide shortly before its publication. Grass knows the importance of this text and charts how both father and son, at two very different periods of time, before World War I and just prior to the Nazi takeover of Danzig, turn to this work for their definition of the Jew. The responses of the father are in two very specific arenas: he founds an athletic club and sings in the church choir "because it was said in the standard work [i.e., Weininger] that the Jew does not sing and does not engage in sports" (170). Likewise, "Eddi" Amsel "let his boy soprano . . . jubilate in Mozart Masses and short arias, and in regard to sports threw himself body and soul in to the game of faustball" (170). The image of the Jew's polluted and polluting discourse is present subliminally within the novel, for the passage from Weininger to which Grass refers reads:

Just as the acuteness of Jews has nothing to do with true power of differentiating, so his shyness about singing or even about speaking in clear positive tones has nothing to do with real reserve. It is a kind of inverted pride; having no true sense of his own worth, he fears being made ridiculous by his singing or his speech.[10]

Thus Grass points—to those knowledgeable in the tradition of literary anti-Semitism, the anti-Semitism secreted within the book, that icon of German culture—to the myth of the faulty, hidden discourse of the Jews, the desire of the Jews to keep their speech masked. He reflects here, in another intertextual link, upon his teacher Alfred Döblin's own ambiguity concerning his Jewish identity, the qualities of his discourse, and the image of the discourse of the Eastern Jew, here not the Jew of Warsaw but of Danzig. He thematizes this, reversing as he often does the standard images of the anti-Semite in his depiction of Jew and non-Jew.[11]

Grass's ironic shifting of stereotypes breaks down at one crucial moment. Grass provides a secret language, a sort of schoolyard Pig Latin, that binds Amsel and Matern, a simple reversal of words which functions as the hidden language of the boys, neither Jews nor non-Jews. Knowing the tradition of the Jews' hidden language, having seen it at work in Weininger and Döblin, Grass nevertheless places the creation of this secret language squarely on the shoulders of the "Jew" Eddi Amsel:

At most little Probst and Heine Kadlubek, the son of a coal dealer, were privileged to listen while Walter Matern maintained a long dark staring silence and Eduard Amsel developed his secret language, giving new names to the new surroundings. "I tnod ekil eht sdrib ereh."
"I don't like the birds here."(89)

This linguistic link established between the two boys is the invention of the Jew who believes in it, who believes that it signifies a real bond between Matern, the silent one, and Amsel, the creator of their secret language. It is, of course, in the moment of Amsel's betrayal, when Matern, joined by a group of Hitler Youth, beat Amsel senseless, that the secret language, the link between friends, is revealed to be merely the Jew's illusion of friendship:

As this first strikes him, it grinds its teeth behind a black rag. From Amsel's red-foaming mouth, a question blows bubbles: "Is it you? Si ti uoy?" But the grinding fist doesn't speak, it only punches. (213)

Grass attempts to redeem the *mauschelnd* figure of Markus by revealing how both Jew and non-Jew, in a specific historical moment, became convinced of the Jews' difference, and more specifically, the difference in their discourse. This could be a conscious reflection of what Grass, the non-Jew, had done in *The Tin Drum*. But it fails as a thematization of this problem since it is still the Jew, the slightly dull and heavy-lidded "Eddi" Amsel, who creates this hidden language. It is a feature of the absence of the center of the Jew, since it distorts the true language of fiction, German, and Grass recognizes this by providing a "translation" of each of these lines into correct, non-reversed German. (This is quite unlike Markus's language in *The Tin Drum*, which while distorted was assumed by Grass to be comprehensible.) Amsel's language is a Jewish invention, and it remains as the Jew's even at the moment of the awareness of Amsel's sense of his own difference. For up to that moment Amsel is a Jew only in a reactive mode, · only in the sense that he, like his father before him, must prove that they were not Jews; at the moment of his betrayal by Matern, his discourse becomes that of the Jew, the marker of difference between his former friend and himself, a discourse which marks the difference between Jew and non-Jew. This is a powerful moment, but some of its power rests on the unstated ·parallel to Weininger's as well as Döblin's image of the discourse of the Jew. And this intertextual relationship, indicated over and over again within the novel through Grass's use of Weininger as the arch-anti-Semite, points toward the spoiled discourse of the Jew. For Grass, perhaps, it is the discourse spoiled at a specific historical moment, when the Jews' parochial identity is abandoned, their sense of difference is suspended, and they desire to become merely German.

This tension within the most important set of works of the early 1960s to deal with the "Jewish Problem" shaped the idea of the Jew in the area of liberal, high culture in Germany. For Grass's work became one of the touchstones for the Germans' understanding of the Jew within the clearly identified political area of liberal ideology. Grass became one of the self-appointed guardians of Germany's liberal tradition. In the 1960 election, Grass went on the hustings, speaking throughout the Federal Republic in support of the Social Democrats. During the election campaign of 1965, Grass wrote his "Transatlantic Elegy" to commemorate the pure but lost German which he was able to find only among the Jewish emigrés when he journeyed across the Atlantic.[12] Grass romanticizes the "Swabian, Saxon, Hessian" of these Jews as that language which remained uncorrupted by the

Nazis. And yet, in the words he places in their mouths, they fear returning to Germany because "my German—it's old fashioned I know—/won't everyone guess, that I was so long . . ." The Jews with their "emigrant and beautifully preserved language" fear to be marked by their speech, by the rhetoric of difference. Indeed it is in the account of the next election campaign of 1969, Grass's *The Diary of a Snail* (1972), that he embeds a further portrait of the Jew, here as survivor, in his recounting of his travels.[13] The connection between Grass's political visibility and his image of the Jew is not lost, even on Grass himself.

Grass's importance in the German Democratic Republic should also not be underestimated. Even though *The Tin Drum* was not to be published officially in the German Democratic Republic until 1987, and then clearly labeled as a historical artifact, it had an extraordinary impact on experimental writers of the 1960s and 1970s through the circulation of illegal copies of this and other works by Grass. For writers, especially Jewish writers, Grass's image of the Jew was a powerful, liberally sanctioned image of the Jew.

Listening to a Jew Listening to Jews

Edgar Hilsenrath and Jurek Becker are two writers whose work exemplifies the "liberal" reaction of writers labeled as Jews to the tradition of the special or hidden quality of the Jews' discourse. The younger of the two, Becker, born in 1937, is the author of what is perhaps the most important representation of the Jew in the literature of the German Democratic Republic. Prior to Becker, as Ruth Angress observed, the standard image was that of Bruno Apitz's *Naked among Wolves* (1958), in which the Jew was represented by an infant child rescued from the death camp by the Communist underground. Becker presents, if not the first speaking Jew as victim (Franz Fühmann does that in his novella *The Jew's Auto* [1962]), the first novel by a Jewish writer in which the Jewish victim of the German comes into full voice.

The world of Jurek Becker's first novel, *Jacob the Liar* (1969), is fully the world of the victim.[14] Becker, who spent his childhood in the Lodz ghetto and then in the camps at Ravensbrück and Sachsenhausen, learned German in East Berlin after the war. His first novel centers on the image of the Jew as victim coping with the world of the Holocaust. The eponymous hero, Jacob the Liar, invents the existence of a radio in the ghetto of the small town in which he lives. The radio becomes the source of hope for all those who are without hope. Jacob, who adopts a small child whose parents have been deported, is torn between the lies that give comfort and the realization of the eventual destruction of himself, the child, and their world. In an extraordinary moment in the novel he takes the child into the basement, where she believes the imaginary radio to be hidden, and recreates, from behind a screen, a "fairy-tale" hour for her. The world of wholeness, of the normal, is recreated in the lies of Jacob, but they are lies that he consciously knows ameliorate the world in which he and the child find themselves.

Becker has taken one of the strongest myths about the polluted and polluting discourse of the Jew, the image of the lying Jew, and reversed it. Weininger's image of the Jew as the natural liar is countered. Jacob lies as a means for survival, not out of any inborn desire to lie but because of the force of circumstance. In retelling the story of Jacob, Becker is forced to create a new discourse for the Jew, at least for the speaking Jew in the novel. He employs a narrator to retell the tale of Jacob's lies, but it is a narrator who is himself creating a tale, not the story of the heroism of the martyrdom in the camps (a literary perspective common to novels on this theme written in the German Democratic Republic) but the tale of the creation of a moment of near sanity through lies in a world gone mad.

The success of Becker's undertaking can be measured in the very fact that the speaking Jews in Becker's novel are given a discourse that, for postwar German critics, seems to be an accurate reconstruction of the discourse of the Jew. Becker's use of German literary devices, such as the intonation of the narrative voice, as well as the "local color" (through the conscious absence of any Yiddishisms) of the Lodz ghetto, creates, for the German reader, the impression of the speaking Jew. Becker's success in this undertaking permits the living Jew, the narrative voice, to recount the events of the "lying" Jew and thus give proof of his ability to command both a "Jewish" discourse and a "German" one.

The act of writing attempts to distance the charge of the silence of the Jews while putting to rest yet another calumny, the image of the lying Jew. Becker's attempt to mirror the world of the victim, of the dead, in *Jacob the Liar* succeeds because we are confronted with the living voice of the narrator at the conclusion of the novel. The pendant to *Jacob the Liar*, Becker's *The Boxer* (1976), is a much more complicated novel; it presents the world of the child not as victim but as survivor.[15] Like *Jacob the Liar*, *The Boxer* depends on the voice of the narrator to place the reader in a specific relationship to the world of the survivor, the created images of the "good" Jew and the "bad" Jew, of the acceptable and the unacceptable solution to the problem of bearing witness.

The plot of *The Boxer* is fairly straightforward. Aron Blank, who calls himself Arno to avoid being again identified as a Jew, has survived the camps and is searching for his son, Mark, who, before the Germans invaded, had been living with Aron's divorced wife. He finds a child called Mark in a hospital for displaced children and identifies him as his missing child, even though the last name is not correct. He raises the child in the turmoil of postwar Germany, living, as did Becker and his father, in the Soviet zone of Berlin. The tale shows the shaping of both father and son by the postwar experience. Emblematic of this experience is the title vignette. The boy is beaten up by a group of toughs, and his father decides to teach him how to box. The new Jew, Arno, needs to have the tools to deal with the new world, tools that Aron lacked. The relationship between father and son, however, deteriorates as the boy grows up. Eventually Mark leaves home, wanders the world, and dies fighting as a Jew in one of the Arab-Israeli conflicts. The novel closes with the narrator, who had reconstructed Arno/ Aron's and Mark's story from his interviews with Aron, becoming aware that Arno's fate was determined through his survival and that surviving can be as much of a hell as were the camps.

Becker's presenting of the survivor as victim and as the "new" Jew is yet another restructuring of the image of the writer. The pseudo-Yiddish tone of *Jacob the Liar* (which has been compared with Shalom Aleichem's romanti- cized reconstructions of shtetl life) presented one language for the speaking Jew. It was not *mauscheln* but the intonation of the Yiddish speaker, an intonation that has its roots as much in the literary tradition of Jewish narrative presented by the premier Christian novelist of the German Demo- cratic Republic, Johannes Bobrowski, and his *Levin's Mill* (1964), as it does in Yiddish.[16] The investigatory tone of *The Boxer* is quite different. The tone is taken from the world of socialist realism, of the narrator as investigative reporter.

But the theme reported is quite the same: the special language of the Jews, the death of the Jews' language in the world of the camps. When Arno/Aron first meets Mark he asks: " 'Did anyone tell you who I am?' The child says: 'No.' 'I am your father. . . . Then you are my son,' Aron says. 'Do you understand?' 'No.' For a few minutes Aron could not understand what Mark could not comprehend. The directress of the hospital had not said a word that he was *meshugge*. He said: 'What don't you understand?' 'That word.' 'What word?' 'The one you said.' 'Son?' 'Yes.' " (64–65).

The word "son" does not exist in Mark's world, since for as long as he can remember he has not been a "son," only a child. What is most striking about this moment in the narrative is that the author's use of indirect discourse embedded in the direct dialogue between father and putative son, a discourse that is to reveal to us the inner working of Arno's mind, is characterized by the use of a Yiddishism, one that is clearly part of German slang but in spite of this is also self-evidently Yiddish. Arno is the Jew as survivor; his son, the child who must develop a new persona. The father's world is determined by his camp experience; the son's is also, but he at least has the potential for some independent growth and change.

After Mark leaves, he writes his father a long letter explaining his action. The core of the letter is his charge that his father's silence had made any relationship between them impossible: " 'You can say that I never spoke to you about this as long as there was a chance. Then I must charge you with having raised me to silence. I know that you are a rather intelligent person, I am evidently one also. Why then did we never speak about these important matters? It wasn't my fault that I can only guess what is going on in your head. I never heard from you' " (285). The silence is the silence between generations, but it is also the silence of the Jew as survivor. Aron is unable to respond. He never answers any of his son's many letters.

For seven years Aron receives his son's letters, one a month until June 1967, when the letters cease. What puzzles Aron is how his son had become a Jew, a Jew who would live on a kibbutz and die fighting for Israel. Who could have "made a Jew out of him?" he wonders. Does not one have the right to choose? "A child of Catholic parents can choose when it comes of age freely to remain or not remain a Catholic. Why then, he asked me, are the children of Jewish parents denied the same right?" (298). Being a Jew denies the possibility of free will. The narrator presents Aron's questions as impossible, and he avoids the most evident of answers. Mark "becomes" a Jew, a "new" Jew because his father remains an "old" Jew, a silent Jew, a Jew condemned to the world that followed the camps. Mark's attempts to "speak" to his father through his letters and Aron's inability to respond are the metaphors for the difference.

Becker claims to incorporate many of his own wartime experiences into his fiction. In an interview given in the late 1970s, Becker speaks about his father's search for him following the war, when he was seven.[17] He reports that his earliest memories stem from this period. After he was found by his father, they went to live in the Soviet zone of Berlin for "reasons which I can only guess. For he would never speak to me of them" (11). Unlike the protagonists of his novel, Becker remained in East Berlin with his father until his father's death in 1972. His sense of identity was as a Jew in the new Communist state. He observes that "he does not know what the signs are which mark one as being Jewish. I know that other claim to identify such signs. I hear that a Jew is one whose mother is Jewish. . . . A human being is one who has human beings for parents, no more, no less" (13). While Becker rejects the particularism of any religious identification as a Jew, he sees himself within a larger literary tradition.

At the conclusion of this interview he observes that after *Jacob the Liar* appeared, reviewers placed him in the tradition of Shalom Aleichem and I. B. Singer. He had, however, been exposed to Shalom Aleichem only through the highly sanitized stage version of his work *Fiddler on the Roof* and had never read any Singer at all. "Now I can imagine, that someone will say after this bit of information: 'See, there we have it! It's the Jewishness in you which the critics recognize. And whether you admit it or not, it's there.' " Becker concludes by observing that perhaps there is a modicum of truth in this: "I don't feel myself as a Jew, but am one in a hundred ways. And so? Why should I try to solve this riddle? Would I be any the wiser? I am afraid not. I am afraid that I would uselessly try to solve the secret, a secret without which my life would be poorer" (18). The secret that Becker senses behind his "Jewish" identity, his identity as a Jewish writer, or at least a writer in a Jewish mode, is the secret language of the Jews, the overcoming of the curse of silence, of his father's silence, and his ability to write this silence out of existence in the fantasies of his prose. For he kills his alter ego, Mark, in defense of a Jewish world. Mark becomes the ideal of the "state of peasants and workers," the German Democratic Republic's motto, by working as a "peasant" (Aron's word) on a kibbutz, and he dies in the defense of that world, just as the heroes of all good social realist novels are programmed to die in defense of the socialist fatherland. *The Boxer*, with its complex narrative mode, its mode of retelling, but a retelling through the probing voice of the questioner, is the exorcism of the silence of the father as Jew and the Jew as father.

Becker's most recent novel, *Bronstein's Children* (1986), is his first return to a "Jewish" theme since his immigration to West Berlin in 1977.[18] In 1976

Becker resigned from the Writers' Union because of Wolf Biermann's exile from the GDR, but he alone of the writers who made this grand gesture was permitted to maintain his citizenship while being granted a long-term visa to "permit" him to live in the West. One simply does not exile writers who are identified in the public eye as Jews. (While Becker did publish a collection of his short stories in 1980, which included a brilliant story about the Nazi ghettos in Poland, "The Wall," this story was written before 1977.)[19] *Bronstein's Children* is without a doubt the most successful work Becker has written in the West. Originally intended to be titled *How I Became A German*, the novel traces two years in the formation of a young Jew in the German Democratic Republic from the perspective of his growing sense of his own conflicts of identity. The plot deals with a family, a father, his eighteen-year-old son, and grown daughter, and their lives in 1973 and 1974 in East Berlin.

The "hero" of the novel, or, at least, its narrator, is the son Hans, who narrates the novel a year after the death of his father Arno in 1973. He attempts to reconstruct the events leading to his father's death and to understand how he has been constructing his life following that event. It is clear from the use of the name Arno for the father that Becker is linking both novels, not in a mechanical sense but in a sense that he is providing the next stage in the "Jewish Question," the development of a Jewish identity in those individuals (unlike all of those in *The Boxer*) who had no firsthand experience of the Holocaust but whose parents (and here, sibling) survived.

The complex plot has at least four major strands, one of which is the central motor force in the novel. (And it is the multistranded complexity of this work which so contrasts with Becker's last novel of the "Jewish Question," *The Boxer*.) Arno and two of his friends kidnap an individual whom they had recognized as a guard at the concentration camp at Neuengamme. They tie him to a bedstead in Arno's country house and proceed to "interrogate" him. Hans has been using the house for assignations with his girlfriend and stumbles across the scene. The second strand links Hans and his Jewish girlfriend Martha, who has become an actress and is starring in a film about the Holocaust. The third strand links Hans and his sister Ella, who is in an asylum, insane, having been horribly mistreated by the family with whom she was hidden (for payment) by her parents when the Nazis entered Poland. The final strand is Hans's attempt to establish himself a year after his father's death, a year he has spent with Martha's family, the nuclear family denied him by the Holocaust but a family deeply marked by the same events that robbed him of his family.

More than survivor guilt marks Hans. For the actions of his father and his friends seem incomprehensible to him. Why not turn the guard over to the authorities who, unlike the authorities in the Federal Republic, were sure to punish him? Is it vengeance that makes them keep him prisoner? Is it the creation of their own little camp with an inmate over whom they have the same control as was held over them? Hans cannot understand these actions and attempts over and over again to interrogate his father and the prisoner. Their rationale, as explained by Arno, is that historical chance has placed them in a land (the GDR) in which this individual will be punished only because one occupying nation rather than another dominates. The Germans ("deutsches Gesindel") are themselves no more trustworthy in the German Democratic Republic than in the Federal Republic. Indeed, Arno later says, the Germans are the most tractable of peoples. They would act not out of belief but because they were told that to convict the guard was their duty. "Order them to eat dogshit and, if you are strong enough, they will soon take dogshit to be a delicacy" (130).

Becker's description of Hans, the narrator, as an athlete, at the very beginning of the novel, forms an epiphany which illuminates the rest of the text, in a manner uncomprehended by the narrator until the conclusion of the work. Hans must complete the swimming test in order to graduate, and his disinterest in doing so reflects one of the images of the Jew in German fiction, the Jew as attempting to avoid any type of physical exertion. And yet Becker plays with this standard theme much more consciously than he did in any of his earlier "Jewish" novels. The scene is set. Hans must take his swimming test and is ordered by one of his schoolmates, in a schoolboy Prussian tone, to take off his swimsuit and shower. Hans's answer is to punch him in the nose, to which the boy's responds, after he gets up, that "he's crazy" (43). The reader is led into the resulting uproar by the teachers who flood into the locker room, and provide a rationale for the incident. The explanation, imagined by Hans to be whispered to his victim by the teacher, is that he's a Jew. "There are slight sensitivities, which we cannot so easily comprehend" (47). The implication is that Hans has not wanted to remove his swimsuit because of his physical difference, because of his circumcised penis. But the chapter ends with the revelation, in the narrator's interior monologue, that he is not circumcised. He had no hidden "Jewish" motivation (in his own understanding of this) to hit his schoolmate, only an objection to his schoolmate's pedantic, Prussian tone. Jews, according to Hans's account of Arno's view, are an invention of those who wish to victimize those labeled as Jews. This powerful scene reveals the reactive moment in Becker's characters; their Jewishness is revealed only in their response to the corrupt world about them. Or so we are led to believe by Hans.

The theme of Jews as different, different because of history, because of the Holocaust, because of the Germans, not because of their own sense of difference, seems to dominate this novel, as it did *The Boxer*. For his set paper, well prepared in advance, Hans has as his *Abitur* theme, "the cell as the means of genetic inheritance" (93).

The image of difference is ironicized. One of his father's friends is a violinist who damns the popular view that all Jewish violinists have to be "Heifetz or Oistrakh." For people "expect greatness from him while he is sadly but an average violinist" (133). Everything having to do with concepts of difference in Hans's world seems reversed. The Nazis are represented by the old man in the cabin stinking of shit (an ironic reversal of the *foeter judaicus*) or by the film actors in their SS uniforms, who play cards with the Jews between takes. But the Jews in the film are played by real Jews because they look like Jews. The realities of his parents, of his mother and father, photographed with real "Jew's Stars" sewn on their clothing, are opposed to the world of make-believe, in which his girlfriend, Martha, plays at being a Jewess, while really being one. This confusion of role and reality suddenly undermines the seemingly clear line between being Jewish as a role assigned by society and having any inherent sense of difference.

Becker destroys the clean line between the construction of categories of difference and the realities of difference in one extraordinary moment, a moment for which we are no more prepared than the revelation that Hans is uncircumcised. Hans has returned to the cabin again and again to speak with the captive. Once, he returns home to find that his father and his friends have gathered in their apartment for a strategy session. The son pulls a set of drawers away from a hidden door, lies on the ground, and listens to his father speak:

The first words that I heard made it clear why they did not feel it necessary to be quiet: they spoke Yiddish. It was incomprehensible to me that father could make himself understood in this language. I wanted to believe that a stranger sat there using father's voice. Not only had he avoided speaking Yiddish in my presence, he never even indicated that he could speak the language. He spoke without clumsiness, without stuttering, as if the words flew to him from one moment to the next. I found that horrid, I felt myself betrayed. He spoke louder than all the others, so that I asked myself whether he counted on my listening and wanted thus to betray his secret to me. Never before was I so against him. . . .

The sound of this language was unpleasant, not merely strange like a normally foreign tongue. This language remained on the border of the comprehensible, and I constantly had the feeling that I only had to strain myself a bit in order to understand it. Perhaps they spoke Yiddish together because they believed that this language was the most appropriate for their undertaking. (221–22)

Suddenly the hidden language of the Jew, the Jew within, surfaces for Hans. Yiddish is the marker of real difference for Becker, the hidden nature of the father as Jew and victim. Hans's constant rejection of special treatment as a "victim of fascism," his uncircumcised penis, his desire to serve as the means by which the guard is rescued, all point to his sense of being a "German." He is aware of his role as a Jew but believes this is an invention of his tormentors, as his father had always told him. Suddenly there is a difference, a sense of strangeness, of the "uncanny," that sense of the self projected into the world and made different. Hans needs to feel like the German he had always believed himself to be. He turns again to the country cabin, to the guard, in order to free him. There he finds his father dead and the guard, who screams upon seeing Hans, "I couldn't do anything; I was innocent" (300) (his cry throughout the novel, but in other circumstances). Hans begins to file off the handcuffs, when the guard says: "He has the key with him." The novel ends with Hans going to his "father and reaching into his pocket, first in the wrong one and then in the right" (302). The true key, the key to Hans's identity, to Arno's sense of self, dies with the father. Becker underlines the sense of change by placing the novel at the time of Walter Ulbricht's death. With the death of a generation, of a father, "missed more in death than treasured in life" (300), Hans will become a German but will also now remain a Jew. He will not be able to abandon, to repress, his identity. This is the answer to Aron/Arno's question in *The Boxer* of "what made a Jew out of him." Becker signals this moment of awareness in his character's sense of difference through the use of the motif of the hidden language of the Jews, but now in a much more highly differentiated mode. For being a Jew is simply being one of "Bronstein's children," and the irony of an inescapable and inexorable sense of difference makes Becker's most recent novel into the most constructive means of dealing with this otherwise destructive theme. For Becker thematizes the hidden language of the Jew in a discourse that is not "Jewish" but clearly German, a German of post-modernistic literary discourse exemplified by his last two "non-Jewish" novels. There is little difference in the complexity of his literary language, of his subtle use of Grassian irony; he is indeed a "German" in his cultural embeddedness but a Jew in his representation of the contradictions of what being German means to the German-Jewish writer.

Hilsenrath and Grass *Revividus*

Edgar Hilsenrath was born in Leipzig in 1926 (and is therefore a full decade older than Becker). In 1938 he fled with his mother and brother to Rumania, where, in 1941, they were sent to the ghetto at Mogiljow-Podolski. Surviving, he emigrated with his family in 1945 to Palestine and from there in 1951 to the United States. In the late 1960s he returned to the Federal Republic and now lives, like Becker, in West Berlin. Hilsenrath is the author of a number of "Jewish" books. His first was his memoir of life in the camps, *Night*, published in German in 1978 but in English translation in 1967. The two novels I will be concentrating on, however, are Hilsenrath's most recent: *Bronsky's Confessions* (1980) and, his best-known and best-selling work, *The Nazi and the Barber* (1977), first published in English in 1971.

Hilsenrath's reception in Germany is as a Jewish writer, a writer with specific insights into the "dilemma" of the "Jewish Question." *Der Spiegel*, in reviewing *The Nazi and the Barber*, could simply comment that "the author knows that which he reports: Edgar Hilsenrath, 51, is a Jew."[20] In 1989 "the Jew Hilsenrath" (according to *Der Spiegel*) published his account of the 1915 murder of the Armenians, *The Fairytale of the Last Thought*, which is described as "an anagram of contemporary history, of his own biography."[21] And again in Rolf Hoppe's recent review of the same novel: "the Jewish novelist Edgar Hilsenrath transforms the Turkish massacre of the Armenians into art."[22] This qualifier was also applied to Becker in a number of the reviews of his first novel, *Jacob the Liar*, and places their identity as Jews and writers as parallel. In his two major novels, Hilsenrath plays with this theme, the question of a German-Jewish identity in contemporary Germany, seeing the question of the definition of the Jew as a problem not for the Jews in Germany and the United States but for their tormentors. Out of this critique of the idea of the Jew comes one of the most successful literary production of recent years, Hilsenrath's *The Nazi and the Barber*.

Bronsky's Confessions provides a fictionalized context for the longer and more involved novel.[23] Like *Night*, it is a highly autobiographical novel, a work that completes the life story of the narrative "I" begun in the concentration camps of the earlier work. In the novel, Jakob Bronsky, a German Jew, arrives as a "displaced person" after the war, in a United States, or at least a New York, or at least a Yorkville, or at least an "immigrant cafe on Broadway and 86th" (75), seemingly populated only by German immigrants and American social outcasts. The novel begins with an ironic exchange of letters in 1938 between Bronsky's father, Nathan, and the American counsel in Berlin, attempting to get papers to enable him and his family to flee Nazi anti-Semitism. The counsel observes, in 1939, that it would not be until the 1950s before their quota as Polish Jews (for Bronsky's father was born in what was Poland in 1939) would enable him to grant them a visa to the United States. Nathan Bronsky's reply, couched in the only use of English to be found in the novel, is: "Fuck America!" (19).

After the horrors of the war, in the 1950s Jakob Bronsky and his parents arrive in America. This Nabokovian world of German-Jewish emigrés centers around the title character and his obsessive desire to write his experiences in the form of a novel, to which an acquaintance gives the perfect title:

"Are you the hero of the book?"

"That could be. I'm writing it in the third person, even though the book is autobiographical."

"Understood," Grünspan says, "In the third person. The hero is a man?"

"Of course. The hero is a man."

"What kind of a man?"

"A lonely man."

"A masturbator?"

"What do you mean?"

"A lonely man is always a masturbator," Grünspan says.

"My book doesn't have anything to do with masturbation. It's a serious book."

"That doesn't make any difference," Grünspan says, "If he is a lonely man, then he is a masturbator." . . .

"Does your book have a title?"

I said, "Not yet."

"None?"

"None. Not even a working title."

"Call your book: The Masturbator."

"The Masturbator?"

"The Masturbator!"

"A best-seller's title," said Grünspan. "If I were in your place, I wouldn't change this title. A first-class title: The Masturbator." (48–49)

The image of the author as self-centered subject, as masturbator, is central to Hilsenrath's image of the Jew in America. Isolated, deprived of normal human contact, languageless, speaking German in an English-speaking world, Bronsky functions on the margins of society, much like the picaro. It is language—for Bronsky, German and its (for him) necessary context, "Culture," and the novel as cultural artifact—that defines Bronsky's world. Bronsky is so tied to German as his means of expressing his experiences of the world, of the Holocaust, that he is unable to see himself in a non-German context, even when this would be necessary to achieve his desired status as a writer. Being a writer for Bronsky means writing in German, and that for Hilsenrath has a very specific rationale:

I said: "You know it's not easy writing in a language which no one wants to speak with me."
"No one?"
"With the exception of a couple of immigrants, whom I happen to know."
"Oh."
"That is one of my worst problems."
"You're talking about German?"
"Yes."
"Then why don't you write in English, a language which everyone understands?"
"I can't."
"Are you dependent on German?"
"Yes."
"I don't understand that."
"Me, neither."
"Aren't you a Jew?"
"But of course."
"Yuh-huh." (105–6)

For Hilsenrath the problem of the Jews' discourse is the problem of the exile's language, a problem that haunts German-Jewish writers in non-German-speaking exile after 1933 (and especially after the *Anschluss* of Austria). The hidden language of the "Jew" is German, not because there is a necessary link between Jews and the German language but because it is the language of the character's childhood as well as his formative experience, the concentration camps.

Hilsenrath's America is parallel to the ghetto in *Night*, in which the inhabitants are reduced to a subhuman level by the forces that keep them in the camp, depriving them of all human needs, such as food. This theme, of

New York as the new inferno, echoes through many of the post-Holocaust visions of America, such as Saul Bellow's *Mr. Sammler's Planet.* For Hilsenrath it is, however, closely tied to the act of writing, the means of communication. Grünspan's title for the novel, a novel that remains unwritten in the course of Hilsenrath's novel, points toward the pollution of the Jews' discourse but a pollution that comes from without, from the blind anti-Semitism of the world in which the narrator finds himself and which he, unlike his alter ego in *Night*, who dies at the conclusion of the novel, survives. But his survival as author is placed within a fantasy of return. The closure of the novel comes with an extensive fantasy in which Jakob Bronsky imagines himself back in Germany, returning "primarily because of my language" (200). His return to his language, German, forms the context for the completion of his novel, for which he cannot find a publisher. He proceeds to feign suicide, to persuade his aged mother to get Max Brod, Kafka's executor, to read his unpublished work. Brod, in this fantasy, sees Bronsky as a "second Kafka" (203), at which point Bronsky suddenly reappears and becomes a media star. In the dreamlike television interview which closes the fantasy and the novel, Bronsky states his case for the Jew as author in contemporary Germany:

INTERVIEWER: "Mr. Bronsky. Do you have something to say to the German people?"
BRONSKY: "I have nothing to say to the old people. They know already."
INTERVIEWER: And to the youth?"
BRONSKY: "To the youth, I want to say that they should read my book."
INTERVIEWER: "Your book on the Jewish Ghetto?"
BRONSKY:: "My book against violence and inhumanity."
INTERVIEWER: "The Masturbator?"
BRONSKY: "The Masturbator." (205)

Bronsky's book remains a "Jews' book" in Germany, and the fantasy that a shared language would create some understanding vanishes. Bronsky's experiences, in the ghetto and in America, are too extreme to be understood by Germans even where the bridge of language exists. But this final chapter is only a fantasy, spun out like all children's fantasies abou their own death and resurrection out of a sense of powerlessness. Bronsky remains in New York, while Hilsenrath returns to Germany to turn his sensed distance into the creativity that produced a series of major novels such as *Bronsky's Confessions,* all of which deal with the German fantasy of the damaged discourse of the Jew and the Jew's creative response.

The Jewish response to the myths spun about the nature of the language of the Jews in the fictions of postwar Germany has its high point in what has been seen as an Evelyn Waugh-like novel of black humor, *The Nazi and the Barber*.[24] The plot is a clear answer to Günter Grass's *Dog Years*. Like Grass, Hilsenrath presents us with two children, born within minutes of each other, friends and rivals during their childhood. Itzig Finkelstein and Max Schulz, Jew and non-Jew, are presented much like the two children in Twain's *Puddinhead Wilson*, seemingly switched at birth. The Jew is blond and blue-eyed with a straight nose and good teeth; the non-Jew is small, dark, thick-lipped, pop-eyed, hook-nosed, and with bad teeth (24). Max is raised within the Finkelstein household, thus escaping his mother, the town whore. There he learns Yiddish, the language of Itzig's father, Chaim, and his wife, Sarah. For Chaim German is merely "a corrupt, destroyed, highfallutin Yiddish," thus reversing the traditional German image of Yiddish as the language of Jews and thieves (23). The narrator, Max, observes that only a few families in Wieshalle spoke Yiddish. Most of the Jews spoke German, having lived in the town for generations. Thus the non-Jew attends synagogue with his friends, learns the Hebrew alphabet seemingly by osmosis, and memorizes the Sabbath prayers.

This linguistic reversal is the irony which Becker points to in *Bronstein's Children*, the irony of the randomness of all human characteristics, even those such as circumcision, traditionally ascribed to the Jew. Max Schulz becomes a Nazi, eventually a concentration camp guard and executioner at Laubwalde, and murders his childhood friend in 1942 (303). Following the collapse of the Thousand Year Reich, Schulz escapes to the West and assumes Finkelstein's identity. While he looks like a Jew and speaks the hidden languages of the Jews, he is missing two signs of Jewish identity: two signs of identity at least in the mind of a non-Jew in 1945. He does not have a camp identification number and he is not circumcised. He accomplishes both in the ruins of postwar Berlin, after which he disappears into the displaced persons' camps as the master barber Itzig Finkelstein.

The newly circumcised Itzig Finkelstein emigrates to Palestine, where he assumes the role of the activist Jew, fighting as part of the Revisionist "Stern Gang" in the War of Liberation. Schulz/Finkelstein's identity is as a German Jew but one who has the linguistic abilities of the Eastern Jew. Indeed, the wife of his employer, "a Prussian Jewess who cannot forget Prussia," (231) to use Schulz/Finkelstein's formula, "looks cross-eyed every time he speaks Yiddish with the clients" (232). While many of the "Yekes" have great difficulty learning Hebrew (one of the salient aspects of the comic stereotype of the German Jew in Israel), Schulz/Finkelstein has none. He buys a Hebrew grammar book and learns the language with alacrity (249). He adds English, the language of the British occupying forces, for good measure ("It's really just like German" [249]). This new Hebrew- and Yiddish-speaking figure marries one of the two survivors of a massacre in the Ukraine, a woman shocked into speechlessness. This motif, so ably used by Jerzy Kosinski in *The Painted Bird,* represents the loss of communicative ability in a world in which interpersonal relationships have absolutely no meaning. Language ability, such as that of Schulz/Finkelstein, is a sign of the enemy, not of the victim. Schulz/Finkelstein's wife regains her speech, and Schulz/Finkelstein eventually dies of a stroke trying to persuade his friends that he was really the murderer Schulz, not the victim Finkelstein. At the moment of death he is beyond language (318). His punishment is to spend eternity suffering the anguish of the six million he helped murder.

To understand the context of the reading of German-Jewish writing in the Federal Republic of Germany today, the relationship between Grass and Hilsenrath, and its critical reception, can be most illuminating. One representation of the Jew which I did not cite in my depiction of Grass's discussions of the Jew comes from his 1979 novel *The Meeting in Telgte.* There should not be (nor is there overtly) a representation of the Jew in this novel of the German Baroque which was written to evoke the history of Hans Werner Richter and the literary association called the Group 47 in the late 1940s and early 1950s. In the account of the end of the third day of the endless literary debates which take place during a meeting of seventeenth-century poets, the poet Filip Zesen wanders along the river, bemoaning his fate as one of the poets who has been forced to remain celibate that evening because of losing a wager. There he sees (through the eyes of the narrator) the following scene:

But no sooner had I caught sight of him standing above the outer Ems, which had dug deep into its sandy bed, than two corpses, tied together, were washed against the bank. Though bloated, they could be recognized as a man and a woman. After brief hesitation—an eternity for Zesen—the pair broke loose from the tangled reeds, spun around playfully in the current, escaped from the eddy, and glided downstream to the mill weir where evening was blending into night, leaving nothing behind except potential metaphors, which Zesen began at once to pad with resounding neologisms. He was so hard pressed by language that he had no time to be horrified.[25]

This passage is full of the "Baroque" flavor of the Hundred Years War and evokes the horrors of a very distant German past. But it is also a direct plagiarism from Edgar Hilsenrath's autobiographical novel of the Holocaust, *Night:*

Two corpses were drifting comfortably down river: a man and a woman. The woman drifted somewhat ahead of the man. It looked like a flirtation: the man constantly trying to snatch the woman but without succeeding. Then the woman drifted a little to the side and grinned at the man. And the man grinned back at her. And he caught up with her; his body touched her.

Both corpses now proceeded to float in a circle; for a while they stuck together as if they wanted to unite. Then they floated downstream, reconciled.[26]

This borrowing was noted in 1987 by Christoph Sieger in the notes to the critical edition of the novel as well as by Andreas Graf in an essay of 1989.[27] Both of these critics seem to see in Grass's "borrowing" only a post-modern playfulness with categories of "reality" and "fictionality."

Let me remind you of another such borrowing in the recent past, the debates about which revealed certain sensitivities in Anglo-American literary criticism. D. M. Thomas's novel of Freud, feminism, and the Holocaust, *The White Hotel* (1981), was not only a best seller but eventually stood at the center of a firestorm of controversy. It was revealed by a close reader of the text that Thomas had appropriated without acknowledgment a long section from Anatoli Kuznetsov's firsthand account of the massacre at Babi Yar for the conclusion of his book.[28] Much discussion in the public press ensued about whether it was appropriate to have "borrowed" such a section without noting its presence in some way, either in an introduction, or in notes, or at least through the appropriate punctuation. Some critics argued that this was a sign of the authenticity of the discourse in the novel, an authenticity which could only be created by using the direct language of the victims.[29] Now this debate was carried out in the public press and it centered on the problem of the language and discourse of the Jew as incorporated into the fictions of the Christian non-participant in the Holocaust. There could be, of course, no resolution of this question, though Thomas himself felt that the questions raised missed the entire problem, which he saw as the ability of a writer to draw on whatever sources of inspiration he needed.[30] Perhaps true, but where did this leave the visibility of Kuznetsov?

The criticism by contemporary West German critics of Grass's "borrowing" from Hilsenrath has certainly not made the front page of any newspaper in Germany. And it most probably will not. For the treatment of Grass's borrowing is as a legitimate, post-modern literary undertaking. Grass's purposeful confusion of "reality" and "narrativity" is stressed by Graf, the subtitle of whose essay is "on the ironic relationship between literature and reality." Might I suggest another reading. For all of the questions raised by Thomas's use of Kuznetsov, it was acknowledged that he maintained the context of Kuznetsov's description of the murders at Babi Yar. Thomas's novel is ultimately about the Holocaust. Günter Grass's "borrowing" is placed in quite a different context. Grass isolates this text and displaces it into the seventeenth century, with an evocation of the post-World-War-II era and the Group 47. He thus brackets the world which Hilsenrath inhabited. This violation of the Jew's authenticity, of the voice of the Jew narrating his own experience, within the literary world of contemporary fiction is marked by Grass's borrowing. The Jew not only vanishes, his voice becomes the authentic voice of the German experience of the seventeenth century or the immediate postwar era.

Hilsenrath's first novel, first published in English translation, was only published with great difficulty in Germany and has only been widely read in the past few years with the appearance of a paperback edition. Grass's novel, *The Meeting in Telgte,* was widely advertised and widely discussed (if rarely read) when it appeared. Grass manages to incorporate and thus make invisible, not only his source, but certainly as important, the context out of which this source springs, the postwar German Jew's struggle to establish his own identity in German culture. Grass's visible Jews are marked by the flaw of the hidden language ascribed to the Jews; his hidden Jew, Edgar Hilsenrath, marks the invisibility of the Jew in the literary world of postwar Germany. As certainly as Markus and Amsel represent the visible Jew with his contaminated discourse in the world of the Danzig Trilogy, so does Edgar Hilsenrath function in Grass's work as the hidden Jew, representing the Jew within postwar "high" culture, neither seen nor heard. For even when they are seen —as in the popularity of Hilsenrath's novel *The Nazi and the Barber*—they are relegated to the world of the past, a world completed and closed. They are not acknowledged as part of the world of the present, taking their themes out of their own experience but casting them in the discourse of the high culture in which they live. Thus *Der Spiegel's* review of Hilsenrath's latest novel evokes "the Jew Werfel" and his novel of the Armenian massacre, in other words a dead Jew is evoked to categorize the living author. But both of them are simultaneously Germans and Jews, except in the eyes of the contemporary critic.

The tension which exists within the world of German culture is mirrored in the work of Grass. His early novels about Nazism react against and thus recapitulate the idea of the Jew taken from the German past. It is in Grass's "non-Jewish" texts, such as *The Meeting in Telgte*, that the problem of the appropriation (rather than the creation) of the Jews' discourse appears. Here the invisibility of the Jew is as upsetting (at least to an American-Jewish Germanist) as is the stereotypes of the Jew in his earlier work.

The problem in German criticism, in the classroom, and in fiction seems to be clear. Is it possible to conceptualize a role for Jews in contemporary German society, a role which given Becker and Hilsenrath's success, they clearly have? Is it possible to see them not as "Jews" but as "Germans" and "Jews" simultaneously? Not in the fantasy of a discredited cultural symbiosis, but rather, and thus even more difficult, in the role of Jews writing about the common past of German, Christian and Jew, in a discourse of high culture today, reflecting the problems and conflicts of contemporary German culture, a culture which evidently still has great problems coming to terms with its "Jews."

Toward Answering the Question: Who Killed the Jewish Writers of Contemporary Germany and Why?

The signs that have been assumed to have a permanent signification as signs of the Jew in postwar German letters, circumcision and the hidden language of the Jews, come to be signs of the German illusions about Jews for writers such as Hilsenrath and Becker. Hilsenrath and Becker would seem, on the surface, to form a most disparate duo. What relates them is their projection of the specific qualities of the discourse of the Jew onto a specific image of the Jew, the Jew as survivor. In some cases this alter ego is glorified, in others it is condemned. In all cases this fictional discourse is distanced from the world of the author, from the choice that he has made to move from a language contaminated with images of his inability to a world in which he can creatively use that very language. Both Hilsenrath and Becker successfully turn the image of the damaged discourse of the Jew against itself by thematizing and satirizing this myth. They thus set the stage for a critique of the invisibility of the Jew in contemporary Germany through their stress on the centrality of a negative symbiosis as the key to an understanding of German-Jewish identity and the contemporary German response.

Why is it that their highly successful works, in terms of both aesthetic as well as popular success, have not been reflected in the image of the Jewish writer in contemporary Germany? Why is it that contemporary criticism does not speak of a German-Jewish literature, as it is so free to speak of the Age of the Great American Jewish Novel? My sense is that Grass could and did use images of the Jew in the 1950s and 1960s which were at first blush understood to be sympathetic and evocative ones, since they were positive stereotypes. It is only with detailed analysis (and perhaps, historical distance), that one can see that the very reason why such images proved to be successful (and this is true of the portrait of the Jew by other "liberal" authors of the 1950s and 1960s) was that these images were, at least in part, the inversion of the negative images preceding them. This is not to say that Grass uses *Stürmer* caricatures in his work. But he uses their polar anti-image, and in it he maintains at least one of the major myths about the Jews, that of the Jews' hidden and secret language. And his "borrowing" from Hilsenrath's novel signals this attitude in a very direct manner. The corpses floating in the river of narrative mark the invisibility of the Jew in German culture. Unseen except as a "source" for the German author, he remains part of the past even though he is quite alive and functioning within Grass's literary world.

When writers such as Hilsenrath and Becker (and one can greatly extend this list) came to portray Jews in fiction, they first had to counter the accepted image of the Jew, as in the works of Grass, an image which fit neither their self-perception nor their understanding of the appropriate manner of dealing with their seemingly contradictory identity as Jews, Germans, and authors. It was not merely that they separated their reality from the fictions about Jews. This would have been all too simple. For what writer confuses his/her own personality with the fictions that personality is able to generate? What they found was that the philo-Semitic world of German liberal politics, the world of writers who in their own minds and in their public actions represented an idealized image of the German writer in a direct continuity to the liberalism (read: Jewishness) of the 1920s (and even earlier) was able to employ images of the Jew that were poisoned. The Jew thus existed only in the past. When Jews (however defined) turned to images of the Jew, they found an uncanny recognition of the forces of evil as well as the forces of good. And given the radical reversal of the image of the Jew with the rise of left-wing anti-Zionism (read: anti-Semitism) in the 1970s, their reading was not wrong.

Writers in the Anglo-American world who understood themselves to be Jews, writers such as the American-Jewish author Philip Roth, in the Zuckerman novels (1979–85), and the British-Jewish author Clive Sinclair, in his extraordinary novel *Blood Libels* (1985), were able to thematize the idea of the hidden language of the Jews. They were able to come to terms with the assumption that as Jews they see the world differently from everyone else and that, as a result, their texts are encoded with hidden "Jewish" messages. What these writers did was to transform the accusation into the stuff of their novels. By writing, they disprove the special nature of the Jews' language as assumed in Western letters. But commentators of both the left and the right did not recognize the cry for universalism within such a satiric representation of particularism. Unlike the Anglo-American experience in which Roth and Sinclair are viewed as Jews, "self-hating Jews," but at least as Jews, Hilsenrath and Becker in Germany are simply denied any special status within their cultural world. They remain simply Jews, not Jews in Germany or German-Jews. And being a "Jew" means being part of the past, not of the present. For to admit that Jews can write about Jewish topics and still transcend such a subject matter and thus be "real" writers, i.e., in the terminology of liberalism, writers about "universal" topics, would violate the liberal view that particularism of any sort is bad. Being a "Jewish" writer in present-day Germany is for present-day Germans (or at least for Germans and their American intellectual clones of the 1970s and 1980s) is an unacceptable, even racist category. And yet it remains the label which is applied to German-Jewish writers. It is such an attitude that easily leads to the view that "Zionism is Racism." To destroy such "racism," they have destroyed the idea of the "Jewish" writer. For such critics, the category of "Jewish writer" exists only for the prewar period. They thus connect the Holocaust with the identifiable place of the Jew in Weimar Germany. If there are no Jews in German culture today, only Germans, then the Holocaust, an attempt to destroy all sense of difference in destroying the Other, succeeded. The new liberal cry, which confuses the sense of the place of the Jewish writer in German culture with the label placed upon the Jewish writer as different by the Nazis, is to eliminate the category of the Jew completely. They have denied identity to contemporary German-Jewish writers dealing with the complexities of the themes of present-day German Jewry in a creative and valuable manner, an identity to no little degree imposed upon them by being Jewish in present-day Germany. Thus writers such as Hilsenrath and Becker return to these themes in order to prove that they really exist as Germans, Jews, and writers. Their cry is that they do exist as Jewish writers in Germany, where they articulate the presence of the most invisible of categories, the cultural Jew. Indeed, the final chapter of Rafael Seligmann's

recent novel of the struggle for identity of a German who is Jewish or a Jew
who is German (and Seligmann is both) evokes the specter of self-hatred as
a means of creating a literary identity. His final chapter, his cry for the
establishment of his fictive personality as a German and a Jew, is simply
entitled "A German Jew," a label which speaks not to the utopian past but
to the conflicted present.[31]

Notes

1. Bernt Engelmann, *Deutschland ohne Juden* (Munich: Schneekluth, 1970); citations are from the translation by D. J. Beer, *Germany without Jews* (New York:
   Bantam Books, 1984).
2. Jack Zipes, "The Vicissitudes of Being Jewish in West Germany," in his and
   Anson Rabinbach, eds., *Germans and Jews since the Holocaust* (New York/
   London: Holmes & Meier, 1986), pp. 27–49.
3. Peter Sichrovsky, ed., *Wir wissen nicht was morgen wird, wir wissen wohl was
   gestern war: Junge Juden in Deutschland und Österreich* (Cologne: Kiepenheuer &
   Witsch, 1985); translated by Jean Steinberg as *Strangers in Their Own Land:
   Young Jews in Germany and Austria Today* (New York: Basic Books, 1986).
4. Henryk M. Broder, "Die unheilbare Liebe deutscher Intellektueller zu toten und
   todkranken Juden," *Semit* 3 (1989): 29.
5. The term is from Dan Diner, "Negative Symbiose: Deutsche und Juden nach
   Auschwitz," *Babylon* 1 (1986): 9–10.
6. *Jewish Self-Hatred: Anti-Semitism and the Hidden Language of the Jews* (Baltimore:
   The Johns Hopkins University Press, 1986; paperback, 1990).
7. Ruth Kluger Angress, "A 'Jewish Problem' in German Postwar Fiction," *Modern
   Judaism* 5 (1985): 215–33. Prior to Angress the studies of this topic have been
   hopelessly utopian in their perspective; see Christiane Schmelzkopf, *Zur Gestaltung jüdischer Figuren in der deutschsprachigen Literatur nach 1945* (Hildesheim:
   Georg Olms, 1983) and Heidy M. Müler, *Die Judendarstellung in deutschsprachiger
   Erzählprosa (1945–1981)* (Königstein: Athenäum, 1984).
8. Günter Grass, *The Tin Drum*, trans. Ralph Manheim (New York: Pantheon,
   1962), p. 99. The original German, which is even more radical in its use of
   mauscheln, is to be found in Günter Grass, *Die Blechtrommel* (Frankfurt a M.:
   Fischer, 1963), p. 85.
9. All references are to the reprint of his collected works: Alfred Döblin, *Reise in
   Polen* (Olten: Walter, 1968). (My translation.) On Döblin and the discourse of
   the Jews, see Hans Peter Althaus, "Ansichten vom Jiddischen. Urteile und
   Vorurteile deutschsprachiger Schriftsteller des 20. Jahrhunderts," in Watler Röll
   and Hans-Peter Bayerdörfer, eds., *Auseinandersetzungen um jiddische Sprache und
   Literatur/Jüdische Komponenten in der deutschen Literatur—die Assimilationskontro-*

verse: *Akten des VII. Internationalen Germanisten-Kongresses*. Göttingen 1985 (Tübingen: Niemeyer, 1986), pp. 63–71.

10. Otto Weininger, *Sex and Character* (New York: G. P. Putnam's Sons, 1906), p. 324.

11. See Lyle H. Smith, "Volk, Jew and Devil: Ironic Inversion in Günter Grass's *Dog Years*," *Studies in Twentieth Century Literature* 3 (1978): 85–96.

12. Günter Grass, *Was ist des Deutschen Vaterland?* (Niewied/Berlin: Hermann Luchterhand, 1965), pp. 11–12.

13. See the discussion (with an unpublished remark by Grass on the source of the portrait of the Jew in *The Diary of a Snail* in the biography of Marcel Reich-Ranicki) in Hans Dieter Zimmermann, "Spielzeughändler Markus, Lehrer Zweifel und die Vogelscheuchen: Die Verfolgung der Juden im Werk von Günter Grass," in Herbert A. Strauss and Christhard Hoffmann, eds., *Juden und Judentum in der Literatur* (Munich: Deutscher Taschenbuch Verlag, 1985), pp. 295–306.

14. *Jakob der Lügner* (Berlin: Aufbau, 1969); *Jacob the Liar*, trans. Melvin Kornfeld (New York: Harcourt Brace Jovanovich, 1975).

15. *Der Boxer* (Frankfurt: Suhrkamp, 1976). See Chaim Shoham, "Jurek Becker ringt mit seinem Judentum. "Der Boxer" und Assimilation nach Auschwitz," in Röll and Bayerdörfer, *Auseinandersetzungen um jiddische Sprache und Literatur*, pp. 225–36.

16. Leah Ireland, " 'Your Hope is on My Shoulder': Bobrowski and the World of the *Ostjuden*," *Monatshefte* 72 (1980): 416–30.

17. Hans Jürgen Schultz, ed., *Mein Judentum* (Berlin: Kreuz, 1979), pp. 10–18.

18. All references are to *Bronsteins Kinder* (Frankfurt a. M.: Suhrkamp, 1986). (My translation.)

19. *Nach der ersten Zukunft* (Frankfurt a. M.: Suhrkamp, 1980), pp. 62–102.

20. "Max und Itzig," *Der Spiegel* (22 August 1977), pp. 137–39. See also Sidney Rosenfeld, "German Exile Literature after 1945: The Younger Generation," in John M. Spalek und Robert Bell, eds., *Exile: The Writer's Experience*. University of North Carolina Studies in Germanic Languages and Literature, 99 (Chapel Hill, N.C.: The University of North Carolina Press, 1982), pp. 333–41; Peter Stenberg, "Memories of the Holocaust: Edgar Hilsenrath and the Fiction of Genocide," *Deutsche Vierteljahrsschrift für Literaturwissenschaft und Geistesgeschichte* 56 (1982), 277–89 and Peter Stenberg, "Remembering Times Past: Canetti, Sperber, and a World that is No More," *Seminar* 17 (1981): 296–311.

21. Edgar Hilsenrath, *Das Märchen vom letzten Gedanken* (Munich: Piper, 1989), reviewed in *Der Spiegel* 36 (1989), p. 233.

22. *Deutsches Allgemeines Sonntagsblatt* (4 August 1989), p. 21.

23. All references are to *Bronskys Geständnis* (Berlin: Ullstein, 1982). (My translation.)

24. All references are to *Der Nazi und der Friseur* (Frankfurt a. M.: Fischer, 1977); the earlier English translation, *The Nazi and the Barber*, trans. Andrew White (Garden City, N.Y.: Doubleday, 1971) has also been consulted.

25. Günter Grass, *The Meeting at Telgte*, trans. Ralph Manheim (New York: Harcourt Brace Jovanovich, 1979), p. 35.

26. Edgar Hilsenrath, *Night*, trans. Michael Roloff (New York: Manor Books, 1974), pp. 278–79.

27. Günter Grass, *Werkausgabe in Zehn Bänden*, ed. Volker Neuhaus, vol. 6: *Das Treffen in Telgte*, ed. Christoph Sieger (Frankfurt a. M.: Suhrkamp, 1987), pp. 37–38 and Andreas Graf, " 'ein leises dennoch' ": Zum ironischen Wechselbezug von Literatur und Wirklichkeit in Günter Grass' Erzählung *Das Treffen in Telgte,*" *Deutsche Vierteljahrsschrift für Literaturwissenschaft und Geistesgeschichte* 63 (1989): 282–94.

28. D. M. Thomas, *The White Hotel* (New York: Penguin Books, 1981). On the "borrowing," see Lady Falls Brown, "The White Hotel: D. M. Thomas's considerable debt to Anatoli Kuznetsov and Babi Yar," *South Central Review* 22 (Summer 1985): 60–79. See also Yevgeny Yevtushenko, "Babi Yar," *The Holocaust Years: Society on Trial*, ed. Roselle Chartock and Jack Spencer (New York: Bantam Books, 1978), pp. 36–45 and James E. Young, *Writing and Rewriting the Holocaust: Narrative and the Consequences of Interpretation* (Bloomington, Ind.: Indiana University Press, 1988).

29. George Levine, "No Reservations: The White Hotel," *New York Review of Books* (28 May 1981): 20–23 and Mary F. Robertson, "Hystery, Herstory, History: 'Imagining the Real' in Thomas's *The White Hotel,*" *Contemporary Literature* 25.4 (Winter 1984): 452–77. See also Ellen Y. Siegelman, "The White Hotel: Visions and Revisions of the Psyche," *Literature and Psychology* 33.1 (1987): 69–76.

30. D. M. Thomas, "On Literary Celebrity," *The New York Times Magazine* (13 June 1982).

31. Rafael Seligmann, *Rubinsteins Versteigerung* (Frankfurt a. M.: Eichborn, 1989).

[15]

The Arab World Discovers Anti-Semitism

Bernard Lewis

Since 1945, certain Arab countries have been the only places in the world where hard-core, Nazi-style anti-Semitism is publicly and officially endorsed and propagated.

In the Western world, since the defeat of the Nazi Reich, anti-Semitism, though by no means dead, is clandestine or hypocritical, and cannot be openly avowed by anyone with serious political ambitions or cultural pretensions. In the Soviet bloc, though extensive use is made of anti-Semitic themes and symbols in both domestic and foreign propaganda, anti-Semitism as such is denounced and condemned, and the war against the Jews is waged under other flags, such as secularist anti-Judaism and socialist anti-Zionism. While the influence of such anti-Semitic classics as Canon Rohling's *Talmud Jew* and the *Protocols of the Elders of Zion* can sometimes be seen very clearly in polemical literature ostensibly directed against Jewish clericalism and Zionism, these works are not cited by name, and copies are apparently not available. In the Western world, where there is no comparable control of publications, these books are still being reprinted, but they are nowadays confined to the lunatic fringe, and their direct influence is minimal.

In the Arab world, by contrast, these two books are the most frequently cited authorities on Jewish matters—not only on Israel and Zionism, but on Jews and Judaism in general; not only in the context of the present time or

Reprinted by permission from *Commentary* (May 1986).

since the beginning of Zionist settlement, but throughout the three thousand years of recorded Jewish history. Nor are these publications confined, as in the West, to the lunatic fringe. They are published by major, sometimes government, publishing houses; they are endorsed and sometimes introduced by prominent political, religious, and intellectual figures; they are quoted on national television and radio programs and in some of the most respected newspapers and magazines; they form the basis of discussions of Jews and Judaism in many school, college, and teacher-seminary textbooks.

In 1970, in a book published by the PLO Research Center in Beirut, the writer, As'ad Razzuq, protested against the use of such tainted materials, which "are regarded with contempt by the civilized world," and which dishonor and discredit the Arab cause. At that time he listed twenty-six books based directly or indirectly on Rohling. His protest had no effect, and since then there have been many more such books. There are at least nine different Arabic translations of the *Protocols*, and innumerable editions, more than in any other language including German. One version, published in 1961, was introduced by the famous and respected author 'Abbas Mahmud al-'Aqqad; another, published in about 1968, was translated by the brother of President Nasser. Until a few years ago, the reader with access only to Arabic would not have known that the authenticity of the *Protocols* had ever been called into question, the sole discordant voice coming from some Marxist critics who reject personal explanations of history, such as those relied upon in the *Protocols*, but without indicating that they are a fabrication.

More recently, a few Arab writers have shown at least some awareness of this, but they still display a curious reluctance to abandon the *Protocols* entirely. One described them as "of questionable authenticity." An article in the Cairo newspaper *al-Ahram* (February 22, 1974) observes judiciously that "the prevailing opinion at the present time is that the *Protocols* are a forged document." This cautious formulation no doubt represents some progress, but leaves a number of questions unanswered, such as who forged them and what they represent. Here the article is remarkably equivocal, and the unwary reader might be left with the impression that of the *Protocols* were not actually fabricated by Jews, they nevertheless accurately reflect the image which the Zionists hold of themselves and which they desire to project to others. For the most part, however, their authenticity has been taken as axiomatic, and Arab writers on Jewish matters have sometimes assigned the *Protocols* the third place among the pillars of Judaism, after the Bible and the Talmud.

The *Protocols* have at different times been publicly recommended or cited by Presidents Nasser and Sadat of Egypt, President 'Arif of Iraq, King Faysal of Saudi Arabia, Colonel Qaddafi of Libya, and numerous other kings, presidents, prime ministers, and political and intellectual leaders. In addition to local use and distribution, agencies in several Arab countries, and latterly also in revolutionary Iran, have undertaken the distribution of the *Protocols* and related literature all over the world, and notably in countries in Africa and in South and Southeast Asia not previously affected.

Clearly, the argument sometimes put forward that the Arabs cannot be anti-Semitic since they themselves are Semites lacks all merit, and indeed the mere use of this argument is in general an indication of either ignorance or bad faith. Semite, like Aryan, is a classification of language, not of race or nationality. The misuse of both these terms originated in the same quarters, and serves the same purpose. In any case, anti-Semitism has never been directed against any but Jews, and this has been well understood by all concerned. The Nazis, who may be recognized as the most authoritative exponents of anti-Semitism, saw no difficulty in simultaneously hating Jews and courting Arabs, and there were not a few Arabs who likewise found no difficulty in responding to that courtship. No people on earth is immune to the universal human disease of ethnic or racial hostility, and the Arabs are no exception.

The question should be put in a different form. Obviously, Arabs are as liable as Germans, Russians, Jews, or anyone else to develop hostilities against other peoples, and their history and literature bear ample testimony to this. But are Muslims subject to what has hitherto been regarded as a specifically and indeed exclusively Christian disease—a certain attitude to Jews arising from the gospel narratives of the foundation of the Christian faith, and inculcated in countless generations of children through education, worship, literature, art, and even music? According to the Qur'an, Jesus was a prophet and not the son of God, and the crucifixion never took place. The prophet Jesus was taken away by God to safety, and a simulacrum or illusion crucified in his place. There is therefore in Muslim theology and literature no accusation of deicide, and consequently no doctrine of collective and hereditary guilt for that crime; nor is there any such intimate relationship with the earlier religion as to make continued Jewish existence a challenge to Muslim verities.

In considering these questions, it may be useful to distinguish three types of hostility which, though they may sometimes overlap and interact, are nevertheless different.

The first of these may be defined as opposition to Israel, and also to the

Zionist movement from which Israel developed. Zionism is an ideology, which men of good faith and good will may accept or reject, without being necessarily inspired by prejudice. Israel is a state, engaged in a political conflict, over real not imaginary issues, with other states and peoples. Such a conflict may generate prejudice; it may be affected by prejudice; but the hostility to which it gives rise is not necessarily, in itself, an indication of prejudice. This point is particularly important in a region where violent language is normal and accepted in the expression of political conflicts or even disagreements.

A second type of hostility, more difficult to define, is what one might call common, conventional, in a sense even "normal" prejudice, sometimes giving rise to "normal" or "conventional" persecution. Hostility to neighbors of another family, another tribe, race, faith, or origin is part of the universal condition of mankind. Relations are always troublesome between majorities and minorities, between neighboring states and peoples, between rulers and ruled. There is no lack of examples in other parts of the world of minority groups, sometimes from a different religion, race, or culture, who play some specific economic role, and are hated and persecuted as a result. The fate of Indians in East Africa and Chinese in Southeast Asia are examples. Hostility to Jews may sometimes be caused, or at least aggravated, by similar causes.

The third type is anti-Semitism—a hatred which is unique in its persistence, its universality, its profundity, and above all its theological and psychological origins. Unlike other forms of ethnic and racial prejudice, anti-Semitism goes beyond mere denigration or even persecution, and attributes to its adversary a quality of cosmic and eternal evil. Conventional prejudice and persecution can be very terrible, but they differ from anti-Semitism as does conventional from nuclear war.

In what follows, the term anti-Semitism will be limited to the third category defined above—that special and peculiar hatred of Jews, which has its origins in the role assigned to Jews in certain Christian writings and beliefs concerning the genesis of their faith, and which has found modern expression in such works as the *Protocols* and similar portrayals of a universal Jewish plot against both God and mankind.

In this specialized sense, anti-Semitism did not exist in the traditional Islamic world. True, Muslim religious and other literature provides ample evidence of prejudice against Jews, and Muslim history records not a few cases of persecution. But—and this is surely the crucial point—these attitudes and these persecutions were not accompanied by the demonological beliefs and conspiratorial fantasies that are characteristic of Christian anti-Semitism in both medieval and modern Europe, and do not differ significantly from the hostility and persecution to which other religious minorities, besides the Jews, have been from time to time subject.

While in Christendom the Jews were the only non-Christian minority, in the Islamic world they were one among several, and in most places not the most important. It is true that the Qur'an and other early Muslim writings express a preference for Christians over Jews. For while the Prophet had few encounters with Christians, he came into conflict with the Jewish tribes of Medina, and this conflict, with the bitterness which it engendered, is reflected in the Qur'an and in the biographical traditions. But the conflict ended in their destruction, not his; and this made it possible for Muslims to adopt a more relaxed and less embittered attitude toward their Jewish subjects.

If the Qua'an and early traditions show far greater hostility to Jews than to Christians, the Muslim law makes no such distinction, but treats both subject religions on a footing of equality with each other. In practice, in medieval and in Ottoman times, Jews often fared rather better than Christians, for the obvious reason that unlike their Christian compatriots, they were not suspected of treasonable sympathies with the Christian enemies of the Islamic empires.

The Islamic society and polity have now existed for more than fourteen centuries, in vast areas of Asia, Africa, and, for long periods, southwestern and then southeastern Europe. Clearly, the treatment of Jews, and the attitude toward them of governments and majorities, varied greatly from time to time and from place to place, in accordance with both internal and external circumstances. While, therefore, it is difficult to generalize, this much may be said with reasonable certainty—that they were never free from discrimination, but only occasionally subject to persecution; that their situation was never as bad as in Christendom at its worst, nor ever as good as in Christendom at its best. There is nothing in Islamic history to parallel the Spanish expulsion and Inquisition or the Russian pogroms, let alone the Nazi Holocaust; there is also nothing to compare with the progressive emancipation and acceptance accorded to Jews in the democratic countries of the Christian and post-Christian West during the last three centuries. While prejudice was always present in Islamic lands, it was often muted, rarely violent, and mostly inspired by disdain and contempt rather than by the explosive mixture of hate, fear, and envy that fueled the anti-Semitism of Christiandom.

The nineteenth and twentieth centuries, however, brought major changes, mostly to the detriment of Jews and also of other non-Muslim minorities and sometimes even of Muslim ethnic minorities. Three factors in particular contributed to the beginning and development of European-style anti-Semitism in the Islamic world. The first of these was the rise to world domination of the European empires, and the consequent enhancement of the influence of the local Christian subject populations within the Islamic states. Much attention has been given by scholars to the transfer and acceptance in the Islamic world of such European notions as liberalism, constitutionalism, and later socialism. But there were other ideas that traveled by the same route, among them anti-Semitism.

Thus it was from their Christian subjects that the Ottomans first heard about the blood libel, previously unknown to Muslim literature and history. European consular and clerical missions, and their local protégés and disciples, played some part in the introduction and propation of these ideas. The years of the Dreyfus crisis, for example, saw the appearance of the first specifically anti-Semitic books published in Arabic: these were translations of anti-Semitic writings produced in France.

The impact of these books was very limited, however. The translations were made by Christian Arabs, and were printed in very small editions. They had only a small effect within the Christian communities, and virtually none outside. And even within the eastern Christian communities, they were resisted by leading Christian Arab writers, who condemned the introduction of this kind of hate literature.

The promotion of anti-Jewish ideologies among the Arabs by Europeans did not end with the Dreyfus affair, though apart from the activities of a few cranky individuals Western countries were no longer involved, at least not until the advent of the Nazis. In the period immediately following World War I, the campaign of anti-Semitism launched by the White Russians produced some repercussions in the Middle East, if of limited extent. But then came Nazi Germany, which from 1933 to 1945 devoted considerable efforts to wooing Arab opinion. These efforts were very successful at the political and strategic levels—in mobilizing Arab support against the common enemies, the Western democracies and the Jews, and in propagating Nazi philosophy about the nation, the party, and the state. They were less successful in promoting Nazi anti-Semitism among the Arabs, who with a few exceptions continued to express their hostility to Jews in traditional

religious and modern political, rather than anti-Semitic, ways. Nazi influence in the Arab world did not end with the collapse of the Third Reich,
but was continued by Nazi émigrés, many of whom found a refuge and new
tasks in Nasser's Egypt and elsewhere.

With the rapid rise of Soviet influence in the Arab countries from the
mid-fifties, this phase came to an end, and anti-Jewish polemics in the
Arabic media acquired a new ideological underpinning and a new vocabulary. One of the stock accusations against the Jew in the Nazi era was that
he was a Bolshevik and a revolutionary, and responsible for the destruction
of Russia by the Soviets. This was of course an unsuitable idea for Soviet
Russia to spread among its new allies and protégés. These charges were
therefore dropped, except in a few places like Saudi Arabia, where they
survive to the present day. Elsewhere, such words as socialist, revolution,
and even Bolshevik became terms of praise instead of blame, and therefore
not appropriate for denouncing Jews. In a grotesque twist, this accusation
was replaced by a new one—that Jews were racist, and Zionism a form of
Nazism.

These charges, previously unknown among the Arabs, spread very rapidly, and their appearance was recognized as a sign of Soviet influence. The
campaign at the United Nations to denounce Zionism as racism, culminating
in the famous resolution of 1975, was clearly a Soviet far more than an Arab
enterprise, and was needed for Soviet domestic as well as international
purposes.[1] Since then, readers and viewers all over the world have been
treated to the strange spectacle of some of Hitler's former allies denouncing
Hitler's foremost victims as racists and Nazis.

The second factor which worsened the position of virtually all religious
and ethnic minorities under Islam was the breakdown and ultimate collapse
of the old political structures and of the loyalties and traditions associated
with them. Tolerance comes more easily from a position of strength. It is far
more difficult when one is defeated, conquered, and subjugated, and when
one's own tolerated subjects seem to be in alliance with the conquering
enemy. The old dynastic and communal system had worked fairly well. The
new patriotic and nationalist loyalties and structures which replaced it,
despite their proclaimed adoption first of libertarian and later of egalitarian
doctrines, were far less able to tolerate any kind of diversity, and far harsher
therefore in their treatment of religious, ethnic, and ideological minorities.
For a while, the resulting hostility was directed more against Christians than

against Jews. But the Jews were fewer, weaker, and far less able to call on the protection of the great powers. They therefore presented a more tempting target.

It is possible that these two developments would in themselves have sufficed to make the position of the ancient Jewish communities in the Arab lands untenable. They were finally and unequivocally doomed by the third factor, the struggle resulting from the growth of the Jewish resettlement in Palestine, the establishment of the State of Israel, and the series of Arab-Israeli wars that followed.

In the early years of the present century there was a movement of liberal patriotism among the urban elite of the Ottoman Empire, in which Muslims, Christians of various denominations and nationalities, and Jews cooperated in a joint struggle to realize shared political objectives. This continued briefly even after the defeat and destruction of the Ottoman Empire, and in the early post-World War I years a few Jews played some role in Arab political activities. This was not, however, of long duration. The new nationalism, which doomed some minorities and endangered all of them, soon affected the Jews as well. The struggle in Palestine removed whatever slender chances there might have been for a recovery. Almost from the beginning of the Palestine Mandate, anti-Jewish feeling grew stronger and stronger, not only in Palestine but, one after another, in most other Arab countries.

From the first, anti-Semitism played some part in this. Thus, for example, a memorandum presented by a group of Arab notables to the British Colonial Secretary in 1921 quotes extensively from the *Protocols of the Elders of Zion*. But this kind of anti-Semitic literature remained a minor element in the Arab propaganda against the Jews, most of which rested on the revival and development of the themes and symbols of traditional Islamic anti-Judaism, and continued to do so, with few exceptions, right through the 1920s and indeed until the 1950s. True, there was some slight increase in the anti-Semitic literature available in Arabic. The *Protocols* were translated several times, as were some other anti-Semitic classics, and some of the books translated at the time of the Dreyfus affair were reprinted in new and larger editions. But this literature was marginal to the main Arab struggle.

It is noteworthy that through the most difficult times in Mandatory Palestine, and even during the period of German connections and powerful Nazi influence, the specifically anti-Semitic element remained minor. While, as we have seen, Nazi political philosophy exercised some influence, and the Nazi war against the Jews won enthusiastic support, there were few, apart from such as the Mufti of Jerusalem and his circle, who espoused the Nazi doctrine of anti-Semitism, and relatively few anti-Semitic works were available in Arabic. Hatred was deep and violent, and expressed in the strongest language, but it was still in the main traditional rather than anti-Semitic in its themes. Even the wars of 1948–49, the establishment of Israel, and the departure of the Palestinian refugees, while they engendered powerful and intense feelings, do not seem to have contributed significantly to the output of published anti-Semitism.

The real change began after the Sinai War of 1956 and was accelerated after the Six-Day War of 1967. During these years, first a trickle and then a torrent of anti-Semitic books, articles, films, radio and television programs, newspaper and magazine pieces, saturated the media in the Arab countries of the Middle East and, to a much lesser extent, affected North Africa. The favorite works were Rohling's *Talmud Jew* and the *Protocols of the Elders of Zion*, which appeared in literally dozens of translations and adaptations, and rapidly came to dominate virtually all discussion of the Jews and Judaism, in the media and in academic circles. In addition to these two, numerous other anti-Semitic classics from continental Europe were translated and adapted, as well as some of the more recent writings of French, British, and North American fascists. Along with the themes and imagery, the Arabic media also adopted the iconography of European anti-Semitism (though it is interesting that in this respect cartoonists seem to follow East European rather than Central or West European models).

So far there has been very little attempt to resist this universal spread and adoption of anti-Semitism, and very little attempt even to provide an alternative source of information for the young Arab reader who may wish to learn something about this peculiar people, the Jews. No doubt, the Arab intelligentsia has its own equivalents of Émile Zola, who would wish to protest against this pollution of the intellectual waters, and, as already noted, there were indeed such in earlier and freer times. But the present political and intellectual atmosphere in the Arab and Islamic world, including the émigré communities, is not conducive to dissent.

Aside from themes borrowed and adapted from Christendom, there are now anti-Semitic innovations that are explicitly Islamic, or at least presented in Islamic terms. The most important of these is the restatement of the story of Muhammad's relations with the Jews. Instead of being a minor nuisance, ineffectual and unsuccessful in their plots against him, Jews are now presented in a role which obviously reflects the narrative of the Christian gospels. They are depicted as a dark and evil force, conspiring to destroy the Prophet, and continuing as the main danger to Islam from that time to this. Given the importance of the biography of the Prophet in Muslim education, the adoption of this theme is by far the most potent instrument for the dissemination of anti-Semitism among the mass of the Muslim population.

An obvious question arises: how is it that while the Arabs did not to any extent adopt European-style anti-Semitism during the struggle in Palestine, the 1936 rebellion led by the Mufti, the alliance with the Nazis, the rise of Israel, and the departure of the Palestinians, they suddenly began to do so in the late fifties, sixties, and seventies? An answer may be found in the wars of 1956 and 1967.

The war of 1948–49 was a hard-fought struggle, which lasted many weeks, and in which Israel won the prize of survival at a high cost. By contrast, the Israeli victories of 1956 and 1967 were swift and overwhelming, and for the vanquished presented a terrible problem of explanation. This problem was made more difficult by the general description, in the Arabic media, of Israelis and Jews in general as cowardly and lacking in all the martial virtues. An article in the Egyptian armed forces weekly of November 16, 1964, remarks: "The Jew in his very soul and character has not the qualities of a man who bears arms. He is not naturally prepared to sacrifice for anything, not even for his son or his wife . . ." An Egyptian literary critic, commenting on the cliché-ridden portrayal of Israelis in fiction and drama, asked: "Before this kind of presentation, I put the question: if the Israelis were really like that, how could they have inflicted a defeat upon us?"

How, indeed? If the Israelis are as corrupt and cowardly as their image in Arabic literature, then their humiliating victories become even more inexplicable, or at least require explanations beyond the normal processes of rational thought. To a rapidly increasing extent, the literature of anti-Semitism has provided such an explanation.

Notes

1. See my article, "The Anti-Zionist Resolution," *Foreign Affairs*, October 1976.

[16]

The Jews of Iran: Between the Shah and Khomeini

David Menashri

In the eleven years since the 1979 revolution, the followers of Ayatollah Ruhollah Khomeini have become the sole rulers of the Islamic Republic of Iran.* This needs saying because the revolutionary movement had begun as a coalition of widely different, even divergent, ideologies, but fairly soon it was monopolized by Khomeini's radical disciples, eventually excluding all other groupings from any share in actual power.

For the new rulers, "Islamic Revolution" was not a mere name but a living reality: *Revolution* signifying profound, comprehensive and rapid change in all spheres of life; *Islamic* signifying its orientation and content.[1] For his disciples, Khomeini's radical doctrine is the sole legitimate interpretation of Islam. As such it is the only appropriate basis for policy-making in foreign and domestic affairs. Inasmuch as Islam covers each and every sphere of the

* This article is based in part on numerous interviews with Jews who have fled from Iran since the Islamic Revolution. Many interviews were recorded on tapes now kept at the Moshe Dayan Center for Middle Eastern and African Studies at Tel Aviv University. I wish to express my gratitude to all my interviewees, even though I am barred from identifying them.

For a comparison of the Islamic regime's treatment of ethnic and religious minorities, see my article: "Khomeini's Policy towards Ethnic and Religious Minorities," in Milton Esman and Itamar Rabinovich (eds.), *Ethnicity, Pluralism and Conflict in the Middle East* (Ithaca: Cornell University Press, 1988), pp. 215–29, copyright © 1988 by Cornell University. I wish to express .my gratitude to Cornell University Press for their permission to include portions of the above-mentioned article in this chapter.

believer's life, "Islamization" was to make every single aspect of life conform to the structure of the ideal society envisaged by Islam. Evidently, this subsumes their attitudes towards minority religions.

Yet the leaders of the "new" Iran have often upheld pragmatic considerations of national interest inherited from the past—sometimes relegating their ideological tenets to second place.[2] This was often so in their policy toward ethnic and religious minorities. Nonetheless, remaking Iran in a mold totally conforming with Khomeini's perception of a true Islamic society remained their main objective. Since the Shah's regime and all its works were "un-Islamic," this meant that past practices needed to be reversed. Since the religious minorities had enjoyed almost total freedom until 1979, political change, let alone the advent of a radical Islamic regime, could only be a change for the worst. Having repaid their benefits by identifying with the Shah's regime now made the danger all the more grave.

1. The Historical Setting

A. The Qajar Legacy. The history of the Jews of Iran, like that of other religious minorities, has been one of suppression, persecution and harassment. This goes back to Zoroastrian times and continues intermittently till the end of the Qajar dynasty (1796–1925). Qajar rule was one long series of persecutions in almost any place where Jews were then residing. Their life was unbearable even when compared with that of the Jews in the Ottoman Empire, who themselves were experiencing hard times at the same period. "Compared to the Jews of Iran," Bernard Lewis writes, "the Jews of the Ottoman Empire were living in paradise."[3]

Travelers supply gloomy descriptions of Jewish life. Their verdict is summed up by the Hungarian-Jewish orientalist Arminius Vambery, who traveled extensively in Iran and Central Asia in the mid-nineteenth century: "I do not know any more miserable, helpless, and pitiful individual on God's earth than the *Jahudi* in those countries. . . . The poor Jew is despised, belabored and tortured . . . he is the poorest of the poor."[4] Speaking of "instances of outrageous oppression which the poor descendants of Israel suffer here [in northern Iran] from their Muhammedan masters," the American Reverend Justin Perkins quotes a Jewish physician who told him in 1836 that "if the Messiah does not appear soon, . . . [the Jews] would be exterminated."[5]

George Curzon gives fuller details of their misfortune in different cities, and then—referring to Iranian Jewry as a whole—goes on to write:

As a community, the Persian Jews are sunk in a great poverty and ignorance. . . . Throughout the Mussulman countries of the East these unhappy people have been subjected to the persecution which custom has taught themselves, as well as the world, to regard as their normal lot. Usually compelled to live apart in a Ghetto, or separate quarter of the towns, they have from time immemorial suffered from disabilities of occupation, dress, and habits, which have marked them out as social pariahs from their fellow creatures. . . . They rarely attain to a leading mercantile position. In Isfahan, where there are said to be 3,700, and where they occupy a relatively better status than elsewhere in Persia, they are not permitted to wear the *kolah* or Persian head dress, to have shops in the bazaar, to build the walls of their houses as high as a Moslem neighbor's, or ride in the streets. . . . As soon, however, as any outburst of bigotry takes place in Persia or elsewhere, the Jews are apt to be the first victims. Every man's hand is against them; and woe betide the luckless Hebrew who is the first to encounter a Persian street mob.[6]

Blood libels and persecutions abound throughout this period. Among the better known were the persecution of the Jews of Tabriz late in the eighteenth century, and the pogrom in Hamadan in 1860. Cases of forced conversion to Islam are very rare in Islamic history, yet "apart from one or two in Morocco and in the Yemen, most of them occurred in Iran."[7] The most notorious was the conversion of the Jews of Meshed in 1839.

Why did the Jews of Iran suffer more than their co-religionists elsewhere in the Muslim world? Part of the reason lay in the fact that they resided in a remote state isolated from the West, among a hostile and fanatic population, with only few travelers witnessing their misfortunes and reporting them to Europe. It was only in the last quarter of the nineteenth century that Jewish organizations in Europe took more of an interest in Iranian Jewry. During the various visits of Naser al-Din Shah to Europe (mainly those of 1873 and 1889), and as a result of pleas by Sir Moses Montefiore and Adolphe Cremieux, there was some improvement. The foundation of the Alliance schools (the first was established in Tehran in 1898) was one result of their involvement.[8]

To all these one must add the hostile and fanatic attitudes of the population and the xenophobic elements in Shi'i Islam. According to Islam, defilement results in ritual impurity. This can come about through sexual intercourse or menstruation; through contact with body wastes or discharges; or with "unclean" things such as wine or carrion. But to fundamentalist

Shi'is, contact with unbelievers also makes "unclean." Therefore, touching their clothes or having food touched by them causes ritual impurity too.[9] Such obsessive concern with pollution, perhaps influenced by Zoroastrian theology, was found only in Iranian Shi'ism. In the late nineteenth century it led to Jews being forbidden to go out on rainy days from fear that the rain or snow would contaminate the Muslims with the impurity of the Jews. Jews could not, of course, use the public *hamam* [bath] or eat in the local *chaykhaneh* [cafe].[10] Referring to such practices, J. J. Benjamin, who traveled in Iran in the mid-nineteenth century, wrote:

1. Throughout Persia the Jews are obliged to live in a part of the town separated from the other inhabitants; for they are considered as unclean creatures, who bring contamination with their intercourse and presence.

2. They have no right to carry on trade in stuff goods. . . .

3. Under the pretext of their being unclean, they are treated with the greatest severity, and should they enter a street, inhabited by Mussulmans, they are pelted by the boys and mobs with stones and dirt.

4. For the same reason they are forbidden to go out when it rains; for it is said the rain should wash dirt off them, which would sully the feet of the Mussulmans. . . .

5. If a Jew enters a shop to buy anything, he is forbidden to inspect the goods, but must stand at a respectful distance and ask the price. Should his hand incautiously touch the goods, he must take them at any price the seller chooses to ask for them.[11]

As noted above, some improvement was noticed in the late nineteenth century due to growing ties with the West and the intercession of European Jewry. The liberal movement of the turn of the century and the Constitutional Revolution helped further to better the status of Jews. But substantial improvement came only with the rise of the Pahlavi dynasty (1925–1979).

B. The Pahlavis. Improvement began under Reza Shah (1925–1941) and continued under his son, Muhammad Reza Shah (1941–1979). It reached its peak in the era of the "White Revolution" (beginning 1963), the "Golden Age" of Iranian Jewry, when Jews enjoyed almost total cultural and religious autonomy, experienced economic progress, and had no less political freedom than their Muslim compatriots.

The following reasons combined to produce this change:

1. The ideology of the Pahlavi Shahs, basing itself on Westernization, secularization and the concept of the nation-state, allowed more room

for Jewish participation. Also it was much easier for the Jews to identify with the secular notion of a nation-state than with a state concept with Islam at its core. Moreover, the process of modernization allowed them to turn their talents to the benefit of society at large—much more so than in the past.

2. The formation of a strong and centralized government made it possible to impose government control on the periphery and to prevent local initiatives against the Jews (as was often the case under the Qajars).

3. The strengthening ties with the West not only gave the Shah an incentive to honor minority rights but also made possible closer ties between Jewish organizations (such as the Joint and Otzar Ha-Torah) and Iranian Jewry, resulting in economic and cultural support for the Jews.

4. The establishment of the state of Israel and its victories over the Arabs imparted a sense of pride and security to Iranian Jews. Furthermore, the emigration to Israel of many of the poorer Jews improved the economic status of the remaining ones and changed their image.

5. Iranian-Israeli cooperation at the inter-state level made a twofold contribution: it caused the Shah to allow the Jews more freedom and caused the Jews to feel more secure. The Shah did not conceal his dislike for his Arab neighbors or his distaste for the PLO. A strong Israel in conflict with the Arabs, was, he felt, an asset to his country. Therefore, while in the Arab countries the conflict with Israel nursed hatred of the Jews, it failed to have a similar effect in Iran.

6. The Shah trusted the Iranian Jews to be loyal to his policy and his dynasty. And, in fact, the Jews were loyal and admired him. Prayers were said for him in the synagogues and any mention of his name drew applause. His desire for history to remember him as the successor of Cyrus the Great reinforced his tolerant approach.

7. Finally, one cannot escape the impression that his support for the Jews stemmed in part from certain concepts of European anti-Semitism. He overestimated the power of world Jewry and believed in the existence of a "Jewish conspiracy" and in Jewish controls of the world media. He held that American Jewry was capable of imposing its will on the President. In 1971, for example, when the Western media criticized the extravagance of the celebrations marking the 2,500th anniversary of the Persian monarchy, he blamed Israel for "allowing" them to take such an attitude.

For two years, just before the fall of the Shah, I lived in Tehran conduct-ing research on Iranian education. I met there a Jewish community which was free, proud and rich. Towards the end of the Shah's rule there were some 80,000 Jews in Iran (about 60,000 of them in Tehran). They consti-tuted no more than 0.25 percent of the total population, but their share in economic, cultural and professional life was much larger. Some 10 percent of the community were believed to be "very rich," and a similar number were in "economic distress." The remaining 80 percent were "well off" and constantly bettering themselves. [12] On per capita terms they may well have been the richest Jewish community in the world. Out of approximately 150,000 students in institutes of higher learning 4,000 were Jews, many of them in the most prestigious institutes and faculties. Their share among Iranian students abroad was even higher. There were 80 Jewish professors at the universities (out of some 4,000) and 600 physicians (from among some 10,000). The literacy rate among Jews was far higher than among Muslims.

The Jews were allowed to have schools of their own and run social and cultural organizations. There were some thirty synagogues in Tehran alone, and Hebrew courses, lectures and other cultural activities took place at many of them. Often, Israelis were invited to lecture at the synagogues, and contributions for Israel were solicited publicly. The Jewish Students' Associ-ation was the only legal student organization. That of Tehran numbered over 1,000 members. There were organizations of Jewish academics, wom-en's organizations, etc.—all highly active. They organized conventions, lectures and tours to Israel, as well as groups for discussing local and Jewish problems. On the same day that Iran voted at the UN to condemn Zionism, I gave a lecture on Zionism to the Association of Jewish Academics of Tehran, which met at a fashionable hotel (i.e., at a location easily accessible to SAVAK agents). When campus disturbances led to student arrests, Jewish students were immediately released; the authorities relied on them to be loyal. [13]

Nevertheless, the new realities also posed grave challenges to the Jewish community. The exit from the *mahaleh* (the Ghetto) made it more difficult for Jewish schools and synagogues to function. This, as well as the more liberal attitudes on the part of the government and some segments of the population and the overall secularization process, made the Jewish commu-nity rather less Jewish than it had been before. The Jewish Agency and the Iranian Jewish Committee (*Anjomane Kalimiyan*) were free to act; if they were not active and not successful enough, they themselves rather than the government were to blame.

With the general trend towards Westernization, the doctrine of the unbelievers' impurity was almost totally forgotten. Those interviewed by the author were not disturbed by it, although they remembered "such stories" from their parents. Some spoke of recent examples, but emphasized that they were exceptional and rare. Those orthodox Muslims who still observed such restrictions often used Jewish terms to explain them: it was their way, they said, to keep *kosher*. A woman who looked after our daughter in Tehran never took food at our place. She brought her own cup to drink water. When she was cooking for us, she used to invite our Jewish neighbor to taste the food and check whether it was properly spiced. She too explained this in terms of both sides keeping *kosher*. A rabbi told me that while Muslim clerics used to eat at his house, they knew he would not eat at theirs. The whole issue no longer disturbed either side too much. But it came to the fore again under Khomeini (see below).

Despite all these changes Iranian Jewry remained aware of its minority status, wary and often enough even frightened of their Muslim neighbors. On many occasions (mainly in small towns, or in the bazaars), they were even threatened, and sometimes insulted and beaten up. There were numerous anti-Jewish articles and even more so anti-Jewish remarks and expressions (n speeches, media reports, cartoons, etc.). But, all in all, considering past practices and the religious nature of Iranian society, they gained security and made progress more than at any earlier time. All those interviewed claimed that there was neither discrimination nor hatred; if anything at all, there was envy. Some Jews transformed Pahlavi into the nickname *Papa-Levi*; alluding to his patronage of the Jews, some radical Muslims said the Shah was a Jew himself.

C. **The Year of Upheaval: Seeds of Calamity.** The revolutionary upheaval (September 1977–February 1979), culminating in the change of regime, caused much concern to the Jews. All their previous assets now turned into liabilities. Their social and economic standing; their identification with the Shah and his policies; and their relations with Israel, Zionism and "American Imperialism" were all being held against them. The weakening of authority at the center, the growing resentment against the rich, the religious ideology of the opposition and the leadership of Khomeini all presaged disaster.

Moreover, precisely at this critical juncture Iranian Jewry was in the midst of an internal power struggle. A sort of "Jewish Revolution" within the *Anjomane Kalimiyan*, the Jewish religious leadership, was under way just before the Islamic Revolution began to loom in the distance. A group of young radical Jewish intellectuals with anti-monarchical, anti-Zionist and leftist tendencies was challenging the traditional leadership, mostly drawn from the rich. In March 1978, after an aggressive election campaign, they were able to topple the old leaders. Since the new *Anjoman* proved unable to function, new elections were called for June. In the campaign, the radicals appeared at the head of a new, anti-Zionist organization called *Jame'eye Roushanfekrane Yahudiye Iran* (the Association of Iranian Jewish Intellectuals), led by 'Aziz Daneshrad and Parviz Isha'yah. Both were members of the *Tudeh* Party and had been jailed under the Shah. Their group lost the election, but the *Anjoman*—not very active at the best of times—was now almost totally paralyzed.[14]

With the outbreak of open opposition to the Shah, many Jews were threatened by their Muslim neighbors. This was not necessarily the result of a deliberate policy on the part of the revolutionary movement, but rather of independent and spontaneous initiatives by individuals. But their action brought home to Iranian Jewry the dangers inherent in times of crisis. The ideology of Khomeini, coupled with many threats and several actual attacks were sufficient to cause deep concern. Warnings sent to many Jews in Tehran in June 1978 added greatly to their anxiety. One of them, signed by a group calling itself "The National Front of Iran's Young Muslims" reads:

O bloodthirsty people, who suck the blood of each one of us Muslims. You have gathered in our Islamic state, taken away the money from us Muslims by means of interest, theft and fraud, and send it to the Zionist state of Israel.

You have seized houses, land, stores, and gardens belonging to us Muslims.

Now your golden dreams have come to an end.

You are hereby warned that you must leave the country as soon as possible, otherwise we shall massacre all the Jews from the youngest to the oldest.

Every age needs its Hitler to take care of the people of deceit and eradicate the offspring of the Jews from the earth, so that our brothers in religion in the Arab countries will live in peace.

Threats intensified after "Bloody Friday" (8 September 1978), when rumors circulated in Tehran that Israeli soldiers had taken part in crushing the demonstrations (see below). Anti-Jewish remarks made by Khomeini himself (then still in Paris) were even more threatening.

Iranian Jewry was compelled to reorganize to face the new realities. The rabbis declared a day of fasting (6 November) and of prayer for the well-being of the country and its Jews. But soon they sensed that more determined action was required. Already during the religious processions on 11 December 1978, i.e., while the Shah was still in power, organized Jewish groups joined the mourning Muslims who marched to demonstrate their opposition to the Shah. They, too, carried anti-Shah banners. On 13 February 1979 (a ·day after the Bakhtiyar government fell) they came out again to demonstrate for Khomeini. It was the Association of the Intellectuals which was instrumental in organizing the protest, as well as in arranging contacts with the leaders of the revolution. Others left the country altogether and/or transferred to the West as much of their wealth as they could. Those who remained kept a low profile and demonstratively shifted their loyalty to the Islamic Republic, trying to buy Khomeini's protection.

2. The Islamic Republic

The ideology of Khomeini is distinctly anti-Jewish. It combines general Islamic tenets, specifically Shi'i dogma and elements typical of modern European anti-Semitism. A study of his writings before his advent to power reveals an extreme anti-Jewish stand. On the very first page of his *Al-Hukuma al-Islamiyya* (The Islamic Government) he points out:

Since its inception, the Islamic movement has been afflicted with the Jews, for it was they who first established anti-Islamic propaganda and joined in various stratagems, and as you can see, this activity continues down to our present day.[15]

Referring to Muhammad's dealing with the Jews of Medina, Khomeini claims that the Prophet "eliminated" the Jews of the Bani Qurayza because they were a "troublesome group, causing corruption in Muslim society and damaging Islam and the Islamic state."[16] Elsewhere he adds:

We see today that the Jews (may God curse them) have meddled with the text of the Qur'an and have made certain changes in the Qur'an they have printed in the occupied territories [the West Bank and the Gaza Strip]. . . . We must protest and make the people aware that the Jews and their foreign backers are opposed to the very foundations of Islam and wish to establish Jewish domination throughout the world.[17]

An earlier book by Khomeini, *Touzih al-Masa'el* (Clarification of the Problems, a guide to Muslims in their daily life) already gives us an inkling of his attitude towards the Jews. There he emphasizes the Shi'i doctrine of the ritual impurity of unbelievers, listing "eleven things which made unclear." He groups together urine, faeces, sperm, dogs, pigs, carrion and unbelievers. In gloss on the latter, he adds: The entire body of the unbeliever is unclean; even his hair and fingernails and [bodily] secretion are impure." There is, however, as Lewis ironically suggests, "some relief": "When a non-Muslim man or woman is converted to Islam, their body, saliva, nasal secretions, and sweat are ritually clean. If, however, their clothes were in contact with their sweaty bodies before their conversion, these remain unclean."[18] The child of an unbeliever is equally "impure." Products which cannot be purified, such as meat and vegetables, must not be bought from infidels. Khomeini singles out the prohibition of working for Jews, and adds that although it is permissible to work under a Jewish foreman it is "a disgrace."[19] Many other invectives form part of his pre-revolution speeches, some directed at Jews and Judaism in general, some specifically at Iranian Jewry. In a speech in 1973, for example, he accused Iranian Jews of "actively supporting Israel," and called upon Iranians to prevent them from doing so "with all their means."[20]

Once the revolution had succeeded, however, there was a radical change in Khomeini's pronouncements regarding the Jews. Venomous attacks gave way to more balanced and tolerant statements. This was in keeping with the new regime's general policy towards religious minorities. (The exception were the Baha'is who were not recognized as a religious minority, but were considered apostates from Islam.)

Initially, the main concern of the new regime was to make sure of the loyalty of the minorities and make them conform to the norms of personal conduct which it thought appropriate to the Islamic Republic. On 29 September 1982, at a meeting between the heads of the Revolutionary Courts and the spiritual leaders of the minority groups, Judge Husayni asked them to respect these norms. Demanding that they refrain from alcohol in public, he made clear to them what the regime expected of them, saying: "At home the minorities can act according to their own customs, but . . . in public places they must conform to norms of the Islamic Republic."[21] This advice was carefully adhered to by the minorities. In the existing revolutionary atmosphere, they thought it wise not to give the authorities any pretext for harassing them.

Official tolerance did not preclude individual acts of persecution or even the execution of some prominent minority leaders—among them Habib Alqanayan, former head of the Jewish community. However, given the large number of executions of men of the old regime, minority groups were not singled out for death sentences beyond their share in the Shah's establishment. The regime stressed emphatically that no one was executed because of his religious belief: Alqanayan's execution did not mean that the regime was against the Jews, just as the execution of many Muslim supporters of the Shah did not mean that it was against Islam.[22] Meeting with the heads of the Jewish community following the execution, Khomeini told them that "Islam does not differentiate between . . . those who hold different faiths." He added: "We distinguish between Jews and Zionists. Zionism has nothing to do with religion."[23] Radio Tehran added that religious minorities in Iran enjoyed "the highest degree of security" and that there was "no room for worry for our religious compatriots" following Alqanayan's execution. His crime "had nothing to do with the fact that he was a Jew. . . . He was an individual who wished to equate Jewry with Zionism."[24] Yet at the same time, the media went on describing Alqanayan as "a Jewish milliardiare" and emphasized his being Jewish.[25]

In practice, however, the religious minorities—mainly Jews, Armenians and Zoroastrians (but not the Baha'is)—came to rely on a measure of tolerance and protection extended to them by Khomeini in keeping with the traditional attitude of Islam towards the *dhimmis* (the protected non-Muslim minorities). They received official recognition as "religious minorities" and were given representation in the *Majlis* (Parliament). There was no governmental campaign of incitement against them, nor was there any systematic harassment.

Jewish freedom of worship was not substantially restricted and Jewish religious holidays were given wide coverage on radio and television—much more so than under the Shah. Some two dozen synagogues were still active in Tehran alone (in 1987) and, given the overall religious atmosphere in the country and the community's need to unite and re-organize, more people visited the synagogues than in the days of the Shah. Although from time to time Muslim clerics came to preach sermons in synagogues, Jewish rituals are not disturbed; on the contrary: people are encouraged to pray. The Ministry of Education supports courses on Bible and Judaism at the synagogues, though it restricts the study of Hebrew. Jewish community leaders, particularly the rabbis, found some of the Ayatollahs (i.e., Muhammad Beheshti,

Musavi Ardebeli and 'Ali Qadusi) to be attentive to their demands and their religious requests were almost always met. A rabbi who had met them several times, spoke to me of Beheshti as one of the "just Gentiles." Ishak Faramandpour (a Jewish member of the first *Majlis*) confirmed this, based on his own experience in the House. He also mentioned 'Ali Akbar Hashemi Rafsanjani (then *Majlis* Speaker and now the President), Bahonar, Lahuti, Bazargan and Ibrahim Yazdi as other revolutionary leaders who had treated Jewish issues fairly.

Yet there were problems. The Jews were made aware of their inferior status as a tolerated minority and felt insecure. Threats against them continued and many Muslims took advantage of Jewish fears and stopped repaying or paying rent to Jews. There were some cases of persecution, mainly in outlying provinces. Also, *kosher* food became much more expensive and harder to find. In one field at least, Jews were clearly discriminated against: in the matter of obtaining exit permits (required after the outbreak of the war with Iraq). A special office dealt with Jewish applications, and turned down most of them. Many were too frightened even to apply. But the main problem was that of cultural autonomy, the rule requiring children to register at the school closest to their residence made it impossible to operate Jewish schools. Most of those interviewed expressed fear of impending "cultural annihilation." In public schools, Jewish children had to participate in morning prayers and be present at sermons and lectures on Islam. Their schools taught them to believe that Islam, as the "last religion," must be accepted by Jews and Christians alike. They were repeatedly told that religion did not necessarily come from parents to children. Moreover, most community leaders had fled the country, and with the departure in 1982 of Rabbi Yedidiya Shofet, they were left without a spiritual leader. The fact that some two-thirds of Iranian Jewry left Iran after 1978 is indicative of these problems and in itself created new ones. (In 1989 there were less than 30,000 Jews in Iran.)

The relatively good relations between the regime and the Jewish minority during the Islamic Republic's first decade existed in many respects on the surface only. At a deeper level, matters were much more complex. There is a palpable conflict between the basic Islamic approach of tolerance towards monotheistic faiths and the many passages of invective against Jews, Christians and Zoroastrians (let alone Baha'is) that appeared so often in the writings and sayings of Khomeini and his closest associates. It is this writer's view that these reveal the true attitude of the regime and are therefore indicative of possible future behavior. Therefore, if and when this happens, the Jewish minority is likely to be the most vulnerable.

Although Khomeini had repeatedly declared that "we distinguish between Judaism on the one hand, and Israel and Zionism on the other," manifestations of anti-Jewish sentiment continue to abound not only among the population at large, but in the pronouncements of senior government officials as well. As is the case in the Arab world, the distinction between Jews, Israel and Zionism is often blurred. There are many references to Israel as a "bunch of Jews" or to its government as "a government of unbelievers, of Jews." In the same vein, all of American Jewry are termed "Zionists." Most striking in this respect is the occasional reference to seventh-century Jews as "the Zionists of Muhammad's time."

There are countless examples of equating Jews and Zionists. Ayatollah Husayn 'Ali Montazeri (designated in 1985 to succeed Khomeini but dismissed in 1989) for example said in one of his Friday sermons in Qum in December 1979 that Judaism had been racist from its inception, and that today's Zionism is a continuation of the same ancient racism. He concluded that the Zionists today are equivalent to the Jews of the past and vice versa.[26] Khomeini himself made a revealing slip in a speech in September 1982. He began by saying that those who follow in the path of Jesus were even worse than the Jews, even though it was perhaps "impossible to say that there is something worse than the Jews." He then pulled himself up, adding quickly: "I mean the Jews of Israel."[27]

Over time, direct attacks on Judaism and Iranian Jewry have become commonplace. A few examples will suffice to illustrate the point:

1. The leading Tehran newspaper, *Kayhan* reported that an Israeli battalion bore the brunt of overpowering the anti-Shah mass demonstrations on the bloody "Black Friday" of 8 September 1978. It added that "many Iranian Jews" fought in the ranks of this battalion and that they were members of "the secret defense organization of Iranian Jewry."[28]

2. Hujjat al-Islam Muhammad 'Ali Allahi, writing in the magazine *Ettela'at* stated that Israel's hostility to Islam is nothing new: "according to the Qur'an testimony, ever since the birth of Islam . . . the corrupt [Jewish] culture . . . a culture of covetousness, a life of usury and interest, treachery, aggression, murder, and sowing divisiveness . . . developed a front against the culture of Islam." He quoted Qur'anic

verses to prove that the Jews are enemies of Islam. Among others he
quoted "the Sura of the Table" (verse 82): "Cursed were the unbelievers of the Children of Israel by the tongue of David, and Jesus, Mary's
son; that, for their rebelling and their transgression. They forbade not
one another any dishonor that they committed; surely evil were the
things they did."[29]

3. One of the operations of the Iran-Iraq war (in February 1984) was
   given the code name "Khaybar" after the Jewish oasis Muhammad
   besieged and conquered in 628. Every Muslim is aware of the significance of this name and its historical connection with the Jews. To
   leave no doubt, President 'Ali Khameneh'i explained in a Friday
   sermon that "Khaybar" was "in memory of the glorious victories of the
   warriors of Islam in the days of the Prophet in their struggle against
   the Jews of that time. . . . [Since] the front opposing us today [in the
   war with Iraq] is a Zionist front, this will serve as a reminder for us of
   the struggle of Islam against the Jews of Khaybar."[30]

4. Since 1979, perhaps a dozen Jews have been executed, among them
   prominent members of the community. Although the regime insisted
   that they were not sentenced because of their Judaism, the nature of
   the charges brought against them has been extremely disturbing. Ver-
   dicts made public in Iran (and one which was smuggled out of Iran
   and reached the writer) reveal that alongside other charges (mainly
   economic offenses), some of them were sentenced for their links with
   the Zionist movement and Israel. Accusations in such general terms
   could easily be leveled against many Jews in Iran.

5. The *Protocols of the Elders of Zion* and venomous anti-Semitic caricatures have often been published in Persian newspapers.[31]

What emerges, then, is a picture of ideologically and religiously motivated rejection of Jews and Judaism, combined with a measure of tolerance
—precarious, to be sure, but so far mostly predominant.

Practical moderation is reinforced by two further factors:

Firstly, the government is fully aware that the Jews do not pose any
political threat; on the contrary, they have proved loyal, like the other
religious minorities; they publicly supported Khomeini while he was still in
Paris; they have strictly complied with the regime's instructions and have
observed Muslim behavioral norms; they have "contributed" to the finances
of the regime, including the war effort; and they have, at regular intervals,

issued statements identifying themselves with the regime and denouncing its opponents. On more than one occasion, Jewish community leaders have harshly criticized Israel and Zionism,[32] endeavoring to lend substance to the argument that there is a difference between Jews and Zionists. They have also brought pressure to bear on Israel not to publicize the problems of Iranian Jewry.

Secondly, in keeping with the characteristic behavior of many revolutionary movements at the point of transition to power, Khomeini's line changed once he was confronted with the harsh realities of running a state.[33] Thus, in the view of this author, his pre-1979 ideology represented Khomeini's true feelings and they were reinforced by the identification of the Jews with the Shah until then. But once in power he could not totally ignore the new-found loyalty of the Jewish minority, nor could he altogether disclaim the traditional responsibilities towards them that devolve upon a "true" Muslim ruler with respect to the monotheistic minorities. Khomeini had had legal training and was "juridically minded." Consequently, he had striven to underpin all his policies by Islamic law and had consistently insisted on strict observance of legal procedures—at least such as he interpreted them. Alongside political considerations, his attitude towards the religious minorities was undoubtedly also shaped by the Islamic code of law prescribing tolerance.

Thus, in its first decade in power the policy of the Islamic regime towards the Jews was one of generating hatred against them, yet preventing it from being translated into violence; making a distinction between Judaism and Zionism, but at the same time systematically blurring the two terms; in short: a combination of instigation and restraint.

This is best illustrated in the following example. In 1986 *Jumhuriye Islami* (the official organ of the Islamic Republican Party) and *Kayhan* both published a lecture given in 1971 by the late Tehran University professor, Amir Tavakol Kambuziya. It appeared under the title—presumably given by the editors—"The Art of the Zionists." The whole lecture is a piece of wild agitation against the Jews, from the inception of their history up to the present. It defines them as "a dirty people" and "enemies of mankind," and goes on: "If we really want to visualize all that has been said about *Ahriman* [the evil deity and the source of all evil in Zoroastrianism] we must envision the Jews." By fraud and trickery they betrayed the peoples among whom they had resided throughout their history. They do not hesitate to destroy mankind (such for instance was the intention of the theories of Freud) as long as they advance their own ends. From the inception of Islam, the author continues, they have "worked against the Prophet, the Caliphs and the [Muslim] people." Quoting anti-Jewish verses from the Qur'an and referring to their "recent crimes" in the Middle East, he advises the Iranian people "to recognize their real enemy." Mentioning Hitler's massacre of six million Jews, he denounces that action as contrary to the principles of Islam, yet claims that "execution" is the only way to block the way of these people.

However, after quoting the lecture in detail, the paper adds the following editorial note: "It may be needless to say so, but in fact it is clear from the context, that the professor in using the term Jews . . . is not speaking of the pious followers of this religion. The professor explicitly and frankly distinguishes between Zionists and Jews." In fact, the editors advise the readers to understand the accusations against the Jews as referring to the Zionists only. Nevertheless, whoever reads the lecture is left with no doubt that the author did indeed refer to Jews whenever he used that term. Could he have referred to Zionists when writing of the stubborn Jews who made life so hard for Abraham or fought the Prophet Muhammad? From his few mentions of Zionists it is also clear that Kambuziya was aware of the distinction between the two terms and therefore meant Jews when he wrote Jews. Moreover, is it conceivable that the editors tried to tell their readers to replace the term Jews with Zionists every single time the former appears in the text? Can one give such an order to the reader as though he were a computer? It seems that the very publication of the lecture, fifteen years after it was delivered, and the inclusion of the editorial note attest to our conclusions stated above.[34]

Conclusion

The Islamic Revolution has signaled a radical change in most fields of Iranian life; for Iranian Jewry it was clearly the end of a period. An era of security, freedom, progress and self-confidence has given way to a period of insecurity, restrictions, regression and fear. Yet, it did not develop into the catastrophe that might have been expected.

Judged against the background of the age-old Jewish experience in Iran, it was the flowering under the last Shah which was exceptional, not the decline under Khomeini. Compared with the lot of Muslim (non-Persian) ethnic minorities and of dissenting political movements, who were mercilessly oppressed, the Jews—who were not proclaimed the "enemies of Allah" —are being treated with tolerance. Even when compared with the situation under the Qajars, the Jewish community is better protected and less perse-

cuted now. Then there was no anti-Jewish ideology, but Jews were nevertheless persecuted; now such an ideology exists, but is not being translated into
violence. Both then and now, the Jews were at the government's mercy to
protect them from popular excesses, although under the present regime the
government also invites those excesses.

But there is no mistaking the fact that the crisis in Iran was also a crisis
of Iranian Jewry. Given the history of persecutions, Khomeini's ideology and
the worldview of his radical disciples, Jews feel threatened. The fact that
two-thirds of the Jewish population, including almost the entire leadership,
have fled the country poses additional challenges. Today, they are being
made aware of their inferior place in the Islamic regime, and so are their
Muslim neighbors.

They have more reasons for concern. The Islamic regime has systematically inflamed mob passions and revolutionary fervor to keep itself alive
(e.g., during the persecution of the Shah's loyalists, the taking of the
American hostages and the Iran-Iraq war); it is liable to turn popular wrath
against the Jews. At such time, the masses are unlikely to distinguish
between Judaism and Zionism. Economic difficulties (aggravated first by the
revolution itself, then by the war and later by the decline in oil prices, until
the recent price increase resulting from the gulf crisis) is likely to further
incite people against the Jews. Jewish history is rife with anti-Semitic resentment at times of economic distress. The persecution of the Baha'is has set
an alarming precedent. In the meantime, however, the precarious combination of instigation and restraint continues to mark government policy.

Notes

1. In the structural sense, the popular uprising against the Shah largely conforms
   with the conditions for a "revolutionary situation" as laid down in the histori-
   graphical literature. But a true revolution also has an aspect of quality and
   content, bringing about lasting and genuine change. It is of course too early to
   judge whether this is true of the Islamic Revolution. The use of the term
   revolution here is meant only to mark it off in the structural sense from the
   typical coups d'état.

2. Thus, although Khomeini denounced Ba'th ideology as anti-Islamic, Ba'th-ruled
   Syria is Iran's closest ally. Or again: in the seventh year of the war against Ba'thi
   Iraq, Iran still kept its embassy in Baghdad and allowed an Iraqi diplomatic
   mission to operate in Tehran.

3. Bernard Lewis, *The Jews of Islam* (Princeton: Princeton University, 1984), p. 166.

4. Arminius Vambery, *The Story of My Struggles* (London: T. Fisher Unwin, 1905), p. 424.

5. Justin Perkins, *A Residence of Eight Years in Persia* (New York: Allen, Morrill & Wardwell, 1843), pp. 298–300.

6. George N. Curzon, *Persia and the Persian Question* (London: Frank Cass, 1892), I, pp. 510–511. For details of Jewish life in specific regions of the country, see I: 165–166, 333, 380; II: 240, 244, 493. For similar descriptions from the mid-nineteenth century, see the accounts of the Jewish traveler J. J. Benjamin, *Eight Years in Asia and Africa from 1846 to 1855* (Hanover: The author, 1859), pp. 211–213. For a fuller discussion of the situation of Iranian Jewry from the sixteenth to eighteenth centuries, see *Pe'amim*, 6 (1980), which is devoted entirely to this topic (in Hebrew).

7. Lewis, pp. 151–152.

8. Ezra Spicehandler, *Contemporary Iranian Jewry* (Jerusalem: The Institute of Contemporary Jewry, 1970), pp. 11–12 (in Hebrew).

9. For details on the laws on purity (*tahara*) and impurity (*naqasa*), see Lewis, p. 33, and the sources mentioned there.

10. David Littman, "Jews under Muslim Rule: The Case of Persia," *Weiner Library Bulletin*, 32 (1979), 7–8.

11. Benjamin, pp. 211–213.

12. Amnon Netzer, "Problems of Cultural, Social and Political Integration of the Jews of Iran," *Gesher* (1979), 69–83 (in Hebrew).

13. This was disclosed to the author by Jewish students in Tehran. A SAVAK general, interviewed by the author following the Shah's fall, confirmed that Jews were *a priori* regarded as loyal (the danger, after all, came from Muslim fundamentalists) and were consequently treated more leniently.

14. For details on this group and the rifts within the Jewish Association, see: Amnon Netzer, "The Jews of Iran, Israel and the Islamic Republic of Iran," *Gesher* (1980), 45–57 (in Hebrew).

15. Ruhollah Khomeini, *Al-Hukuma al-Islamiyya* (n.p.: 1970), p. 7 (in Arabic); *Velayate Faqih* (the Persian version). This and the following quotations are generally based on Hamid Algar's translation, *Islam and Revolution* (Berkeley: Mizan, 1981). However, the author preferred translating *ubtuliyat bil-yahud* (in Arabic) or *gereftare yahud* (in Persian) as "afflicted with the Jews" and not "to contend with them," as Algar did.

16. Khomeini, *Al-Hukuma al-Islamiyya*, p. 83.

17. Ibid., p. 121.

18. Ruhollah Khomeini, *Touzih al-Masa'el* (Tehran: 1962), pp. 15, 18; Lewis, p. 34.

19. Khomeini, *Touzih al-Masa'el*, pp. 18, 324–325, 509.

20. For some examples of many anti-Jewish expressions in Khomeini's speeches, declarations and interviews before the revolution, see: Algar, pp. 180, 196.

21. *Kayhan*, 30 September 1982, *Ettela'at*, 23 October 1982. (See also an interview by the Minister of Islamic Guidance, 'Abdul Majid Ma'adikhwah, with the

Islamic Republic News Agency, 29 May 1982, reported in the British Broadcasting Corporation's Summary of World Broadcasts (Middle East and Africa), 1 June 1982.

22. *Ettela'at*, 10 May 1979; Radio Tehran, 11 May—as reported in U.S. Foreign Broadcast Information Service, Daily Report, Middle East and North Africa (DR), 16 May 1979.

23. Based on an interview with one of the participants in the meeting. Khomeini's guidelines were also quoted by Radio Tehran, 15 May 1979 DR, 16 May 1979.

24. Radio Tehran, 15 May 1979 DR, 16 May 1979.

25. *Ettela'at*, 10 May 1979.

26. Ibid., 29 December 1979.

27. *Jumhuriye Islami*, 20 September 1982.

28. *Kayhan*, 12 June 1979.

29. *Ettela'at*, 28 February 1984.

30. *Kayhan*, 25 February 1984. *Majlis* Speaker, Hujjat al-Islam 'Ali Akbar Hashemi Rafsanjani pointed out a similar connection in a speech in the House: *Kayhan*, 26 February 1984.

31. See, for example, the article headlined: "The Protocols of the Meetings of the Learned Elders of Zion" in *Imam* (London), 4, no. 2 (February 1984), 14–15.

32. For instance, when the credentials of the Jewish *Majlis* deputy, Khosrow Naqi, were being discussed in the House on 21 February 1982, he declared that he rejected "Israel's right to exist" and regarded it as an "appendage of Imperialism" (*Ettela'at*, 22 February 1982). Rabbi Uriel Davoudi, the head of the Jewish rabbinical court, stated in September 1982 that Iranian Jews condemned Israel, and that "Israel is not part of us." Referring to the Beirut massacre of September 1982, he noted that "the Jewish community [of Iran] condemns *all* Israel's actions" (*Kayhan*, 30 September 1982; *Ettela'at*, 25 September 1982). Similar views expressed by Davoudi were cited in *Ettela'at*, 25 September; and a statement along similar lines by the Jewish student organization was quoted in *Kayhan*, 19 September 1982.

33. For an analysis of the change in Khomeini's ideology in transition from opposition to power, see my book: *Iran: A Decade of War and Revolution* (New York: Holmes & Meier, 1989), pp. 386–395. See also my article, "Khomeini's Vision: Nationalism or World Order," in D. Menashri (ed.), *The Iranian Revolution and the Muslim World* (Boulder: Westview Press, forthcoming).

34. The lecture was first published in the literary supplement of *Jumhuriye Islami* (*Sahifeh*, No. 31) and was reprinted in the weekly *Kayhan* (*Kayhan Hava'i*, 12 March 1986).

[17]

German Reunification and the Jews

Sander L. Gilman

Immediately after November 9, 1989, my personal trepidation about the future of the new Germany seemed an adequate Jewish response to the sudden, unpredictable changes in what had seemed to be an immutable political solution to the "German Question."[1] The very changes in what had seemed for forty years a rigid status quo evoked specific memories of the past. In Israel, Shimon Peres stated that "on the one hand, what is happening there brings forth great hope. On the other hand, no one among us is free of the memories of the Second World War . . . When we hear of a united Germany, we must ask: What kind of Germany will it be? A Germany with an army, without an army? A demilitarized Germany, an undermilitarized Germany?"[2] Peres's feeling about what was occurring in Germany, like mine, was cast in an image of a prewar Germany as *the* military power in Central Europe. And that image from the past was linked by Jews throughout the world to only one event in both German and Jewish history—the Shoah. It is to this focus of the relationship between Jews, in Germany and the rest of Europe, to the path of German history, that I shall return.

The emblematic survivor of the Shoah, Eli Weisel, shared Peres's view. While greeting the collapse of the wall as a "moving and rewarding experience," he too asked: "What next? Will this unexpected turn of events lead to a reunification of Germany? . . . Will a united, powerful new Germany break away from the conquest-thirsty demons that dominated the old Germany? I cannot hide the fact that the Jew in me is troubled, even worried.

372

Whenever Germany was too powerful, it fell prey to perilous temptations of ultranationalism."[3] It seemed that Wiesel's reading of German history was specifically Jewish. A. M. Rosenthal, of the *New York Times*, evoked that past, a past that in the West seemed only to be evoked in a Jewish self-consciousness of German reunification when he wrote: "I search through the endless newspaper columns about the German wave rolling toward unification, but I cannot find any of the words I am looking for. . . . And when leaders of so many nations issue their carefully crafted statements about how the will of the German people must be honored, the words are not there either. These are some of the words: Jew, Auschwitz, Rotterdam, Polish *untermenschen*, Leningrad, slave labor, crematorium, Holocaust, Nazi."[4] Rosenthal's complaint was not lodged solely against the Germans, but against all who spoke about German reunification without evoking the Shoah.

The very thought of an undivided Germany evoked the militaristic past of Germany for many in Europe and the United States, but not in an undifferentiated way. For Jews in Israel and the United States, for survivors of the Shoah and those untouched by the Shoah, the German past is the Shoah. But the Shoah means something quite different to Jews, in the United States or in Europe, and to the non-Jewish Germans. We share the same past, but we give it quite different meaning. What I would like to do in this chapter is to examine this Jewish response, including my own, and attempt to understand it.

Let me begin with A. M. Rosenthal's charge of the absence of the past in the discussion of German reunification during the fall of 1989. This silence was linked by him and many others to an image of the Germans (ironically) as the product of their history, condemned by it to eternally recapitulate it. Certainly in both the GDR and the FRG there have been constant and direct evocations of the past, but always within specific political contexts. Helmut Kohl, the Chancellor of the Federal Republic, on a November 1989 state visit to Poland wrote in the guest book at Auschwitz that "the warnings emanating from this place must never be forgotten. Unspeakable hurt was inflicted on various peoples here, but above all on European Jews, in the name of Germany."[5] Accompanied on this trip to the new Poland by Heinz Galinski, the head of the official West German Jewish organization, Kohl seemed to many listeners to have crafted his eloquent words for Soviet and American media consumption. And for this audience the assumption was that the evocation of the Shoah as well as the trip to Auschwitz was necessary. Willy Brandt's trip to Poland had marked the opening of the FRG to the East. Helmut Kohl's belief about those "blessed by being born too late" to have experienced the Shoah drew his statement at Auschwitz into question for Jews and non-Jews alike. His evocation of the Shoah seemed a ritual evocation of the past, a past from which he felt himself and the German people separated. Indeed, in this context it was the very evocation of the Shoah that was troubling.

But what did the reunification of German have to do with me as an American Jew? I knew that the Berlin wall and the division of Germany had nothing directly to do with any sort of punishment of the German people for the Shoah. I knew that the Berlin wall which symbolized the difference between the FRG and the GDR was an artifact of the cold war. It had less to do with Auschwitz than with Westminster, Missouri, where Churchill coined the term "iron curtain." The association of the wall with the punishment of the Germans seemed to be a specifically Jewish response to the meaning of November 9, 1989. As Nea Weissberg-Bob, a "Jew with a German passport" (her description) who teaches in West Berlin lamented: "I am horrified at reunification. The wall as a symbol of partition was a just punishment. I couldn't be sorry for that. I do not wish them a nationalist rejoicing. I would have preferred continuation of a second Germany, like Austria."[6] Henry Ashby Turner, the noted Yale historian of contemporary Germany was right when he claimed that "many who worry about unification think the Germans have not been sufficiently punished for their country's past misdeeds. There are many problems inherent in the idea of collective guilt, but suffice it to say that Western conceptions of justice are incompatible with the punishment of innocent members of a nationality committed by compatriots. Moreover, how can Germans born since 1945 be held culpable for what happened before then?"[7] Moreover, Turner was not alone in stating this position. Moshe Zimmerman, the respected head of the Institute for German History at the Hebrew University in Jerusalem was, of course, right that "reunification [of the two Germanys] is not going to take place in its old forms."[8] But are we all a "bunch of idiots," to use Zimmerman's felicitous phrase, for worrying about the meaning of German reunification. Was our response irrational?

When I was in both West and East Berlin in December 1989, there was the sense of a new age having begun on November 9, 1989. The idea that dominated this city where Hegel taught for so very long was not of an end to history, but rather an absolute break with the past, a break as complete as the abyss between West and East that the wall had come to represent. How radical the shift of German identity implied by the collapse of the wall was, could be read in the statement made by Walter Momper, Mayor of West Berlin, on November 10, the day after the wall fell, proclaiming that November 9 should be made a national holiday.[9] (November 9, 1990 became such a holiday in Berlin, with a somewhat more somber Momper unveiling a plaque to commemorate the breaching of the wall.) A Social Democrat, whose government represented a so-called traffic light (i.e., green-red) liberal-left coalition of the Social Democrats and the Alternative List (the Greens), Momper had spent the evening of November 9, 1988, of one year before, in commemoration of the fiftieth anniversary of *Kristallnacht*, the burning of the German synagogues and the looting of Jewish shops by the Nazis. In 1988 November 9 was already a memorial day in West Berlin and a moving one, as in the rest of the Federal Republic. A year later, in the passion of the moment, the past vanished. A new national symbol, the opening of the wall, claimed the day for the new "German" history; its association with the history of the Jews in Germany was effaced. The replacement of one idea of history with another did not happen with the fall of the wall. It was a long process, a process that had to do with the shift of the generations in both Germanys and the gradual erosion of an already repressed memory of the Shoah.

I have already mentioned the incompleteness of both West and East Germans coming to terms with the Shoah. The association between the absence of a period of true mourning among the Germans—after 1945—meant that the reconstruction of both Germanys took place without having to deal with the Shoah except in the most extrinsic manner. In the FRG, the *Wirtschaftswunder*, the economic miracle of the early 1950s, meant that the focus was on the rebuilding of Germany; in the GDR, the official line from the founding of the state was that the GDR was not a successor state to Nazi Germany and indeed its inhabitants were as much the victims of the Nazis as were the Austrians. (We might note the rising xenophobia in Austria during the late 1980s.)[10] In the FRG during the late 1960s a new generation confronted their parents over the question of guilt, but the issue of the Shoah was never confronted. The problem of anti-Semitism became submerged in the debate about capitalism. This confrontation never took place in the GDR, where the illusion of seamless transition from Ulbricht to Honecker took place. With the late 1980s a third generation has appeared in both the FRG and the GDR—and it is this generation who will dominate the newly reunified Germany. And it is the question of the German past, more than anything else, which silently lurks in the background for this generation. As one young West German student said to me in the summer of 1989: "In Berlin, I'm a German, a good European. When I travel abroad, even to France or England, I sense that I am seen as a "bad" German. I bear the stigma of history." The mode of dealing with the stigma of the past has been, however, different in the FRG and the GDR.

Ironically, one of the keys to the national identity of the GDR was its relationship to the Jews. The official line in the GDR was that the Shoah was the doing of a state which ceased to exist in 1945 and, therefore, the GDR was not part of that "Germany" which was responsible for the Shoah. This position was linked to the break with the State of Israel when it was decided in the Eastern block that "Zionism was racism." During the fall of 1989, Benjamin Netanyahu, then the Israeli Deputy Foreign Minister expressly linked "the question of the resumption of relations" between the GDR and Israel to the "question of the historical responsibility for the Holocaust."[11] On February 8, 1990, the government of Prime Minister Hans Modrow recognized "the responsibility of the entire German people for the past" and stood ready to "provide material support" in the form of reparations.[12] This view was seconded during the first session of the newly elected (and first and only freely elected) *Volkskammer* in mid-March 1990, which under the leadership of a conservative government, accepted responsibility "for the humiliation, expulsion and murder of Jewish men, women and children."[13] This support would have been given after the same model as the reparations given by the government of the FRG some forty years ago. These payments would have included direct reparations to those who have claims on the East Germans because of activities which took place in that area of Germany (such as those inmates at Buchenwald or the forced laborers at the chemical works at Buna) and a full third of the cost of the resettlement of European refugees in Israel after 1949 (a sum of $300 million). These negotiations between Jewish organizations and the government of the GDR, which began under Erich Honecker in 1974, were a spin-off of the American recognition of the GDR. This now means that the newly reconstituted Federal Republic of Germany will have to consider a new wave of reparations payments during the 1990s. The debate about the inclusion of some mention of the Shoah in the revised German constitution, which arose immediately prior to the beginning of December, 1990, placed the extent of these reparations in question. Little or no attention has been given to this question in the discussion about the meaning (financial and otherwise) of German reunification since reunification in the fall of 1990.

Can we as American Jews claim from this third generation of non-Jewish Germans the same response to the Shoah which we as victims or as the children of victims feel? This is the major coloration of an American-Jewish as well as a German-Jewish understanding of the reunification of Germany. Most Jews here and abroad of my father's generation and mine still need the Shoah not to be a past event; we need it to be a part of our daily reality. Our mourning is for parents and grandparents, for brothers and uncles. For many Jews this daily reminder of the Shoah was present in the wall, the scar which marked the division of Germany. That scar, as real on the body of Germany as the tattoo on the arm of the concentration camp prisoner, became a mark, not of the cold war division of Germany (as it was understood by many Germans) but of German guilt for the Shoah. It was the Wailing Wall of modern Jewish history, marking for Jews outside of both German States, the living awareness of the Shoah. It was as real a sign of the guilt of the Germans as we Jews could hope for—and yet it was one which had intrinsically nothing to do with the Shoah. It was our Jewish reading of the map of contemporary Europe as a reflection of the German past, a reading not shared by either the superpowers then or now nor by the Germans themselves. When this reading is publicly ignored or discounted, when we sense the gradual moving of our experiences into the past, we are anxious, we are distraught. And this is a correct, a natural, a necessary response to a shift in the understanding of German history.

The question of the meaning of reunification for Jews must be focused. I have stressed my response as an American Jew to this shift. For me, its meaning is symbolic; for the Jews in the newly reconstituted Germany it is real. Let me turn to asking what reunification will mean to the Jews who live and who will continue to live in this new Germany. Let me begin with a glance at the GDR.

In the GDR Jews existed as the exemplary victims of fascism, but as such were invisible as Jews. Hermann Kant, the ousted head of the East German Writers' Union, has noted that when the issue of anti-Semitism came up in the 1950s and he and others circulated a small questionnaire asking fellow students to say if any of their professors was Jewish, "The answer was 'no.' Nobody knew," Mr. Kant said. "We did it to prove there was no anti-Semitism."[14] What this anecdote actually shows, was the total repression of the idea that there were Jews still present in the GDR and that any position which acknowledged their presence was taboo. With all the emphasis on the destruction of fascism in the GDR, the racist underpinnings of fascism were never stressed, since anti-Semitism was, according to official theory, merely a reflex of state fascism not its essence, and with the abolition of fascism and its roots, capitalism, anti-Semitism had to vanish. Thus no real emphasis on the reality of the Shoah in the daily awareness of the citizens of the GDR took place. The *Gemeinde,* the official representative body of the some 200 Jews who live in East Berlin, was seen as a state mechanism and was linked to an anti-Zionist campaign early in the 1970s. In November 1989, Irene Runge, a spokesperson for the East Berlin Jewish community, saw the sign of a real shift in the GDR with the unrolling of "The Israeli flag in front of East German television [cameras] and they show[ed] it . . ."[15] In the mind of the East German Jews there was a link between the recognition of Israel and the acknowledgement of German guilt for the Shoah. The political importance of this movement, from a community that had studiously ignored its relationship with Israel for over two decades, is evident.

The Jewish presence in the GDR is small but extraordinarily important.[16] In the GDR Jews are on the one hand invisible and other the other hand highly visible. Indeed it is often said that "Jews in the GDR have become a 'protected species'."[17] The Jewish organizational structure in the GDR did receive many more privileges as "victims of fascism." They were marked with a higher degree of career mobility than the general population and were given direct privileges, such as the ability to travel to the West, shared by few of that population. One indicator of this special status was the treatment of the dissident novelist Jurek Becker, who was exiled from the GDR along with a number of other intellectuals in 1976 following their objection to the forcible expulsion of Wolf Biermann. Becker, a Jew who survived the Lodz ghetto, is the author of *Jacob the Liar,* the most widely read account of the Shoah in the GDR. In many ways Becker's novel was the first public acknowledgement in the GDR of the role of the Jews as the primary victims of the Nazis. Of all of the writers exiled in 1976 only Becker was given a permanent visa which permitted him to keep his GDR citizenship and return to the GDR on visits to his family. His status as a visible Jew provided him with a type of privilege which his fellow dissidents did not share (even those such as Thomas Brasch who were, like him, Jewish).

By September 1990 many of these Jews, such as the eighty-one year old Steffi Spira, the sister of the famed actress Camilla Spira, had rethought their own identity. She had spent her youth in Mexico in a circle of Communist intellectuals which included Anna Seghers and returned after the war to the GDR where she became very visible in cultural circles. She joined the struggle against the Honecker regime in the fall of 1989 and rejected the old regime for its "treason" to the cause of socialism. She remains staunchly anti-Nationalistic, a view espoused by German-Jews as diverse as Daniel Cohn-Bendit, (Danny the Red of 1968 Paris student revolt) on the left, and Julius H. Schoeps, the leading conservative German-Jewish academic specialist on contemporary Jewry. All retain their sense of doubt about the mission of a new national German state and the role which Jews will or do play in it.[18] This view is shared by most of the Jews in the former territory of the GDR, but all of these have the additional stigma of having been "privileged" in the GDR as returned exiles.

The very word "privilege" now marks the difference between the "good" German and the "bad" German in the GDR. Any individual who was "privileged" under the old regime is now seen as compromised. Privilege, whether it was owning a hunting lodge or the ability to more easily travel to the West, has become a public litmus test in the GDR. (Even Christa Wolf, the leading oppositional writer in the GDR, who was talked about in November 1989 as a potential candidate for the presidency of a newly constituted GDR, has been publicly defamed because of the type of automobile she was said to drive.[19]) Günter Kunert saw this as a striving of the "crowds in Leipzig and East Berlin . . ." ". . . for an existence without fear or deprivation—a normal existence. And they are answered by writers and intellectuals who, having never known such deprivation, call for a purified, revitalized socialism."[20] In 1990 such privileges are seen as a sign of the special relationship which the Jews had with the now detested party apparatus under Walter Ulbricht and Erich Honecker. Everyone with "privilege," whether directly part of the destructive and exploitive inner circle of power (such as Erich Honecker) or whether "privileged" through the foreign income generated by creative activities (such as Christa Wolf), is the enemy. Jews, whose "privilege" came through their status as "victims of fascism" were likewise lumped with everyone else. Those without privileges have been suddenly redefined as part of the opposition to the old order. Real opponents, real victims of the State were only those without economic privilege. It was only that small group of the privileged (among them the Jews) who controlled the state; everyone else was an exploited captive of the system. We must remember that almost two and a half million citizens of the GDR freely sought membership in the now detested Socialist Unity Party.

This fantasy replicates almost exactly the mindset in both German states in the late 1940s in which the entire German people were seduced and held captive by a small number of madmen, specifically those identified and punished at Nuremberg. It is a view espoused by Henry Ashby Turner, but not shared by me. For him it was only "a band of political criminals led by a master demagogue [who] exploited adverse circumstances to win the backing of millions of Germans, gain control of the country and set in motion a program of conquest and genocide."[21] But while Turner's view is that a small number of "evil" Germans seduced a nation, many of us—students of the history and culture of Germany—view the presence of anti-Semitism as the central focus of European, that is, Christian culture. We see the rise of the Nazis as a response that articulated those feelings of hate directed against the Jews. Indeed, many of us see in the attempt to "identify the guilty" in the GDR a similar attempt to exculpate the general citizenry from responsibility for the actions of their leaders. It was not us—it was Hitler or Honecker—who made us do it! (This is in no way to set these two moments in history as parallels, only to acknowledge the all too human response to place the blame beyond one's self.) For many of us it is not the question of a German "national character" but a German "national culture" which we see at the root of the Shoah. And it is the real working through of these past feelings in the new Germany, not merely the forgetting of the past, which creates part of the anxiety many of us feel.

Hermann Kant's claim of the invisibility of the Jews as a sign of the absence of anti-Semitism (if it were ever true) has been quite reversed and the sudden visibility of "Jews" becomes a means of discrediting the old order. Thus the sudden interest in both West and East German (as well as the foreign) media in the fall of 1989 in the "ethnic" makeup of the party leadership of the past and the present. When Gregor Gysi became head of the party in early December 1989, the fact that he was "Jewish" was immediately noted by the media in the FRG and abroad. In fact Gysi's father, Klaus Gysi, when he was the Secretary of Religious Affairs, served in a capacity which reflected more the atheistic bias of the government rather than any "Jewish" commitment (either religious or ethnic) on his part. Gregor Gysi was not a member of the *Gemeinde,* the official organization of the Jews in the GDR. But he was labeled as "Jewish" in the media. Even more striking to me was the reporting in both East and West about the disappearance in East Berlin of the state secretary who was in charge of the foreign currency reserves of the GDR. Alexander Schalck-Golodkowski was the civil servant in charge of economic relationship with the West, who was accused by the reform government of Hans Modrow of having maintained secret foreign currency accounts for the party in Swiss banks. When a order for his arrest went out early in December 1989, the story was reported in the West German *Bild Zeitung* with the word "Schieber," blackmarketeer, prominently featured in a banner headline. Historically, this word has racist overtones in German. Even the serious media, such as the *Frankfurter Rundschau* reported that Schalck-Golodkowski had fled—where else but to Israel under the Law of Return.[22] When he showed up in West Berlin a few days later and placed himself in the hands of the West German authorities (who, by the way, refused to extradite him to East Berlin because the economic crimes he was accused of were not crimes in the FRG), no further mention was made of his "Jewish" connection.

In the newly emerging press in the GDR relatively little of this discourse about the "Jewish" identity of some of the leaders of the old order appeared. The self-censorship about ethnic identity, so well instilled during the past forty years, meant that such references were assumed to be "fascist." It was only in the February 21, 1990 issue of the by now independent, left-wing newspaper *Junge Welt* that reports of the rise of anti-Semitism were circulated in the GDR—but they were accounts of anti-Semitism in the Soviet Union.[23]

Understanding who has been labeled as a Jew in the GDR is of interest in understanding the construction of Jewish identity in the public sphere during the past half year. But one must also note that the self-identification of some of the younger Jews in the GDR has shifted radically over the past two to three years. At the beginning of the 1980s, with the exception of the members of the *Gemeinde*, few acculturated Jews in the GDR identified themselves as "Jews." Beginning in late 1988 more and more of these ·individuals came to identify themselves as Jews in the public sphere. Major cultural figures wholeheartedly announced that they were Jews. One of the leading theater critics of the GDR, Christian Trilse, in 1988 published a series on the history of the Yiddish theater in Germany in the leading theater magazine, *Theater der Zeit*. He signed these as Christian Jochanaan Trilse, signaling for the first time in public his Jewish ancestry. As their identification with the goals of the socialist state diminished, as it did with many intellectuals during the 1980s, these "Jews" saw a return or a rediscovery of their "Jewish" identity, within a completely secular model. This model had no particular anti-Socialist stigma in the GDR.

The increased visibility of the Jews in the GDR and the FRG is a sword which cuts both ways. Thus there was an official claim that there had been an increase in the number of anti-Semitic incidents in GDR during the past few years, incidents which were ignored by the government. That many of these incidents actually did occur, can not be doubted. And certainly their existence was assumed by writers outside of the GDR such as George Steiner, when he asked in a note whether "Jew-hatred, in the persistent eschatological sense, [would] smoulder into heat? Already [in December, 1989] there are ugly signals from Hungary and East Germany."[24] In speaking with a number of Jews in East Berlin over the past three years, their impression was of an increase in the activities of "skinheads," mostly adolescents, who adopted the Nazi attitudes, style and dress of their compatriots in the FRG.[25] Hans Coppi, Jr., a social worker who has worked with the East German police, puts the number of skinheads in the GDR at between 5,000 and 10,000.[26] Their visible, aggressive presence was felt in early March 1990 with the first major public demonstration in East Berlin. In the fall of 1989, the secretary of the Erfurt Jewish organization received daily calls from a man who said: "The ovens of Buchenwald are waiting for you again." In 1988 there had been 44 prosecutions for fascist (including anti-Semitic) activities in the GDR while by the end of 1989 the number had increased to 144.[27] (This may indeed indicate an increase in activity; it may, however, merely indicate an increase in the official sensitivity to such activities as well as the courage to report activities which officially should not have taken place in a socialist state.)

Without a doubt the most outrageous and widely publicized act was the smearing of fascist slogans on the huge Soviet war memorial in Treptow, a suburb of East Berlin, at the beginning of January 1990. As a result a mass demonstration called by the Socialist Unity Party filled the streets of East Berlin with 250,000 people. They rallied "against Nazis" and for a "humanistic offensive."[28] At the time a rumor was also circulating that the Modrow government had either committed this act of desecration (after the model of the Nazi burning of the *Reichstag*) or at least was using it for their own political ends. What was clear was that the manipulation of the rhetoric of the past was being used to attempt to justify the reinstitution of a secret police reputedly to control fascist groups. The discredited "Stasi," the old secret police, was to be replaced by a new secret police dedicated to fighting fascism. This ploy did not work, for the evocation of the past was not powerful enough to overcome the absolute separation of the reality of the present from the shadow of the past.

What was evoked on the streets of East Berlin at the beginning of 1990 was the fear of the encouragement and sponsorship of East German neo-fascist groups through the political right wing in the FRG. For very few in the GDR in the midst of the final year of its existence, reunification meant the emergence of powerful neo-fascist forces latent in East Germany. In the winter of 1990 they seemed, for many, simply part of the fear-mongering against the West. The reform groups in the GDR, such as the New Forum, the Citizens' Movement for Democracy Now, and Democratic Upsurge, were in general opposed to reunification and had, as Barbara Einhorn and Mary Kaldor report in the British the *New Statesman & Society,* "an explicit commitment to socialism, democratic and green—to a socialist GDR, based on the rule of law within a perspective of global responsibility."[29] They were little interested in the fearful echoes from the distant historical past; this was in no way part of their agenda. Save the trees was their cry; not remember the Shoah. The conservative parties, which won the first free election held in the GDR in March 1990, did not raise the issue of the Shoah, of German responsibility, or reparations, as part of their platform. Indeed, the one party which mentioned this, at least in its campaign literature during the election campaign, was the P[arty for] D[emocratic] S[ocialism], the newest version of the old Communist Party (SED). Before the election, the head of the party, Gregor Gysi made a direct appeal to the leadership of the American Jewish community to support the PDS in order to assure the continued memory of the Shoah within German political culture. Following the election, and in the period leading up to the general elections of early December 1990, little discussion of the Shoah took place in reunited Germany. The meetings between German and Polish officials in early November 1990 and the state visit of the President of the Soviet Union at the same time, two moments in which the Shoah could have been meaningfully evoked, passed without a mention.

The dismissal of the past was part of the agenda of the forces of the German right in the FRG before reunification and the tiny right wing in the GDR has clearly been influenced by the West German right. Brutally eliminating the past is part of the very successful political platform of the West German neo-fascist Republican Party again under the leadership of Franc

Schönhuber. With 23,000 members its influence is substantially greater than its membership. The party held 11 seats of West Berlin's 138 seat city council at the time of reunification. The dismissal of the Shoah by the party is closely linked to its xenophobic and antiforeign views. The Republicans have focused on the Turkish, Jugoslavian, and "asylum-seeking" populations, with surprisingly familiar arguments about the economic consequences of permitting too many strangers into the West German economy. There are 4 million "foreigners" in the FRG or about 6.8% of the population in 1990. (In 1939 there were 210,000 Jews or less than 1% of the population in all of Germany.) But in the mind of the Republicans this influx of foreigners causes "racial conflict, growing criminality, more unemployment, and social and cultural tensions."[30] It was precisely these claims, of course, that were made earlier in the century about the presence of Jews in Germany. And that link remains in the popular mind. In the fall of 1989, stimulated by the fall of the wall, an eleventh grader at a school in Beuel in the FRG reported that one of her fellow students said that "there were too many foreigners already in West Germany, and then he said there were too many Jews again, and I just stared at him with anger."[31] The public image of the "foreigner" and the image of the "Jew" are often associated by the far right. Graffiti in Turkish neighborhoods in West Berlin, such as "Zyklon B" or "off to Auschwitz" directly evoke the Shoah. Jewish inhabitants of West Berlin understand comments such as "Just wait until we've gotten rid of [Heinz] Galinski —because then your time here has come as well" not merely as threats against the Turks but also as threats against themselves as "foreigners."[32]

What is never said quite aloud is that the Jewish community in West Germany has become quite foreign. For over the past twenty years a large number of Russian Jews who landed in Vienna and did not or could not go on to Israel or the USA settled in West Germany and especially in West Berlin. Approximately 2,000 out of the 6,000 Jews now in West Berlin are from Eastern Europe and these are mostly the younger members of the *Gemeinde*. The relationship, by the way, between the older members of the West Berlin *Gemeinde* under Heinz Galinski and these younger families is quite strained. The irony is that many of the older members of the *Gemeinde* were themselves Displaced Persons from the East, like the parents of the German-Israeli novelist Lea Fleischmann, who had chosen to remain in Germany after the war. It is this generation of Eastern European Jews, now acculturated into German society, who feel themselves the most threatened by the new arrivals from the East.[33] As the anonymous leader of a small

Jewish community commented in October 1990: "It's the old internal conflict between German Jews and Jews from the East. They are different from
us and much more different from the Germans. We get along well with the
Germans."[34]

With the absolute limitation to 80,000 on the number of Soviet citizens,
who will be able to enter the USA in 1991, the resettlement of Soviet and
Eastern European Jews in the FRG has increased. Most of the Jews who have
decided to move to try to move to Germany are young professionals, engi-
neers, physicians, musicians, whose skills could not be employed in Israel
and who see a much better chance for a meaningful life in the Jewish
Diaspora. The growing sense of the instability of Israel among Soviet and
Eastern European Jews has not been helped by Yitzhak Shamir's public
statement about the need of a "big" Israel to accommodate a "big immigration" of Soviet Jews. Even though Shamir has altered his position for
American consumption, and even though less than 1% of the new arrivals
from the Soviet Union chose to settle on the West Bank, the impression has
been left that it will be the Soviet Jews who will be bearing the brunt of the
Intifada.[35] (The number of Soviet Jews who came to Israel in October 1990
alone was 21,000.) With the religious parties in Israel also raising the
question of whether the acculturated Jews returning from the Soviet Union
are "real" Jews or not, the sense of welcome has been even more damp-
ened.[36] More and more Jews opted for political asylum status in this new
reunified Germany.

On September 14, 1990 the government of the Federal Republic halted
the immigration of Soviet Jews into East Berlin after some 40,000 Soviet
Jews had arrived during the summer months. An official in Bonn informed
Annetta Kahan, the director of East Berlin's office for foreigners, that
"We're not taking over any old burdens from East Germany—refugees, Jews,
anything."[37] By the end of October 1990, the rhetoric of the old anti-
Semitism, the anti-Semitism keyed to the fearsome image of the *Ostjude* had
reappeared. The state of North Rhine-Westphalia stated that it was willing
to take in some 500 Jews, warning that the admission of too many Soviet
Jews could foment "a new anti-Semitism."[38] During the fall of 1990, a new
group was added to the list of stigmatized categories in Germany: the "Zonies"
or the "Ossies," the inhabitants of the GDR itself. This anti-GDR feeling is
especially evident among many West German intellectuals, who knew that
their side was right all along, or at least since last November. This sense of
the innate inferiority of the inhabitants of what has come to be called the

"new federal states" has resulted in a sense of self-hatred. A friend from Berlin wrote to me in October 1990 that this "new East German self-hatred has appeared, or more likely has now become visible: 'Ach wir sind ja so mickrig'—we're so crumby, they moan." Indeed, much of the older stereotype of the Jew has become evident in the image of the Zonie. Just as the Jews' accent was thought to mark them as inferior, the Saxon accent now marks the Zonies as different. A young clerk at the town hall in Bad Harzburg observed: "A lot of Zonies come over here and we're slowly getting used to them. It takes time to get used to their Saxon dialect. It's a foreign country there, sort of like Bavaria."[39] As a result of this internalized sense of inferiority the attacks, both verbal and physical, on the "Fitschis," as they are pejoratively called, the Cuban, Vietnamese, and Mozambique guest workers in the GDR, have increased. (They are called "people from Fiji" because the inhabitants of the GDR, in a grotesque reversal of their own sense of isolation, see every foreigner as the inhabitant of some exotic island.) But the rhetoric is not the rhetoric of the German colonies; it is the rhetoric of anti-Semitism. The skinheads in "the new federal states" not only shout "foreigners out" but follow it up by crying "Juda verrecke!," the cry of anti-Semites from the middle of the nineteenth century. When ethnic Germans in present-day Poland speak of the Poles as "being lazy, given to theft and preferring to trade rather than do productive work" they employ the pejorative word "schachern," a stock word of German anti-Semitism about Jewish unproductivity.[40] Still each day during the fall of 1990, a few Jews arrived in the newly reunited Berlin. They lined up before the former Nazi Ministry of Propaganda, now the Advisory Center for Foreign Jews, to wait and see if they will be granted asylum.

When the question of the "foreigners" is evoked by the right wing, with all of the rhetoric of the Nazi past, the hostile image of the Jew is simultaneously evoked. Among the new citizens of the FRG from the GDR, from the USSR and Poland, this image immediately evokes the double image of the Jew as historically embedded in the nationalistic and religious movements of the East as well as the image of the privileged Jew, the Jewish Bolshevik from whom they fled. Thus the Republicans as well as the skinheads have a most fertile field in the FRG, especially in the former territory of the GDR in the foreseeable future if the government, whether right or left, is unable to solve those problems of unemployment and housing associated with "foreigners."

The "question of German reunification" is no longer a question, it is a reality. There is a new, reunified Germany under the old West German constitution. When I was a graduate student in Germany, I secretly smiled at those members of the exile organizations of Silesians or Pomeranians who marched on June 17 every year to proclaim their desire to reclaim their homeland. I no longer laugh. When the Chancellor of the FRG saw the political advantage to a quick and clean reorganization of Europe and when I see the potential consequences of a conservative government in the FRG playing the *Gesamtdeutsche*, the united German card, then I wonder about the past, and about the "Jewish Question." Helmut Kohl's evocation of German "confederation" was done in the light of a specific political advantage for him and his party. The federal elections in the FRG were held in the fall of 1990 and Kohl's strategy worked. These "new" Germans, those who have already voted against socialism with their feet in leaving the GDR, Rumania, Poland, and the Soviet Union, voted in a conservative manner. The disillusioned former citizens of the GDR joined them in their move to the right.

The word "reunification" had always seemed to me a bit of historical jargon from a distant past, evoked as part of the emotional rhetoric of contemporary politics but not really believed in by the politicians who used it as an aspect of *Realpolitik*. But then too, I had always heard the phrase, "the Jewish Question," as a historical fossil, an artifact from the pre-Shoah past. But the "Jewish Question" is back with us in the form of questions about the future of the Jewish communities in Germany, in terms of the structure of the relationship between a new reunified Germany and Israel. Reunification evokes much in the mind of the Jew. But it is always tied to the Shoah, a past which is alive for Jews in a way that it is not for others. One can see this in the brilliant Anglo-Jewish novelist Clive Sinclair's Swiftian proposal in the summer of 1989 that the soon to be emptied GDR would be a good place to resolve the problem of Israeli-Palestinian conflict: "When East Germany has been vacated by its former inhabitants, offer it to either the Israelis or the Palestinians as their homeland. This will solve the territorial dispute of both the Israelis and the Palestinians (two people in a single room), ensure that Germany will never be reunited and be a final reparation for their crime. Perfect!"[41] Even in our fantasies Jews, especially those outside of the FRG and the GDR, seem to have needed the division of Germany as a sign of the living presence of the past.

What can we American Jews do to mitigate our evident sense of anxiety, an anxiety which is to a certain degree a correct response to the generational shift within both Germany as well as to the political developments in the new Germany?

• First and primarily, we must be aware that our response as Jews outside of the FRG and the GDR—of doubt, hostility, suspicion—is both our reflection of our past but also a reasoned reaction to present events. It is neither sour grapes nor are we all a "bunch of idiots." There has been a real change of generation in Germany. We American Jews are not sure what this change will mean. There is and will continue to be evidence of unworked-through nationalistic feelings in Germany that are historically and intimately bound to the image and idea of the Jew. These feelings do and should make us, as they make large numbers of Germans such as Günter Grass (as he stated in his February 1990 lectures at the University of Frankfurt), anxious enough to take these threats seriously.[42] The West German "basic law," the constitution, provides certain guards against splinter parties and against racism. These safeguards must be built into any reunified Germany. They will protect not only Jews in the new state but all minorities.

• Second, we must be aware that our primary focus for the present moment should be on Jews, no matter how defined, in Germany. A. M. Rosenthal, in his moving column in the *New York Times*, asked that the intellectuals of the American-Jewish community speak out on the issue of the meaning of German reunification.[43]

• Third, we, as American Jews, must be aware that the creation of a new Germany will impact quite directly on the meaning of the Shoah in the eyes of the world. It will continue to be the obligation of Jews, even more than in the recent past, to keep the meaning and memory of the Shoah alive. It will be our obligation to teach the Shoah, as we teach the going out from Egypt, as a living part of Jewish experience.

• And lastly, we, as American Jews, must be constantly aware that our feelings are not necessarily the feelings of most non-Jewish Germans. Their joy and our anxiety are different responses to the same events. As we must respect their sense of their own present, they must recognize that our response is also valid.[44]

Notes

1. Revised comments to the American Jewish Committee's Colloquium on German Reunification, Wednesday, March 7, 1990.

2. *Washington Times* (November 14, 1989), p. A9.
3. *New York Times* (October 17, 1989): p. A39.
4. Ibid. (February 4, 1990: p. E23.
· 5. Ibid. (November 15, 1989): p. A14.
6. Ibid. (September 25, 1990): p. A10.
7. Ibid. (February 11, 1990): p. E25.
8. *Atlanta Journal and Constitution* (November 24, 1989): p. A13.
9. This is evoked by Eli Weisel in his piece in the *New York Times* (October 17, 1989), p. A39.
10. *New York Times* (October 7, 1990): p. A18.
11. Ibid. (January 29, 1990): p. A10.
12. Ibid. (February 9, 1990): p. A10.
13. *Newsweek* (May 7, 1990): p. 44.
14. *New York Times* (December 11, 1989): p. A7.
15. *USA Today* (November 14, 1989): p. 6A.
16. In addition to the official members of the *Gemeinde*, there are probably another 100 to 300 Jews in East Berlin as well as another 100 or so East Germans who could be labeled as Jewish.
17. Robin Ostow, *Jews in Contemporary East Germany: The Children of Moses in the Land of Marx* (New York: St. Martin's Press, 1989), p. 113.
18. *New York Times* (September 25, 1990): p. A10.
19. On this problem of the intellectuals in the GDR in a time of transition, see the remarks made by the GDR writer Monika Maron, reprinted in the *taz* (February 6, 1990): p. 11.
20. Günter Kunert, "Comments on the State of Europe," *Granta* 30 (1990): 161.
21. *New York Times* (February 11, 1990): p. E25.
22. *Frankfurter Rundschau* (December 6, 1989): p. 2.
23. *New York Times* (February 21, 1990), p. A6.
24. George Steiner, "Comments on the State of Europe," *Granta* 30 (1990): 132.
25. Ostow, op. cit., p. 119.
26. *Newsweek* (May 7, 1990): p. 44.
27. *Times* (London) (December 16, 1989): p. 3.
28. See the reporting in *Junge Welt* (Berlin-East) (January 4, 1990): pp. 1-3.
29. Barbara Einhorn and Mary Kaldor, "Germany beyond the Wall," *New Statesman & Society* (17 November 1989): p. 15.
30. *St. Louis Post-Dispatch* (December 4, 1989): p. 12A.
31. *Washington Post* (November 15, 1989): p. A23.
32. These examples are cited in a letter from Y. M. Bodemann, Berlin, printed in the *SICSA Report* 3 (Winter 1989–90): 3.
33. J. Dornberg, *The New Germans—Thirty Years After* (New York: Macmillan, 1976), p. 140.
34. *Washington Post* (October 25, 1990): p. A28.
35. *New York Times* (February 8, 1990): p. A3.
36. Ibid. (February 12, 1990): p. A3.
37. *Washington Post* (September 14, 1990): p. A21.

38. Ibid. (October 25, 1990): p. A25.
39. *New York Times* (September 23, 1990): p. A14.
40. Ibid. (October 4, 1990): p. A17.
41. Clive Sinclair, "Kicking *tochis*—In praise of bad behaviour," *Jewish Quarterly* (London) (Winter 1989): 4.
42. Günter Grass, *Two States—One Nation?*, trans. Krishna Winston (San Diego: Harcourt, Brace, Jovanovich, 1990).
43. *New York Times* (February 4, 1990): p. E23.
44. See Günther Gillessen's account of "Jewish Anxiety in the Light of German Unification," in the *Frankfurter Allgemeine Zeitung* (February 14, 1990): 34.

Notes on Contributors

Jeremy Cohen holds the Melton Chair of Jewish History at the Ohio State University, and is Associate Professor of Jewish History at Tel Aviv University. His publications include *The Friars and the Jews: The Evolution of Medieval Anti-Judaism* and *"Be Fertile and Increase, Fill the Earth and Master It": The Ancient and Medieval Career of a Biblical Text*, both winners of the National Jewish Book Award.

Nicholas de Lange teaches Rabbinics at Cambridge University. His book *Origen and the Jews* was published in 1976. He has edited texts of Origen in the French series *Les Sources Chrétiennes*, and written a number of specialized studies on early Christianity, Judaism, and anti-Semitism.

Leonard Dinnerstein is Professor of History at the University of Arizona. He is currently engaged in a study of the history of American anti-Semitism. Among his published works are *The Leo Frank Case*, *America and the Survivors of the Holocaust*, and *Uneasy at Home: Anti-Semitism and the American Jewish Experience*.

Andrew Ezergailis is Professor of History at Ithaca College. He is the author of *The 1917 Revolution in Latvia*, *The Latvian Impact on the Bolshevik Revolution*, and numerous articles on Soviet, Russian, and Latvian topics. Presently, he is working on a study of the Holocaust in Latvia.

Sander L. Gilman is the Goldwin Smith Professor of Humane Studies at Cornell University. He is the author of *Jewish Self-Hatred* and the forthcoming study of outsiders in the literary world, *Inscribing the Other.*

R. Po-chia Hsia is Professor of History at New York University. His publications include *Society and Religion in Munster, The Myth of Ritual Murder: Jews and Magic in Reformation Germany,* and *Social Discipline in the Reformation: Central Europe 1550–1750.* He also edited *The German People and the Reformation.*

Steven T. Katz is Professor of Near Eastern Studies and Jewish Studies at Cornell University. He is the editor of *Modern Judaism* and the author of *Historicism, the Holocaust, and Zionism,* published by New York University Press.

Ruth Kluger (formerly ANGRESS) was born in Vienna. She was educated at Hunter College and the University of California at Berkeley. She has taught in the German Departments of the University of Virginia and Princeton University, and is presently Chairwoman of the German Department at the University of California at Irvine. A former editor of *The German Quarterly,* she has written on Lessing, Kleist, Stifter, Schnitzler, Baroque poetry, and German-Jewish literary relations.

Moshe Lazar is Professor of Drama and Comparative Literature at the University of Southern California. His areas of special interest include civilization in the Middle Ages and the twentieth century, and Jewish topics in the context of Romance literatures. Among his books are *Amor courtois et "fin'Amors", Almerichi: La Fazienda de la otra Mar, Le jugement dernier* (French and Provençal Play), and a series on medieval Spanish-Jewish thinkers. He is currently writing a book entitled *Satan's Synagogue.*

Bernard Lewis occupied the Chair of History of the Near and Middle East, University of London, from 1949 to 1974, and was Cleveland E. Dodge Professor of Near Eastern Studies, Princeton University, from 1974 to 1986. His books have been translated into nineteen languages. They include *The Arabs in History, The Assassins, The Middle East and the West, the Jews of Islam, Semites and Anti-Semites, The Political Language of Islam,* and *Race and Slavery in Islam: An Historical Enquiry.*

David Menashri is currently Senior Research Fellow at the Moshe Dayan Center and Senior Lecturer in the Department of Middle East and African Studies at Tel Aviv University. He has also done research in his native Tehran (1975–77), as well as being a Fellow of the Department of Middle Eastern History at Princeton University (1984–85), Visiting Professor at Cornell University (1985–86) and the University of Chicago (1989–90). The recipient of numerous awards and grants—including the Landau Prize (1974, 1983) and the Fulbright (1984)—he has published *Iran in Revolution: The Islamic Republic in Action* (in Hebrew), *Iran: A Decade of War and Revolution*, and a forthcoming study of *Education and the Making of Modern Iran*.

Alexander Orbach is Associate Professor of Religious Studies at the University of Pittsburgh. He has written on the emergence of a secular Jewish intelligentsia in the Russian Empire in the second half of the nineteenth century *(New Voices of Russian Jewry)*, and on the evolution of Jewish politics at the turn of the century.

Pinchas Hacohen Peli was a regular columnist on Jewish topics for the *Jerusalem Post*. He served on the faculty of the University of the Negev and was a Visiting Professor of Jewish Studies at Cornell University during 1986–87.

Walter H. Sokel, Viennese born, has taught at Columbia, Stanford, Harvard, Hamburg, and Freiburg. He is now Commonwealth Professor of German and English Literature at the University of Virginia and has received NEH and Alexander-von-Humboldt fellowships. He is currently Honorary President of the Kafka Society of America, a member of the American Academy of Arts and Sciences and the International P.E.N. Club, and a former member of the Executive Council of the Modern Language Association of America. His publications include books on German Expressionism and Franz Kafka, an anthology of German Expressionist drama in English translation, and numerous articles on German and comparative literature and intellectual history.

Guy Stern is Distinguished Professor in the German and Slavic Department of Wayne State University. A specialist in German and comparative literature of the eighteenth and twentieth centuries and in exile studies, he has published extensively in those fields. Among his recent books are *War, Weimar and Literature* and *Literature in Exile*. He holds advanced degrees from Columbia University and has taught at his alma mater, at Denison University, and the University of Cincinnati. He was honored with a Festschrift, and also with the Grosses Verdienstkreuz and the Goethe Medal from the Federal Republic and the Goethe Institute, respectively.

Liliane Weissberg is Associate Professor of German and Comparative Literature at the University of Pennsylvania. She is the author of *Geistersprache: Philosophischer und literarischer Diskurs im späten achtzehnten Jahrhundert,* as well as the editor of Dorothea Schlegel, *Florentin: Roman—Fragment— Varianten* and of a forthcoming critical edition of early Romantic letters for the German Klassiker Verlag. She is currently completely a book on Rahel Varnhagen, Dorothea Schlegel, and Henriette Herz, entitled *Writing One's Self.*

Index

Printed in the United States
31018LVS00002B/45

9 780814 730560